BUILDING
LIBRARY
COLLECTIONS

BUILDING LIBRARY COLLECTIONS

Fifth Edition

by

Wallace John Bonk
and
Rose Mary Magrill

The Scarecrow Press, Inc.
Metuchen, N.J. & London
1979

Library of Congress Cataloging in Publication Data

Bonk, Wallace John, 1923–
  Building library collections.

  A revision of the work by M. D. Carter and others.
  Includes bibliographies and index.
  1. Collection development (Libraries) I. Magrill,
Rose Mary, joint author. II. Carter, Mary Duncan,
1896–   Building library collections. III. Title.
Z687.B66 1979   025.2'1   79-11151
ISBN 0-8108-1214-2

In Memory of
Mary (Duncan) Carter Isbell
(1896–1978)

Late Professor Emeritus of Library Science
The University of Michigan

TABLE OF CONTENTS

PREFACE

This fifth edition of *Building Library Collections* has been prepared with the same objective in mind that motivated the co-authors on earlier editions—to produce a text that can introduce common principles, accepted procedures, unresolved questions, and current selection and acquisition tools for a general collection development course.

In addition to the usual updating of bibliographies and selection aids, this edition has been partly rewritten and rearranged. Those who are familiar with earlier editions may find an outline of these changes useful.

As in the previous edition, the first several chapters (nine in this case) comprise a section we have called "selection." Chapter one, which gives a historical review of selection principles, is unchanged, except that the checklist of selection principles which was formerly appended to it has now been moved to the appendices at the end of the book. The second chapter, which deals with the varying collection development environments of different types of libraries, has been substantially rewritten and updated. Chapter three, on community analysis, is basically a new addition to the text. Part of a chapter in previous editions was devoted to studying the community, but the topic has now become of such concern to librarians that we thought it deserved its own chapter. The fourth chapter, on subject selection, and the fifth, on book selection aids, remain essentially unchanged, except that the list of selection aids appended to chapter five has been thoroughly reviewed and updated. Chapter six, on selection of non-book formats, has been largely rewritten and its list of selection aids has been revised and updated. Chapters six (censorship) and seven (publishing) have been updated where appropriate. Another new addition is the concluding chapter in the first section, dealing with resource sharing. Cooperative acquisitions and storage projects have been discussed briefly in previous editions, but a more extensive presentation of contemporary networking developments and their relations to collection development seemed required in this edition.

Two chapters still comprise the section on acquisitions. Both follow the basic arrangement of previous editions, but they have received considerable revision, updating, and additions.

The three chapters in the third section are almost completely new to this edition. Collection evaluation and weeding had been restricted to part of a chapter in the previous edition, and there was so much material to be covered on collection maintenance that both of these topics grew to demand chapters of their own. Brief comments on preservation were added as a last chapter, since so much of the current discussion of collection deterioration has relevance for collection building.

The appendices of this edition are changed considerably from those of the last edition. We are still reprinting, of course, the statements on intellectual freedom issued by the American Library Association. We have, however, dropped all of the excerpts from selection policies which had appeared in earlier editions and have substituted a general set of guidelines for collection development policies produced by the Resources and Technical Services Division of the American Library Association. We had hoped to include as the last section in the appendices the official statement on instructional materials selection of the American Association of School Librarians, but permission could not be obtained.

We wish to extend our appreciation to Judith F. Krug, Director of ALA's Office for Intellectual Freedom, for permission to reprint the ALA statements on intellectual freedom. The same grateful acknowledgment goes to William I. Bunnell, Executive Secretary of the Resources and Technical Services Division, for permission to reprint that division's collection development policy guidelines. For advice and encouragement throughout the preparation of this new edition, we owe thanks to our colleagues in the School of Library Science of The University of Michigan, particularly Professors Helen D. Lloyd, Constance Rinehart, and Rose Vainstein.

Ann Arbor
August, 1978

PART I

SELECTION

CHAPTER 1

The Principles of Selection for Public Libraries

Introduction

Public librarians are occupied in performing many different tasks each day. They open the library every morning, hasten to compile yesterday's statistics, straighten desks and clear them for the day's action, see that the process of returning books to the shelves gets under way, and greet the first users with the fresh enthusiasm which a new day brings.

The average person, viewing the day-to-day operations of a library, might well ask which of all the jobs being done is the most important one. Is it answering reference questions? helping some reader to understand the intricacies of the library's card catalog? receiving books from a dealer and checking all the invoices and order slips? cataloging books?

The fact is that the fundamental task of the librarian is so unobtrusive that the observer might miss it—or, seeing it being performed, might misinterpret what the librarian is about. The department head, sitting quietly at a desk with a copy of *Publishers Weekly*, the circulation librarian, turning over the pages of *Kirkus Reviews,* the head librarian reading through the review section of *Library Journal:* these unspectacular activities represent the most important job of the librarian—the selection of those materials which he/she judges will be best for the library.

When all is said and done, the major task of any library is to supply those materials which the individual user will find valuable and useful. The amount of satisfaction a reader finds in a library depends directly upon the materials the librarian has available for his/her use. If the librarian manages consistently to choose things of no interest or use to readers, he/she cannot expect them to be satisfied with the library.

A librarian's interpretation of what is best for the library will vary, however, with the purpose which the librarian envisages the library as serving. The librarian might feel that the dissatisfaction of readers would have to be borne if that dissatisfaction arose from the fact

1

that they could not get things which they wanted, but which the librarian believed were unsuitable to the purposes of the library. Various librarians may arrive at contradictory judgments concerning the value of any given item, and these opposing views become understandable the moment one realizes that the disagreeing librarians hold differing views of the library's purposes. What is best for the amusement of the reader may not be best for that reader's education or enlightenment, and individual librarians may emphasize different aims in their own libraries. Before a discussion of principles can be profitably embarked upon, it is necessary to consider the purposes which the principles are intended to implement and to consider the various ways in which librarians have interpreted these purposes.

Purposes of the Public Library

The public library's broadest purpose has been expressed in various ways. Perhaps it can be summarized best by calling it the educational or civilizing aim. This view sees the library as attempting to provide people with information and knowledge which it is hoped will lead to wisdom and understanding. The Reverend Thomas Bray felt that collections of books, spread about through a country, would "ennoble [people's] minds with principles of virtue and true honor, and file off that roughness, ferocity and barbarity, which are the never failing fruits of ignorance and illiterature." This view of the library sees it as an "open door," through which people can participate in all the accumulated wisdom of the race. Underlying this aim of the library is the faith accepted by our society that reading is a good thing, that it leads to desirable ends, and that it has the power to alter people for the better. This educational aim has been advanced by leaders of the public library movement in the United States since its inception.

Another purpose of the library in our kind of society might be called the civic aim. The public library offers citizens of a democracy the means by which they may become informed and intelligent citizens. The emphasis here lies not so much on their improvement as "liberally educated" human beings as on their improvement as functioning parts of a free society. Thomas Jefferson believed that the people of a country would never consent to the destruction of their liberties if they were informed and that nothing could do more good toward making them informed than the establishment of a small circulating library in every county. Where the people have the responsibility for electing public officials, it becomes imperative that they do their voting from knowledge, not from ignorance. Furthermore, individual citizens may be called upon to take some part in community affairs—even though it may be only as a member of some local committee—and it is certainly desirable that they be informed in order that they may act their part intelligently.

In addition to these aims, many people believe that the library justly serves very utilitarian purposes: that, in addition to improving individuals as citizens and as humanely-educated persons, it should also help them improve themselves in their jobs. Gerald Johnson summarized this view in the following way: "Its sole reason for being [in the minds of some] is to help people get along in the world, to help school children get better grades, to help business men make more money, to help preachers write sermons that will keep the congregation awake." Thus, some librarians will buy materials which will enable the mechanic to improve himself so that he can become a foreman, which will enable the saleswoman to teach herself to become an accountant, which will enable people to improve their "occupational mobility."

There is an aim which has been strongly supported by some and is still looked upon with some suspicion by others, but which has been supported even in the creation of such a library as the Boston Public. That aim might be called the "recreational" aim. It is seen as a perfectly legitimate purpose for a public library. Indeed, at the second session of the 1876 convention of American librarians in Philadelphia (at which the American Library Association was founded) William F. Poole (of periodical index fame) delivered an address entitled "Some Popular Objections to Public Libraries." After dispatching the fear of taxation and the belief that governments had no duty but to protect life and property (and so, though they could support police, courts, and penitentiaries, they could not support libraries), he dealt with the final objection he felt important: it was the belief that libraries are only for the cultured and the scholar, and that, therefore, public libraries are not necessary. He noted that libraries were condemned for promising to raise the level of the population, but after they open, the bulk of reading is in prose fiction, not history or philosophy. He remarked "I do not lament or join in the clamor raised over the statistics of prose fiction circulated at public libraries."

The discussion following his speech is an entertaining one. Mr. Edmands remarked that he had seen no definite proof that novel reading elevates the taste of those who read it, while Mr. Morris was firm in noting that he had known of not infrequent instances of young people who read novels for two or three years and then began reading English literature and history. Mr. Kite, of the Germantown Friends' Free Library, said his rules allowed no novels in the library. He reported that his readers—half of whom were factory workers—asked for novels, but that he was almost always able to keep them from reading them by recommending other, more wholesome books. His parting shot is worth memorializing: "Perhaps one might get rest from reading Dickens, but I cannot say what the effect of novels really is, since I have never read one myself.''

Pool of the Y.M.C.A. (not Poole of the periodical index) gave a criterion for selecting novels which may be of interest to our own generation: ''We reject all those that are immoral, sensational, or trivial, such works as fill the mind with false, wild ideas of life.'' Mr. Yates had a simple remedy for the problem of young people reading novels. He left the decision with the parents. When they notified the library that their children ''were becoming intoxicated with too much novel reading, their cards were cancelled forthwith.''

By this time the novel is pretty firmly installed in most libraries, but there are still some traces of the Puritan opposition to ''pleasure literature,'' as opposed to edifying literature. The authors have heard that there are some libraries which will buy only a certain number of novels each year (and a pretty modest number, at that), and that no amount of requests from the patrons will move them to add another fiction title. (One could, we suppose, raise the question: is ''Make Friends with Your Nerves'' or ''Twenty Easy Ways to Seduction'' really more serious reading than *War and Peace* by Tolstoy?)

The *Minimum Standards for Public Library Systems, 1966* gave the following statement of public library purposes: (1) facilitating informal self-education of all people in the community; (2) enriching and further developing the subjects in which individuals are undertaking formal education; (3) meeting the informational needs of all; (4) supporting the educational, civic, and cultural activites of groups and organizations; (5) encouraging wholesome recreation and constructive use of leisure time.

Candor demands that one admit that not all of these aims are subscribed to with equal enthusiasm by all librarians. As a consequence, one must expect a certain degree of variation in the interpretation of selection principles. In the discussion which follows, this divergency of opinion will be illustrated.

Some Traditional Principles of Selection

(1) *Select the Right Materials for the Library's Readers.* The first question is, who are the library's patrons? Is the library to serve only those who actually come to it today? Or should the librarian attempt to provide for all those who may come some day? Should the librarian, to put it another way, select for present clientele only, or also for some potential clientele (however that potential group may be defined)?

One of the underlying principles of the free public library is that it is open to all. This statement implies that the librarian has the responsibility for selecting for all the members of the community—even though they may not come to the library at the moment—since they are all welcome to come. Some librarians believe that this ideal is a central tenet to be observed in determining the library's selection policies. They do not interpret this first principle—the right materials for the library's readers—as requiring that the librarian serve only those who come to the library. Rather they feel that it imposes on the librarian the responsibility for reflecting in the library collection all the manifold interests of this potential community-wide clientele.

Even if the librarian agrees with this view, there are still two approaches to carrying it out which could be taken. One is the passive approach: let those who come, come; the library will have a good collection to serve them so that future readers will find the material they want. The other is the active approach: buy through the whole range of subjects, but proselytize to increase the use of the library by those not now using it.

One of the arguments advanced for the inclusion in the library collection of a whole range of non-book materials has been that these materials will serve to attract to the library the person who is not interested in reading books. If the library is truly to serve the entire community, proponents of this view argue, then it must assume the task of providing access to ideas for those to whom books are not an effective medium for the communication of ideas.

Another traditional statement of principle which reflects this conviction that the library should serve the whole community—and not merely the group of present readers—runs as follows:

(2) *See to it that No Race, Nationality, Profession, Trade, Religion, School of Thought, or Local Custom Is Overlooked.* Again, if one accepts this principle, it is argued that one buys in these areas even though members of these particular groups may not be active present users of the library. They are all potential users, and their possible future interests should be anticipated.

One can move from this broadening of the selector's range—which is based upon the make-up of the community—to an even wider principle:

(3) *Every Library Collection Should Be Built up According to a Definite Plan on a Broad General Foundation.* The librarians who advocate this approach have advanced the view that the library collection has its own needs, apart from the needs of the community which it serves. These librarians feel that the selector has a responsibility to the collection itself and should attempt to round it out. Such a collection

would have material on all subjects, whether or not there were any groups in the community interested in the various subjects, either as active or potential users.

There are some very practical problems involved in the acceptance of this principle, which have led many librarians to abandon any attempt to carry it out, even though in theory they consider it good. If the library is limited in funds, as most libraries are, if it is not one of the behemoth collections, the librarian may well have cause to hesitate before attempting to build the well-rounded collection. If item "A" is purchased because it has intrinsic worth, expounds its subject brilliantly, is highly authoritative, but does not represent a present reading interest in the community, then item "B," which is of interest to the community, cannot be purchased. The librarian may then ask: Can one justify the use of limited funds to buy materials which *may* be used some day? Can one justify spending limited funds to build the ideal, the well-proportioned, the balanced collection, when there is not enough money available to buy all the materials present readers want?

Some librarians have preferred to concentrate on the bird in the hand. They would accept the following principle as primary:

(4) *Demand Is the Governing Factor in Selection.* Librarians who accept this principle would abandon the effort to complete a well-rounded collection, as they would also abandon the effort to buy for potential, rather than actual users. Although they would buy some materials as part of the basic collection, they would concentrate on trying to supply those materials which their present readers need. Other factors than demand would be considered, but demand would be the over-riding factor. In attempting to carry out this policy, continuing acts of judgment on the librarian's part would be necessary. If some items are to be bought for the basic collection—in addition to those in demand—the librarian would have to determine the percentage of the budget which was to be allocated to building the general collection. This balancing of the two pressures would have to be decided by the librarian on the basis of a series of factors: knowing which way the decision had gone the previous week, and the week before that, and the month before that; knowing how much money was left; knowing of any heavy seasonal buying which might lie ahead—the list could be extended considerably.

There is another set of principles to be considered. These are concerned more with the quality of the titles selected than with questions as to the group for whom one ought to buy. Basing selection on demand raises this issue: Will we apply some standard of excellence in selection, or will we buy anything asked for, regardless of its quality? Melvil Dewey advocated the purchase of the *best.* Emphasis on the best underlines a point of view which sees the library as the primary source in the community for serious, educational materials. It is a view held by those librarians who are interested in increasing the use of the library for sober ends, who feel that the library has an important role to play as pedagogue to the nation. These librarians, emphasizing as they do the educational purpose of the library, endorse the principle that

(5) *Materials Acquired Should Meet High Standards of Quality in Content, Expression, and Format.* Librarians committed to this view would emphasize authoritativeness, factual accuracy, effective expression, significance of subject, sincerity of the author's purpose, and responsibility of the author's opinions. They would resist buying anything which failed to meet these standards, even if it were in heavy demand. Such a conviction has led to a de-emphasis in some libraries of fiction, particularly light fiction. Some libraries even limit the number of current fiction titles which will be purchased in a given year, regardless of the demand for additional titles. The classics of fiction would be stocked by these libraries even if demand for them were not great. Those librarians who feel strongly the importance of the library as an educational force rejoice in the increase in non-fiction reading reported in recent years.

The problem of fiction in the library is not a new one, and an effective statement of this issue was made in the 1875 report of the Examining Committee of the Boston Public Library:

> There is a vast range of ephemeral literature, exciting and fascinating, apologetic of vice or confusing distinctions between plain right and wrong, fostering discontent with the peaceful, homely duties which constitute a large portion of average men and women's lives, responsible for an immense amount of the mental disease and moral irregularities which are so troublesome an element in modern society—and this is the kind of reading to which multitudes naturally take, which it is not the business of the town library to supply . . . Notwithstanding many popular notions to the contrary, it is not part of the duty of a municipality to raise taxes for the amusement of the people, unless the amusement is tolerably sure to be conducive to the higher ends of good citizenship. The sole relation of a town library to the general interest is as a supplement to the school system; as an instrumentality of higher instruction to all classes of people.

It is interesting to note that our own time also sees much concern expressed over the deleterious social effects of the reading of certain kinds of novels, which are judged to be pernicious. Legislative committees—both at the national and state level—have held hearings which discussed the degree to which certain paperback books could be held accountable for the "immense amount of mental disease and moral irregularities'' which plague our age, as they apparently plagued Boston in 1875.

The view of the public library as primarily an instrumentality of education is not universally accepted. At the other extreme are those librarians who see the public library as being largely a source of entertainment for people. They would enunciate their major principle, perhaps, in the following manner:

(6) *Our Purpose Is the Same as the Parks Department's.* These librarians view the library as one of the recreational agencies of a city. They will buy heavily where there is public demand and will not be greatly interested in the quality of the material. They would probably agree with F. B. Perkins, who made the following statement in the 1876 report of the U.S. Bureau of Education:

> The first mistake likely to be made in establishing a public library is choosing books of too thoughtful or solid a character. It is vain to go on the principle of collecting books that people ought to read, and afterwards trying to coax them to read them. The only practical method is to begin by supplying books that people already want to read, and afterwards to do whatever shall be found possible to elevate their reading tastes and habits. Most of those who read are young people who want entertainment and excitement, or tired people who want relaxation and amusement.

This group might approve wholeheartedly of the traditional principle which asserts

(7) *Do Not Hesitate to Install a Mediocre Book Which Will Be Read in Preference to a Superior Book That Will Not Be Read.* This principle does not imply, of course, that all those librarians who accept it would buy books which are patently trash, but they will emphasize the demands of the community, as opposed to the demands of quality. They would assert as a principle that

(8) *Quality of Materials Must Be Related to the Other Two Basic Standards of Selection—Purpose and Need.* Since their purpose is primarily to furnish recreational reading, and since their public expresses a need for such materials, they will abandon the building of an ideal collection.

In this matter, there are librarians who cannot embrace either extreme. They see the library as performing a variety of tasks, which in turn demands a variety of materials. They would argue that

(9) *The Collection Is Inclusive and Contains Whatever Materials Contribute to the Purposes of the Library.* Such librarians would agree with William F. Poole that it is important to remember, if one is

trying to select the best, that there are as many kinds of best as there are kinds of readers. They might ask, as Charles Cutter asked, "Best in what? in style? in interest? in instructiveness? in suggestiveness? in power? Best for whom? for the ignorant? for people in general? for college graduates? for the retired scholar?" Since these librarians attempt to serve all those various categories of readers, they would be willing to accept a variety of materials, whose standards of quality might vary as the titles are seen to be useful for one group or another.

Such librarians will look carefully at each title in the process of selecting, decide for which type of user it was intended, and then apply the appropriate standards of quality. A library built on this principle might indeed include the classics of fiction, but it might also include popular materials. The extent to which it will include material representing such disparate categories will depend upon the judgment of the librarian, who will have to weigh a whole complex of local factors. A librarian accepting this view might conclude that the statement "Our purpose here is the same as the Parks Department's," need only be changed to "*One* of our purposes here is the same as the Parks Department's," to make it acceptable.

This middle-of-the-road position was not restricted to Poole. William I. Fletcher stated it ably in the 1876 report of the U.S. Bureau of Education:

> No question connected with public libraries has been so much discussed, or is of such generally recognized importance, as that of the kinds of reading to be furnished. On the one hand, all kinds of arguments—from the political one, that it is not the province of government to furnish the people with mere recreation, to the religious one, that it is wicked to read novels—have been urged against the admission of any but the very highest order of fictitious works; while, on the other hand, the sweeping assertion is made by some that the public library cannot refuse to supply whatever the public sentiment calls for. The mean between these two extremes is doubtless the true view of the case. The managers of public libraries are not less bound to control and shape the institution in their charge so as to produce the best result than are the managers of the school system. To say that calls for books should be accepted as the indications of what should be furnished, is to make their office a merely mechanical and perfunctory one. In such communities as we are especially considering [manufacturing communities], adherence to such a principle as this would make the library a mere slop shop of sensational fiction. But in avoiding the Scylla of unlimited trash, the Charybdis of too high a standard must be equally steered clear of.

While the judgments of the past are being called to bear witness, let the following words of Charles Cutter—who also summarized this problem in his colorful and effective rhetoric—be introduced as evidence:

> When you have a perfect people you can afford to have only perfect books, if there are such things. When you have a homogeneous public you can hope to have a stock of books exactly fitted to them all, and no book shall be unfitted to any one of them. But so long as there is a public of every diversity of mental capacity, previous education, habits of thought, taste, ideals, you must, if you are to give them satisfaction or do them any good, provide many books which will suit and benefit some and will do no good, perhaps in some cases may do harm, to others. It is inevitable. There is no escape from this fundamental difficulty. . . .
>
> Select your library then, as Shakespeare wrote his plays, the highest poetry, the deepest tragedy, side by side with the comic and the vulgar . . . To sum up, what I have been trying to show is the great diversity in very many respects of those who come to the library, the consequent diversity of the best each can read, the necessity of providing many different kinds, qualities, degrees of good books, the impossibility of limiting one's choice to any one degree of good, lest it should be too high for some and too low for others.

The emphasis in the statements by both these gentlemen is on service to the individual reader, pointing out that one cannot select for some abstract mass of readers who are all statistically alike. It contrasts strongly with a view held by many librarians today, which makes of the library one of the media of mass communication, trying to reach large groups of readers with the same message, presented in the same form. This school of thought would envision selection as a process of applying the results of reading studies of large groups to the groups which make up the reading public of a given library, rather than emphasizing and considering the individual differences among members of the groups. Ralph A. Ulveling, former Director of the Detroit Public Library, commented on this tendency in 1959:

> But the public library is not one of the mass communication media and should not organize its fundamental services on a mass basis. Ten years ago, when I was a member of the United States National Commission for Unesco, I tried, within the limits of my persuasiveness, to have libraries so recognized. Eventually it became clear to me that a precise distinction which I now recognize as sound and proper, kept libraries out of the mass communication category. To that body a mass medium is one through which a message is distributed widely in a single form. All listeners hear identical words coming out of the radio or from the TV. The monthly magazine brings the same pictures and the same articles at the same time into all homes that subscribe for

it, regardless of its usability at the time it comes. But the public library, unlike motion pictures or any of these, should provide an individualized service for every patron who comes to it. Thus it is not a mass medium providing one message for all, but it is rather a medium for serving masses of individuals with a prescription service whereby each gets the precise thing that is best suited to his particular needs, to his ability, to his interests, and to his background.

It may be well at this point to remark that there are two types of libraries to which the principles are addressed: (1) the ideal library, which exists as an abstraction (and to which the general principles apply directly and fully); and (2) the actual library which exists in a particular community (and to which the general principles must be adapted). It is this distinction which leads us to consideration of another factor of signal importance in effective selection.

In any judgment of materials, the librarian has to consider not only the abstract principles of selection, but the community of readers which the particular library serves. An informed and intelligent judgment cannot be made if there is insufficient knowledge of the community, either the general community (in the case of the librarian who tries to meet potential demand as well as present demand), or the specific group of present readers (in the case of the librarian who tries to supply those books which present readers want). It is therefore most important that the librarian

(10) *Know the Community.* Knowledge of the community consists of two kinds of information: (1) general information which applies to any community; (2) the specific reading interests and needs of a particular community. The general information is the kind which can be gathered from general reading interest studies of adults—which it is assumed will apply, to some degree at least, to any community of adults. These studies are attempts to describe the general reader, who is, of course, a statistical abstraction. Many efforts have been made to outline the nature and needs of this statistical personage.

Douglas Waples and Ralph Tyler's *What People Want to Read About* (1931) made one of the first serious attempts to apply social science research methods to reading interests. They demonstrated that the factors which made for differences in reading interests were—in order of importance—sex, amount of schooling, occupation, environment, age, and time spent in reading. The more of these factors any two groups have in common, the more alike their reading interests will be. The selector, armed with the data gathered by Waples and Tyler—and by other studies of special groups of readers—could then proceed to select materials which would appeal to people fitting into the various categories outlined and could feel some certainty that the materials chosen would be of interest to their readers—at least to the degree that their readers fitted into categories.

Various other studies have revealed—as further clues to the selector—that women read more fiction than men; that men tend to read more on business and public affairs; that women do more recreational reading, while men do more work-related reading; that the higher the level of education, the more reading that is done; that the largest single category of non-fiction reading is biography and autobiography, followed by social problems and self-help books; but that, taken as a whole, the question of reading interests of adults can be most simply answered by saying that readers delve into every conceivable subject, and that they read most heavily in what is readily available. The general information revealed by such studies will form a useful background for the librarian who is charged with selecting books and will enable him/her to exercise a more informed judgment as to the potential usefulness of any given item.

In addition to the general studies, which apply in part to any community, the librarian has the task of determining what the readers of a particular community want or need. This task may also be divided into two parts: (1) a general study of the community, which will reveal its broad outlines—educational level, occupations, distribution by ages, sex, etc.—all of which will form a measure of the degree to which that community fits the pattern of the "general reader's community" as revealed by the various reading surveys; and (2) a study of the actual users of the library, which will reveal their particular reading interests and relevant sociological data. The actual techniques for determining these facts have been outlined in various places. A discussion of the details of community study will be presented in a subsequent chapter. At this point, it is only necessary to point out that intelligent selection demands a reasonable knowledge of the community and of the library's readers.

The social turmoil of the 1960s and the unfortunate impact of the recession of the early 1970s have led to renewed—and occasionally quite agitated—discussion of the public library's purpose in a society which seems in total flux. A few voices have gone so far as to declaim gloomily that the public library is obsolete and will disappear under the waves of social change. More voices have expressed the view that the public library needs to look closely at its methods for meeting the new needs of the community, including new and quite different informational needs. Some have proposed a new "advocacy librarianship" in which librarians would not only furnish information concerning the agencies which could help the disadvantaged, but would go with them and help them fight their way through the red tape and endless mazes of bureaucracy.

These information services are not conceived of as a mere extension of current reference practices. The library would concentrate on materials which would assist in the solution of current, local social problems. One library tried to suggest the nature of the new services by the name, "*Community* Information Service" (italics added). These centers would collect information regarding all the pressing social and civic problems of *that* community, as well as information about the programs of social and local governmental agencies—and those of state and federal—which were created to help the citizenry. Rather than just collecting and sitting back to help those who came to seek the information, the library would actively seek out those who needed the information. Very probably they might not be library users, and, if they were, they would not expect to find this new kind of help in the public library. "Outreach" was the cry of the hour, and it summarizes well the efforts of librarians who sincerely wanted to bring their institutions into the forefront of those trying to meet the urgent needs of the community. The attention of these librarians naturally turned to a consideration of the purposes of public libraries.

The history of American librarianship shows clearly the emergence of tensions between those who profess the ideal and those who stress the realities of community service to particular readers, between the librarians who would select by intuition or some knowledge of the abstract general reader and those who want factual data on their own community and the individual readers who use their libraries. American library history also shows that librarians have come to believe that the library tries to accomplish a number of purposes. It is equally clear that the individual librarian may emphasize one or another of these purposes, either because the need is greater in his/her community or because of his/her own interests and temperament. The fact seems to be that two libraries of the same size, in two towns much alike, can be two very different institutions, reflecting the succession of judgments and choices made by librarians in selecting the materials which make up the collection. Some lament this lack of uniformity, some applaud this existence of many mansions in the house of librarianship. What seems most essential is that librarians recognize the causes of this variety and understand their own convictions—that they make judgments and choices from a clearly realized point of view and not from some nebulous, imprecise feelings which they have never translated into real understanding.

The best way of assuring that such clear realizations will be achieved is to have a written statement of selection policy. This statement should include an outline of the general purposes that the library is attempting to serve, as well as a statement of those specific aims which arise out of the particular community's needs. The statement of purpose might well be followed by a determination of the standards of selection to be applied to materials being considered for purchase. Such a statement should be prepared by the librarian and the Library Board, should be formally adopted by the Board, and—equally important—should be reviewed periodically. Some librarians, particularly those in small libraries, have questioned the need for such a written statement. Although its actual necessity in the small library may not be incontrovertible, its advisability seems obvious, since it cannot help but make clear the many areas in which it is easy to be vague.

The need for periodic revision is important. While it is true that the general purposes of the library are relatively stable, the particular aims arising out of the nature of the local community may very well alter with the passage of time. Librarians have the responsibility for being alert to changing populations, new community problems, and all the changes which come with the growth of communities.

In the course of this chapter, we have talked about public libraries as if they were all identical units. It is important to note, however, that size of library has an impact on selection problems, and that the interpretation of a given principle may vary as the size of the library changes. In addition, the procedure for selecting will vary as size of library changes. The following discussion attempts to point out some of the major variations.

The Large Public Library

The large public library serves the most heterogeneous public. It runs the gamut from children to the aged, from college graduates to those with little formal education (including a large number who are now students at one level or another, with their special curriculum-created demands), from those interested in the most utilitarian how-to-do-it books to those concerned with the most abstruse subjects. It must provide materials in every Dewey class and must represent both the popularization for the uninitiated and the more advanced work for the knowledgeable. The general principles apply most directly and without modification to the large public library—conceived of an as abstract unit.

But it must be remembered that the metropolitan public library consists of both the large central collection and a group of smaller branch libraries, whose communities of readers form distinct reading groups. Selection for the branch will be governed by the nature of the community each branch serves. Neighborhood branches may vary from those located in upper-income, upper-educational level areas to those situated in low-income, low-educational areas. Thus there will be a variety of types of collections in the various branches. In general, branches will not try to maintain extensive reference collections, will stress the more popular type of reading, will not store little-used materials, and will not attempt to provide materials for scholarly research. The central library—in addition to its popular reading collection, which might be thought of as a branch library within the main building—may have very extensive collections serving special research interests, such as business reference libraries, historical collections, music departments, and the like, in which the materials would include the highly specialized and the scholarly.

The major problem of selection in the large metropolitan library is to create a method of selection which will adequately reflect this variety of types of users and types of materials. Generally speaking, large libraries have as their major decision the determination of which titles they do not want to buy. Their financial resources might enable them to buy annually the entire production of new trade titles, if they wished to have only one copy of each of the titles issued in this country. It is their central concern, then, to select out of the total available output that part which will be found useful in their various collections, branch and central.

Organization of Selection in Large Public Libraries

In metropolitan libraries there are large professional staffs, heavy subject departmentalization and specialization, and large branch systems with generalists in charge of the individual branch libraries. In such systems it would be difficult to involve each member of the professional staff in selection simultaneously. Organization in the form of a selection department is needed, therefore. This department is responsible for checking and circulating reviews to staff members, acquiring approval copies of books and other materials for review, and, after the selection is made, compiling lists of materials approved for purchase, where such lists are used.

Since the department heads are specialists in their respective fields, they check the selection aids for material related to their subjects. These specialists have the advantage of knowing their collections well and being able to concentrate upon a relatively narrow area of subject material. The branch collections and the collection for popular or home reading in the main library make up another aspect of the selection process. One system for selecting employs rotating committees, representative of both the departments and the branches. These committees hold meetings at regular intervals to consider titles on the lists compiled by the selection department. Materials are reviewed by members of the committee, the reviews being based upon examination of items sent to the library on approval and also upon published reviews. Approval copies are usually secured from the wholesaler or bookshop which supplies the library with the bulk of its materials, or—more frequently—directly from the publishers. The head of the selection department requests certain titles, selected in advance from publishers' announcements or from such aids as *Publishers Weekly* or *Kirkus Reviews*. Copies of materials discussed at the meetings are available for examination by the branch librarians after each meeting.

One plan for securing prepublication copies for review purposes is known as the Greenaway plan. It originated in an agreement made by Emerson Greenaway, librarian of the Philadelphia Free Library, with Lippincott to receive one copy of each trade title at the same time as the general reviewers did. This facilitated staff reviewing and prepublication ordering of multiple copies. Many other publishers agreed to adopt the plan, other publishers offered their own versions of the plan, and many libraries have availed themselves of this service.

At a selection meeting, any item that is not approved by the committee is marked accordingly on the list, and, if the committee vote has not been unanimous, a minority report is often given. Materials which are not approved are not bought. This decision is not necessarily final, and the question can be reopened.

An alternate method used in some of the large public libraries is to have materials which have been sent to the library on approval evaluated by the department heads, who prepare reviews which are made available to the branch librarians. They in turn select from this master list. The branch librarians read the librarians' notes prepared by the department heads, examine the approved items, and place orders for their individual branches.

The Medium-Sized Public Library

Like the large public library, the medium-sized library deals with a wide variety of readers. The range of interests may not be as large as that of the metropolitan area, with its many industries, national groups, commercial and social organizations, and so forth, but the users of the library are still a much more heterogeneous group than those of a college, school, or special library. The librarians of a medium-sized public library have the advantage of being able to know the individual users more personally than the staff of a central library in a large city and can thus be more immediate in selecting to meet reader interests.

The major problem of selection for the medium-sized library arises from its more limited budget. It becomes imperative that selection be very carefully done. By exercising judgment, the medium-sized library can buy the significant titles issued in any year, but any flagging of attention to selection will result in wasteful choices. If a large library were to buy a few dozen titles which turned out to be little used, the impact on the budget would be minor. The medium-sized public library cannot afford to spend any of its limited funds on materials whose usefulness in that library is limited. A large part of its collection must be built of things that will be used intensively.

Recently a new demand has been falling on these libraries, and it has occasioned discussion among librarians as to the extent of their responsibilities in selection. With the development of junior colleges in communities, with the activities of university extension centers, with the tendency of college students to return home more frequently during the semester, there has arisen a demand for materials which will support the courses these students are taking. The librarian of the medium-sized library, already hard pushed to make the budget meet present demands, pressed by the evergrowing number of high school students crowding into the public library, now is asking if the library really must buy readings in sociology and history and economics and linguistics, and all the whole range of courses in the college curriculum, to satisfy the students who come to the library asking for what are essentially as-signed readings for specific courses. In a sense, the librarian is being asked to make the library partly a reserve reading room for college students.

As one might expect, the response to this demand has been varied. Some librarians have decided against attempting to provide such materials. If a given book meets a demand by the general reader, and also happens to be on a course reading list, they will be glad that it serves a dual purpose. But even here, problems arise. If there are many students taking a course for which this book is required reading, will the librarian then duplicate copies to satisfy the extra demand, which is above and beyond the call by regular library patrons? Those librarians who are resisting this pressure feel that it is the college's responsibility to buy multiple copies of reserve books—or, at the least, to be willing to send copies on interlibrary loan to the besieged public library.

Other librarians have felt that this is a legitimate responsibility of their libraries. These students are part of the community; they have a special interest: why should this be any different from buying books for the special interests of the garden club, which may be studying nematodes, and for whom the library will buy titles? It has been argued that, if public librarians buy for this year's Sociology I reading list, they will discover—as college librarians discover—that next year the list will have been changed, and the books which they bought will go unused. Proponents of such buying point out that this is essentially what happens to any book that is bought because it is in current heavy demand. The best-selling novel, for example, which may have been bought in multi-ple copies, will probably not be heavily read after a year—or perhaps two. But this obsolescence does not mean that one will refuse to buy the title, if it meets the standards of selection.

Organization of Selection in the Medium-Sized Public Library

In many medium-sized public libraries, all of the professional librarians on the staff participate in the selection of library materials. They bring to selection a knowledge of the existing collection as well as a knowledge of reader interests and preferences. Two methods of checking selection aids are in common use. In some libraries, all the aids are checked by staff members according to their subject specialties. These specialties may reflect the formal educational background of the librarian or they may be based on hobbies or personal reading interests. In other libraries, one staff member is made responsible for checking a single selection aid. In either case, the selections are coordinated by the chief librarian, who checks recommended materials in the light of the overall collection and the budget.

Few libraries of this size have selection meetings. Those which do are obliged to base their consideration of titles upon reviews, rather than upon actual examination, since approval copies are seldom available to libraries of this size. Cooperative selection might obviate this difficulty. It has been experimented with in several areas with some success. Some metropolitan libraries have opened their selection meetings to the librarians in suburban areas. This method gives the librarians of medium-sized libraries a broader view on which to base their own selection. It also points the way to regional cooperation and extended interlibrary loan. Several large public libraries distribute their weekly or fortnightly lists to other libraries.

The Small Public Library

The small public library—as a statistical abstraction—has been characterized as being largely a fiction lending library. It is usually staffed by a part-time person, often without any library training, open only on a part-time basis, and it has a very small budget. It will have few of the standard selection tools, and the untrained librarian may not be familiar with the range of aids available—if, indeed, the library could afford to purchase them. The over-riding factor in selection will probably be demand, and the best-sellers are likely to be the library's main stock in trade. If the librarian has training, he/she may experience frustration because many of the principles of selection simply cannot be implemented due to the budget limitations.

The need for some kind of program aimed at improving the library service of the small library has long been recognized. Many states provide workshops for the untrained librarians of these small libraries to help them learn about such matters as selection. State agencies provide consultant service to aid the librarians in the solution of their problems, distribute lists of materials selected by the state agency, and furnish loans of extensive collections to those libraries whose budgets are limited. Recently much emphasis has been placed on the federated system, regional libraries, or county library systems, to make available to the smallest library the resources commonly associated with only the large metropolitan libraries. A larger system will have the money to hire a full-time, professionally-trained headquarters staff and to buy the necessary selection aids. Thus it will be able to supply the expensive selection process for the small library.

Organization of Selection in the Small Public Library

Selection in the small public library may be restricted to a single person, as there may be only one librarian on the staff. The librarian is obliged to check possible titles, select titles for purchase, and order them. In such a library members of the library board and patrons with special backgrounds and interests can help. The wishes of library borrowers are likely to carry more immediate weight in the small public library than in other types. The librarian relies entirely on the checking of selection aids. With a small budget, the aids are few. Heavier dependency is placed on the use of state library extension agency lists, one weekly book review (frequently the *New York Times Book Review*), and "The Book Review" section in *Library Journal* and/or *The Booklist*.

Standards for Library Service

When variations in interpretation of the principles can result even in one type of library as size of unit varies, there is a danger that eventually the feeling may grow up that "anything goes," because nothing is really fixed, firm, and certain. As early as the ALA Midwinter Meeting of 1916, a committee was appointed to study the possibility of "grading" libraries as to the quality of service given, after having classified them by population served, amount of taxable property, size-of-area, etc. There was considerable controversy about this concept, but pursuit of the idea continued. In 1933, standards were written for public libraries. These consisted of a brief general statement including commentary on staff, book collection, measurement of the use of the library, and required income (a minimum of $1.00 per capita). The statement was endorsed by several state library associations.

As the depression continued into the thirites, it became evident that libraries needed more specific statements of standards in order to furnish them with the same type of guidelines used by other social service agencies. The National Planning Resources Board paved the way for the later *Post-War Standards for Public Libraries*, published by ALA. It was an ambitious and detailed statement. The 1956 standards announced that the effort to write standards for small libraries had been abandoned, and that the new standards were intended for systems of libraries large enough to provide a budget which would support the level of service defined as minimum by the standards. (Roughly put, it was the level of service of metropolitan libraries.) This did not meet with the complete approval of the librarians of smaller public libraries, who felt, one suspects, that they had been thrown to the city hall wolves with no defense for their service. One result of their dissatisfaction was the preparation of ''interim'' standards for small public libraries. The 1966 standards retained the emphasis on systems.

In the development of standards, there has been a growing effort to minimize purely quantitative measures and to establish some kind of qualitative measures. This effort did not meet with immediate acceptance despite the work of many committees, which spent many hours of devoted labor. If one attempts to move away from such quantitative measures as the size of the reference collection or the number of reference staff and attempts to develop meaningful quantitative measures for *quality* of reference work, one will soon discover the complexities involved in trying to find objective measures for operations evaluated by subjective judgments.

About 1971, the Standards Committee of the Public Library Association began the task of preparing a new set of standards to replace those of 1966. The changes in society in the 1960s, mentioned earlier, led the committee to question the utility of its charge and the procedure for writing new standards. It held a series of hearings and committee meetings in 1972 and 1973 which led to (1) a change in the name of the PLA Standards Committee to the PLA Goals, Guidelines, and Standards Committee; (2) the publication of ''Community Library Services—Working Papers on Goals and Guidelines'' in *School Library Journal*, September 1973; (3) the publication of ''Goals and Guidelines for Community Library Services'' in the *PLA Newsletter*, June 1975; (4) approval by the PLA Board at the Detroit Conference, June 1977, and publication in *American Libraries*, December 1977, of ''A Mission Statement for Public Libraries; Guidelines for Public Library Service.'' Guidelines will be developed by the committee, based on reaction to the ''Mission Statement.'' *American Libraries*, October 1977, announced the awarding of a $140,000 grant (from the Office of Library and Learning Resources of the U.S. Office of Education) for a 21-month research project on ''The Process of Standards Development for Community Library Services.'' Work was to have begun in October 1977, so we suggest that those who are reading this chapter (which should appear in September 1979) watch for publication of the results of the study, which is scheduled to end in May 1979.

Whatever the difficulties involved in creating meaningful standards, the effort is bound to continue because there is a strongly-felt need for common benchmarks by which comparisons can be made among libraries of the same group. Thus, in the late 1970s, there were, in addition to the effort of the public librarians, standards for college, correctional institution, junior college, hospital, school, special, and state libraries. The Association of College and Research Libraries was also discussing the creation of standards for university libraries. Standards have been written for individual services such as those to children and young adults and for bookmobile service. A number of these sets of standards are under revision, and the reader interested in them is reminded to seek out the latest edition. The standards include many more topics than selection of materials, but it is suggested that the sections on selection in each set of standards be read, and that the several statements be compared.

The next chapter will take up some of the differences among the other types of libraries, which have an effect on selection.

Conclusion

This presentation of principles has attempted to stress the relationship of the librarian's conception of the library's purpose to his/her attitude toward selection principles, the eternal need for judgment, and the continual balancing of one principle against another in terms of the immediate library situation. To be a good selector is not an easy job. It requires a great deal of time and thought and effort and intelligence. The librarian cannot avoid responsibility for constant judgments in selecting because the principles do not furnish automatic machinery for deciding whether or not to buy a given item; they do not furnish a yardstick against which materials can be placed and a numerical reading of fitness taken; they cannot be applied blindly. There is no mathematical formula for successful selection. There is no easy road to the building of library collections.

BIBLIOGRAPHY

Allerton Park Institute, 9th, 1962. *Selection and Acquisition Procedures in Medium-Sized and Large Libraries*. Edited by Herbert Goldhor. Urbana, University of Illinois, Graduate School of Library Science, 1963. 139p. Ten papers on a variety of topics.

American Library Association. Resources and Technical Services Division. Resources Section. Collection Development Committee. "Guidelines for the Formulation of Collection Development Policies." *Library Resources and Technical Services*, 21:40–47, Winter 1977.

Berelson, Bernard. *The Library's Public*. New York, Columbia University Press, 1949. 174p. Classic review of research on public library use.

Blackshear, Orilla T. *Building and Maintaining the Small Library Collection*. Chicago, American Library Association, 1963. 11p. (Small Libraries Project Pamphlet No. 5)

Bone, Larry Earl. "The Public Library Goals and Objectives Movement: Death Gasp or Renaissance?" *Library Journal*, 100:1283–1286, July 1975.

Bone, Larry Earl and Thomas A. Raines. "The Nature of the Urban Main Library: Its Relation to Selection and Collection Building." *Library Trends*, 20:625–639, April 1972. Argues for greater depth in collections of main urban libraries.

Boyer, Calvin and Nancy L. Eaton. *Book Selection Policies of American Libraries; An Anthology of Policies from College, Public and School Libraries*. Austin, Texas, Armadillo Press, 1971. 222p. Reprints 31 policy statements.

Broadus, Robert N. "The Applications of Citation Analyses to Library Collection Building." In *Advances in Librarianship*, Vol. 7, pp. 299–335. New York, Academic Press, 1977.

Broadus, Robert N. *Selecting Materials for Libraries*. New York, Wilson, 1973. 342p. Textbook which focuses on selection in a medium-sized public library. Gives considerable emphasis to subject selection.

Broderick, Dorothy. *An Introduction to Children's Work in Public Libraries*. New York, Wilson, 1965. 176p.

Brown, Eleanor Frances. *Library Service to the Disadvantaged*. Metuchen, M.J., Scarecrow Press, 1971. 560 p.

Bundy, Mary Lee. *The Library's Public Revisited*. College Park, University of Maryland, School of Library and Information Service, 1967. 84p.

Carrier, Esther Jane. *Fiction in Public Libraries, 1876–1900*. New York, Scarecrow Press, 1965. 458p. Historical review of librarians' attitudes toward fiction.

Casey, Genevieve. "Alternative Futures for the Public Library." *Library Scene*, 3:11–15, June 1974.

Crum, Norman J. *Library Goals and Objectives: Literature Review*. Washington, D.C., ERIC Clearinghouse on Library and Information Sciences, 1973. 39p. (ED 082 794)

Davies, D. W. *Public Libraries as Culture and Social Centers: The Origin of the Concept*. Metuchen, M.J., Scarecrow Press, 1974. 174p. Historical review.

Ditzion, Sidney H. *Arsenals of a Democratic Culture*. Chicago, American Library Association, 1947. 263p. Early history of American public libraries.

Drury, Francis K. *Book Selection*. Chicago, American Library Association, 1930. 369p. Old, but useful discussion of points to consider in building library collections.

Ennis, Philip E. *Adult Book Reading in the United States; A Preliminary Report*. Chicago, National Opinion Research Center, 1965. 111p.

Enoch Pratt Free Library, Baltimore. *How Baltimore Chooses; Selection Policies of the Enoch Pratt Free Library*. 4th ed. Baltimore, 1968. 60p. Includes policies for adult, young adult, and children's materials.

Evans, Charles. *Middle Class Attitudes and Public Library Use*. Littleton, Colo., Libraries Unlimited, 1970. 126p.

Futas, Elizabeth. *Library Acquisition Policies and Procedures*. Phoenix, Ariz., Oryx Press, 1977. 406p. Reprints, among other examples, a number of public library policy statements.

Gaver, Mary V. *Background Readings in Building Library Collections*. Metuchen, N.J., Scarecrow Press, 1969. 2v. Collection of previously-published articles from a variety of sources.

Goldhor, Herbert. "A Note on the Theory of Book Selection." *Library Quarterly*, 12:151–174, April 1942.

Gregory, Ruth W. and Lester B. Stoffel. "Collection Building and Maintenance." In *Public Libraries in Cooperative Systems: Administrative Patterns for Service*, pp. 148–196. Chicago, American Library Association, 1971.

Haines, Helen. *Living with Books*. 2d ed. New York, Columbia University Press, 1950. 610p. Classic work on selection.

Harris, Michael. *The Role of the Public Library in American Life: A Speculative Essay*. Urbana, University of Illinois, Graduate School of Library Science, 1975. 42p. (Occasional Papers No. 117)

Hartford (Conn.) Public Library. *Book Selection Policy Statement*. Rev. ed. Hartford, Conn., 1972. 14p.

Jennison, Peter S. and Robert N. Sheridan. *The Future of General Adult Books and Reading in America*. Chicago, American Library Association, 1970. 160p. Collection of six papers.

Kujoth, Jean S. *Libraries, Readers and Book Selection*. Metuchen, N.J., Scarecrow Press, 1969. 470p. Forty-four articles reprinted from 28 journals.

Library School Teaching Methods: Courses in the Selection of Adult Materials. Edited by Larry Earl Bone. Urbana, University of Illinois, Graduate School of Library Science, 1969. 137p. Papers from a conference.

Lipsman, Claire K. *The Disadvantaged and Library Effectiveness*. Chicago, American Library Association, 1972. 208p. Report of a research study.

Long, Harriet G. *Public Library Service to Children: Foundation and Development*. Metuchen, N.J., Scarecrow Press, 1969. 162p.

Lyman, Helen H. *Literacy and the Nation's Libraries*. Chicago, American Library Association, 1977. 212p. Developing Public Library Programs to Serve the Illiterate. Includes discussion of collection development.

McNiff, Philip J. "Book Selection and Provision in the Urban Library." *Library Quarterly*, 38:58–69, January 1968. Discusses building of collections for advanced students and professionals.

McPheron, Judith. "On to the Tumbrels; or, Let's Put Quality in Its Rightful Place." *Wilson Library Bulletin*, 49:446–447; 455, February 1975. Argues for collection of popular materials in public libraries.

Martin, Lowell A. *Baltimore Reaches Out: Library Service to the Disadvantaged*. Baltimore, Enoch Pratt Free Library, 1967. 54p.

Martin, Lowell A. *Library Response to Urban Change; A Study of the Chicago Public Library*. Chicago, American Library Association, 1969. 313p.

Merritt, LeRoy Charles. *Book Selection and Intellectual Freedom*. New York, Wilson, 1970. 100p. Illustrates the writing of selection policies in public libraries.

Milwaukee Public Library. *Book Selection Criteria: Milwaukee Public Library System*. Milwaukee, 1975. 227p. (ED 121 335)

Murison, William J. *The Public Library: Its Origins, Purpose, and Significance*. 2d ed., rev. and reset. London, Harrap, 1971. 244p.

Polacheck, Dem. "A Method of Adult Book Selection for a Public Library System." *RQ*, 16:231–233, Spring 1977. Experiences of Stark County District Library, Canton, Ohio.

Public Library and Federal Policy. Westport, Conn., Greenwood Press, 1974. 349p. Reviews history and makes recommendations.

Public Library Association. "Goals and Guidelines for Community Library Services." *PLA Newsletter*, 14:9–12;14, June 1975. Includes rationale behind the "Goals and Guidelines" statement.

Public Library Association. *A Strategy for Public Library Change: Proposed Public Library Goals—Feasibility Study*. Allie Beth Martin, project coordinator. Chicago, American Library Association, 1972. 84p. Formed the basis for much of the discussion of new public library standards.

Public Library Association. Audiovisual Committee. *Guidelines for Audiovisual Materials and Services for Large Libraries*. Chicago, American Library Association, 1975. 35p. Includes quantitative guidelines.

Public Library Association. Goals, Guidelines, and Standards Committee. "A Mission

Statement for Public Libraries; Guidelines for Public Library Service: Part I.'' *American Libraries*, 8:615–620. December 1977. Draft version published for review and comment.

Public Library Association. Standards Committee. ''Community Library Services— Working Papers on Goals and Guidelines.'' *School Library Journal*, 20:21–27, September 1973.

Public Library in the Urban Setting. Edited by Leon Carnovsky. Chicago, University of Chicago Press, 1968. 108p. Papers from the 32nd Conference of the Graduate Library School, August, 1967.

Public Library of Cincinnati and Hamilton County. *Book Selection Policy*. 3d rev. Cincinnati, 1971. 31p. Detailed selection policy statement.

Public Library Policies; General and Specific. Rev. ed. Edited by Ruth M. White and Eleanor A. Ferguson. Chicago, American Library Association, 1970. 108p. (Public Library Reporter, no. 9) Guide to formulation of policy statements.

Shera, Jesse H. *Foundations of the Public Library*. Chicago, University of Chicago Press, 1949. 308p. Analysis of the causes of the American public library.

Smith, Ray. ''Book Selection and the Community Library.'' *Library Quarterly*, 33:79–90, January 1963.

Social Responsibilities and Libraries: A Library Journal/School Library Journal Selection. Compiled and edited by Patricia G. Schuman. New York, Bowker, 1976. 402p. Reprints fifty articles.

Spiller, David. *Book Selection: An Introduction to Principles and Practice*. 2d ed. rev. London, Clive Bingley, 1974. 142p. British viewpoint.

Toronto Public Library. ''Policies and Practices for Selection and Care of Materials in the Toronto Public Libraries.'' In *Public Libraries in the Urban Metropolitan Setting*, edited by H. C. Campbell, pp. 277–289. London, Clive Bingley, 1973.

Tulsa (Okla.) City-County Library System. *Materials Selection Policy*. Tulsa, Okla., 1973. 29p. (ED 092 158)

Voos, Henry. *Information Needs in Urban Areas*. New Brunswick, N.J., Rutgers University Press, 1969. 90p.

Wellard, James H. *Book Selection; Its Principles and Practice*. London, Grafton, 1937. 205p. Discusses selection principles in relation to public library objectives.

Wheeler, Joseph L. and Herbert Goldhor. *Practical Administration of Public Libraries*. New York, Harper and Row, 1962. 571p. Several chapters consider aspects of collection development.

Wilson, Louis R. *The Practice of Book Selection*. Chicago, University of Chicago Press, 1940. 368p. Collection of papers by various authors.

CHAPTER 2

Variations by Type of Library

Sooner or later at almost any meeting of librarians, one is bound to hear a librarian declare: "But in our situation. . . ." This phrase usually heralds an invocation of that great truism, "Circumstances alter cases," to justify some practice which other librarians have questioned. There is always the danger, of course, of being so far influenced by local demands that generally accepted professional standards may be ignored. It is tempting to use the appeal to "our situation" to justify a departure from sound practice, and the librarian must always be on guard to support informed professional judgment against local influences. The appeal to local conditions has been used on occasion as a defense of unwillingness to change, to grow, to depart from the old ways. Nevertheless, much as this appeal to local conditions may be misused, it is essential to have a close knowledge of and a respect for the local factors which must be taken into account in building a library collection. Legitimate adaptations of the general principles must be made, as libraries vary by size and type. They are not departures from professionally accepted standards, but necessary modifications, amplifications, or variations of them.

One of the primary factors influencing the building of a collection is the type of library. Public, university, college, school, and special libraries may generally adhere to the same group of basic principles of collection development, but the specific objectives of these types of libraries are not identical. The libraries operate in different environments, serve different groups of people, and often collect different types of materials. This chapter discusses some of the variations in objectives, clientele, type and volume of material collected, and organization of selection procedures found in different types of libraries.

THE UNIVERSITY LIBRARY

University libraries exist to support the teaching, research, and public service programs of the university. Collection development in these libraries is influenced by the breadth of the university's curriculum, the levels (undergraduate, graduate, advanced graduate) at which various disciplines are taught, the numbers of students who choose particular majors and degree programs, the fields of research pursued by faculty and graduate students, and the number and type of outreach, extension, or other public service programs offered. University libraries are so closely tied to their parent institutions that every financial, administrative, or academic decision made by the university has potential impact on the library. When the university decides to start a new degree program or to support a previously unemphasized area of research, the library must respond. Because of this relationship, the clientele and operating environment of the university library must be discussed in terms of the university's clientele and environment.

Higher education occupied a very favorable position in the nation's priorities from 1957 to the late 1960s. Many people began to view education—the more of it, the better—as the solution to all scientific, technical, and social problems. This led to public support of funding. Faculty members were recruited, programs were expanded, students were encouraged to enroll for ever higher degree programs, and libraries received great increases in materials budgets and money for new buildings. Although academic institutions of all sizes felt the effects of this, publicly supported institutions—especially the small and medium-sized ones—were affected the most. Many state colleges expanded their programs and enrollment, assumed the name "university," and began to build libraries that would rival—at least in total size if not in richness of holdings—the collections of major universities. Libraries which had never tried to do more than support the teaching programs of their parent institutions were asked to provide research materials in a wide variety of fields.

Beginning in the late 1960s, the environment in which university libraries operated changed sharply. Enrollments in most academic institutions have stabilized—declining in some cases, growing much below projected rates in others. Because of a decline in the population age group from which college and university enrollments are most often drawn, universities are attempting to appeal to older students, part-time students, and even students who do not wish to pursue a formal degree program. Budgets for faculty, buildings, and library resources have been affected by the lack of enrollment growth, the general pessimistic mood about the value of higher education to individuals and society, and the rising inflation rate, which has become of increasing concern in the late 1970s. All of these factors—changing student body, fluctuating fiancial support, and shifting objectives of the parent institutions—affect university library collection development policies and procedures.

There is no such thing as a typical university library collection, but certain general comments can be made about the characteristics of such collections. First of all, university library collections tend to be large. Membership in the Association of Research Libraries, an organization which includes the largest libraries in the United States and Canada, is determined partly by number of items held in the collection. In 1976–77, only eleven of the 105 member libraries were not located at universities. (The exceptions included national libraries of both countries, a few large public libraries, and a few endowed research libraries.) The smallest ARL university library reported holdings that year of 906,741 volumes; the largest (Harvard) reported 9,547,576 volumes; the median for university members was 1,656,275 volumes. In general, the more research is (and has been traditionally) a major priority of a university, the more likely the library is to hold a collection of scholarly, little-used, rare, and expensive items. Such libraries buy materials in many languages, in every type of print format (books, journals, government documents, technical reports, privately-issued works, microforms, etc.) and many types of nonprint formats (audio and video recordings, data files on magnetic tapes, etc.). Since content is likely to be the major reason for adding an item to a research collection, format (assuming the format does not inhibit access to the content) is a relatively unimportant consideration. The range of subjects covered in a university library collection will be *at least* as broad as the teaching and research interests of faculty and students and will probably be even broader, since many university librarians acquire some materials as a contribution toward the library resources of the nation or region. Breadth, depth, and variety are key characteristics of university library collections.

Organization of Selection in University Libraries

Earlier editions of this book have described a typical approach to the organization of selection in university libraries. The various academic departments are theoretically responsible for selection in their subject areas, while the library staff remains responsible for the fields of general bibliography, for those areas not covered by departments, for special materials such as periodicals and documents, and for overseeing the general development of the collection. A "selection officer," "chief bibliographer," or "head of selection and bibliography" assumes the responsibility for directing a group of librarians who attempt to see to it that the general collection is kept sound in all of its many constituent parts. They watch the buying of the departments, trying to prevent unnecessary overlapping, suggesting titles for purchase which the departments may have missed, or buying titles which they feel must be procured. This selection group works with dealers' catalogues, trying to pick up out-of-print items which should be in the collection. In general, the selections officer is responsible for the development of the collection as a whole and for the coordination of all the widely-dispersed sources of orders. This procedure is still followed, essentially, in some university libraries. In other libraries, however, the academic environment of the 1960s and 1970s has brought about changes in organization.

Blanket Orders and Approval Plans

Several developments in university libraries in the 1960s—a rapid increase in materials budgets without an equal increase in staff, pressure to collect in subject areas not previously emphasized in a library's collection, requests for materials from countries and in languages not formerly collected—led to the acceptance in many libraries of blanket orders and approval plans. In general, a blanket order plan is one in which a publisher agrees to supply everything published (within specified limits of the plan), generally without return privileges for the buyer; and an approval plan is one in which a dealer assumes the responsibility for selecting and supplying, subject to return privileges, all materials fitting the library's profile specified in terms of subjects, levels, formats, price, etc.

Many university libraries adopted blanket order and approval plans in the 1960s. Some libraries had as many as 30 or 40 separate plans operating at once, covering both foreign and domestic publications. In some cases, rather large percentages of the book funds were spent through this method, although other libraries were very selective in their choice of plans. Librarians were encouraged to consider blanket plans when their selection procedures reached the point where decisions on individual titles had become perfunctory, when they were already acquiring almost all new publications in specified subject areas, or when the regularly appropriated budget seemed to be covering easily the purchase of current imprints. Such conditions are most likely to be found in large university libraries during times of economic prosperity and least likely to be found when, as in the 1970s, budgets are tight and priorities must be reviewed.

As a tool to improve selection, blanket order and approval plans have been praised for offering more systematic coverage of current publishing in fields of interest than the older method of relying on faculty selection. Faculty members need not be excluded from the selection process under a blanket plan; but since they do not have to initiate orders, any negligence on the faculty's part will not be reflected in an unbalanced collection. According to supporters, approval plans simply mean that the faculty members or librarians who want to select books can do it with the book in hand. Opponents of approval plans point out that reviews will not be available at the time of selection and emphasize the natural human tendency to take the path of least resistance by accepting a marginal book that has already arrived, rather than taking the trouble to reject and return it.

Some of the proponents of blanket plans seem to view the jobber's staff as an extension of the library's staff. When materials are needed in a language that few, if any, library staff members can handle easily, jobbers can be instructed to select and ship. If, as supporters claim, blanket order and approval plans mean that the library staff spends less time on current acquisition, then they ought to be able to spend more time on evaluating the collection, identifying weak areas, and doing retrospective buying. Of course, some experienced librarians have warned that there may be no good reason to change a system which employs competent and experienced local selectors and works well. Blanket order and approval plans cannot alone solve the problems of inefficient selection and acquisition procedures.

Collection Development Policies

In recent years university libraries have tended to adopt more formal approaches to selection policy and procedure. Written statements of selection and acquisition policies and budget allocation formulas are evidence of this trend. Before 1970, few voices were heard in support of developing written policies for large university libraries; since 1970, the professional literature has been filled with advocates airing their views, examples of policy statements from individual libraries, and organizational pronouncements and guidelines. The publication in 1977 by the American Library Association's Resources and Technical Services Division of "Guidelines for the Formulation of Collection Development Policies" put a strong stamp of approval on this type of collection planning. Boyer and Eaton, in their 1971 compilation of policies, defined a selection policy as one which specifies the "intellectual framework within which decisions are made," the community to be served, who has authority for selection decisions, acceptable physical and intellectual quality, and methods of handling problem materials or controversial subjects. They described an acquisitions policy as one which gave a detailed listing, subject by subject, of the depth of collection which a library hoped to acquire. The collection development policy, as outlined by RTSD, would include the main features of both selection and acquisition policies. (The variety of points which might be covered in a written policy are evident in the RTSD "Guidelines," in the examples reproduced in Boyer and Eaton, and in a 1977 collection of policies by Futas.)

Advantages cited by the advocates of written collection development policies include the benefits which come from the drafting process, the improved communication which results, and the contribution such a policy can make to overall library planning. The process of writing a policy usually brings to light important information about traditional, but unrecorded, policies and procedures; it forces the staff to examine what the library is trying to do and to set priorities within the ubiquitous budgetary restraints. A written policy enables each selector to have a better idea of what the others are doing, which in the long run ought to ensure consistent and balanced collection growth. Sometimes a written policy may be used to resist pressures from very vocal segments of the library community; at other times it may serve to remind selectors of the needs of the quieter members of the community. A written policy has great potential as a means of communication with other libraries (assuming that standard terminology is used). Special interlibrary loan arrangements, cooperative acquisition agreements, and other kinds of resource-sharing projects have stimulated the development of written policies.

Opponents of written policies usually cite as major disadvantages the staff time and expense involved in getting agreement on a policy. They point out the confusion of purpose evident in some policies—should it be a working, public relations, or defense document?—and argue that there is very little that a written policy can accomplish. A collection development policy does not answer all selection and acquisition problems and can only serve as a general guide in making decisions about individual items. In addition to confusion about the intended audience for a written document, there is disagreement about how futuristic the document should be. Does a policy describe the situation as it is, does it describe what the library is able to do, or does it describe what the library should be doing—the ideal situation? Review and revision of a written policy must be a constant concern of the staff. The collection development policy will be a useful tool only if it is kept current; the development process is a continuous one.

Budget Allocation Formulas

Another, and related, manifestation of the formalization of collection development procedures which has occurred in university libraries in the 1970s is the increased interest in budget allocation formulas. Allocation of funds in the materials budget to subjects or academic departments is not a new development in academic libraries, but the need to rationalize the allocation of limited funds has redirected attention toward this control device. Allocation formulas are related to written collection development policies in that both reflect a concern for planning and establishment of priorities, the two ought to be consistent with each other, and the process of producing one in a given library often leads to work on the other.

Allocation systems vary with the allocation unit used, the factors used to determine amount of allocation, and the weight assigned to each factor. Allocations may be made on the basis of administrative unit (departmental library, undergraduate library, special collection, etc.); form of material (monographs, serials, microforms, etc.); broad subject; specific subject; academic unit; individual or group responsible for selection (individual librarians, departmental faculty, etc.); or language or country of publication. Each possible division of the funds has its advantages and disadvantages. Those methods which allow more flexibility (such as assignment to broad subjects) tend to allow less monitoring and control. Factors on which allocations are based may include strength of existing collection, number and cost of books currently being published, number of faculty members, number (and level) of students, number (and level) of courses, circulation counts, interlibrary loans, inflation rates, and subjective ratings of the importance of a discipline. In a given formula, any factor may be assigned a weight to represent its importance in the allocation decision. For example, a graduate student may be assigned higher weight than an undergraduate and a faculty member may be given more weight than a graduate student. (The assumption underlying this practice is that the weights represent relative need for library resources.) From all the possible combinations of allocation units, factors, and weights, librarians in a given university must reach agreement (and convince the faculty that their decision is correct) on the best combination for their situation. The method of allocation used in one institution might be completely unsuitable for another.

Collection Development Offices and Committees

In addition to collection development policies and budget allocation formulas, other evidence exists of a move toward more formal coordination and control of collection development in university libraries. In some large university libraries collection development responsibilities have been assigned to a separate, permanent collection development office. The collection development officer who heads this unit often reports directly to the head of the library and sometimes holds the title of assistant or associate director. Activities of the collection development unit may vary from those primarily involved in coordination of the selection activities to others which are of a controlling or policy-setting nature. When university libraries do not have a collection development office (and sometimes when they do), they are likely to have a collection development committee made up of staff members from various units of the library. Roles of these committees vary as much as do the roles of collection development offices. Committees or offices may be asked to identify areas where policies or procedures are lacking, draft policy and procedure statements, conduct surveys of the collection, produce budget allocation formulas, coordinate selection with academic departments, or approve requests costing more than a specified amount. In addition to general collection development committees, some libraries also have separate serials committees to review serial selection procedures and to coordinate and control serial requests.

The Role of the Faculty in Selection

In all academic libraries (university, college, and school), it has been customary for the faculty to take part in selection. Indeed, in some libraries, librarians have been restricted to selecting only general reference materials and those items not covered by departmental subject lines. The arguments for giving the faculty a prominent role in selecting materials seem good ones: (1) After all, they are the subject experts. They have degrees in their fields, which represent considerable reading and study. They know the past and present scholars in their respective fields; they know the major works and can evaluate a new contribution to the subject. (2) They teach the courses, so they know which readings will be required for the students, they know what kinds of materials will be needed for term papers, they know when they change the emphasis in a course or add new units.

One can then visualize the ideal faculty selector: he/she knows the current productive scholarship, knows fully what the library has in the field, knows the sources of information for new materials and uses them, is accurate in transcribing information about a title when requesting its purchase and even checks to see that the item is not already in the library, is not narrow in his/her interests, but notices important related materials, has some interest in selecting for students as well as researchers, and so orders materials with a wide range of complexity for different groups of students—the major in the subject, the minor, the interested layperson.

The ideal faculty selector is, like all ideal creatures, something of a rare bird. The realities of experience have taught us that not all faculty members will participate in selection. Some are interested but do not have the time. They try to do a good job in the classroom, which means many hours each week spent in preparation; they are free with time for interviews with students; they participate in departmental and college committees; they have families which demand some time; they take part in community activities; they read their professional literature and try to keep up with the world outside their field. They simply do not find enough hours to do systematic and continuing work on building the collection.

There are those who do not participate because they are not interested. Some are indifferent, some are lazy. Others have come to rely on the library to have what they want and see no need to make an effort which could only duplicate the work already done by the librarian. Some adhere to the practice of lecturing and asking the students to do their reading in a list of books which will be reserved for that purpose, and so they are not concerned with building the collection for independent study.

It is true, too, that it is growing very difficult for any working teacher to find enough time to keep up with the professional and scholarly literature. Many readers find that reviews must substitute for the books they will never have time to read; much journal reading becomes a scanning of title pages, with only occasional dipping into selected articles.

There is some reason to feel that some of the difficulty in building general collections is attributable to a narrowing tendency of advanced education. The expertise becomes more and more restricted in scope. As a college sophomore, for example, the student may have taken the survey course in English literature, which sweeps from the Anglo-Saxons to modern times in two brief semesters. As a senior, the same student may take a survey course in eighteenth-century literature, which covers the century in two semesters. As a graduate student, he/she may take two semesters to study the criticism of the Age of Queen Anne. As a doctoral student, he/she may produce a dissertation devoted to one very small segment of that microcosm. Such narrowing of interest may lead to a somewhat parochial view, so that the professor may be truly interested in only a small part of his/her field.

Surveying the realities of much faculty selection in practice (at any level of education), some have argued for giving librarians the major responsibility for selection. Indeed, at many institutions this has actually happened without planning and continues to be a noticeable trend in large university libraries. Librarians usually have studied at least one subject major and are supposed to have had a good general liberal education; many are dedicated readers, who use their own collections to expand their own education. The number of librarians with graduate training in academic disciplines seems to be increasing, especially in large university libraries.

Furthermore, librarians are trained in using sources of information about new materials and can often identify needed materials before the faculty hears of them. This is true primarily because faculty are likely to rely on their professional journals, all of which are notoriously late in reviewing. Librarians watch publishers' announcements, national bibliographies, issues of library periodicals which list forthcoming materials, and all the multitude of specialized sources which are part of the librarian's armamentarium. It is this kind of knowledge which has enabled librarians with masters' degrees in a field like history to give good service as heads of chemistry libraries. They know how to find information; that is their stock in trade.

Librarians are also likely to watch the whole range of demands or needs and see where gaps exist or are being created. They see the collection in a way that the individual faculty member or department is not likely to see it, and they will try to ensure that all interests are represented, even if those interests are not loudly expressed.

Clearly, however, it is desirable that both faculty and librarians cooperate in building the collection, each bringing to the task special skills and knowledge. There should be constant and continuing communication across the barriers separating the library staff from the faculty and departments from each other. Unfortunately, there are some blocks to easy cooperation which have grown up with time.

There are occasional faults on the faculty side which lead librarians to suspicion of faculty suggestions—and sometimes to openly expressed hostility. One university librarian received a request from a very powerful department, asking that the library purchase a very expensive reprint of a massive set of source materials originally published in the 1880s. The purchase involved several thousand dollars, so the librarian sent the request to the selection officer for checking. The selection officer first went to the catalog—to discover what one can guess: the library had bought the set in 1880. Chalk up one cause of doubt concerning the faculty's judgment.

In another university, a chemical experiment supported by a grant had reached a point at which the researchers needed a certain piece of information. A literature search did not turn it up, and so the main experiment was sidetracked while special equipment was built to run a subsidiary experiment to determine the data needed. It had been completed before the chemistry librarian got wind of the whole affair and had the sad duty (or satisfaction?) of reporting that the results had been obtained in Germany 40 years earlier and were available in the library, but had not been found by the experts.

The faculty have sometimes hardly endeared themselves to the librarian, or encouraged cooperation, by the openly expressed belief that librarians are really rather low-powered clerks, without much in the way of brains or training, who are competent enough to stamp a date due card or collect a fine, but hardly able to make an informed judgment. This may certainly be true of some librarians, but it is hardly the way for faculty to obtain whole-hearted support from the library staff.

The faculty do individually sometimes take a very parochial view of the library. They see only their own needs and are not at all concerned with other parts of the collection. This is a natural enough state of affairs but it may lead them to condemn the librarian for trying to ensure that the needs of all parts of the faculty and student body are satisfied. It is also true that there is usually a small group of very vocal and active faculty members who demand materials, but there is a larger group who never order anything and yet will criticize the library staff at faculty meetings for not having what they need.

Librarians have made their contributions to the problem with a few faults of their own. They sometimes tacitly hold, or openly express, the belief that the faculty are really a pretty ignorant bunch when it comes to knowing anything about selection; that they are a selfish lot, not caring a whit whether any other faculty or student need is met; that when they are not ignorant, they are lazy—and careless as well. Librarians ask how else one can explain the books ordered under sub-title (by the expert, no less!); the authors all garbled, misspelled, or with works wrongly attributed to them; and they point to the agonized screams for purchase of titles which have been in the library for months. Some librarians have unjustly concluded that faculty cannot be trusted at all.

Librarians in academic libraries of any type need the cooperation of the faculty. Librarians must be fully aware of the curriculum, the collection, the faculty interest, and the composition of the student body. They need to get out of the library and talk to the faculty, watch the departments for the appearance of new courses and the hiring of new faculty, and attempt to learn as much as possible about how courses are taught. The library staff bears the responsibility for the collection and should have the final authority in making decisions concerning it, but they must know their community well in order to make the best decisions.

Special Problems in University Libraries

Because universities emphasize both teaching and research, the university library must try to supply materials needed for classes currently being taught, while at the same time building collections that may be of use to researchers in the future. A conflict between these priorities often arises in times of severely limited budgets. When large numbers of students demand more duplicate copies of reserve books, it is hard to justify expensive purchases for which there may be no immediate demand. On the other hand, some research materials must be bought and preserved now or they will be unavailable in the future. The balancing of research needs against teaching needs (or future needs versus current needs) is an unresolved issue in many university libraries.

Serial publications, which are increasing in volume and cost, pose another problem for university libraries. In some disciplines, especially the scientific ones, the serial form of publication (journals, newsletters, monographs-in-series, etc.) is the most important printed source of information. University libraries must acquire or at least provide prompt access to long runs of domestic and foreign serials. In recent years, the costs of acquiring, processing, and storing these serials have absorbed larger and larger percentages of the materials budget. In some academic departments, almost the entire allocation for library materials is designated for serials. Although university librarians are giving much attention to the collection development posed by serials, as yet no totally satisfactory solution seems to have been found. One popular approach is to develop cooperative projects (which will be discussed in a later chapter) to handle the less frequently-used serials.

THE COLLEGE LIBRARY

The library of the liberal arts college generally has three major functions: (1) to support the curriculum with materials in those subjects taught by the college; (2) to provide a basic collection aimed at the development of the "humane," the "liberally educated" person, apart from curricular requirements; (3) to support a degree of faculty research. To serve these functions, the library must provide a fairly wide range of new scholarly monographs in English (covering all the academic disciplines it is supporting), a carefully-chosen periodical collection, an extensive reference and bibliography collection, and nonprint materials needed to support teaching efforts.

The typical college library has a much smaller and more homogeneous community of users than the average university library. In an institution without graduate programs, there is likely to be a narrower range of academic specialization represented in the student body. Faculty members will probably be graduates of specialized doctoral programs, but some of them at least have left the specialization of the university and chosen to teach in a program with a broad, liberal arts emphasis. The assumption is made, although it may often be false, that college faculty members place a higher priority on teaching than on research. In most colleges, the number of faculty, staff, and students is small enough that librarians can know most of the faculty and many of the students individually and can follow rather closely the interests and needs of their users.

Since the college library is not intended primarily for research, but for use of students in undergraduate education, it will not require the expenditure of funds for the more remote materials of narrow subject scope and intense specialization. Since it does not support a curriculum encompassing the special technical fields (medicine, engineering, agriculture, nursing, dentistry, etc.), it will not need the highly specialized materials of these fields. Since it is not a public library serving a wide variety of publics, it may tend to base its selection on the value and authority of a given title, rather than on its popular appeal. In the various subject fields, it need not emphasize the popularizations, intended for the less skilled or less informed reader, although it may feel a responsibility for general works, introductory to a field, intended for the college student who is not specializing in that field but who wishes some knowledge of it as part of a general education.

College library collections vary widely in size but tend to be small in comparison with university research collections. The size, as well as the nature of the collection, is governed by the range of academic programs offered and the availability of other library resources in the area. The latest set of standards for college libraries (published in 1975 by the Association of College and Research Libraries) recommends that a college library should "provide prompt access" to a basic print collection of 85,000 volumes, to which should be added 100 volumes for each full-time faculty member, 15 volumes for each full-time student, 350 volumes for each undergraduate major or minor field, and several thousands of volumes (rising as the level of instruction rises) for each graduate program which might be offered by the institution. Of course, the emphasis in these standards is on the number of items to which faculty and students have quick and easy access, as opposed to the number of items which the college library actually owns. Some college libraries own as few as 20,000 volumes while a few others have collections approaching the half-million mark. The average college library collection is well below that size.

Organization of Selection in College Libraries

In the college library participation in selection is likely to be widely dispersed. In addition to the entire library staff, the members of the faculty and sometimes students are encouraged to select in their subject fields. Because the group involved can be large, it is important that overall planning be done and the decisions on selection policy be set down in writing. A written collection development policy is just as important in a college library as in any other type of library. The remarks made earlier about collection development policies in university libraries also apply here.

Because the college library collection should be centered on the curriculum, it is particularly important that library staff and faculty members work together. Some of the difficulties mentioned in connection with faculty selection in university libraries may apply here, but college selection should lean heavily on all faculty members, and full participation should be encouraged by the heads of departments.

As it becomes unwieldly to have all the faculty participating in this activity without direction or coordination, it is typical that each faculty member make recommendations to the department head or to the departmental library committee. The general college library committee, which may also become involved in this process, should be made up of members of the faculty who are genuinely interested in assisting in developing the collection and who represent the college faculty as a whole.

Although the ideal situation is to have intelligent faculty participation in selection, ultimate responsibility lies with the librarian and the professional staff. In certain college libraries, the selection of general materials is made by the professional library staff, which meets at regular intervals after perusal of the various reviewing media. As in the university situation, it is assumed that librarians have expert knowledge of sources for selection, knowledge of the overall collection, and will consider every order in the light of the needs of the library as a whole and its place as part of the total educational apparatus of the institution.

Blanket orders and approval plans are seldom used in college libraries; the smaller the materials budget, the less likely they are to be used. The college librarian has the assets of close acquaintance with the library community and the potential of good communication with and cooperation from the faculty, and the liability of a rather limited materials budget. Under those circumstances, common sense holds that selection decisions can best be made by librarians and faculty. Larger college libraries will probably maintain some standing orders, but more are not likely to collect any subject in the depth that makes a blanket order or approval plan economical.

Special Problems of College Libraries

Liberal arts colleges, most of which are privately supported, have had a difficult time in recent years. The shock of adjusting to rising expectations for academic programs and library holdings in the early 1960s, followed so quickly by the reassessment and retrenchment required in the 1970s, has caused the closing of a number of institutions and lowered the expectations in many others. The pressures of unpredictable enrollments, stable or declining budgets, inflation—all of which had serious effects on university libraries—are affecting college libraries even more drastically. With the increase in publishing (which has been evident worldwide for at least the past decade), college libraries with fairly small materials budgets have had trouble buying all they might be expected to acquire, judged on the basis of their academic programs. Summaries of expenditures made by college libraries in recent years show that acquisition rates have gone down. When financial troubles hit small institutions, where there seems to be less budget surplus to absorb new cuts, libraries and their materials budgets are likely to be hard hit.

Periodicals also cause problems in college library collections. They are expensive to acquire initially and represent a continuing drain on library resources, since they may continue indefinitely (no library starts a subscription with the idea of keeping it only a year or two) and require expensive recordkeeping, binding, and shelf space. Periodicals are, however, an important part of a collection which supports instruction, and no library can afford to cut too much its subscription list or its holdings of back files. How a library approaches this problem will probably depend on the other resources available in the area and on the views of faculty and students about using backfiles in microform.

Because they are not primarily research collections, college libraries must be weeded regularly and carefully. This is necessary because of the limited amount of storage space available to most college libraries and also because the collection is intended to be a working collection for undergraduates. Keeping the collection lean by removing superseded editions and other outdated material actually improves service by improving access to the better, more current materials.

THE COMMUNITY COLLEGE OR JUNIOR COLLEGE LIBRARY

The typical community college has a broad mission. Most try to prepare students for the third and fourth years of college, offer terminal courses in vocational and technical fields, and provide adult and continuing education programs for the community. This diversity of purpose leads to diverse course offerings. Since the purpose of the learning resource center (as libraries in community colleges are generally called) is primarily to support the curriculum, those responsible for collection development face a greater challenge than one might expect.

Another result of the diversity of purpose is a more heterogeneous student body, representing varying ages, interests, academic backgrounds, and degrees of academic intention. There may be less rigidity in admission standards, which will have an effect on the materials purchased, in that many of them may have to be fairly elementary. At the same time, some students will be as academically talented and ambitious as the average student in a competitive liberal arts college, and their needs must be met, too.

Although private junior colleges have a long history, most publicly-supported community colleges have been established since

World War II. There was a rapid proliferation of two-year post-secondary institutions in the 1960s, coupled with growth in their enrollments. One effect of the newness of many of these institutions has been their ability to experiment with new types of library service, and to work toward closer integration of library materials with the instructional program. They tend to encourage integration of books, films, filmstrips, tapes, and other of the newer media into a single instructional program. The fact that most two-year institutions have chosen to use the term "learning resources" rather than "library materials" is an indication that they are trying to avoid the traditional print orientation of most university and liberal arts college libraries. (The latest set of standards for the two-year college library, published in 1972 by the Association of College and Research Libraries, is titled "Guidelines for Two-Year College Learning Resources Programs.") The impact on the selection process of widespread use of nonprint materials is obvious.

Organization of Selection in Community College Libraries

In spite of the fact that it may use different terminology for most things connected with the library and its collection, the two-year college library typically organizes its selection procedures in a manner similar to that of the four-year college library. Cooperation between librarians and faculty is important and procedures are usually set up to encourage faculty participation and suggestions. Faculty involvement in collection development is particularly desirable in an institution with such a wide range of courses (from the traditional academic disciplines to technical apprenticeship programs), great diversity in student abilities and needs, and relatively small library staff.

THE SCHOOL LIBRARY MEDIA CENTER

School library media centers have a responsibility to both faculty and students. For the students, they must supply materials related directly to course needs, but they must also provide what are sometimes called "enrichment" materials. The latter form that part of the collection which aims at the liberal education of the student, going beyond strictly curricular needs to provide materials which will educate in a broader sense. Through the school library media center, students gain experience in locating, evaluating, and using information which they comprehend through their reading, listening, and viewing skills. For the faculty, these centers provide instructional materials for use in the teaching of specific courses, as well as materials needed for the teachers' own professional growth and development.

In addition to supporting objectives which range from supplying rather specific classroom-related needs to promoting broad general education/personal development goals, the typical school library media specialist must build a collection to fit a diverse clientele. Whereas the student body in four-year colleges and in universities is relatively homogeneous (all sharing at least a high school education, all having met the entrance requirements of the college or university, all being reasonably adequate readers), the school library media specialist is faced with much less uniformity in the student body. The spread in the elementary schools is staggering—from those who are just learning to read, through those who are skilled and practiced readers, listeners, and viewers. But junior and senior high schools offer an even greater range of potential users, for there are students who have moved a good distance into intellectual maturity and those who have still not learned to read. In fact, with each grade level the span of reading abilities increases. The school library media specialist not only needs to provide materials supporting each area of a broad curriculum; he/she also has to provide a greater variety of levels of treatment of these subjects than either college or university librarians.

Recent developments in education have created the potential for even more diversity in the clientele of school library media centers. Students who were formerly enrolled in special education programs, sometimes housed in separate buildings, are increasingly being integrated into regular classrooms—a practice sometimes referred to as "mainstreaming." This means that media specialists, as they build their collections, must now consider the needs of children with serious physical, emotional, and learning difficulties. To do this successfully they must know more about how various kinds of handicaps—of seeing, hearing, etc.—interfere with learning and prevent the use of traditional library materials.

On the basis of a simple count of items held, individual media centers in schools will have smaller collections than most individual libraries of the types previously discussed, but the variety of holdings may be much greater. Collections in schools are likely to contain materials such as books, periodicals, newspapers, pamphlets, microforms, films, filmstrips, videotapes, videocassettes, slides, transparencies, audiotapes, audiocassettes, audiodiscs, posters, prints, maps, globes, models, games, toys, and specimens—preserved or live. In addition to the materials themselves, the media center must acquire and supply the equipment to play and/or project many of the media. Some of the more expensive media—films, videotapes, etc.—may be supplied at the district level, as may the more extensive collections of professional materials for faculty and staff.

Organization of Selection in School Library Media Centers

In general, the principles and procedures of collection development in a school library media center are the same as those for other libraries, even though media specialists operate under different objectives and deal with different materials and clientele. For example, the current standards for school library media centers (*Media Programs: District and School,* ALA, AECT, 1975) state that selection should be guided by a selection policy (presumably written) which has been developed with consideration for and input from all those concerned with the media center—the media center staff, administrators, faculty, students, and representatives of the community—and approved by the board of education. (Recent developments, such as a 1976 court decision involving the Strongsville, Ohio, City School District, reemphasized the importance of formal, written and officially-approved selection policies and procedures for handling complaints.) A policy statement should recognize the influence on collection development of such factors as the abilities and strengths of the faculty; the courses taught and the methods used to teach them; the media resources which are already available in the community; the characteristics and quality of the materials and related equipment which are available for purchase; and the budget allocated to support the program. The application of the traditional principles of selection in a school library media center requires acceptance of the concept that facts and ideas can be transmitted in a variety of media and ought to be offered to students in the most effective medium available.

Selection should be a cooperative process, involving faculty, students, staff and others, and coordinated by the media specialist. If the school has followed the recommendations of the 1975 standards and has developed a detailed selection policy, endorsed by the appropriate legal authority, the organization of the selection process may already have been spelled out from the district level. If the school has no established process, one should be developed which both provides for wide participation by those who have the knowledge and skill to contribute to the process and makes clear that the final responsibility for selection rests with the person who must account for the budget.

Having as many interested individuals represented in the selection process as possible is important because each type of potential selector has unique strengths. Media specialists are best able to say what is in the existing collection and what materials are available on the market. Also, because of their training in both the traditional skills of librarianship and audiovisual techniques, they know how to locate additional information on materials and equipment. Teachers know their own subject fields and their students' capabilities. In addition, experience has shown that the teachers who help select materials for the media center are also the ones who use it most often with their students—after all, they naturally tend to use what they know. Students are the final judges of what interests them and appears to be directed at their levels of comprehension, and they can make important contributions to the selection process. In some schools parents and members of the community are brought into the selection process, particularly at the policy-making level.

Allocation of the funds available for materials and equipment will be determined, at least partly, by district practices. For example, the media center may receive designated, or line-item, allocations and be required to maintain separate accounts for textbooks, library books and pamphlets, periodicals and binding, audiovisual materials, and audiovisual equipment. Informal allocation of those funds to academic departments or grade levels may be possible at the discretion of the media specialist. *Media Programs: District and School* gives recommendations for minimum number of items of each type which should be in a school's basic collection, as well as the number of items to which the users should have access through district, regional, or state arrangements. These standards offer some idea of how much weight should be given to the various formats when budgets are proposed.

Some media centers operate the selection process through selection committees, organized separately for faculty, students, curriculum areas and/or grade levels. In other schools the media specialist sets up a procedure for routing reviewing journals, other selection aids, and preview copies or prints to those who will participate in selection and collects recommendations from them directly. When there is more than one media specialist in the school, each may work directly with certain departments or faculty members.

Large school districts often maintain evaluation and selection sections which assist individual media centers. The purpose of such district-level units is generally to improve the quality of the media collection in the district, but some attempt to do this through maintaining centralized control of most selection and acquisition, while others concentrate on assisting the efforts of individual media centers. Such units may coordinate policies by, for example, taking the lead in developing written policies, or they may establish and supervise procedures. Typical activities might include organizing district-wide selection committees, developing approved buying lists, maintaining examination centers where media specialists may preview materials before purchase, building professional collections on library science and educational technology, or conducting workshops to improve the evaluation skills of media specialists. The present trend for district-level units is toward decentralization—giving greater control to the individual media centers, while emphasizing facilitating activities at the district level.

Special Problems in School Library Media Centers

Selection of materials for a school library media center is filled with potential problems. Currently controversies exist over the demand versus value approach to selection, the inclusion of materials suspected of racial, ethnic, sexual, or other stereotyping, the reevaluation of present collections, and the range and amount of materials on current social problems which should be included in a collection.

Although most experienced media specialists advocate applying typical general criteria (authority, scope, format, authenticity, treatment, arrangement, special features, cost, etc.) when choosing individual items for a school library media center, problems may arise over the interpretation of these criteria. For example, should the principle of popular demand as a basis for selection overrule the principle of quality? In other words, is it more important to add to a collection materials which interest children, will be used by them, possibly may even be demanded by them (the Nancy Drew books, for example) than to add high-quality, well-reviewed, possibly award-winning materials for which there is no detectable demand? Some people feel that a media center ought to collect anything that a student will read; others advocate buying only the best—in terms of traditional literary standards.

In the last decade many people have been concerned about the subtle influences which library materials may have on children. This concern has been expressed in several ways. One way has been to attempt to expose children to a broad range of social issues through media. Until recently those who produced and selected books for children, particularly young children, tended to try to shield the children from complex and difficult personal and social problems. That practice has changed drastically in the last decade. Now any problem discussed in adult books—drug addiction, child abuse or abandonment, mental illness, unwed parents, etc.—is likely to be treated in a realistic way in children's books. Although the materials are now available, there is still controversy about how much and at what age children should be exposed to realistic discussions of social problems.

Other adults are concerned with how the media transmit views of society to children. They look upon any book, film, or other form of media, even those which claim to be pure entertainment, as a potential influence on children's values, and demand that every item considered for a media center be criticized in terms of the values explicitly or implicitly presented in them. These adults have been particularly critical of the stereotypes—racial, ethnic, sexual, etc.—found in children's books and have attacked the problem in two ways: through pressure on producers and selectors to make more nonstereotyped materials available, and through efforts to have materials currently in children's collections reevaluated in terms of their own criteria. Since so many books (including a number considered to be classics) have been attacked, controversy still rages over whether or not reevaluation of materials is actually censorship under another name. All sides in this controversy present persuasive arguments—a situation which leaves the media specialist in a particularly difficult position. Most experts agree that selection should be a positive decision—that is, materials should be bought because they match the needs of the school and meet the selection criteria—but applying that principle is easier said than done.

THE SPECIAL LIBRARY

The special library has the most restricted purposes and homogeneous clientele of any of the types of libraries discussed thus far. It is created for very specific purposes—often to support the research or business activities of one particular company. It exists to serve a relatively small group in their work. The range of subjects may be very restricted—indeed, the library may concern itself with one narrow subject area—but the variety of forms and types of materials may be great, including such items as monographs, journals, pamphlets, internal and external technical reports, theses, reprints, conference proceedings and transactions, lab notebooks, archival material, photographs, clippings, slides, films, etc. The budget is usually adequate, and, in libraries serving corporations, special needs in terms of purchase are more readily supported by the parent company.

Selection is often difficult, however, because the regular trade bibliography is usually not so significant. For example, in the case of a library serving a chemical corporation, emphasis is on such materials as research reports, government documents, and the whole paraphernalia of research, which is hard to find out about and difficult to come by. The librarian must become thoroughly informed about the field in order to contact such sources of information directly, rather than depending on the standard selection tools. There will be great pressure for the immediate acquisition of all important materials, and this, added to the scattered nature of the producers and the lack of general bibliographic aids, will make the selection process somewhat more hectic than usual.

As in other types of libraries, written policies may be needed—specifying depth and extent of subject coverage, types of materials collected, exchange agreements, and other special considerations—although the special librarian is more likely than most to point out the inflexibility of a written policy. Many special librarians prefer to rely on specific purchase requests and can be counted on to give any suggestion from the clientele full consideration. Some librarians also consider it advisable to have a library committee consisting of specialists who can advise on purchases.

THE SPECIAL COLLECTION

Special collections sometimes exist as separately administered and financed organizations, such as a privately-endowed research library, but they may also be units within university, college, public, or special libraries. These collections typically are restricted to a well-defined (and possibly narrow) subject area, emphasize the needs of researchers, and attempt to build comprehensive collections of primary, as well as secondary, materials.

Development of these collections generally ignores the evaluation of individual titles and concentrates on determining the existence of anything within the subject boundaries of the collection. The only factor limiting collection development for such libraries is the amount of money they have to spend and, of course, the availability of material. In highly specialized collections, identification of the existence of an item is tantamount to selection.

When a public library, for example, decides that it will finally follow the dictum so often enunciated and begin collecting local history, there is going to be a natural alteration in the librarian's "evaluation" of the materials for that collection. He/she will not be interested in the literary quality of the diaries and letters of early settlers—the library wants them all. The librarian may gather up bushel baskets of play bills, yards and yards of the account books of early businesses, acres of old newspapers ... and these are all justifiable, for they are meeting a different kind of purpose than that envisioned in the selection of individual titles for the general reader.

Take, as another example, a library that decides that it is going to build a special collection dealing with labor-management relations in a given industry. The focus of attention is again suddenly changed—one is no longer concerned with getting *only* the best books on the subject. One wishes to build a *comprehensive* collection, reflecting all the varied aspects of labor-management relations. Certainly one will want the objective histories and analyses written long after the fact, but one will also want the contemporary record, no matter how biased, violent, or partisan the accounts may be. The library will try to build files of union newspapers, management serials, the pamphlet publications of both, and will, of course, try to acquire any archival material which either side will surrender. The letters, diaries, journals, memoranda of the leaders of the labor and management groups, of individual workers and minor executives—all these materials will be sought to provide the background for researchers into the history of the subject. When such a library's selection officer reads *Publishers Weekly*, he/she will order anything new that is listed, without waiting for reviews—for this collection is to be as extensive, inclusive, and as full as possible. The books and other materials derive their value not only from intrinsic worth but from their relationships to other materials in the collection and for the light they may shed on minor—as well as major—points. The assumption underlying the building of such a collection is that it is not intended for the use of the "general reader," but for the specialized researcher. The definitive studies whose writing such collections are created to assist cannot be based on a few general, even if excellent, popularizations.

Another example may perhaps be allowed. On the University of Michigan campus, there is a special library of early American history, the William L. Clements Library. It is a collection of *source* materials, not of secondary sources. That is, the books on its shelves describing, let us say, a battle in the American Revolution, were written *at that time*. The library is not interested in collecting modern works about the social customs of early America; it tries to buy the books printed in early America which reveal social customs. It does not refuse to buy a book because the author's style is defective—it is interested in collecting all it can find that was published in the period it covers. It is block buying—by period.

This type of buying is not restricted to any one type of library, nor is it only characteristic of large libraries. The smaller college and public libraries may have only one single special collection, but as much care and time may be lavished on it as on the dozens of special collections of the largest institutions. The special library serving business or industry may resemble the special collection in a university library in the type of acquisitions policy which is followed. Even the smallest public library may make some attempt at collecting local history.

CONCLUSION

Emphasis has been placed in this chapter on describing the differences which exist among the various types of libraries, for it is clear that the general principles of selection will be interpreted differently as the function of the library changes. To say that librarians will select "the best" does not say anything about the way in which the interpretation of what is best will vary. It is obvious that the "best" book on nuclear energy will turn out to be different as one moves from the elementary school library through the public library to the special library of a company engaged in nuclear research. The principle remains the same,

48

Building Library Collections

but the results of its application will vary widely. The standards for judging the individual title must depend directly upon the type of reader being served and on the kinds of service which the library feels it should give. It would be a useful task—but a rather extensive and perhaps laborious one—to take each of the statements of principle outlined in the checklist of selection principles appended to the first chapter and to interpret its meaning for each of the various types of library. Even without undertaking such a project, it is perhaps clear enough that the general principles serve only as general prescriptions for practice, which must be related to the specific nature of the individual institution.

BIBLIOGRAPHY

General

ACM Conference on Space, Growth and Performance Problems of Academic Libraries. Chicago, 1975. *Farewell to Alexandria; Solutions to Space, Growth, and Performance Problems of Libraries.* Edited by Daniel Gore. Westport, Conn., Greenwood Press, 1976. 180p. Ten essays with implications for collection development.

Allerton Park Institute, 9th, 1962. *Selection and Acquisition Procedures in Medium-Sized and Large Libraries.* Edited by Herbert Goldhor. Urbana, University of Illinois, Graduate School of Library Science, 1963. 139p. Ten papers on a variety of topics.

American Library Association. Resources and Technical Services Division. Resources Section. Collection Development Committee. "Guidelines for the Formulation of Collection Development Policies." *Library Resources and Technical Services,"* 21:40-47, Winter 1977. See Appendix C.

Baughman, James C. "Toward a Structural Approach to Collection Development." *College and Research Libraries,* 38:241-248, May 1977. Emphasizes the use of structure of subject literatures in collection development.

Boyer, Calvin J. and Nancy L. Eaton. *Book Selection Policies in American Libraries: An Anthology of Policies from College, Public, and School Libraries.* Austin, Texas, Armadillo Press, 1971. 222p. Reprints 31 policy statements.

Broadus, Robert N. "The Application of Citation Analyses to Library Collection Building." In *Advances in Librarianship,* Vol. 7, pp. 299-335. New York, Academic Press, 1977.

Buckland, Michael K. *Book Availability and the Library User.* New York, Pergamon, 1975. 196p. Considers, among other questions, how many titles a library should have.

Clarke, Jack A. "A Search for Principles of Book Selection, 1550-1700." *Library Quarterly,* 41:216-222, July 1971. Historical review.

Futas, Elizabeth. *Library Acquisition Policies and Procedures.* Phoenix, Ariz., Oryx Press, 1977. 406p. Reprints 26 policies and parts of 56 others.

Gaver, Mary Virginia. *Background Readings in Building Library Collections.* Metuchen, N.J., Scarecrow Press, 1969. 2v. Collection of previously-published articles from a variety of sources.

Kujoth, Jean S. *Libraries, Readers and Book Selection.* Metuchen, N.J., Scarecrow Press, 1969. 470p. Forty-four articles reprinted from 28 journals.

University and Research Libraries

Association of College and Research Libraries. "Guidelines for Branch Libraries in Colleges and Universities." *College and Research Library News*, 36:281–283, October 1975. Includes brief comments on collection development.

Association of Research Libraries. Office of University Library Management Studies. *SPEC Kit on Acquisition Policies in ARL Libraries*. Washington, D.C., 1974. 132p. Examples of statements from several university libraries.

Association of Research Libraries. Office of University Library Management Studies. *SPEC Kit on Collection Development in ARL Libraries*. Washington, D.C., 1974. 132p. Examples of various kinds of guides, job descriptions, plans, and other official documents related to collection development.

Bach, Harry. "Why Allocate?" *Library Resources and Technical Services*, 8: 161–165, Spring 1964. Concise statement of pros and cons.

Brazell, Troy V., Jr. "Comparative Analysis: A Minimum Music Materials Budget for the University Library." *College and Research Libraries*, 32:110–120, March 1971.

Bryant, Douglas W. "The Changing Research Library." *Library Scene*, 4:2–4, 15, September 1975. Review of problems facing large university libraries, with specific references to development at Harvard.

Burton, Robert E. "Formula Budgeting: An Example." *Special Libraries*, 66:61–67, February 1975. Presents an example based on a university library.

Byrd, Cecil K. "Subject Specialists in a University Library." *College and Research Libraries*, 27:191–193, May 1966. Experiences at Indiana University.

Clapp, Verner W. and Robert T. Jordan. "Quantitative Criteria for the Adequacy of Academic Library Collections." *College and Research Libraries*, 26:371–380, September 1965. Presents a formula for estimating collection adequacy.

Coleman, Kathleen and Pauline Dickinson. "Drafting a Reference Collection Policy." *College and Research Libraries*, 38:227–233, May 1977. Includes copy of policy drafted at San Diego State University.

Converse, W. R. M. and O. R. Standers. *Rationalizing the Collections Policy: A Computerized Approach*. Calgary, Alberta, University of Calgary Library, 1975. 8p. (ED 105 861)

Coppin, Ann. "The Subject Specialist on the Academic Library Staff." *Libri*, 24:122–128, 1974. Brief state-of-the-art review.

Danton, J. Periam. *Book Selection and Collections: A Comparison of German and American University Libraries*. New York, Columbia University Press, 1963. 188p. Comprehensive discussion of the philosophies underlying collection development in university libraries.

Danton, J. Periam. "The Subject Specialist in National and University Libraries, with Special Reference to Book Selection." *Libri*, 17:42–58, 1967.

DePew, John N. "An Acquisitions Decision Model for Academic Libraries." *Journal of American Society for Information Science*, 26:237–246, July–August 1975.

Downs, Robert B. "Collection Development for Academic Libraries: An Overview." *North Carolina Libraries*, 34:31–38, Fall 1976. Brief review of major issues.

Drake, Miriam A. "Forecasting Academic Library Growth." *College and Research Libraries*, 37:53–59, January 1976. Illustrates use of two quantitative forecasting techniques in a university library.

Edelman, Hendrik. "Reduction, Reduction, Reduction, Reduction; Some Observations on Collection Development." *Cornell University Library Bulletin*, no. 195:8–10, May 1975. Experiences at Cornell.

Edelman, Hendrik and G. Marvin Tatum, Jr. "The Development of Collections in American University Libraries." *College and Research Libraries*, 37:222–245, May 1976. Trends of the past 100 years.

Ettlinger, John R. T. "Nation-Wide Rationalization of Acquisition Policies in Canadian College and University Libraries: Are Total World Coverage and Nonduplication of Resources Part of an Impossible Dream?" Paper presented at the Canadian Association of College and University Libraries Workshop on Collection Development, Sackville, New Brunswick, Canada, June 16–17, 1973. 24p. (ED 087 492)

Evans, G. Edward. "Book Selection and Book Collection Usage in Academic Libraries." *Library Quarterly,* 40:297–308, July 1970. Shorter version of study cited next.

Evans, G. Edward. "The Influence of Book Selection Agents upon Book Collection Usage in Academic Libraries." (Ph.D. Thesis, University of Illinois, 1969). 159p. Investigates selection by librarians, faculty, and through blanket order-approval plans.

Evans, Glyn T. "The Cost of Information About Library Acquisition Budgets." *Collection Management,* 2:3–23, Spring 1978. Factors which influence the budget and information needed.

Fussler, Herman H. and Julian L. Simon. *Patterns in the Use of Books in Large Research Libraries.* Chicago, University of Chicago Press, 1969. 210p. Based on studies at the University of Chicago.

Gold, Steven D. "Allocating the Book Budget: An Economic Model." *College and Research Libraries,* 36:397–402, September 1975.

Goyal, S. K. "Allocation of Library Funds to Different Departments of a University—An Operational Research Approach." *College and Research Libraries,* 34:219–222, May 1973.

Hall, Mary M. "Theoretical Considerations of Selection Policy for University Libraries: Their Relevance to Canadian University Libraries." *Canadian Library Journal,* 23:89–98, September 1966. Discusses from a Canadian viewpoint the issues raised by Danton (1963).

Hamlin, Arthur T. "Book Collections of British University Libraries; An American Reaction." *International Library Review,* 2:135–173, April 1970. Similarities and differences between British and American collections.

Hanes, Fred W. "Another View on Allocation." *Library Resources and Technical Services,* 8:408–410, Fall 1964. Reaction to Bach (1964).

Haro, Robert P. "The Bibliographer in the Academic Library." *Library Resources and Technical Services,* 13:163–169, Spring 1969. Use of subject specialists in large university libraries.

Haro, Robert P. "Book Selection in Academic Libraries." *College and Research Libraries,* 28:104–106, March 1967. Results of a survey of 67 libraries.

Haro, Robert P. "Some Problems in the Conversion of a College to a University Library." *College and Research Libraries,* 30:260–264, May 1969.

Hlavac, R. W. "Book Selection in University Libraries." *New Zealand Libraries,* 34:109–113, June 1971. Emphasizes New Zealand's special problems.

Holley, Edward G. "What Lies Ahead for Academic Libraries?" In *Academic Libraries by the Year 2000; Essays Honoring Jerrold Orne,* edited by Herbert Poole, pp. 7–33. New York, Bowker, 1977. General predictions about academic libraries and the environment in which they will operate.

Humphreys, Kenneth. "The Subject Specialist in National and University Libraries." *Libri,* 17:29–41, 1967. Outlines roles and qualifications.

Illinois State Library. "Collection Development Policy." *Illinois Libraries,* 54:824–838, November 1972. Detailed policy statement.

Knightly, John J. "Library Collections and Academic Curricula: Quantitative Relationships." *College and Research Libraries,* 36:295–301, July 1975. Study of curricular similarity and collection duplication in 22 state-supported universities in Texas.

Kohut, Joseph J. "Allocating the Book Budget: A Model." *College and Research Libraries,* 35:192–199, May 1974.

Kohut, Joseph J. and John F. Walker. "Allocating the Book Budget: Equity and Economic Efficiency." *College and Research Libraries,* 36:403–410, September 1975. Response to Gold (1975).

Kosa, G. A. "Book Selection Trends in American Academic Libraries." *Australian Library Journal,* 21:416–424, November 1972. Trends from late nineteenth century to 1970.

Kraft, Margit. "An Argument for Selectivity in the Acquisition of Materials for Research Libraries." *Library Quarterly,* 37:284–295, July 1967.

Lane, David O. "The Selection of Academic Library Materials; A Literature Survey." *College and Research Libraries,* 29:364–372, September 1968.

Lane, David O. *Study of the Decision-Making Procedures for the Acquisition of Science Library Materials and the Relation of These Procedures to the Requirements of College and University Library Patrons.* Chicago, American Library Association, 1967. 123p. (ED 047 712) Identifies five levels of decision making.

Leach, Steven. "Growth Rates of Major Academic Libraries: Rider and Purdue Reviewed." *College and Research Libraries,* 37:531–542, November 1976.

Lopez, Manuel D. "A Guide for Beginning Bibliographers." *Library Resources and Technical Services,* 13:462–470, Fall 1969. Practical suggestions.

McGrath, William E. "An Allocation Formula Derived from a Factor Analysis of Academic Departments." *College and Research Libraries,* 30:51–62, January 1969. Suggested method for book fund allocation.

McGrath, William E. "Determining and Allocating Book Funds for Current Domestic Buying." *College and Research Libraries,* 28:269–272, July 1967. Proposes an objective method.

McGrath, William E. "A Pragmatic Book Allocation Formula for Academic and Public Libraries with a Test for Its Effectiveness." *Library Resources and Technical Services,* 19:356–369, Fall 1975.

Magrill, Rose Mary and Mona East. "Collection Development in Large University Libraries." In *Advances in Librarianship,* Vol. 8, pp. 1–54. New York, Academic Press, 1978. Literature review emphasizing the last two decades.

Martin, Murray. "Budgeting Strategies: Coping with a Changing Fiscal Environment." *Journal of Academic Librarianship,* 2:297–302, January 1977. Based on a hypothetical university library budget.

Michalak, Thomas J. "Library Services to the Graduate Community: The Role of the Subject Specialist Librarian." *College and Research Libraries,* 37:257–265, May 1976.

Montgomery, K. Leon and others. "Cost-Benefit Model of Library Acquisitions in Terms of Use." *Journal of the American Society for Information Science,* 27:73–74, January–February 1976. Project at the University of Pittsburgh.

Northwestern University Library. *An Acquisition Policy for the Northwestern University Library, Evanston Campus.* Rev. ed. Evanston, Ill., 1972. 205p.

Olsson, A. L. "Developing a Selection Policy for the National Library." *New Zealand Libraries,* 34:51–53, April 1971.

Orne, Jerrold. "Current Trends in Collection Development in University Libraries." *Library Trends,* 15:197–334, October 1966. Contains eight papers on collection development at specific universities.

Osburn, Charles B. "Planning for a University Library Policy on Collection Development." *International Library Review,* 9:209–224, 1977. How and why to develop a written policy.

Perkins, David L. and Carol Bedoian. *Manual for Collection Developers.* Northridge, Calif., California State University Libraries, 1975. 113p. (ED 116 681) Example of one library's procedures.

Pierce, Thomas J. "An Empirical Approach to the Allocation of the University Library Book Budget." *Collection Management,* 2:39–58, Spring 1978.

Pratt Institute. *Service Policies: Access, Collection Development*. Brooklyn, New York, 1976. 48p. (ED 124 126)

"Problems of Acquisition for Research Libraries." Issue edited by Rolland Stevens. *Library Trends*, 18:275–421, January 1970. Includes ten articles on acquisition of various types of materials and collections.

Ramer, James D. and Joseph Boykin. "The Book Budget in Academic Libraries." *Southeastern Librarian*, 16:40–43, Spring 1966. Experiences at University of North Carolina at Charlotte.

Reid, Marion T. "Coping with Budget Adversity: The Impact of the Financial Squeeze on Acquisitions." *College and Research Libraries*, 37:266–272, May 1976. How ten ARL libraries adjusted.

Rice, Barbara A. "The Development of Working Collections in University Libraries." *College and Research Libraries*, 38:309–312, July 1977. Argues that working collections must replace comprehensive collections.

Richter, Edward A. "Academic Library Acquisitions Policy." *New Mexico Libraries*, 2:95–99, Winter 1970–71. Points covered in typical policies.

Rogers, Rutherford D. and David C. Weber. *University Library Administration*. New York, Wilson, 1971. 454p. Chapter 5 covers book collections.

Schad, Jasper G. "Allocating Book Funds: Control or Planning?" *College and Research Libraries*, 31:155–159, May 1970. Proposes allocating for specific collection needs.

Schad, Jasper G. and Ruth L. Adams. "Book Selection in Academic Libraries: A New Approach." *College and Research Libraries*, 30:437–442, September 1969. Ways to take advantage of faculty subject expertise.

Schad, Jasper G. and Norman E. Tanis. *Problems in Developing Academic Library Collections*. New York, Bowker, 1974. 183p. Thirty case studies covering a variety of problems.

Simmons, Peter. *Collection Development and the Computer; A Case Study in the Analysis of Machine Readable Loan Records and Their Application to Book Selection*. Vancouver, B.C., University of British Columbia, School of Librarianship, 1971. 60p.

Skelley, Grant T. "Characteristics of Collections Added to American Research Libraries, 1940–1970: A Preliminary Investigation." *College and Research Libraries*, 36:52–60, January 1975.

Sloan, Elaine C. "The Organization of Collection Development in Large University Research Libraries." (Ph.D. Thesis, University of Maryland, 1973). 192p. Based on study of 11 ARL libraries.

Stanford University. Libraries. *Book Selection Policies of the Libraries of Stanford University*. Compiled by Peter A. Johnson; edited by E. M. Grieder. Stanford, Calif., 1970. unpaged.

Stueart, Robert D. "Area Specialist Bibliographer; An Inquiry Into His Role." (Ph.D. Thesis, University of Pittsburgh, 1971). 200p. Based on a survey.

Taggart, W. R. "Book Selection Librarians in Canadian Universities." *Canadian Library Journal*, 31:410–412, September–October 1974. Reviews trend toward full-time selection personnel.

Taggart, W. R. "Preparing a Collections Policy for the Academic Library." *Canadian Association of College and University Libraries Newsletter*, 4:53–56, September 1972. Experiences at the University of Victoria.

Texas. University at Austin. The University of Texas at Austin General Libraries. *Collection Development Policy*. Austin, 1976. 207p.

Thompson, James. *Introduction to University Library Administration*. 2d rev. ed. London, Clive Bingley, 1974. 164p. Chapter 4 covers collections. British viewpoint.

Tuttle, Helen W. "An Acquisitionist Looks at Mr. Haro's Bibliographer." *Library Resources and Technical Services*, 13:170–174, Spring 1969. Response to Haro (*LRTS*, 1969) on subject bibliographers.

Urquhart, J. A. and N. C. Urquhart. *Regulation and Stock Control in Libraries.* Stocksfield, Northumberland, Oriel Press (Routledge and Kegan Paul), 1976. 154p. Introduction discusses broad issues of academic library collection development.

Voigt, Melvin J. "Acquisition Rates in University Libraries." *College and Research Libraries,* 36:263–271, July 1975. Presents a model for estimating necessary minimum annual acquisition rate.

Voigt, Melvin J. "Case Study of the California Experience in Library Collection Building." Paper presented at the Institute on Acquisitions Procedures in Academic Libraries, University of California at San Diego Libraries, August 25–September 5, 1969. 30p. (ED 043 345) Development of collections at nine University of California campuses.

Vosper, Robert G. "Collection Building and Rare Books." In *Research Librarianship; Essays in Honor of Robert B. Downs,* edited by Jerrold Orne, pp. 91–111. New York, Bowker, 1971. Development of collections in the largest American university libraries.

Ward, K. Linda. "Collection Policy in College and University Libraries." *Music Library Association Notes,* 29:432–440, March 1973.

Webb, William H. "Collection Development for the University and Large Research Library: More and More Versus Less and Less." In *Academic Libraries by the Year 2000: Essays Honoring Jerrold Orne,* edited by Herbert Poole, pp. 139–151. New York, Bowker, 1977.

Liberal Arts Colleges and Undergraduate Libraries

Association of College and Research Libraries. "Standards for College Libraries." *College and Research Libraries News,* 36:277–279; 290–301, October 1975. "Standard 2" concerns collections.

Braden, Irene A. *The Undergraduate Library.* Chicago, American Library Association, 1970. 158p. (ACRL Monograph No. 31) Case studies of undergraduate libraries at six universities.

Buckeye, Nancy. "A Plan for Undergraduate Participation in Book Selection." *Library Resources and Technical Services,* 19:121–125, Spring 1975. Followed by critical responses from three academic librarians.

Carlson, James F. "Book Selection and the Small College Library." *Learning Today,* 4:37–43, Fall 1971.

Dearnaley, Carolyn and Paul Bixler. "A Latin American Collection." *Wilson Library Bulletin,* 42:417–421, December 1967. Building an area studies collection at a liberal arts college.

Farber, Evan Ira. "Limiting College Library Growth: Bane or Boon?" *Journal of Academic Librarianship,* 1:12–15, November 1975. Considers how a college library should differ from a university library.

Horny, Karen. "Building Northwestern's Core." *Library Journal,* 96:1580–1583, May 1, 1971. Describes development of a 30,000-volume noncirculating collection primarily for undergraduates.

Jenks, George M. "Book Selection: An Approach for Small and Medium-Sized Libraries." *College and Research Libraries,* 33:28–30, January 1972. Describes process at Bucknell University.

Lyle, Guy R. *Administration of the College Library.* 4th ed. New York, Wilson, 1974. 320p. Two relevant chapters.

Lynch, Beverly P. "The Changing Environment of Academic Libraries." *College and Research Libraries,* 39:10–14, January 1978. Covers trends in financing, admissions, and curriculum; also applicable to universities.

Massman, Virgil F. "Changes That Will Affect College Library Collection Development." In *Academic Libraries by the Year 2000; Essays Honoring Jerrold Orne,* edited by Herbert Poole, pp. 152–164. New York, Bowker, 1977.

Massman, Virgil F. and David R. Olson. "Book Selection: A National Plan for Small Academic Libraries." *College and Research Libraries,* 32:271–279, July 1971. Proposes a national blanket plan.

Muller, Robert H. "The Undergraduate Library Trend at Large Universities." In *Advances in Librarianship,* Vol. 1, pp. 113–132. New York, Academic Press, 1970. State-of-the-art review with selective bibliography.

Scherer, Henry. "The Faculty and the Librarian." *Library-College Journal,* 3:37–43, Fall 1970. How teachers and librarians in liberal arts colleges work together on collection development.

Stiffler, Stuart A. "A Footnote on Confusion: Book Selection in the Smaller College Library." *Ohio Library Association Bulletin,* 40:17–18, July 1970.

Stiffler, Stuart A. "The Librarian, the Scholar, and the Book Collection." *Library-College Journal,* 3:37–41, Summer 1970. Outlines a selection rationale.

Stiffler, Stuart A. "A Philosophy of Book Selection for Smaller Academic Libraries." *College and Research Libraries,* 24:204–208, May 1963.

Voigt, Melvin J. "The Undergraduate Library; the Collection and Its Selection." Paper prepared for the Institute on Training for Service in Undergraduate Libraries, University of California at San Diego Library, August 17–21, 1970. 26p. (ED 042 476)

Wingate, Henry W. "The Undergraduate Library: Is It Obsolete?" *College and Research Libraries,* 39:29–33, January 1978. Reviews trends in separate undergraduate collections on university campuses.

Junior Colleges/Community Colleges

Agbim, Ngozi. "Library Resources for Community Colleges." *Bookmark,* 36:98–101, Summer 1977. Procedures used at La Guardia Community College Library (N.Y.).

Allen, Kenneth W. and Loren Allen. *Organization and Administration of the Learning Resources Center in the Community College.* Hamden, Conn., Linnet Books, 1973. 187p. Chapter five touches on collection development.

Association of College and Research Libraries. "Guidelines for Two-Year College Learning Resources Programs." *College and Research Libraries News,* 33:305–315, December 1972. Contains a section on materials.

Bach, Harry. "The Junior College Library Collection." *California Librarian,* 33:88–99, April 1972. General discussion.

Canadian Association of College and University Libraries. *Standards Recommended for Canadian Community College Libraries.* Ottawa, Canadian Library Association, 1973. 8p.

Dale, Doris Cruger. "The Community College Library in the Mid-1970's." *College and Research Libraries,* 38:404–411, September 1977. Review based on visits to 31 campuses during 1975–76.

Mitchell, Bonnie J. and others. "Junior College Materials." *Choice,* 6:28–33, March 1969. Problems of selecting technical and vocational materials.

Olsen, Humphrey A. "Building the Book Collection." *Library Trends,* 14:156–165, October 1965. Special problems of junior colleges.

Veit, Fritz. *The Community College Library.* Westport, Conn., Greenwood Press, 1975. 221p. Contains several relevant chapters.

School Library Media Centers

American Association of School Librarians. *Media Programs: District and School*. Chicago, American Library Association; Washington, D.C., Association for Educational Communications and Technology, 1975. 136p.

American Association of School Librarians. "Policies and Procedures for Selection of Instructional Materials." *School Media Quarterly*, 5:109–116, Winter 1977. Revision of AASL's 1970 official statement on the selection process.

American Library Association. Young Adult Services Division. Research Committee. *Media and the Young Adult; A Selected Bibliography, 1950–1972*. Chicago, 1977. 138p. Almost 400 titles dealing with attitudes, information needs, and media use of young adults.

Baker, D. Philip and David R. Bender. "An *SMQ* Feature: Marketing, Selection, and Acquisition of Materials for School Media Programs." *School Media Quarterly*, 6:97–132, Winter 1978; 6:171–201, Spring 1978. Contains six papers based on a 1976–77 survey of school media programs, media producers, and distributors.

Baskins, Barbara H. and Karen H. Harris. *The Special Child in the Library*. Chicago, American Library Association, 1976. 199p. Collection of articles on providing library materials and services for handicapped and gifted children. Includes a section on selection criteria.

Belland, John. "Factors Influencing Selection of Materials." *School Media Quarterly*, 6:112–119, Winter 1978. One of the papers based on the 1976–77 survey (see Baker and Bender for citation to complete series).

Bomar, Cora Paul and others. *Guide to the Development of Educational Media Selection Centers*. Chicago, American Library Association, 1973. 112p. (ALA Studies in Librarianship No. 2) Gives overview of such centers and discusses how, why, and where to establish them.

Brown, James W. and others. *Administering Educational Media: Instructional Technology and Library Services*. 2d ed. New York, McGraw-Hill, 1972. 449p. Chapter 9 covers selection.

"Children's Book Selection." *Library Journal*, 98:3693–3694, December 15, 1973. How students were brought into the selection process at an elementary school.

Coachman, Dorothea L. "Some Personal Observations on Building the Humanities Collection." *School Libraries*, 21:18–21, Winter 1972. Experiences of the Hanover Park (N.J.) High School.

Council on Interracial Books for Children. *Human (and Anti-Human) Values in Children's Books; New Guidelines for Parents, Educators, and Librarians*. New York, Council on Interracial Books for Children, 1976. 280p. Discusses criteria used by the Council when reviewing books and illustrates these with analysis of 235 books published in 1975.

Cullinan, Bernice E. and Carolyn W. Carmichael. *Literature and Young Children*. Urbana, Ill., National Council of Teachers of English, 1977. 180p.

Davies, Ruth Ann. *School Library Media Center: A Force for Educational Excellence*. 2d ed. New York, Bowker, 1974. 484p. Chapter 5 and Appendix H cover media selection.

Delaney, Jack J. *The Media Program in the Elementary and Middle School*. Hamden, Conn., Linnet Books, 1976. 222p. Chapters on selection and ordering.

Florida State Department of Education. *Criteria for Instructional Materials Selection*. 1975 Adoption. Tallahassee, 1975. 19p. (ED 101 753) Prepared for middle and secondary schools.

Freeman, Patricia. *Pathfinder: An Operational Guide for the School Librarian*. New York, Harper and Row, 1975. 325p. Brief discussion of the media collection.

Gerhardt, Lillian. *Issues in Children's Book Selection.* New York, Bowker, 1973. 216p. Reprints 29 articles from *Library Journal* and *School Library Journal.*

Gillespie, John T. *A Model School District Media Program.* Chicago, American Library Association, 1977. 207p. (ALA Studies in Librarianship No. 6) Case study of Montgomery County, Maryland.

Gillespie, John T. and Diana L. Spirt. *Creating a School Media Program.* New York, Bowker, 1973. 236p. Includes chapters on media selection and acquisition and a detailed appendix: "Specific Criteria for Selecting Educational Media."

Hartz, Frederic R. "Selection of School/Media Materials." *Catholic Library World,* 47:425–429, May–June 1976. Brief review of factors involved.

Hicks, Warren B. and Alma M. Tillin. *Developing Multi-Media Libraries.* New York, Bowker, 1970. 199p. Emphasizes collection development in schools.

Iowa State Department of Public Instruction. *Selection of Instructional Materials: A Model Policy and Rules.* Des Moines, 1975. 19p. (ED 116 691) Intended as a model for schools developing a local policy.

Johnson, Mary Frances K. "Media Selection: Six Concerns." *Catholic Library World,* 47:416–417, May–June, 1976.

Jones, Milbrey L. *Survey of School Media Standards.* Washington, D.C., U.S. Office of Education, 1977. 259p. Summarizes national, regional, and state standards for personnel, resources, expenditures, facilities, equipment, etc.

Liesener, James W. *A Systematic Process for Planning Media Programs.* Chicago, American Library Association, 1976. 166p. Emphasizes identifying needs and setting priorities.

McKeon, Helen. "Book Selection Criteria of Children's Book Editors and Elementary Classroom Teachers." (M.Ed. Thesis, Rutgers University, 1975). 115p. (ED 116 136) Results of a questionnaire survey.

Maryland State Department of Education. Division of Library Development and Services. *Guidelines for the Review and Selection of Textbooks and Instructional Materials.* Baltimore, 1976. 12p. (ED 126 909) Guidelines for developing policies and procedures.

Mazzola, Agnes L. "Developing Collections in School Library Media Centers: A Joint Partnership Between Teachers and Library Media Specialists." *Bookmark,* 36:6–10, Fall 1976. How one high school got wide involvement in the selection process.

Measel, Wes and L. Lucille Crawford. "School Children and Book Selection." *American Libraries,* 2:955–957, October 1971. Use of students as reviewers and selectors.

Michigan Association for Media in Education. Intellectual Freedom Committee. *Selection Policies: A Guide to Updating and Writing.* n.p., 1977. 69p.

Moss, Carol E. "Budgeting for Media Selection and Ordering." *Catholic Library World,* 47:423–424, May–June 1976. Brief review of general considerations.

Nickel, Mildred L. *Steps to Service; A Handbook of Procedures for the School Media Center.* Chicago, American Library Association, 1975. 136p. Includes sections on selection and ordering.

Ohio Association of School Librarians. Intellectual Freedom Committee. *Materials Selection Policies for School Media Centers—Aids for Writing.* Columbus, 1976. 16p. Includes two sample policies and a bibliography of aids to writing.

Prostano, Emanuel T. and Joyce S. Prostano. *The School Library Media Center.* 2d ed. Littleton, Colo., Libraries Unlimited, 1977. 218p. Covers collection building.

Rudman, Marsha K. *Children's Literature; An Issues Approach.* New York, D. C. Heath, 1976. 433p. Takes the position that children's books are a powerful means of communicating ideas. Each chapter covers an issue such as divorce, sex, old age, war, race, etc.

Saunders, Helen E. *The Modern School Library.* 2d ed., rev. by Nancy Polette. Metuchen, N.J., Scarecrow Press, 1975. 237p. Focuses on secondary schools.

Shapiro, Lillian L. *Serving Youth: Communication and Commitment in the High School Library*. New York, Bowker, 1975. 268p. Includes a selective list of selection tools in appendix.

"The Strongsville Decision." *School Library Journal*, 23:23–26, November 1976. Court case in Ohio, involving censorship of books in a high school.

Vandergrift, Kay E. "Selection: Reexamination and Reassessment." *School Media Quarterly*, 6:103–111, Winter 1978. Reviews traditional statements on selection in light of the 1976–77 survey (see Baker and Bender for citation to complete series).

Van Orden, Phyllis. "Promotion, Review, and Examination of Materials." *School Media Quarterly*, 6:120–132, Winter 1978. One of the papers based on the 1976–77 survey (see Baker and Bender for citation to complete series).

Wilkinson, J. P. *Canadian Juvenile Fiction and the Library Market*. Ottawa, Canadian Library Association, 1976. 87p. Study of the buying patterns of school and public libraries.

Woolls, Blanche. "Forty Items Per Student; An Investigation of Alternatives in Collection Design." *School Media Quarterly*, 4:116–120, Winter 1976. Suggests a formula for determining collection adequacy.

Special Libraries and Special Collections

Annan, Gertrude L. and Jacqueline W. Felter. *Handbook of Medical Library Practice*. 3d ed. Chicago, Medical Library Association, 1970. 411p. Includes a section on selection and acquisition.

Association of Hospitals and Institution Libraries. *Standards for Library Services in Health Care Institutions*. Chicago, American Library Association, 1970. 25p. Includes statements about collections.

Beatty, William K. "Technical Processing: Selection, Acquisition, and Weeding." In *Handbook of Medical Library Practice*, 3d ed., edited by Gertrude L. Annan and Jacqueline W. Felter, pp. 71–92. Chicago, Medical Library Association, 1970. Brief coverage of a number of topics.

Bloomquist, Harold and others. *Library Practice in Hospitals; A Basic Guide*. Cleveland, Case Western Reserve University Press, 1972. 344p. Several chapters deal with collection development.

Bradley, Carol J. *Reader in Music Librarianship*. Washington, D.C., NCR/Microcard Editions, 1973. 340p.

Burnett, Alfred D. "Considerations on the Support of Antiquarian and Other Special Collections in University Libraries." *Journal of Librarianship*, 5:203–213, July 1973. Argues for supporting such collections and suggests ways. British viewpoint.

Chen, Ching-chih. *Applications of Operations Research Models to Libraries: A Case Study of the Use of Monographs in the Francis A. Countway Library of Medicine, Harvard University*. Cambridge, Mass., MIT Press, 1976. 212p. Discusses implications of book-use models for selection.

Cohen, Jackson B. "Science Acquisitions and Book Output Statistics." *Library Resources and Technical Services*, 19:370–379, Fall 1975. How to plan and control development of science collections.

Cramer, Anne. *Printed Materials: Selection and Acquisition*. Salt Lake City, Network for Continuing Education, Intermountain Regional Medical Program, 1972. 63p. (Hospital Library Handbooks, no. 3) (ED 072 834) Practical suggestions for small libraries.

DeVore, Helen L. "Acquisition Policy." *Special Libraries*, 61:381–384, September 1970. Policy of the Environmental Science Services Administration.

Gnudi, Martha T. "Building a Medical History Collection." *Medical Library Association Bulletin*, 63:42–46, January 1975.

Grattan, Mary C. "Collection Development in Texas State Agency Libraries: A Survey with Recommendations." *Special Libraries,* 68:69–75, February 1977. Summarizes responses from twenty special libraries.

Gulker, Virgil. *Books Behind Bars.* Metuchen, N.J., Scarecrow Press, 1973. 120p. Selection of materials for a prison library.

Harleston, Rebekah M. and Carla J. Stoffle. *Administration of Government Documents Collections.* Littleton, Colo., Libraries Unlimited, 1974. 178p. Basic text covering a variety of topics, including selection and acquisition.

Haugh, I. W. S. and Mona E. Going. "Book Provision for Hospital Libraries." In *Hospital Libraries and Work with the Disabled,* 2d ed., edited by Mona E. Going, pp. 123–133. London, Library Association, 1973.

Krummel, Donald W. "Observations on Library Acquisition of Music." *Music Library Association Notes,* 23:5–16, September 1966.

Manual of Law Librarianship: The Use and Organization of Legal Literature. Edited by Elizabeth M. Moys. Boulder, Colo., Westview Press, 1976. 733p. Emphasizes types of materials needed and has one chapter on acquisition.

Mount, Ellis. *University Science and Engineering Libraries; Their Operation, Collections, and Facilities.* Westport, Conn., Greenwood Press, 1975. 214p. Contains a chapter on collections.

Myers, Mildred S. and William C. Frederick. "Business Libraries: Role and Function in Industrial America." *Journal of Education for Librarianship,* 15:41–52, Summer 1974.

Nichols, Harold. *Map Librarianship.* London, Clive Bingley, 1976. 298p. British viewpoint.

Opello, Olivia and Lindsay Murdock. "Acquisitions Overkill in Science Collections— And an Alternative." *College and Research Libraries,* 37:452–456, September 1976. Argues for stricter selection criteria.

Pacey, Philip. *Art Library Manual.* New York, Bowker in association with Art Libraries Society, Great Britain, 1977. 423p.

Phinney, Eleanor. *The Librarian and the Patient.* Chicago, American Library Association, 1977. 352p. "An Introduction to Library Services for Patients in Health Care Institutions." Includes selection of materials.

Roper, Fred W. "Selecting Federal Publications." *Special Libraries,* 65:326–331, August 1974. Emphasizes value of written policies.

Schwartz, James H. "Accessibility, Browsing, and a Systematic Approach to Acquisitions in a Chemical Research Company Library." *Special Libraries,* 62:143–146, March 1971. Development of a new acquisitions policy.

Schwartz, James H. "Technical Books: Appraisal of Selection Policy and Use by Creative Chemists." *Special Libraries,* 65:58–60, February 1974. Related to previous article by same author.

Sewell, Winifred. *Reader in Medical Librarianship.* Washington, D.C., NCR/Microcard Editions, 1973. 382p.

Sinha, Bani K. and Richard C. Clelland. "Application of a Collection-Control Model for Scientific Libraries." *Journal of the American Society for Information Science,* 27:320–328, September–October 1976. Operations research approach.

Sloan, Elaine. *Collection Development and Selection Decision-Making of the Smithsonian Institution Libraries; A Survey of the Curators of the National Museum of Natural History and the National Museum of History and Technology, September 1970–June 1971.* Washington, D.C., Smithsonian Institution Libraries, 1971. 56p. (ED 059 732)

Spaulding, F. H. and R. O. Stanton. "Computer-Aided Selection in a Library Network." *Journal of the American Society for Information Science,* 27:269–280, September–October 1976. Procedures followed by the Bell Laboratories Library Network.

Special Libraries Association. Illinois Chapter. *Special Libraries: A Guide for Management.* New York, Special Libraries Association, 1975. 74p. Includes a chapter on acquisition.

Special Library Association. Newspaper Division. *Guidelines for Newspaper Libraries.* Reston, Va., American Newspaper Publishers Foundation, 1974. unpaged. Several sections cover acquisition and processing.

Strauss, Lucille J., Irene M. Shreve and Alberta L. Brown. *Scientific and Technical Libraries: Their Organization and Administration.* 2d ed. New York, Becker and Hayes, 1972. 450p. One chapter covers selection of books and journals.

Truelson, Stanley D. "Selecting for Health Sciences Library Collections When Budgets Falter." *Medical Library Association Bulletin,* 64:187–195, April 1976. Summary of selection problems.

Wainright, Jane and Jacqueline Hills. *Book Selection from MARC Tapes.* London, Aslib Research and Development Department, 1973. 48p. (ED 083 991) Results of a pilot project involving several special libraries in Great Britain.

Ward, K. Linda. "Collection Policy in College and University Libraries." *Music Library Association Notes,* 29:432–440, March 1973. Development of a policy for the music library at the University of Western Ontario.

Werner, Mona M. "Collection Development in the Division for the Blind and Physically Handicapped, Library of Congress." *Catholic Library World,* 47:418–419, May–June 1976. Brief review.

Werner, O. James. *Manual for Prison Law Libraries.* American Association of Law Libraries, 1976. 120p.

White, Robert C. "Map Librarianship." *Special Libraries,* 61:233–235, May–June 1970.

Blanket Orders and Approval Plans

Axford, H. William. "The Economics of a Domestic Approval Plan." *College and Research Libraries,* 32:368–375, September 1971. Compares approval plans with traditional selection and acquisition methods.

DeVilbiss, Mary Lee. "The Approval-Built Collection in the Medium-Sized Academic Library." *College and Research Libraries,* 36:487–492, November 1975. Study conducted at California State Polytechnic University.

Dobbyn, Margaret. "Approval Plan Purchasing in Perspective." *College and Research Libraries,* 33:480–484, November 1972.

Dudley, Norman. "The Blanket Order." *Library Trends,* 18:318–327, January 1970. Results of a survey of large university libraries.

Evans, G. Edward and Claudia White Argyres. "Approval Plans and Collection Development in Academic Libraries." *Library Resources and Technical Services,* 18:35–50, Winter 1974. Study conducted in nine libraries.

Gamble, Lynne. "Blanket Ordering and the University of Texas at Austin Library." *Texas Library Journal,* 48:230–232, November 1972.

International Seminar on Approval and Gathering Plans in Large and Medium Size Academic Libraries, 1st, Western Michigan University, 1968. *Proceedings.* Edited by Peter Spyers-Duran. Kalamazoo, Mich., Western Michigan University Libraries, 1969. 142p. Includes papers on operating programs.

International Seminar on Approval and Gathering Plans in Large and Medium Size Academic Libraries, 2d, Western Michigan University, 1969. *Advances in Understanding Approval and Gathering Plans in Academic Libraries.* Edited by Peter Spyers-Duran and Daniel Gore. Kalamazoo, Mich., Western Michigan University, 1970. 220p. Collection of papers.

International Seminar on Approval and Gathering Plans in Large and Medium Size Academic Libraries, 3d, West Palm Beach, Fla., 1971. *Economics of Approval Plans.* Edited by Peter Spyers-Duran and Daniel Gore. Westport, Conn., Greenwood Press, 1972. 134p. Collection of papers.

McCullough, Kathleen. "Approval Plans: Vendor Responsibility and Library Research; A Literature Survey and Discussion." *College and Research Libraries*, 33:368–381, September 1972.

McCullough, Kathleen and others. *Approval Plans and Academic Libraries; An Interpretive Survey.* Phoenix, Ariz., Oryx Press, 1977. 154p. Report of a 1975 survey of 144 libraries.

Meyer, Betty J. and John T. Demos. "Acquisition Policy for University Libraries: Selection or Collection." *Library Resources and Technical Services*, 14:395–399, Summer 1970. Experiences at Ohio State University.

Morrison, Perry D. and others. "A Symposium on Approval Order Plans and the Book Responsibilities of Librarians." *Library Resources and Technical Services*, 12:133–145, Spring 1968. Includes three papers.

Rebuldela, Harriet K. "Some Administrative Aspects of Blanket Ordering: A Response." *Library Resources and Technical Services*, 13:342–345, Summer 1969. Argues with Thom (1969).

Rouse, Roscoe. "Automation Stops Here: A Case for Man-Made Book Collections." *College and Research Libraries*, 31:147–154, May 1970. Experiences at Oklahoma State University.

Steele, Colin. "Blanket Orders and the Bibliographer in the Large Research Library." *Journal of Librarianship*, 2:272–280, October 1970. British view of American practices.

Thom, Ian W. "Some Administrative Aspects of Blanket Ordering." *Library Resources and Technical Services*, 13:338–342, Summer 1969. Points out problems.

Wedgeworth, Robert. "Foreign Blanket Orders: Precedent and Practice." *Library Resources and Technical Services*, 14:258–268, Spring 1970. Survey of dealers.

Wilden-Hart, Marion. "Long-Term Effects of Approval Plans." *Library Resources and Technical Services*, 14:400–406, Summer 1970.

CHAPTER 3

Studying the Library's Community

Becoming familiar with the community to be served is an accepted requirement for today's librarian. A library's selection of materials, its special services, its whole operation, are aimed at providing a specific community (the citizens of a town, the faculty and students of a school or college, the researchers of a company) with what it needs and wants. Although much of the literature on community analysis is directed primarily toward public libraries, no one would claim that detailed knowledge of the community being served is important for public libraries only. All types of libraries have their unique service communities, and academic and special librarians have just as much reason as public or school librarians to know their communities and to engage in planning based on that knowledge. The definitions of community may be somewhat narrower and the sources of community information used will differ, but the basic procedures for study are much the same.

The idea of studying the community is not new, of course. Librarians have long been admonished to know the community, and Joseph L. Wheeler, in his *The Library and the Community* (published by the American Library Association in 1924), gave an excellent summary statement on the community survey. In the 1950s the Library-Community Project of the American Library Association, supported by the Fund for Adult Education of the Ford Foundation, carried on a program of community studies in several towns. This project resulted in a handbook for community study by librarians (*Studying the Community,* ALA, 1960) which may have encouraged more librarians to undertake what has been so widely praised but so infrequently practiced.

In the past several years, librarians have shown a renewed interest in the purposes, procedures, problems, and applications of community analysis for library purposes. Part of the credit for renewing that interest surely belongs to the Public Library Association (PLA). Since the early 1970s, the PLA, working primarily through its Goals, Guidelines and Standards Committee, has wrestled with the problem of revising its 1966 standards for public library systems. For many years PLA (like other library organizations developing type-of-library standards) has published statements of standards which generally specified the levels of certain input variables (books, money, staff, etc.) thought to be necessary for an effective public library operation in a community. The PLA standards committee which started work in 1970 considered that approach to be no longer appropriate and recommended instead that standards for public libraries be based on information needs of the community, without any attempt to predetermine the type of library or information service which should be meeting those needs. The committee took the position that community library service should be studied and planned as a totality and that the public library should take the lead in coordinating this effort. Under such assumptions, standards would be based directly on the local community's unique needs and resources; establishing standards would involve determining local needs and quantity and quality of local resources *before* establishing service priorities and developing programs. All the activities and discussions associated with these efforts at standard revision by PLA and its committee have stimulated workshops, articles, and reports, focusing attention on the importance of librarians becoming sensitive to the unique characteristics and special needs of their libraries' communities.

There are any number of reasons why libraries (as well as other social agencies, such as schools) are feeling pressure to conduct planning (both long and short-range) on the basis of community analysis. The increasing demand by the public for an accounting of how public funds are spent is one aspect of the pressure. If one accepts the assumption that each community is unique, it becomes necessary to reexamine a library's stated (or unstated) goals and objectives in order to justify the services and collections being developed for that unique community and eventually to justify the funds being spent on those services and collections in terms of the community's needs. Unless librarians know a great deal about their individual communities and the special demands of those communities, they will probably have a difficult time proving that they have allocated their budgets in the way most appropriate for their particular libraries.

Most communities, whether they are political units or academic units, are changing, and some are changing very rapidly. If librarians do not examine their communities and their services regularly, they may find that they are trying to do things which are no longer needed or expected from the library. (Knowing about the total library resources available to their clientele will help librarians determine appropriate priorities.) The traditional ways in which librarians have absorbed information about their communities from living and working in them over long periods of time are no longer effective. Librarians seldom work in communities very much like those in which they grew up or went to school, or even very much like those in which they previously worked. Systematic and regular study of the community is a desirable part, and to some librarians—who argue that the professional competence of the staff is demonstrated through the use of community study and planning—it is an essential part of a librarian's activities. Designing good library service within the restrictions of community and financial resources can be an exciting challenge.

Planning the Study

It is clear that librarians, whether they work in a public, academic, or special library, must know something about their users to function effectively. But just what kind of information they must have, and to what degree of statistical sophistication it must be developed, are matters which are not quite as clear. Alert and intelligent librarians can learn a great deal about the library's users simply by using their eyes and ears in their daily stint at the public desk. For a public librarian, a careful perusal of the local newspapers and a reasonable amount of contact with the community through service club membership, PTA, church groups, etc., will broaden his or her knowledge of and understanding of the town and its people. The same result may be achieved by academic librarians who read all university, college, school, or departmental publications, participate in local institutional committees and other activities, and maintain informal contacts with faculty and students. Over a period of time, by using intelligently all opportunities for learning, the librarian can become highly informed. What need would there be for such a librarian to do a more formal study?

Part of the answer lies in the choice of the adjective "formal." A formal investigation can provide a systematic view of the community; it enables librarians to rearrange what they already know in a larger framework, while adding data gathered especially for the project. Librarians may identify new groups, spot areas of the community not well served, or pick out groups in the community which are not making use of the library. In the very act of organizing the topics which community study will try to cover, librarians may discover aspects of the town's life which had not occurred to them before.

A formal community study is costly in staff time and money and must be as carefully planned as any other major research project. As with any research project, the community study begins with a delineation of the questions which need to be answered. What does the library staff really need to know about the community? If the library staff has an interest in more information than it is practical to collect, then what will be the precise purpose (or purposes) of the study being planned?

Stating the questions and defining the priorities help determine the estimated cost and time schedule. Without the careful completion of this first step, the whole project may be doomed to failure.

Typical questions to be addressed in a study of the community have been outlined by a number of groups having an interest in and need to know about the community (social agencies, citizen action groups, academic researchers, local and area governmental planning bodies, etc.). A few examples of handbooks developed by such groups for use in community study are included in the bibliography at the end of this chapter. While they offer many excellent suggestions for library planners, there are some characteristics of the community that are likely to be of more interest to librarians than others. Librarians will probably want to know first of all about the demographic characteristics of the community. Who lives in the area served by the library? What is the age distribution of the population? Has the number of individuals in each age group been increasing or decreasing in recent years? How many racial or ethnic groups are represented in the population and in what numbers? How much formal education has the typical resident of the community had? What percentage of the population is currently enrolled in school? How much income do the people in the community earn? What kinds of jobs do they hold? Knowing how the individuals in a community organize themselves to carry out the activities of their lives is also very important. How is the local government organized? What kinds of social, religious, educational, and cultural agencies have been established? How do people organize for social and recreational activities? Academic librarians will ask similar questions about their academic communities. How many faculty and students is the library supposed to serve? What courses do they teach? What courses do they take and in what numbers do they enroll? Are changes in enrollment expected? What research projects do they plan? What extracurricular activities are operated on the campus? These are a few of the broad questions which may lead to the specific questions of interest to a given library staff.

Proceeding with the Study

An essential step in community analysis, one that should be taken as early in the process as possible, is the study of published reports of other investigations. Time and money can be saved by avoiding unnecessary duplication of effort in data collection, by knowing ahead of time about possible mistakes and inadequacies which may occur in community studies, and by having available good models for planning the study. A related step is to determine how many of the questions can actually be answered from a re-analysis of data already collected by the library as part of its normal operations (information on occupation of borrowers, circulation patterns, etc.).

When the purpose of the community study has been established and all relevant reports and other literature have been assembled, the question of who is to direct and carry out the study must be answered. An initial answer may be to bring in an expert or consultant firm—an individual or a team trained in the techniques of collecting, analyzing, and interpreting community data. Such consultants may appear to be expensive, since their fees can be seen as lump sums, but they will probably produce results relatively quickly and offer the added advantage of access to comparative data. Most libraries do not have sufficient staff to undertake a highly formalized survey, and even if they did, most librarians are not trained for this work.

However, there are sometimes advantages to the self-study approach to community analysis, in which the library staff assumes primary responsibility for planning and directing the study. This approach may take longer and actually cost more because of all the staff time devoted to the effort, but the added skills gained by the staff members and the deeper sense of involvement and interest probably generated among those who will eventually have to apply the findings of the study may more than compensate for these disadvantages.

Other ways to approach the planning include using a combination of experts drawn in to advise on specific parts of the project and of staff members who will do most of the work. It is also possible and sometimes very desirable for libraries to cooperate with other agencies, governmental units, or citizen groups to community analysis and planning projects. Regional planning agencies gather much information which may assist in library planning, and in some regions they have carried out studies specifically designed to determine library use and needs. Academic librarians sometimes find themselves involved in campus-wide or system-wide planning projects and may use that opportunity to make detailed studies of their own library communities.

Whether the planning of the community study is done by the library staff, by outside experts, or by some combination, the actual gathering of the data may involve many other people. There is much to be said for having a community survey carried on by the members of the community. If the library can enlist the aid and expertise of citizens, faculty or students, it will reduce the burden on its staff and involve some members of the community in a library activity, thus spreading an awareness of the library's existence where it may not have been strongly realized before. This also promotes an educational end by having the citizen-participants learning something about their own community. When the survey results are completed, these people will form a useful part of the library's own resources.

Collecting Information

In general, the information to be collected in community studies can be gathered through examining reports and other documents, through questioning people in the community, and through systematic observation. Published materials and library records can supply a great deal of information for a relatively small expenditure of time and money. For questions about demographic characteristics of the community, compilations of the U.S. Bureau of the Census are essential. The decennial census of population and housing provides a thorough tabulation of the social and economic characteristics of the population, broken down by counties, standard metropolitan statistical areas (SMSA), census tracts, and, in some cases, by block. Detailed business censuses of regional and large municipalities covering manufacturing, retail trade, and other industries are also now available. In addition, state and local agencies sometimes supplement and update these with estimates and projections of their own. The structure of the community can be studied through agency reports, organization yearbooks, maps, directories, surveys conducted for other purposes, organization files, newspapers, and community histories. Knowing what groups are operating in a community and knowing what people constitute their membership can tell a great deal about a community. Most of the necessary materials should already be in the library's collection.

The documentation available to librarians in schools, colleges, or universities will be extensive. Academic institutions regularly produce bulletins, calendars, directories, time schedules, summaries of class enrollments, and other pieces of information needed for day-to-day operation. In some institutions reports from faculty committees and minutes of faculty (and board) meetings may give the careful reader the earliest clues on prospective changes in the curriculum or organization of the institution. In addition, librarians may be able to learn much from institutional histories, reports from the executive officer to the governing board, and various long-range plans.

When existing documents will not answer all questions, people who have the answers may be asked to supply them. This can be done through informal interviews with community leaders and others who have specialized knowledge, through formal interviews with a random sample of citizens, or through written questionnaires distributed to a random sample of users and/or non-users of the library. When the questionnaire or interview method is followed, great care must be taken to see that the questions are worded in a way that will be understood by all those being questioned and that will, at the same time, bring in the information actually needed for library planning. Following-up the first responses by contacting all those people in the sample who did not initially respond is essential if the summary of views expressed in the interviews or questionnaires is to be really representative of the community. Much useful information can be gathered from a well-designed interview or questionnaire survey, but the time and cost required to do the job properly may surprise many who are inexperienced in the use of these methods.

Observation sounds like a very informal way to gather information about a community, but systematic observation requires as much careful planning as a questionnaire or interview survey. Those participating in the project must first decide what kinds of people, events, places, etc. are to be observed and must then try to construct a tally sheet or observation checklist to be used by all those who are to be involved in the systematic observation. Of course, informal observation of the community can and should be done regularly by all librarians. Local newspapers, radio, television, and sources of books—bookstores, newsstands, etc.—might be observed to discover what kind of informational or recreational materials are available to the community and how the community makes use of these resources. Physical aspects of the community being observed can conveniently be recorded on slides or video tape and shared with all those involved in the project.

Using the Study

When all these data are gathered and analyzed, the librarian has to decide which of the facts are significant for the library, and what it can do to meet the problems revealed. All the findings piled up in the report of the survey do not equal a decision as to what the library should do. But the findings may indicate what groups make up the community and what those groups are doing and which activities the library might be able to support with appropriate materials; they may reveal certain areas of the city or elements of its population which are not now being served effectively; they may reveal reading interests which could be used as a guide to book selection; they may reveal data useful in planning new buildings or guiding the selection of staff for the various branches.

However, collection development is the area of library activity which may be most directly affected by the discovery of the community's interests. To be fully useful, the analysis and interpretation of the data gathered on the community must go beyond averages and broad generalizations and look at subgroups of communities, identified both by place of residence and by common interests. In collection development, it is necessary to relate the interests of special groups to their other characteristics (age, educational level, etc.) in order to determine how best to supply the materials that they need. Sometimes the differences between library practice and public expectation are concerned with the form in which the library supplies materials as well as with the subject areas emphasized. When the study reveals discrepancies between the library's collecting policy and the community's concerns, arrangements must be made to fill the gap. Sometimes resource sharing arrangements set up locally, regionally, or even nationally will cover the apparent gaps; on other occasions, local collection policies should be changed. In any case, findings of a community analysis should be studied in the context of total information resources available to a library's clientele before priorities are set and policies adjusted.

Libraries involved in community study gain many benefits beyond the obvious ones of being able to adjust collections and services more precisely to the interests and needs of the community. Allie Beth Martin summarized these benefits nicely in her contribution to the January 1976 issue of *Library Trends,* which was devoted entirely to the topic of community analysis.

> Planning and goal setting will be based on total community needs from the widest perspective—not the tunnel vision of the library. Change can be managed more responsibly; that is, the need for change can be better anticipated in time to make positive adjustments. The library will acquire new advocates among planners, governmental representatives and citizens in the process of the community analysis. A broader understanding of financial needs will result. The library will also gain a better understanding of the activities and problems of agencies and organizations. Cooperation will thus be more natural and practical.

Many librarians who have been through successful community analysis projects would agree with these statements and would join in emphasizing the importance to libraries of community analysis.

BIBLIOGRAPHY

Albright, John B. "A Bibliography of Community Analyses for Libraries." *Library Trends,* 24:619–643, January 1976. Annotates 81 studies.
Altman, Ellen and others. *A Data Gathering and Instructional Manual for Performance Measures in Public Libraries.* Chicago, Celadon Press, 1976. 171p.
American Library Association. Library-Community Project. *Studying the Community.* Chicago, American Library Association, 1960. 128p. Manual for community surveys by librarians.
American Library Association. Young Adult Services Division. Committee on Outreach Programs for Young Adults. *Look, Listen, Explain. Developing Community Library Services for Young Adults.* Chicago, American Library Association, 1975. 24p. Presents techniques for investigating a community in order to learn about information needs of young adults. Aimed at the beginning librarian.

Association of Research Libraries. Office of University Library Management Studies. *SPEC Kit on User Statistics and Studies*. Washington, D.C., 1976. Examples of statistical data collection on level and type of library user in large research libraries.

Association of Research Libraries. Office of University Library Management Studies. *SPEC Kit on User Surveys*. Washington, D.C., 1976. Compilation of user assessment techniques used in large research libraries.

Atkin, Pauline. "Bibliography of Use Surveys of Public and Academic Libraries, 1950–Nov. 1970." *Library and Information Bulletin*, 14:1–82, 1971.

Bachus, Edward J. "Studying a Branch Library Service Area." *Library Journal*, 103:144–145, January 15, 1978.

Bates, Marcia J. *User Studies; A Review for Librarians and Information Scientists*. ERIC, 1971. 57p. (ED 047 738)

Beasley, Kenneth E. "Librarians' Continued Efforts to Understand and Adapt to Community Politics." *Library Trends*, 24:569–581, January 1976. Brief historical review.

Benford, John Q. "The Philadelphia Project." *Library Journal*, 96:2041–2047, June 15, 1971. Report of a survey involving school and public library clientele.

Berelson, Bernard. *The Library's Public*. New York, Columbia University Press, 1949. 174p. Classic review of research on public library use.

Blasingame, Ralph and Mary Jo Lynch. "Design for Diversity: Alternatives to Standards for Public Libraries." In *Studies in Library Management*, vol. 3, edited by Gileon Holroyd, pp. 11–35. London, Linnet Books, 1976. Earlier version of this paper was published in *PLA Newsletter*, 13:4–22, June 1974. Discusses the differences between "place communities" and "interest communities" and the implications of these differences for library planning.

Bloss, Meredith. "Standards for Public Library Service—Quo Vadis?" *Library Journal*, 101:1259–1262, June 1, 1976. Describes efforts of Public Library Association to develop new standards.

Bundy, Mary Lee. "Factors Influencing Public Library Use." *Wilson Library Bulletin*, 42:371–382, December 1967. Report of a survey.

Bundy, Mary Lee. *The Library's Public Revisited*. College Park, University of Maryland, School of Library and Information Services, 1967. 84p. Contains papers by students on various parts of the library's public—adolescents, labor, radical right, etc.

Bundy, Mary Lee. *Metropolitan Public Library Users: A Report of a Survey of Adult Library Use in the Maryland-Baltimore-Washington Metropolitan Area*. College Park, University of Maryland, School of Library and Information Services, 1968. 130p.

Burns, Robert W., Jr. "Library Use as a Performance Measure: Its Background and Rationale." *Journal of Academic Librarianship*, 4:4–11, March 1978. Discusses assumptions, basic steps, and methodology of user studies.

Burns, Robert W., Jr. and Ron W. Hasty. *A Survey of User Attitudes Toward Selected Services Offered by the Colorado State University Libraries*. Urbana, University of Illinois, Graduate School of Library Science, 1975. 51p. (Occasional Paper No. 121)

Campbell, Angus and Charles A. Metzner. *Public Use of the Library and Other Sources of Information*. Ann Arbor, University of Michigan, Institute for Social Research, 1950. 84p. Report of a study conducted for the Public Library Inquiry. See also Berelson (1949).

Carpenter, Ray. "A Study of Adult Public Library Patrons in North Carolina." *North Carolina Libraries*, 35:24–36, Spring 1977. Summary of a survey conducted in 1971.

Carpenter, Ray L. *A Study of Public Library Patrons in North Carolina*. Chapel Hill, N.C., n.d. 18p. Results of the 1971 survey. Subtitle: "Socioeconomic, Media Use, Life Style Characteristics of North Carolina's Public Library Clientele."

Casey, Ann D. *General Reference Sources for Accessing Census Bureau Data; An Anno-tated Bibliography*. Rev. Washington, D.C., U.S. Department of Commerce, Bureau of the Census, 1978. 13p.

Childers, Thomas. *The Information-Poor in America*. Metuchen, N.J., Scarecrow Press, 1975. 182p. Comprehensive review of research. Appeared earlier as *Knowledge/Information Needs of the Disadvantaged*, U.S. Office of Education, 1973.

Colorado Market Research Services, Inc. *A Survey of the Attitudes, Opinions, and Be-havior of Citizens of Colorado with Regard to Library Services*. Denver, Colorado State Library, 1973–74. 5v.

Columbia University. School of Library Service. *Knowing the Community*. New York, Columbia University, School of Library Service, Community Media Librarian Pro-gram, 1975?. 20p. Subtitled: "A Manual for Investigating and Identifying Informa-tion Needs in Neighborhoods."

"Community Analysis and Libraries." Issue edited by Larry Earl Bone. *Library Trends*, 24:429–643, January 1976. Issue contains fourteen articles, most of which are also cited individually in this bibliography.

Conant, Ralph W. *A Study of the Professional, Business, and Economic Service Needs of the Residents of the Suburban Library System; A Report to the Suburban Library System*. Hinsdale, Ill., Ralph W. Conant and Associates, 1973. 87p.

Conway, James and others. *Understanding Communities*. Englewood Cliffs, N.J., Prentice-Hall, 1974. 253p. Procedures for gathering the kind of information about public opinion which could be useful to educational administrators.

Coughlin, Robert E. and others. *Urban Analysis for Branch Library System Planning*. Westport, Conn., Greenwood Press, 1973. 167p. Uses data gathered in Philadelphia.

Croneberger, Robert and Carolyn Luck. "Analyzing Community Human Information Needs: A Case Study." *Library Trends*, 24:515–525, January 1976. Describes a Detroit Public Library project.

Cuyahoga County, Ohio, Regional Planning Commission. *Changing Patterns, a Branch Library Plan for the Cleveland Metropolitan Area: A Report to the Cleveland Public Library and the Cuyahoga County District Library*. Cleveland, 1966. 162p.

Daniel, Evelyn H. "Performance Measures for School Libraries: Complexities and Poten-tial." In *Advances in Librarianship*, Vol. 6, pp. 2–51. New York, Academic Press, 1976. State-of-the-art review; useful for any type of library.

Davis, James R. "The New Students: What They Read." *College and Research Li-braries*, 36:216–221, May 1975. Analysis of reported best-sellers from college bookstores.

DeProspo, Ernest R. "The Use of Community Analysis in the Measurement Process." *Library Trends*, 24:557–567, January 1976. Suggests how decision-makers may use study results.

DeProspo, Ernest R. and others. *Performance Measures for Public Libraries*. Chicago, American Library Association, 1973. 71p. Results of a study sponsored by the Public Library Association.

Dewdney, Pat. "Citizen Participation, an Experiment in London, Ontario." *Canadian Library Journal*, 34:157–163, June 1977. How citizens helped study the community.

Eberhart, W. Lyle, "A Closer Look: Gallup Survey of American Adults Assesses the Role of Libraries in America." *American Libraries*, 7:206–209, April 1976. Brief review of findings presented in *The Role of Libraries in America* (1976).

Eisner, Joseph. "Finding Out What They Think of Us." *Wilson Library Bulletin*, 51:400; 428–429, January 1977. How the Plainedge (N.Y.) Public Library used direct-mail techniques to survey citizens.

Ennis, Philip H. *Adult Book Reading in the United States*. Chicago, National Opinion Research Center, University of Chicago, 1965. 111p. Based on national survey data.

Ennis, Philip H. "The Study of the Use and Users of Recorded Knowledge." *Library Quarterly*, 34:305-314, October 1964. Brief state-of-the-art review.

Ernst and Ernst. *Clevelanders' Opinions and Use of the Branch System, Cleveland Public Library; A Documented Survey with Recommendations.* Cleveland, 1972. 2v.

Evans, Charles. "A History of Community Analysis in American Librarianship." *Library Trends*, 24:441-457, January 1976. Reviews earlier studies.

Evans, Charles. *Middle Class Attitudes and Public Library Use.* Littleton, Colo., Libraries Unlimited, 1970. 126p. Survey conducted in Oceanside, California.

Fasick, Adele M. and Claire England. *Children Using Media; Reading and Viewing Preferences Among the Users and Non-Users of the Regina Public Library.* Toronto, University of Toronto, Faculty of Library Science, Centre for Research in Librarianship, 1977. 79p. Findings from interview survey of 540 children, conducted in 1976.

Ford, Geoffrey. "Research in User Behavior in University Libraries." *Journal of Documentation*, 29:85-106, March 1973.

Freebairn, Mark R. and Rita Palmer. *A Survey and Analysis of Reading Habits and Library Use Patterns of the Central City Residents of Salt Lake City, Utah.* Provo, Utah, Brigham Young University, Graduate Department of Library and Information Science, 1972. 168p.

Freeman, James E. and others. *Public Library Use in Denver: An Analysis of Denver Citizen, Business, and Government Use of a Community Information Resource.* Denver, Denver Urban Observatory, 1974. 171p.

Fuller, Muriel L. "Looking at Your Community." *Illinois Libraries*, 57:76-82, February 1975. Basic review of why and how to study a community.

Gallup Organization. *Role of Libraries in America; Report of a Survey Conducted by the Gallup Organization, Inc. for the Chief Officers of State Library Agencies.* Frankfort, Kentucky Department of Library and Archives, 1976. 155p. Results of a national survey.

Gallup Organization. *The Use of and Attitudes toward Libraries in New Jersey: Study Conducted by the Gallup Organization, Inc. for the New Jersey State Library.* Trenton, New Jersey State Library, Department of Education, 1976. 2v.

Garrison, Guy. "The Metropolitan Matrix of Libraries and Users." *Library Trends*, 23:193-205, October 1974. Discusses studies of selected communities.

Goldhor, Herbert. *A Public Opinion Survey of the Evansville Public Library.* Urbana, University of Illinois, Graduate School of Library Science, 1959. 12p. (Occasional Paper no. 56)

Gotsick, Priscilla. *Assessing Community Information and Service Needs.* Morehead, Ky., Morehead State University, Appalachian Adult Education Center, 1974. 23p. (Library Service Guide No. 2) Guide to collecting and interpreting information.

Govan, James F. "Community Analysis in an Academic Environment." *Library Trends*, 24:541-556, January 1976. Brief state-of-the-art review.

Groombridge, Brian. *The Londoner and His Library.* London, Research Institute for Consumer Affairs, 1964. 124p. Survey of both users and non-users of public libraries in metropolitan London.

Grundt, Leonard. "Metropolitan Area Library Problems: An Annotated Bibliography." In *The Metropolitan Library*, edited by Ralph W. Conant and Kathleen Molz, pp. 299-327. Cambridge, Mass., MIT Press, 1972.

Hamburg, Morris and others. "Library Objectives and Performance Measures and Their Use in Decision-Making." *Library Quarterly*, 42:107-128, January 1972. Covers some of same points as Hamburg (1974).

Hamburg, Morris and others. *Library Planning and Decision-Making Systems.* Cambridge, Mass., MIT Press, 1974. 274p. Applies operations research techniques to such problems as incorporating data about the community into decision-making.

Hays, Timothy and others. "The Patron Is Not the Public." *Library Journal*, 102:1813–1818, September 15, 1977. Report of a survey in the Piedmont area of North Carolina.

Howard, Edward N. "Toward PPBS in the Public Library." *American Libraries*, 2:386–393, April 1971. Shows how the Vigo County (Ind.) Public Library used a survey of community information resources to set its own service priorities.

Indiana Library Studies; Reports. Peter Hiatt, general editor. Bloomington, Indiana State Library, 1970–71. Series includes 19 reports; several are studies of information needs—adults, students and young adults, handicapped, state government, etc.

Javelin, Muriel C. "Analyzing Information Needs of Local Community Organizations: A Case Study." *Library Trends*, 24:527–539, January 1976. Report on Nassau (N.Y.) Library System project.

Johnston, Harold G. *Detroit Metropolitan Library Research and Demonstration Project*. Detroit, Wayne State University Libraries, 1969. 173p. Survey of main library of Detroit Public Library.

Knight, Douglas M. and E. Shipley Nourse. *Libraries at Large*. New York, Bowker, 1969. 664p. Includes discussions of a variety of user studies; covers non-specialists' needs as well as those of researchers.

Kronus, Carol L. "Patterns of Adult Library Use: A Regression and Path Analysis." *Adult Education*, 23:115–131, Winter 1972.

Kunz, Arthur H. "The Use of Data Gathering Instruments in Library Planning." *Library Trends*, 24:459–472, January 1976. Examples drawn from experiences of the Nassau-Suffolk (N.Y.) Regional Planning Board.

League of Women Voters of the United States. *Know Your Community*. Washington, D.C., League of Women Voters of the United States, 1972. 47p. Basic guide to community study.

Liesener, James W. "The Development of a Planning Process for Media Programs." *School Media Quarterly*, 1:278–287, Summer 1973. See also next citation.

Liesener, James W. *A Systematic Process for Planning Media Programs*. Chicago, American Library Association, 1976. 166p. Techniques for determining needs and priorities in a school.

Lin, Nan and William D. Garvey. "Information Needs and Uses." In *Annual Review of Information Science and Technology*, Vol. 7, pp. 5–37. Washington, D.C., American Society for Information Science, 1972. Bibliographic review.

Lipsman, Claire K. *The Disadvantaged and Library Effectiveness*. Chicago, American Library Association, 1972. 197p. Report of a project which included community analysis of low-income areas of fifteen cities.

Little, Arthur D., Inc. *The Role of the Public Library in Maine: Consumer Needs and Attitudes Towards Public Libraries in Maine*. Cambridge, Mass., Arthur D. Little, Inc., 1970. 289p. Report prepared for the Governor's Task Force to Study Library Services in Maine.

Little, Arthur D., Inc. *The Urban Central Library: Development Alternatives for San Francisco*. Cambridge, Mass., Arthur D. Little, Inc., 1970. 209p.

Lyman, Helen H. *Literacy and the Nation's Libraries*. Chicago, American Library Association, 1977. 212p. Contains section on community assessment.

Lyman, Helen H. *Reading and the Adult New Reader*. Chicago, American Library Association, 1976. 259p. Characteristics and reading interests of new readers; building collections for such readers.

Martin, Allie Beth. "Studying the Community: An Overview." *Library Trends*, 24:433–440, January 1976. Emphasizes the values of community assessment.

Martin, Lowell A. "Community Analysis for the Library." In *Library in the Community*; Papers Presented Before a Library Institute at the University of Chicago, August 23–28, 1943, pp. 201–214. Chicago, University of Chicago Press, 1944.

Martin, Lowell A. *Deiches Fund Studies of Public Library Service*. Nos. 1–4. Baltimore, Enoch Pratt Free Library, 1963–74. Three of the studies deal with students' needs; the fourth reviews reading habits and needs of Baltimore adults.

Martin, Lowell A. *Library Response to Urban Change; A Study of the Chicago Public Library*. Chicago, American Library Association, 1969. 313p.

Martin, Lowell A. "User Studies and Library Planning." *Library Trends*, 24:483–496, January 1976. Brief comments on the variety of studies which have been done and their value.

Martyn, John. "Information Needs and Uses." In *Annual Review of Information Science and Technology*, Vol. 9, pp. 3–23. Washington, D.C., American Society for Information Science, 1974. Bibliographic review.

Massey, Morris E. "Market Analysis and Audience Research for Libraries." *Library Trends*, 24:473–481, January 1976. Marketing expert shares techniques from that field.

Mathews, Virginia H. "Adult Reading Studies: Their Implications for Private, Professional and Public Policy." *Library Trends*, 22:149–176, October 1973.

Measuring the Quality of Library Service: A Handbook. Compiled by M. G. Fancher Beeler and others. Metuchen, N.J., Scarecrow Press, 1974. 208p. Reprints selections from 21 articles and reports on library use. Includes annotated bibliography of 17 items.

Monat, William R. "The Community Library: Its Search for a Vital Purpose." *ALA Bulletin*, 61:1301–1310, December 1967. Shorter version of Monat, *The Public Library and Its Community*.

Monat, William R. *The Public Library and Its Community; A Study of the Impact of Library Services in Five Pennsylvania Cities*. University Park, Pennsylvania State University, Institute of Public Administration, 1967. 162p. (Pennsylvania State Library Monograph Series No. 7) Summarizes findings from Altoona, Erie, Pottsville, Lancaster, and Williamsport.

Monat, William R. "The Role of the Social and Behavioral Sciences in Determining Library Operation and Impact." *Library Trends*, 24:583–596, January 1976. Application of social and behavioral science methods to library community analysis.

Monroe, Margaret E. "Community Development as a Mode of Community Analysis." *Library Trends*, 24:497–514, January 1976.

Montgomery, James G. *Scarborough Public Library User Survey*. Scarborough, Ontario, Scarborough Public Library Board, 1972. 67p.

Morse, Philip M. *Library Effectiveness: A Systems Approach*. Cambridge, Mass., MIT Press, 1968. 207p. Operations research approach to studying users in the MIT Science Library.

National Board of the Young Women's Christian Association of the U.S.A. *Look Beneath the Surface of the Community*. New York, Bureau of Communications, National Board, YWCA, 1968. Basic manual.

Newhouse, Joseph D. and Arthur J. Alexander. *An Economic Analysis of Public Library Services*. Lexington, Mass., Lexington Books, 1972. 135p. Study of the Beverly Hills (Calif.) Public Library.

Orr, Richard H. and others. "Development of Methodologic Tools for Planning and Managing Library Services: I, Project Goals and Approach," *Medical Library Association Bulletin*, 56:235–240, July 1968. Community analysis in a special library or academic setting.

Palmini, Cathleen. *Better Libraries Create Better Cities; A Study of Urban Needs*. Prepared for the Urban Library Trustees Council by the Library Research Center. Urbana, University of Illinois, Graduate School of Library Science, Library Research Center, 1972. 47p. Discussion of urban trends affecting libraries, based on statistical sources and previous user studies.

Palmour, Vernon E. "Planning in Public Libraries: Role of Citizens and Library Staff." *Drexel Library Quarterly*, 13:33–43, July 1977. Entire issue is on various aspects of library measurement.

Palmour, Vernon E. and Marcia C. Bellassai. *To Satisfy Demand: A Study Plan for Public Library Service in Baltimore County*. Towson, Md., Baltimore County Public Library, 1977. 247p.

Parker, Edwin B. and William J. Paisley. *Patterns of Adult Information Seeking*. Stanford, Calif., Stanford University, 1966. Review of previous research.

Parker, Edwin B. and William J. Paisley. "Predicting Library Circulation from Community Characteristics." *Public Opinion Quarterly*, 29:39–53, Spring 1965.

Peil, Margaret. "Library Use by Low-Income Chicago Families." *Library Quarterly*, 33:329–333, October 1963. Report of a survey.

Price, Jacob M. *Reading for Life: Developing the College Student's Lifetime Reading Interest*. Ann Arbor, University of Michigan Press, 1959. 271p. Includes review of college library use studies as well as general discussions of reading by college students.

Public Library Association. "Goals and Guidelines for Community Library Services." *PLA Newsletter*, 14:11–12, June 1975. Includes rationale behind the "Goals and Guidelines" statement.

Public Library Association. Goals, Guidelines, and Standards Committee. "A Mission Statement for Public Libraries; Guidelines for Public Library Service: Part I." *American Libraries*, 8:615–620, December 1977. Draft version published for review and comment.

Ridgefield Library and Historical Association. *The Ridgefield Library Self-Study Report*. Ridgefield, Conn., 1973. 72p.

Rike, Galen. *Statewide Library Surveys and Development Plans; An Annotated Bibliography 1956–1967*. Springfield, Illinois State Library, 1968. 105p. (Research Series No. 14)

Rzasa, Philip V. and John H. Moriarity. "The Types and Needs of Academic Library Users: A Case Study of 6,568 Responses." *College and Research Libraries*, 31:403–409, November 1970. Summarizes responses to a library user's questionnaire at Purdue University.

Sanders, Irwin T. *The Community: An Introduction to a Social System*. 2d ed. Ronald Press, 1966. 549p. Undergraduate textbook emphasizing the components of communities.

Schlessinger, Bernard S. and others. *Users and Uses of the New Haven Free Public Library; A Survey*. Hamden, Conn., 1972. 144p.

Soules, Gordon. *What People Want in a Library*. Vancouver, B.C., Gordon Soules Economic and Marketing Research, 1975. 150p. Survey conducted for the Burnaby (B.C.) Public Library.

Strain, Paula M. "Engineering Libraries: A User Survey." *Library Journal*, 98:1446–1448, May 1, 1973. Example of community analysis in a special library.

Stroud, Janet G. and David V. Loertscher. "User Needs and School Library Services." *Catholic Library World*, 49:162–165, November 1977. Community analysis in a school setting.

Symbiotic Situation: Brown County, Aberdeen, and Alexander Mitchell Public Library. n.p., July, 1977. Example of a community study done in South Dakota.

Tauber, Maurice F. and Irlene R. Stephens. *Library Surveys*. New York, Columbia University Press, 1967. 286p. Includes chapters on surveys of various types of libraries and library functions.

Tobin, Jayne C. "Study of Library 'Use Studies'." *Information Storage and Retrieval*, 10:101–113, March–April 1974. Analysis of the kinds of studies which have been reported in the literature.

Toronto Public Libraries. *Goals, Objectives, and Priorities*. Toronto, 1975–76. Several documents from the "Goals, Objectives and Priorities Study" of the TPL. Include comments from staff members, consultants, and citizens. Cover both adult and juvenile service.

Townley, Charles T. *Identification of Information Needs of the American Indian Community That Can Be Met by Library Services*. Minneapolis, Minn., National Indian Educational Association, Library Project, 1975. 330p. Final report on a project funded by U.S. Department of Health, Education, and Welfare.

Vainstein, Rose. "Teaching the Elements of Community Analysis: Problems and Opportunities." *Library Trends*, 24:597–618, January 1976. State-of-the-art in library education.

Voos, Henry. *Information Needs in Urban Areas: A Summary of Research in Methodology*. New Brunswick, N.J., Rutgers University Press, 1969. 90p. Comprehensive review of research.

Warncke, Ruth. "Analyzing Your Community: Basis for Building Library Service." *Illinois Libraries*, 57:64–76, February 1975. Basic article on why and how to conduct a study.

Warner, Edward S. "Constituency Needs as Determinants of Library Collection and Service Configurations: An Approach to Measurement." *Drexel Library Quarterly*, 13:44–51, July 1977.

Warner, Edward S. and others. *Information Needs of Urban Residents*. Rockville, Md., Baltimore Regional Planning Council, 1973. 283p. Report of a study done in the Baltimore urban area.

Warren, Donald I. "Six Kinds of Neighborhoods: Parochial, Diffuse or Stepping Stone? Different Strokes for Different Neighborhoods, a Community Leader's Handbook." *Psychology Today*, 9:74–78;80, June 1975.

Warren, Roland L. *The Community in America*. 2d ed. Chicago, Rand McNally, 1972. 418p. Emphasizes the types of relationships which develop between people and social organizations existing in the same location.

Warren, Roland L. *Studying Your Community*. New York, Free Press, 1965. 385p. Practical manual for interested citizens.

Webb, Kenneth and Harry P. Hatry. *Obtaining Citizen Feedback: The Application of Citizen Surveys to Local Governments*. Washington, D.C., The Urban Institute, 1973. 105p. Discusses use of citizen surveys, potential disadvantages and possible procedures.

Wilson, Robert A. and Roger Figura. *The Library Listens: Delaware Library Association Survey 1973. A Survey of Present Use and Future Needs*. Newark, University of Delaware, Institute of Urban Affairs, 1974. 66p.

Wood, D. N. "User Studies; A Review of the Literature from 1966 to 1970." *Aslib Proceedings*, 23:11–23, January 1971. Bibliographic essay.

Zweizig, Douglas. "Predicting Amount of Library Use: An Empirical Study of the Role of the Public Library in the Life of the Adult Public." (Ph.D. Thesis, Syracuse University, 1973). 366p.

Zweizig, Douglas. "With Our Eye on the User: Needed Research for Information and Referral in the Public Library." *Drexel Library Quarterly*, 12:48–58, January–April 1976.

Zweizig, Douglas and Brenda Dervin. "Public Library Use, Users, Uses: Advances in Knowledge of the Characteristics and Needs of the Adult Clientele of American Public Libraries." In *Advances in Librarianship*, Vol. 7, pp. 231–255. New York, Academic Press, 1977. Reviews findings of those studies which concentrated on people (as opposed to circulation studies).

CHAPTER 4

Selection by Subject

In Chapters 1 and 2, it was pointed out that the interpretation given to the principles of selection is affected by the type of library applying them. The librarian who applies the general principles to the several subject fields will discover that interpretations of the principles are also necessary here. These adjustments and alterations do not mean that the basic principles are abandoned. It merely means that more specific judgments have to be made in the light of the sometimes considerable differences in the types of material issued on the various subjects. Let one example of extremes suffice to illustrate the problem: Are the same tests for truth to be applied to the novel describing a future utopia as are applied to a treatise on chemical reactions?

In this chapter, the general tests for non-fiction will be discussed, followed by a section devoted to some of the problems in the specific subject areas. Literature will be dealt with as a separate entity, and the chapter will conclude with a discussion of the selection of translations and editions.

The Criteria for Evaluating Non-Fiction

The first question which may be raised in selecting a new non-fiction title is "Who is this author?" Does the author have any qualifications which fit him/her for dealing with the subject—is he/she by education, occupation, or experience in a position to produce anything of value? For example, if the author has written other books on the subject, produced a film or filmstrip, written the script for a television documentary, etc., the librarian can check to see how they were received by the knowledgeable.

After the authority of the author has been established, the scope of the item should be ascertained. Does it treat the whole subject—or part of it? Does it concern itself with the history of the topic—or some present aspect of it? Is its treatment (either of the whole subject or part of it) exhaustive or brief? Once its scope has been determined, it should be compared with items already in the library to decide if it really makes a contribution to the collection in terms of the material it covers.

Next the selector should attempt to ascertain the manner in which the material is treated. Is there anything in the writing itself which recommends the material? Is the style clear, or muddied and tortured? Does the author organize the ideas so that the reader can follow the thought easily, or is it disjointed and confusing? Does the text have vitality and interest, or is it characterized by tedium and monotony? If the item popularizes a technical subject, is it done with accuracy and care, or has it oversimplified so much that it is really misleading? Does the author attempt to summarize the facts only, or is the material presented in such a way as to support some thesis he/she is committed to? (This does not necessarily mean that the author has done wrong: many books and films have an important contribution to make by advancing arguments for consideration in the social sciences, in science, in musical or literary criticism, etc. If the author has very strong convictions, however, the evidence may be manipulated to suit his/her ends. The librarian must look for evidence of bias in the treatment of the material, trying to decide whether the author is fair-minded or a strong partisan.)

The physical features of the book may also play a role in deciding whether or not the item makes a positive contribution to the collection. The typography should be reasonably clear and readable. Some printing jobs—and particularly with the new methods of reproduction—may reduce the usefulness of a book because of blurring, smearing, too light an impression, and general sloppy appearance. Most often, of course, a title will be available in only one edition. If the text is important, there is nothing the librarian can do except blink at the poor typography and sympathize with the future readers of that particular book. The presence of important illustrations, maps, bibliographies, or significant appendix material may provide the library with materials not elsewhere available and may be reason enough for the purchase of a book whose text is only adequate, but whose special features are invaluable. (Special features of non-book materials are taken up in the next chapter.)

The date of the material may be very important—especially in certain of the subject fields. In literature, of course, one does not exclude *Tom Jones* from purchase because the text was written in the eighteenth century—but perhaps this is too painfully obvious an example. If the book is old, however (and a recent imprint date may conceal a text which actually dates back, substantially unchanged, for half a century), and the field is one which changes rapidly, the librarian would want to decide if an historical treatment were important to the library, or whether the library had not better pass the title by in favor of one including more modern scholarship. The date an item was produced is also important in considering films, filmstrips, documentary videotapes, and other non-book forms.

An important consideration in selecting non-fiction involves the kind of user for whom the material would be useful. Would it serve the needs of the general patron, the beginning student of the subject, the advanced scholar? It might happen that a really brilliant treatment of a subject by a sound authority would be exactly suited to a kind of person which the library does not serve. The utility of its purchase by such a library is certainly highly dubious.

In general, the selector seeks to identify those items which will have permanent value (remembering always that some materials will be important because they deal with a topic of current interest), while trying to eliminate those which are unimportant, trivial, or deliberately distorted. In the selection of non-fiction, a sound knowledge of the subject involved is the central requirement for adequate selection.

PROBLEMS IN THE SELECTION OF BOOKS IN THE SEVERAL SUBJECTS

Religion

The field of religion—like those of politics, economics, and literature—represents an area in which people have strong convictions, a fact which complicates selection, since the titles published sometimes reflect these profound attachments to particular points of view. Since the truths of religion are, in the minds of many people, of a kind which are not susceptible of objective demonstration, the judgment of materials in the field runs into something like the problem of evaluating literary materials. What criterion of truth—in the sense of physical reality—does one bring to a work of religious revelation? Since the librarian may have strong personal convictions on the subject, it may be very difficult to be impartial when confronted with material which holds views on religion very different from his/her own—and hence very shocking. This general problem will color the whole process of selection and should be borne in mind as the following more specific problems are discussed.

One of the difficult problems in selecting religious materials arises out of the polemical. No irony or sarcasm is intended in remarking that religion has bred many disputatious items, some of them quite violent. If the public library tries to carry out its purpose of presenting the various points of view on matters of controversy, it may find itself buying materials which bitterly attack one or another of the organized churches. Such items do exist, and there may well be demand for them from some members of the community. In considering polemical works, it seems reasonable to demand that they contain no distortions or misrepresentations of fact, that there be no attacks made on the basis of emotional opposition alone, without substantiating evidence.

A second area which causes some difficulty is the unsolicited gift to the library, often periodical materials. Many of these periodicals are of a polemical nature, especially those issued by the more energetic proselytizing groups. Many are quite vocal in demanding that their gift be represented on the open magazine racks—they may even return regularly to make sure that their gift is there, not buried somewhere in the stacks of the library. The general rule should be that gifts meet the same requirements for selection as the library's own purchases. If the magazine does not meet the standards of objectivity, utility, and general interest, it could be rejected. However, the protagonists of violent religious literature are themselves liable to be rather violent in their attempts to spread their particular version of the truth, and there is no rule which will enable the librarian to handle this problem easily. The touch of the diplomat may be needed in the attempt to show the zealous that the library does not consider their materials suitable for the public library's shelves.

If one asks whether the library collection should serve as a sort of Sunday school library, i.e., one in which people can come to prepare themselves for membership in a given church, the answer seems fairly clear. Materials which are of an instructional nature, materials which are intended to catechize the aspiring member of one particular church, are too specialized for the general interest of the community. They are properly the province of the church concerned or of the religious bookstore.

Another category which is liable to be troublesome is the popularization—of Bible stories, of lives of Christ or the saints, either in books or films—and the religious "self-help" book. Some of these are characterized by lack of good taste, by sweeping and unfounded generalizations, by suppression of all details which do not support the author's thesis. The style is often a nauseous blend of weepy bathos and the most superficial sentimentality. It is precisely this category of religious literature which is liable to be most in demand, rather than the scholarly histories of religion, the treatises on theology, or the collections of sermons. If librarians operate on the theory that the library must supply whatever its patrons demand, regardless of quality, they will find a good part of the budget for religious literature being spent on materials of no real worth or permanent interest. The librarian who wishes to build a collection which represents intrinsic worth would find such a situation distressing and will be much less friendly to the cheaper kind of popularization. The solution to the problem—or the compromise which is arrived at—will depend on the librarian's conception of the purposes of the library.

Other areas in which decisions will have to be made include, first, the amount of technical material which will be bought—sermons, exegeses, manuals for theological study, doctrinal materials, etc. This question is no different in this field than in other subjects: how much specialized material will the library purchase for the worker in the field or for the scholar? It is a long-standing admonition that libraries will buy at least some materials which will benefit the whole community only indirectly through their use by doctors, lawyers, ministers, and other professionals whose work is of importance to the community.

Secondly, the library will have to decide how much material it will buy to represent the non-Christian religions, and what type of material it should be. Some librarians have inclined to the view that the sacred writings of all the major religions of the world ought to be in every library; others have felt that the demand for such materials would not justify their high cost to the ordinary collection. The size of the community, the interests of the library's users, and the amount available for purchase of materials in the area of religion are certainly all factors which will weigh in the decision made.

In the selection of editions of the Bible, the librarian must be aware of the various inclusions or exclusions of books which result from the acceptance or rejection of certain writings as canonical materials. The Bible is also available in a wide variety of formats, each with its own special advantages or usefulness, as well as the variety of English translations available. There are various kinds of materials supplementary to the study of the Bible which the library will also have to review for purchase: concordances, atlases, interpreter's editions, dictionaries, films, filmstrips, recordings, etc.

Philosophy

Just naming some of the topics covered by the Dewey classification in the field of philosophy suggests a major problem: ontology, cosmology, epistemology, teleology, positivism, nominalism. The very words for the topics bring to mind the fact that technical philosophy is a very technical subject, indeed. The public library will have to decide just how far it wishes to go in presenting the authoritative—but very difficult—treatment of these specialized philosophical discussions. The average public library—omitting from consideration the central reference collections of the large metropolitan libraries—will probably not find such materials of great value to its readers. Hence, these topics are more likely to be represented by popularizations, if at all, which brings the librarian face-to-face with the usual problems involved in selecting a popular treatment of a specialized subject, The librarian who is not trained in philosophy will have to have recourse to those selection aids which record the judgments of the informed.

A second issue to be decided is the extent to which individual philosophers will be represented by their own works. It may be found more useful to buy expositions of the philosopher, or to content oneself with having the various philosophers represented largely in histories of philosophy. In purchasing histories, the library will have to decide whether it will satisfy itself with a few general histories of Western and Eastern philosophy, or whether it will buy more in the way of histories covering shorter periods in greater detail.

Psychology

At least five areas raise problems in selection for the psychology section. The first is the old problem of the popularization for the general reader versus the technical work. Its solution involves the same considerations as to the purposes and the type of reader as are true in other fields.

The second problem area arises in the field of mental health. There are many "pseudo-scientific" materials available, which often have great popularity, as they assure harried citizens that they too can learn to live at peace with their nerves or can think their way to success. Librarians will have to weigh the demand for such items against their own conception of the demand for quality and authority in any material.

A third problem comes from the materials on the occult sciences: numerology, astrology, palmistry, spiritualism, fortune telling, crystal gazing. These subjects are given credence by many people, while their claims to authenticity are scornfully rejected by others. The library will have to ask itself how much of its money it is willing to divert to fields which are considered highly dubious by many, but defended zealously by their adherents. Refusing a request for the purchase of an item in this area presents a problem: how does the librarian tell a patron in any acceptable manner that he/she is asking for material which the library will not buy because the librarian believes that the field is charlatanry? No diplomatic librarian would make such a blunt reply, perhaps, but this field does illustrate the general problem which is faced less extremely in every field: someone has to make decisions as to the quality and reliability of materials, and these decisions will not always be acceptable to some of the library's users.

The fourth problem involves the "case study" type of material, in which the problems (particularly the sexual ones) of individuals are presented in what is often graphic detail. The case study is no longer restricted to technical materials intended for the use of psychiatrists or psychoanalysts: such titles have been published for the general public. With the spread among the general population of greater knowledge of psychology (not all of it very thorough or precise, to be sure), the more lurid details of personal development have lost some of their power to shock and dismay. But some people in every community, and many people in some communities, would be disgusted and revolted by case studies which their more sophisticated neighbors could take in stride. The librarian will have to decide the extent to which such materials would be useful in the community for serious study of human problems. It is true that even some of our wilder modern novels have not approached the frankness of some of the sober works on human sexuality. Those sober works are intended to be used as such, however. Certainly there is considerable need for clear and reliable information on the problems of the human sex life, but the area does present possibilities for turmoil in the community.

One example of the power of such items to disturb the even tenor of the librarian's life may perhaps be permitted. A sixteen-year-old boy took a case study of sex problems out of a public library. After he had read it, he brought it to his mother with the horrified remark that it made him feel as if he had fallen into a pit of slime. The next morning the librarian received a telephone call from a friendly member of the board. "Hang on to your hat," he said, "the police are on the way over to get the names of all the people who have read book X." That conversation had hardly been concluded when the phone rang again. This time it was the mayor, who wanted the librarian to be in his office at 11:00 A.M. to explain why the library was distributing pornography. The mayor's call was followed by a call from the president of the library board, who notified the librarian that her presence was required at an emergency session of the board that afternoon. The next call was from the editor of the local newspaper—a good friend and supporter of the library—who wanted to know the real story concerning the alleged purveying of obscenities by the library.

The mother had been busy on the phone that morning, calling the police, the mayor, the members of the library board, the newspaper, and her minister, attacking the library almost hysterically. She was intensely disturbed because of the damage which she felt the library was doing to her son and other young people of the community.

The outcome of this particular case is not important in itself, nor is it cited to discourage librarians from buying books in this potentially controversial field. It is introduced only to indicate that the problem is not an academic one. Buying of such books—like the buying of any other—should be done on the basis of a clearly realized position which can be explained and defended.

A fifth problem area overlaps the case study somewhat: it is the area of abnormal psychology, ranging from the psychoses, through the neuroses, to what many consider problems of social deviation (as, for example, homosexuality). Technical medical materials on the problem of the abnormal mind do not appear to fall into the province of the ordinary collection intended for the "home reader." But this area is one in which greater understanding on the part of society seems desirable. The library may well wish to have some items intended for general readers, which will help them understand the problems of the insane or the seriously neurotic. Materials dealing with such deviations from generally accepted behavior as homosexuality certainly do present a difficult decision for the librarian. The problem cannot be resolved by any general prescription: its solution depends once more on the kind of community the library serves and the usefulness which such materials would have to the particular library's users. The general faith that knowledge is always better than ignorance might be invoked here, but it is probably true that some of the readers of such books—as one librarian has put it—will not use them for the light they may shed on their own problems, but rather for the titillation they may provide. It is truly a vexing issue. One can only hope that librarians will be neither neurotically prudish nor neurotically scatological.

The Social Sciences

The various social sciences also present areas of potential difficulty in selection. Law, political science, economics, social welfare, sociology, education: the simple listing of some of the subjects covered by the Dewey 300 class is enough to invoke the realization that selection here often involves considerable care. Many of the items in these fields may reflect strong convictions on the author's part. Economics, to take one example, is frequently presented with overtones which are not entirely scientific. Periodically people rush into print with commentary on the educational system or educational theories which is more distinguished for its heat than its light. Materials on the legal aspects of civil rights—racial problems or freedom of speech—are not always presented with the calm, judicial manner or scrupulous concern for facts which one might expect in matters of law. The whole field of political theory—democracy, communism, fascism, anarchism, etc.—presents opportunity for slanted or propagandistic materials. The distant, cold eye of the scientific sociologist may distress those not accustomed to seeing the assumptions of their lives and their society put through the terrible mill of objective analysis. Unorthodox views of society, of mother, of love, of social structure can be encountered among the sociologists, as well as among the political theorists.

In the social sciences librarians should sharpen their perceptions, looking for reliable, unbiased, factual accounts. They should try to decide whether a given item helps to clarify problems, or whether it confuses issues by presenting stereotyped, emotional, or deliberately distorted arguments. When conflicting social values are presented in books or other materials, librarians will have to decide how to represent them in the library: shall an attempt be made to balance opposing views? Shall some views be considered so far outside the accepted pale that they will be banished from the library? Librarians should inspect the author's qualifications carefully and be concerned with the up-to-dateness of the contents. They must expect to find instances of propaganda, dogmatism, polemics, partisanship, and personal bias—and perhaps might only conclude that this really ought to be one of the livelier sections of the library collection, that its contents ought to encourage discussion and excitement.

Science

In an age of science, it seems appropriate that the library should have a good collection of materials which explain to the lay reader the general nature of science and the scientific method, as well as the central aspects of the several sciences. The major problems involve the selection of sound popularizations of science for the general user, and keeping the collection up-to-date, since science is characterized by continual change. The popularizations should be done with scholarship and accuracy, appeal of presentation, and must somehow succeed in presenting highly technical and complex matters in a manner which will not baffle the non-scientist. Such works are by no means easy to come by.

The majority of librarians come to their work without a background in science. Many of them have publicly expressed their feelings of insecurity in trying to select in an area in which they are not only untrained, but in which many of them feel alien and uncomfortable. They are forced to rely on the aid given them by the selection tools to an even greater extent than is true in many other subjects. When these aids are deficient, most librarians would probably feel in no position to dispute or question. Perhaps in this field, more than in any other, the humanistically-trained librarian ought to call on informed specialists from the community for help in selection. This is a resource always available, but not always used. Relying on the scientific periodicals for authoritative reviews of current popularizations will ordinarily not be too happy a solution: their reviews often run very late, and they are not likely to devote space to the popular treatment of a specialized subject.

To summarize briefly: in the sciences, the public librarian seeks to identify materials written with scholarship and accuracy by a person qualified by education and training to speak with authority on the subject; which contain either new material or replace outmoded items; which are presented in a style having some appeal to the user and which are timely in terms of the subject, or timeless in terms of treatment. After all, the average librarian is probably an "average library user," i.e., well-educated, intelligent (we trust), and with a reading and viewing and listening experience considerably broader than the average member of the community (who is not, it must be remembered, an "average library user"). Many of the aspects of the popularization can be judged by librarians. As persons without scientific specialization, but with a good general education, they can judge how successfully the popularization was able to make the subject clear to them. The matter of authority can also be estimated by using the ordinary searching procedures of the reference librarian. The accuracy of the facts presented may be the major area in which they feel they cannot judge, and here they can consult the reviewing media or ask a person trained in that field of science to aid in evaluation. The problems of selection in the sciences may be exacting, but they are not insurmountable.

The Fine Arts

One of the impelling pragmatic reasons for careful and effective selection in the fine arts is the high cost of many of the materials. A mistake in choosing in this field can be very expensive indeed. The prices of books of paintings reflect the high cost of good color reproduction. Unfortunately, it is also true that some highly priced books are by no means so well reproduced as others. The librarian will then need another skill—the ability to judge the quality of reproduction, in slides and films as well as books.

The cost of art materials has often caused the smaller library to pass them by, even though the librarian may have felt that his/her small community would have appreciated them as much as the metropolis, and perhaps even more. Since the smaller community is not likely to have the museums and art galleries which are available to the city dweller, the only chance a citizen of the small town may have to see works of art easily would be in the form of the art book. Where the budget is very limited, librarians have sometimes been enabled to buy such expensive materials through the aid of a Friends of the Library group or other community organization. This is, of course, something of an administrative problem, but it has a close relationship to selection policy. If librarians find sources for support, they must then be ready to select.

Whether or not the library can afford to embark on the purchase of expensively illustrated books of individual artists, it ought to represent in its collection at least the history of art in its various aspects. These histories may serve as selection aids for the librarian interested in purchasing either books of reproductions or reprints for circulation.

If the library circulates framed prints of famous paintings or even—mirabile dictu!—framed originals (by local artists usually), there will arise the problem of selecting the paintings for the circulating collection. Here one might wish to approach the circulating collection historically (representing the major painters of all periods, perhaps with examples of the various periods of each painter); from the point of view of family acceptability; or perhaps even from the interior decorator's view (which pictures have the largest assortment of neutral colors to fit every decor?).

In selecting circulating prints, the librarian will also have to decide at what level of quality to draw the line. As in the case of books, there may be demands for the popular, prettified, wholesome type of dime store art. How "high" shall the standard be? Or—to put the converse—how "low" may we sink? Some patrons might be much more profoundly moved by a charming picture, slickly executed, of a boy and his dog, with the boy carrying the light burden of fishing rod, freckles, and carefree youth into a blue summer day, than by any Botticelli goddess on a half shell. What stand shall the library take?

The field of music also offers a number of areas for decision. Shall the library stock only books about music and musicians, or shall it also embark on the collecting of phonograph records and the printed music itself? In the field of books, shall the library carry only general works, or technical works also on harmony, counterpoint, composition, orchestration, conducting, etc.? Shall it concern itself only with materials on the classical composers and composers of serious contemporary music, or shall it also buy works on popular music? Shall it restrict its purchase of phonorecords to the classics—or include the popular contemporary singer? How will the librarian evaluate the comparative excellence of the various recorded versions of a given work? Shall the librarian select a few titles from all the major composers, plus many of the more popular items by lesser composers, or should he/she attempt a fuller representtion of all the works of only the really major composers? These questions are all raised, not to be answered ex cathedra, but to call attention to areas in which decisions will have to be made. Further discussion of the problems involved in selecting recordings will be found in the chapter devoted to selection of non-book materials.

History

In selecting works on history, authority and accuracy are prime requisites. In addition, clarity of presentation and an effective style should be sought. The best historical writing has often been of distinguished literary quality. The tradition of fine writing in history is so well established that it seems reasonable to ask that new titles meet this requirement.

One of the problems in historical writing is bias on the part of the author, which colors his/her interpretation of the facts. This is especially true in studies of the very recent past, such as the Vietnamese War or Watergate. But even on past issues—the Civil War, Andrew Jackson's administration, Napoleon—one can find startlingly partisan histories, especially startling when one considers that they were written very long after the events.

The distribution of the collection by historical periods will call for decisions on the selector's part. How much of ancient or medieval history should be bought? Should we be satisfied with a general history of the Italian Renaissance, or will the library buy volumes on limited aspects of the various Italian states of the period? Will the library buy heavily in the area of the American Civil War, in which a very large body of material is available? How far will the library go in purchasing in the subject matter of World War II, on which an almost incredible quantity of contemporary material has appeared? At what point can the multiple contemporary works on important historical events be replaced by broader treatments?

The library will also have to decide on the proportion of scholarly to popular treatments of history. Will it insist on books which make new contributions based on examination of the source material, or will it prefer books based on secondary sources, but perhaps more popular in treatment?

In addition to historical periods, decisions are needed concerning the extent and depth of coverage of areas outside North America and Western Europe, Shall one buy heavily in the history of South America? Australasia? Africa? What about individual countries like Upper Volta? Sikkim? Sarawak? Does one include histories of cities like Djakarta? Rangoon? Timbuktu? (or its charming neighbor, Goundam?)

Literature

The problems involved in evaluating a work of creative imagination are quite different from those met with in evaluating factual materials. In this field, we are enmeshed in matters of taste, in matters of esthetic response, in matters of artistic discrimination—none of which is very susceptible of objective verification. One can ask about a book or filmstrip on physics, "Is it accurate? Is it up-to-date? Is it authoritative?" What does it mean to ask if a novel is "accurate"? Yet traditional statements of tests for fiction have asked the librarian to consider whether a given novel is "true to life," whether it "blurs the hard-won line between right and wrong," whether "the psychology of its characters' acts rings true." One can only ask, true to whose version of life? Blurs the line between right and wrong drawn by which of the many groups who define that line differently? The acts of the characters "ring true" according to which school of psychology?

There are, of course, certain less controversial areas of judgment: the plot and structure of a novel or a play, the effectiveness or woodenness of the dialogue, the clarity or obscurity of the style, the authenticity of setting and facts in historical novels or plays, the effectiveness with which dramatic interest is sustained. Even here, the standards of judgment are less objective and more often a matter of personal response to the imponderables of style and presentation than is true in non-fiction. It is in this field especially that the judgments of many informed readers are useful for adequate selection, in order to avoid the acceptance or rejection of a book, film, videotape, or spoken record on the basis of the esthetic response of one individual.

The first general question in selecting literature involves level of quality. Shall the library attempt to select only great literature? or good literature? or popular literature? The problem of judging the quality of a work of literature is not as simple as might be desired. What makes a novel good? Or, to make the problem more difficult, what makes it great? It is obvious enough that the style, the structure, the characterization, the problems presented all play a part, but it is very difficult to get at the elusive quality which makes a novel lasting and important, which distinguishes the work of a master craftsman from the work of a master creator. If one simply lists some of the novels which are generally agreed to possess great distinction (*Pride and Prejudice*, *Moby Dick*, *The Scarlet Letter*, *War and Peace*, *Crime and Punishment*, *Tom Jones*—to name only a few), one can recognize that they represent greater diversity than uniformity. The simplest definition of a great work of art is probably that it is one which has appealed to many people over a long period of time. Let us assume, then, that in the selection of a novel just off the press we are not going to be able to decide with any degree of certainty that we are faced with a great novel. Only time will determine that fact.

Let us settle then for trying to decide a lesser question: is this a good novel? As far as the present authors can tell at this moment in time, a reasonably secure answer to that question can only be based on ascertaining the judgment of a group of readers who are informed, well-read, and esthetically sensitive. If a large group of intelligent and perceptive critics rush into print with high praise, one can conclude that the title has something to offer the reader. Unfortunately, the history of criticism will reveal that works which later achieved fame were not always well received at their first appearance, and some works which were later to fall into the discard were extravagantly praised on their first publication. There does not appear to be any crystal ball which will enable one to foresee such results, and the librarian is left with the conclusion that, uncertain as it is, there is no present mechanism which can supplant the judgment of the informed reader.

A special problem is found in the best-selling novels. A study of best-sellers over a period of several generations will reveal that a great many of the titles have faded into obscurity. Some librarians have been loath to buy novels which would become obsolete after a year or two, while others have decided that they will buy every best-seller and duplicate freely. They feel that great popular interest in a title is in itself sufficient grounds for purchase, particularly since it is so difficult to get agreement as to whether or not a novel is "really" good.

This problem of the best-seller is part of the larger problem of the light, recreational type of novel versus the classic or standard novel. How much money should the librarian spend on westerns, mysteries, and science fiction? How many light romances are justified? How much—to generalize the question—of the popular should be acquired as compared with the cultural? The answer to these questions—as was pointed out in Chapter 1—will depend on the view librarians take of the purposes of the library. If they are convinced that it has an important educational purpose, that it should attempt to stock serious materials for the sober student of life and society, they may well reject light, ephemeral, popular fiction. Some librarians have tried to make an economic compromise by buying the services of those companies which specialize in supplying rental collection types of novels. Some libraries do not charge rental, but pay the cost themselves. They feel that by not processing the titles, they provide a constantly revolving collection of light fiction without heavy expense and without adding those ephemeral novels to the permanent collection. Other libraries rigidly restrict the number of fiction titles which will be purchased in any given year. A very practical problem involved in this area of the popular title is the number of copies to purchase. Here the librarian must function like a bookseller and attempt to predict the "market" for a given title. When a large library buys 800 copies of a title for its main and branch libraries, it is investing a considerable sum in the library's guess that this title will be in heavy demand. A librarian needs a sound knowledge of the reading interests of his/her public in order to make successful estimates of the number of copies needed.

A problem area which was mentioned in Chapter 1 concerns the modern naturalistic novel, which has placed heavy emphasis on the less pleasant aspects of human life and which often concerns itself with sex almost to the exclusion of any other aspect of human life. Some recent writers have begun to react unfavorably to the novel which resembles the psychiatrist's case book more than it resembles a piece of creative fiction. These critics do not object to the presentation of ugly or distorted human beings per se, but they suggest that the writer must do more than describe psychological problem cases, that he/she has the obligation to use this material for literary ends. Librarians have diverged in their treatment of these novels, and the same titles have been bought in some libraries while they were being scornfully rejected by others.

In the field of drama, the library will have to decide whether it feels that anthologies of plays are sufficient to satisfy the demand for this type of literature, or whether the library will buy separate plays. It may also be faced with the decision as to whether it should buy multiple copies of plays for the use of play-reading groups. The number and range of plays by the standard and classic playwrights will have to be decided, as will the extent to which the library will buy copies of current Broadway successes.

Poetry represents a field of literature long held in the highest regard and not read extensively in our day. The library will have to weigh the relative values of presenting poetry largely in anthologies, in the separate collected works of authors, or in individual volumes of poetry. In the field of contemporary verse, the library will have to decide how far beyond the very major writers it wants to go, and to what degree it will invest in the works of the more obscurantist of contemporary authors. It may also decide to set some standard of quality, which would rule out the newspaper versifier.

The library may also feel some concern for representing important foreign literature, either in the native language or in translation. The great classics of the major European countries will probably represent no major problem, but how far should the library go in buying foreign authors who are not widely known in this country, yet who may be very significant on the contemporary scene in their native land?

The best insurance the library can have to assure selection of literature of good quality is to have a staff which is itself well-read, which has developed a sense of discrimination based on knowledge of the best that has been written, which is familiar enough with the reviewers of literature to know which represent informed and able judgments. In this area of taste, however, one cannot expect to find precise and rigid standards. This difficulty does not mean, of course, that it is desirable for librarians to respond by shrugging their shoulders and abandoning any attempt to discriminate.

Conclusion

Answers to the problems of selection in the various subject fields are arrived at by taking into consideration the purposes of the library, the type and size of library, and important local factors in determining how the general principles will be applied. Librarians solve these problems in various ways. The authors of this work have their own personal convictions as to what the only true, eternal, and justifiable solutions are. But, alas, librarians whose judgments they respect do not agree with them in every case. On the other hand, librarians whose judgments they also respect do agree with them on some of these issues. Where does this state of affairs leave the librarian? With, we hope, the realization that the selection of books is not a mechanical process to be done unconsciously by fixed rule and by rote, and that the only person who can decide any of these problems for a given library is the librarian employed in that library. Only that person has enough knowledge of all the factors which go into decisions to make sound judgments.

EDITIONS

The question of selection of editions has attracted the attention of librarians for some time. It is recognized that the physical appearance of a book will have its effect on prospective readers, either attracting or repelling them. The qualifications of a "good" edition, however, include more than mere physical makeup. The addition or omission of special introductions, notes, and illustrations should be observed. Changes in the text are a part of revised editions and are especially important in text-books and scientific or technical material. In a reprint, the text remains the same even though the physical make-up may be drastically changed. This is especially true of the unabridged paperback editions that are put out by the same publishers as the hard cover editions. Both abridged and enlarged editions should be evaluated for possible library purchase.

A knowledge of book production and an appreciation of book design and typography will assist librarians in the selection of editions. A correctly proportioned page is pleasing to the eye and easier to read. Sufficient margins are necessary to achieve this effect and also to facilitate rebinding. Acceptable margins are usually wider at the outside edges and the bottom than the inside and the top. Colorful bindings add to the attractive appearance of books on the shelves. Size can be an important factor because neither very large nor very small books are convenient for shelving or circulating. The esthetic appreciation that arises from examining a truly beautiful edition is one of the great satisfactions of working with books. The inclusion of some fine editions adds considerably to the collection. But for the average circulating book, durable and sound book manufacture should be combined with "the beautiful." Since popular fiction will be read in any edition that is available, some libraries purchase paperbacks as added copies and discard them when they are worn out or the demand abates. A certain number of expendable copies should be supplied for titles already approved for inclusion and in great demand.

The librarian should develop the ability to compare editions quickly in relation to these factors and also in relation to the library's budget. The selection of an appropriate edition also raises the old question of "Best for whom?" For the general reader? the scholar? the researcher? In selecting editions, it is necessary to go much farther than merely selecting the latest one. Just as in general book selection, knowledge of the library clientele is important. The ordinary reader, who has just seen a Shakespearian play on television, would probably be more interested in an attractive, illustrated edition than in an elaborately footnoted edition intended primarily for the student or scholar.

Ideally, the librarian should examine actual copies of the various editions and then make the decision as to which to purchase for a particular book collection and for a specific use. Unfortunately, selection from first-hand inspection cannot usually be done, and it is necessary to rely upon various printed aids. There are notes on editions in the Wilson Standard Catalog series. The *Reader's Adviser* lists various editions and frequently adds annotations. Selected bibliographies in books on special subjects indicate editions and current aids should not be forgotten.

TRANSLATIONS

The selection of translations of foreign books into English can present a variety of problems. The qualifications of the translator, the types of material to be translated, and the potential readers of translations are all matters which the librarian must take into consideration. The primary responsibility of the translator may be said to be to interpret the meaning of the original, rather than to translate literally. It is generally agreed that translators should be faithful to the original in that they attempt to produce the same emotional reactions. The ideas and the style of the original work should also be maintained. The carrying over of style and mood from one language to another requires great skill.

To this quality of complete bilingual ability, one must add the capacity to write fluently in the language into which the book is being translated. Sympathy for the material being translated and some knowledge of the literary and historical background are distinct assets. Familiarity with the locale, the manners and customs of the people, as well as with the literary history of the author and the work, give the translator added advantages. These qualities are part of the background of the translator who aims to recreate a book in another language in such a way that it will affect the reader in the same way as the original.

The type of material also has a bearing on the way it should be translated. It may range from the simple and factual to the literature of the scholar. There are intermediate types, intended for that large amorphous audience, the general reader, which composes the largest group of readers of the public library. General readers are frequently not aware—or, if they are, are not concerned with the fact—that they are reading a translation; they are primarily concerned with the subject matter. The aim of the translator would then be to reproduce this material from another language in as readable a form as possible.

Translation of literature for the scholar is another matter. Here the style is just as important as the content, if not more so. Translations of scientific or technical material must presuppose a good knowledge of terms on the part of the translator, as well as close adherence to the original.

Who are the readers that the librarian should keep in mind when selecting translations? First, there is the reader who is interested in the literature of a given country, but who never intends to learn the language. If the spirit of the original is retained, a free translation would be satisfactory. The student who is learning a language frequently adds to his/her knowledge by reading the literature of that country in translation. In this case, a careful and reasonably literal translation in good English is best because it will help the student to understand the grammar and correct use of idiom. The scholar, on the other hand, may want different translations of the classics for comparison and study. If it is a Greek classic, he/she will want the translation to be close to the original with frequent use of characteristic idioms.

The names of the translators are frequently given on the title page, and the day of the hack translation is almost over. The hastily produced, stupidly literal translation of a popular foreign book, issued in an unattractive, cheap edition, is now a thing of the past. It is unfortunate that more credit is not given to the translator, for a satisfactory translation requires meticulous work combined with ability and considerable scholarly and linguistic background.

To judge a translation adequately, the critic must also be fluent in both languages. Lacking this ability, the librarian will have to depend on the reviewing media and the selection aids for evaluation of translations.

BIBLIOGRAPHY

Asheim, Lester. *The Humanities and the Library*. Chicago, American Library Association, 1957. 278p. Discusses collection building and reference work in religion, philosophy, art, music, and literature.

Baughman, James C. "A Structural Analysis of the Literature of Sociology." *Library Quarterly*, 44:293–308, October 1974.

Benton, Rita. "Nature of Music and Some Implications for the University Music Library." *Fontis Artis Musicae,* 23:53–60, April 1976.

Brandon, Alfred N. "Selected List of Books and Journals for the Small Medical Library." *Medical Library Association Bulletin,* 65:191–195, April 1977.

Broadus, Robert N. *Selecting Materials for Libraries.* New York, Wilson, 1973. 342p. Part five (pp. 157–325) is devoted to selection by subject—biography, history, geography, social sciences, religion, philosophy, art, music, literature, fiction, science and technology.

Cojeen, Robert H. "International Business Publications in the Seventies." *Choice,* 15:21–30, March 1978. Bibliographic essay.

Haines, Helen E. *Living with Books; The Art of Book Selection.* 2d ed. New York, Columbia University Press, 1950. 610p. Part four (pp. 249–567) deals with selecting biography, history, travel, nature and science, social sciences, religion, philosophy, essays, poetry, drama, and fiction.

Harmon, Robert B. *Developing the Library Collection in Political Science.* Metuchen, N.J., Scarecrow Press, 1976. 190p.

Huck, Charlotte S. *Children's Literature in the Elementary School.* 3rd ed. New York, Holt, Rinehart and Winston, 1976. 785p. Standard textbook.

Kosa, Geza A. "Book Selection Tools for Subject Specialists in a Large Research Library: An Analysis." *Library Resources and Technical Services,* 19:13–18, Winter 1975.

Line, Maurice B. and Stephen Roberts. "Size, Growth, and Composition of Social Science Literature. *International Social Science Journal,* 28:122–159, 1976.

MacPherson, Mary. "Historiography: Its Implications for Building Library Collections." *Canadian Library Journal,* 33:39–45, February 1976.

Malinowsky, H. Robert and others. *Science and Engineering Literature: A Guide to Reference Sources.* 2d ed. Littleton, Colo., Libraries Unlimited, 1976.

Martin, Murray S. "The Series Standing Order and the Library." *Choice,* 10:1152–1155, October 1973. Problems to anticipate.

"Music and Fine Arts in the General Library." Issue edited by Guy A. Marco and Wolfgang M. Freitag. *Library Trends,* 23:321–546, January 1975.

Natunewicz, Chester F. "Classics in Translation." *Choice,* 10:1331–1347, November 1973. Discusses criteria and suggests editions.

Reader's Adivser. 12th ed. New York, Bowker, 1974–77. 3v. Especially useful for identifying important authors and editions of standard works. Stronger for humanities than for other fields.

Rogers, A. Roberts. *The Humanities: A Selective Guide to Information Sources.* Littleton, Colo., Libraries Unlimited, 1974. 400p. Covers philosophy, religion, visual arts, performing arts, language and literature.

Schlueter, Paul. "Building a Basic Collection in Religion and Literature: A Suggested Collection for Academic Libraries," *Choice,* 12:1533–1538, February 1976. Bibliographic essay.

"Science Materials for Children and Young People." Issue edited by George S. Bonn. *Library Trends,* 22:415–529, April 1974. Includes thirteen papers on selection criteria, reviewing tools, periodicals, reference materials, audiovisual materials, etc.

Sheehy, Eugene P. *Guide to Reference Books.* 9th ed. Chicago, American Library Association, 1976. 1015p. May be used to locate guides to the literature and basic bibliographies of various subject fields.

Walford, A. J. *Guide to Reference Material.* 3d ed. London, Library Association, 1973–77. 3v. May be used to locate guides to the literature and basic bibliographies of various subject fields.

White, Carl M. *Sources of Information in the Social Sciences; A Guide to the Literature.* 2d ed. Chicago, American Library Association, 1973. 702p. Contains chapters on history, geography, economics and business administration, sociology, anthropology, psychology, education, and political science.

Monographic Series

Baer, Eleanora A. *Titles in Series: A Handbook for Librarians and Students.* 3rd ed. Metuchen, N.J., Scarecrow Press, 1978. 4 vols. Brings information up to January 1975. Includes foreign.

Books in Series in the United States, 1966–1975: Original, Reprinted, In-Print, and Out-of-Print Books, Published or Distributed in the U.S. in Popular, Scholarly, and Professional Series. New York, Bowker, 1977. 2486p. Supplement, 1977. 1000p. Basic volume covers information gathered up to summer of 1976; supplement adds 10,000 titles identified after that date.

U.S. Library of Congress. *Monographic Series.* Washington, D.C., 1974. Appearing quarterly and in an annual cumulation, this compilation contains "Library of Congress printed catalog cards representing all monographs cataloged by the Library as part of series." Alphabetical by title of series.

CHAPTER 5

The Selector and Book Selection Aids

If a standard for evaluating the book selector were to be constructed, what qualities could be outlined as a measure against which the individual selector could judge his/her own fitness for the task? This list of qualities, to be sure, might not be found completely in any one individual, or the individual might find that he/she possessed all of them, but in varying degrees. The list of characteristics that follows does not permit the inference that the failure to have all of them means failure in selection. They are listed to provide a picture of what the ideal selector might be like.

A Profile of the Ideal Selector

First, the selector would have full and detailed information about all the titles being currently issued. He/she would have read every current book in every subject field for which he/she is responsible, since it is obvious that in order to select the best titles from a group of books, the librarian must know each book in the group. He/she would, therefore, have developed some system for covering the field of current publishing. He/she would, in addition, have full knowledge of each writer's previous works and their worth, and would know the authors of each subject and their relationship to one another and to the total subject. He/she would have a clear picture of the development of the literature of each field and could fit current titles into this pattern. He/she would know all about all publishers; their specialties, strengths, and weaknesses, their past triumphs or transgressions, and would know what to expect from any book bearing a particular publisher's imprint.

The selector's own subject knowledge would be vast and constantly increasing. He/she would have extensive education in each field for which he/she was responsible for selection, so that he/she could competently judge the accuracy, reliability, and authority of any given book.

In addition, the selector would be intimately familiar with the people the library served, would know the level of education and reading sophistication of each and could decide accurately which books would be of interest to and of suitable difficulty for each reader. His/her information about the reading interests of the whole community would be detailed and exact. He/she could estimate the reading difficulty of books accurately and match them to the reading skills of his/her users. The selector would be familiar with the problems of the community, with current affairs and with the needs of the citizenry. There would be no group in the community whose activities were unknown to him/her, and his/her eyes would continually be watching for books which would serve and support those activities.

In his/her selection of materials, the selector would maintain perfect impartiality and freedom from bias. Materials would be selected on the basis of their worth and not on the basis of any extraneous factors. He/she would be able to understand and appreciate all the variety of attitudes held by the various groups and individuals in the community. and would represent them all in the selection. He/she would not hesitate to buy books reflecting unpopular or unorthodox ideas, and would be careful to buy titles representing the various positions on controversial subjects.

The selector would, of course, know what his/her own library had on every subject, and in selection would be able to answer accurately the question as to what any given book had to add to the information already in the library. The selector would—in short—be intelligent, educated, informed, courageous, honest, and impartial.

Some Pragmatic Considerations

These, then, are the qualities possessed by our paragon. It is obvious that we are describing a superhuman creature. There are certain realities of life which militate against the production of such a theoretically desirable personage. In the first place, it would be rarely, if ever, in our complex world that we would find a person whose specialized subject knowledge is universal.

Furthermore, if the selector makes the attempt to keep up with all current publishing, it will quickly become apparent that the task is beyond any single individual's abilities and time. In the United States alone, the annual publishing output of trade titles passed the thirty-seven thousand mark—to say nothing of the production of the other English-speaking countries. Covering the field at first hand is simply impossible. Any one individual can do no more than take a sampling. If we add to this reading the millions of books published in the past, it becomes even more painfully obvious that no single individual can hope to read more than a tiny part of the universe of books.

But, granting that the librarian cannot read everything, and granting that intimate knowledge of every subject is impossible, he/she can work constantly to improve his/her acquaintance with books. The first person to receive the benefits of adult education which a library affords ought to be the librarian. Librarians would do well to take Corinne Bacon's advice to know books through a constant perusal of them. It is impossible to pass by her pungent remark without quoting: "Someone has said that the librarian who reads is lost. The librarian who doesn't read isn't worth finding."

Our paragon would also select books from a position of absolute impartiality and freedom from bias. All agree that book selection should be objective. But—to return to the problem raised in the preceding chapter—is this humanly possible? Take, as an example, a potential librarian who learned to read at an early age, and who enjoyed having books read to him/her as a child; who has been exposed to the most appropriate books at each age and reading level; who loved the children's classics and the best contemporary children's literature. In college, this individual majored in English literature and read widely in various other literatures. It is only natural that he/she should have built up certain reading preferences along with special knowledge of the best literature. Will this person be able to sympathize with the taste of the reader of mystery or western stories? Will he/she not have developed a rather exalted literary standard by which to judge books?

Assume that this individual comes from a family which is financially secure, that his/her whole political environment has been that of ultraconservatism; he/she genuinely reveres the doctrines of laissez-faire, of personal independence, of sturdy self-reliance, mistrusts welfare governments, dislikes change in the political or social apparatus. How will this person be able to look impartially on the writings of liberal economists, whom he/she sincerely believes to be tools of Incarnate Evil?

Theoretical personal characteristics of this kind could be outlined in greater detail, but this much should suffice to point out that every librarian is a human being with a full set of preconceptions, of blind spots, of passionate adherence to a philosophy of some sort. Is it really possible to set these personal convictions aside to judge a book's value to one's users objectively?

It is not advocated that the librarian abandon personal opinions and point of view. But he/she can attempt to imitate our paragon and recall that, when selecting books, he/she is selecting for others. When the librarian sits down to select, it is important to remember that he/she is now functioning—not as a private person selecting personal reading—but as a professional selector, choosing what others will find of interest and value, however dull or valueless the selector might find it in his/her present state of enlightenment.

This kind of problem is by no means restricted to libraries, and it may be well to remind ourselves that it is the same difficulty which any human institution faces. Every human organization must devise some system which can be operated successfully by people who are competent and even gifted, but not perfect. If the library cannot be staffed by book selectors who are all perfect, is there no system we can devise to accomplish satisfactory book selection?

Aids to Effective Selection

If it is impossible for the individual librarian to cover the whole field of current publishing, it is possible to fall back upon the helpful principle of division of labor. In a large library, various members of the staff can be assigned to follow particular aspects of the publishing output. In the small library, the librarian will have to rely upon the various book selection aids, which represent a coverage of current publishing by many people, reporting their pooled judgment of the best being published. If it is impossible for each librarian to be a specialist in every subject, it is possible to divide the labor once again, and let those on the staff who are specialists in a subject be responsible for selection in that subject. If there are subject areas in which the library does not have a person with training, the book selection aids can be called upon for help, since their lists in the various subjects will represent the judgment of people who are informed in those fields. If it is difficult for individual librarians to suppress their own convictions in selecting, the use of committees, whose members will represent a variety of attitudes, will serve as a useful protection against personal bias, since the other members can serve as a counterbalance if one selector goes too far afield.

There are many book selection aids which can assist the average librarian to do a satisfactory job. They vary in the speed with which they cover current publishing, in the type of book listed, in the kind and amount of information given for each title, in the type of library for which they are intended, in format, frequency, and usefulness. The librarian must know the various aids and their special characteristics. Even when approval copies of new books can be examined or the books seen in galley proofs in advance of publication, the librarian will want to read the reviews.

Advance notices may be seen in the advertising pages and forecast lists of *Publishers Weekly, Library Journal,* and *Forthcoming Books,* or in the announcements of individual publishers. After the bare bibliographic bones—author, title, publisher, date, and price—have been noted, the title should be checked in *Kirkus Reviews,* which carries informal and informative reviews approximately six weeks before publication date. In "The Book Review" section of *Library Journal* are

found signed reviews written by librarians, useful because the evaluation is made in terms of type of collection or type of library. Many of the
reviews appear in advance of publication.

About the time of publication, the title appears in the *Weekly
Record* published by Bowker, if the publisher has sent in a copy of the
book in advance of publication date. At about the same time, reviews
appear in the weekly book review sections of such newspapers as the
New York Times, Washington Post, and those of other major metropolitan areas. Local newspapers which publish book reviews should be read
regularly also, as these reviews will be reflected in library requests.

Weekly periodicals frequently carry lively and critical reviews.
Time, New Yorker, Newsweek, and the *Saturday Review* feature one or
more reviews and give brief and pertinent annotations about other books.

All of the reviewing media mentioned above present timely reviews either before publication or near the date of publication.

Let us now turn our attention to reviews which appear after
publication, but which can still be used as aids to the selection of current
books.

The American Library Association's guide to current books is
the *Booklist. The Book Review Digest,* published by the Wilson Company, lists new books after a substantial number of reviews have
appeared. General periodicals, notably *Atlantic* and *Harper's,* have
excellent book review sections, but are inclined to review books after
publication date. The scholarly journals also contain reviews, although
they generally appear long after the book is published.

There are also aids for the selection of basic collections, which
can be used for retrospective buying to fill in gaps and strengthen the
library in the various subject fields. The American Library Association
and the H. W. Wilson Co. have been responsible for the development of
basic book selection aids for various types of libraries. That pioneer
librarian, Melvil Dewey, envisioned an *A.L.A. Catalog* as early as
1877, the year after the organization of the A.L.A. Its historical background has been traced by Russell E. Bidlack in his article "The Coming Catalogue; or, Melvil Dewey's Flying Machine." The catalog was
originally published as a government document by the Bureau of Education and bears the imprint date of 1893, although it did not make its
appearance in final form until 1894. Its full title was *Catalog of the
"A.L.A." Library; 5,000 Volumes for a Popular Library Selected by
the American Library Association and Shown at the World's Columbian
Exposition.* The books listed were displayed at the exposition at
Chicago, and the preparation of the catalog was under the direction of
Mary S. Cutler, Vice-Director of the Albany Library School.

This was the forerunner of the *A.L.A. Catalog; 8,000 Volumes*

for a Popular Library, with Notes (1904), which was prepared by the
A.L.A. in cooperation with the New York State Library and the Library
of Congress for the St. Louis World's Fair. The *ALA Catalog, 1926; an
Annotated Basic List of 10,000 Books,* was followed by periodic polyennial supplements. Aimed at informing the librarian of the smaller
public library, this annotated basic list was selected cooperatively by
some four hundred librarians and was limited in its inclusion to a selection of standard and popular titles available at the time.

Growing up beside the later supplements of the *ALA Catalog*
was the former *Standard Catalog* series of the H. W. Wilson Company.
The present *Public Library Catalog* was published at first in eight
separate sections which were brought together into a single, non-fiction
volume in 1934. As in the case of the *ALA Catalog,* the selection of
titles was a cooperative venture, with a number of librarians taking part.
About one-fourth of the titles were starred for first purchase by small
public libraries or those with limited book funds. The *Fiction Catalog*
was first published in 1908, and is kept up-to-date by new editions and
by supplements. Its purpose is to serve as a buying list of the best fiction
for library use. Mention must also be made of the *High School Library
Catalog, Junior High School Library Catalog,* and the *Children's
Catalog.*

There are several aids to the selection of books for junior college
and liberal arts college libraries. The most recent college lists are *Books
for College Libraries* (A.L.A., 2d ed., 1975), which includes a selected
list of 40,000 titles, and A.L.A.'s current reviewing medium, *Choice.*
Two older basic lists are (1) *Catalog of the Lamont Library* (1953),
which was intended to support the particular needs of the Harvard
undergraduate program, and (2) the *Shelf List of the University of
Michigan's Undergraduate Library* (1958–62). For junior colleges,
older lists include Frank J. Bertalan's *Junior College Library Collection*
and James Pirie's *Books for Junior College Libraries.*

A librarian charged with building a collection for a new college
library will have need of retrospective tools, as well as guides to current
publishing. Checking the *Lamont Library Catalog* and the *University of
Michigan Undergraduate Shelflist* as well as *Books for College Libraries* for a given subject would provide a broader review of past titles
than using any one of them alone. All three were developed with somewhat different aims, and thus complement each other. An excellent
older list, Charles B. Shaw's *List of Books for College Libraries* (1931,
and its 1931–38 continuation, 1940) may be used profitably for retrospective buying; in retrospective acquisition, care must be exercised to
avoid selection obsolete materials.

An annotated list of the book selection aids appears at the end of
this chapter.

Summary

Most librarians must depend upon the various selection aids for their information about new titles. It is important, therefore, to consider whether there are any weaknesses in this system for aiding librarians in their choice of titles. Various studies have revealed that most of the reviews of books tend to be favorable, which might cast some doubt upon their objectivity. This tendency to praise is accounted for in part by the fact that only those books considered worthwhile are chosen for reviewing, and omission constitutes a negative review. It is certainly true that many books are never reviewed, and the librarian depending upon the general reviewing media would never become aware of their existence. Furthermore, if the conscientious librarian wants to read a number of reviews, in order to form a more sound judgment of a book, he/she may well be disappointed. Except for the very popular titles—particularly in non-fiction—only a bare minimum of reviews are likely to appear, and some titles may not be reviewed at all. It is also well to recall that the reviewer for the general periodical or newspaper does not have the particular needs of a given library in mind when the review is written—indeed, it is highly unlikely that the reviewer is thinking of library problems. These are real limitations upon the usefulness of the reviewing media, and yet the system appears to work reasonably well. It seems safe to say that the really significant titles of any given year receive full attention, and that the librarian will not be seriously misled by the reviews, in spite of their limitations. He/she may develop various techniques for compensating for the weaknesses of the reviewing system: as one wit put it, if one can find only favorable reviews, one can start judging a book on the basis of the degree of enthusiasm expressed by the reviewer. A consistent reading of the various media over a period of time will reveal their individual characteristics and enable the librarian to make these adjustments.

In this chapter, the librarian who selects books has been urged to have a personal knowledge of books, to continue developing his/her knowledge of subject fields (a task which ought to be considered a lifetime part of the librarian's job), to know the general reading interests of people and the special interests of his/her own community. The librarian ought to have the courage to implement the principles of book selection with honesty and impartiality, avoiding arrogance on the one hand and an unprofessional subservience on the other. It is to be hoped that balanced, sane, and informed judgments will be made. When the librarian feels that his/her own knowledge is weak, or suspects that personal bias is creeping into selection, recourse should be had to that composite judgment of many librarians and critics which is embodied in the various book selection aids.

BOOK REVIEWING AND ANNOTATIONS

Facility in reviewing books should be a part of every librarian's background, for books are the librarian's business, and he/she should be eager and willing to talk to groups or individuals about books. The ability to talk about and write about books is an important adjunct to successful librarianship. The art of annotation and of book reviewing should be acquired by anyone who has a lively interest in books and who wishes to share that interest with others.

There are some skills to be acquired which will facilitate the preparation of reviews and annotations. Reading with reasonable speed and comprehension, ability to exercise a balanced and informed judgment, and to summarize for the use of others will play a part in the process. As long ago as 1885, William E. Foster of the Providence (R.I.) Library observed that the librarian had to develop the ability to skim the book, to get at the kernel of it, and to place it in the literature of its subject.

First of all, the evaluator—in reviewing a book for library selection purposes—should obtain an overall impression of the book by examining the information on the book jacket, the table of contents, and the preface. Aside from the publisher's blurb, the book jacket usually gives some information about the author which can be supplemented from other sources, as well as listing some of the other books which the author has written. It may also furnish a summary of the book. The table of contents gives the plan of the book, and the preface indicates what the author is trying to do.

By reading a few chapters—a hundred pages or so—and scanning the rest of the book, it is possible to determine its style, scope, content, form, structure, and the manner of treatment of the subject. The librarian's purpose, then, is to get the gist of the book. In order to do this, he/she must cultivate the ability to glean its main points swiftly, comprehensively, and accurately, always keeping in mind its potential library use. He/she should attempt to place the book in the class to which it belongs and then compare it with other books on the same subject in an attempt to determine whether it is a necessary or valuable addition to the collection. At this point, a recommendation for purchase or rejection of the book should be made. This usually takes the form of a written annotation or book note giving reasons for the decision.

Annotations

An annotation or book note is a brief, compact characterization of the book, either descriptive or critical. There are two types of annotations—the librarian's note and the reader's note. The librarian's note is intended to help librarians decide whether the book should be added to the collection and to point out the groups of people to whom it will appeal. The reader's note, however, assumes that the book is already in the library and that there is a potential reading public for it. It is written to attract readers.

There are a few points which both types of book notes have in common. They should both be discriminating and impartial, based on definite knowledge of the book. The scope of the book, information about the author, and an explanation of the title—if it is not self-explanatory—should appear in both types. If the material has appeared serially or has been used in lectures, this fact should also be indicated.

The divergence comes in the kinds of information included. In the librarian's note, both favorable and unfavorable criticism has its place. Special points of interest for the librarian are the appeal to certain groups of readers and the possible influence of the book. The note should include a comparison with other books of the same type. In nonfiction, the matter of arrangement is often of importance: Are there appendices which may be useful and important? Is there an index? In the case of fiction, it is inadvisable to give the plot, but important to give some idea of the place of the book in literature.

The reader's note should appeal to the reader for whom the book is intended. The writer of the reader's note must be able to discern the essential part of the book and disregard the immaterial, while at the same time distinguishing both intellectually and sympathetically the kinds of readers to whom the book will appeal. When the writer of the note describes the book, he/she should recreate the spirit and atmosphere in such a way that the people who would like such a book are attracted to it, and, conversely, those who would not enjoy such a book are not.

After the note is written, it should be reread, to make sure that words have not been wasted and that the material is suitably phrased. Since an annotation is frequently limited to from fifty to one hundred words (readers' annotations may be restricted to 25 words or less), every word must count. Ability to eliminate non-essential words and phrases and still reflect the spirit of the book is an accomplishment which comes with practice.

Although the language and style of the reader's note should fit the character of the book, this may be carried too far. For example, in writing a note about a book that is poetic in style, be sure that a clear idea of its content is given, that the writer has not been carried away into the realms of the precious. An annotation describing *Wisdom and Destiny,* by Maurice Maeterlinck, might read: "An individual philosophy of life which is rare, delicate, and fragile, beautiful as a floating mist." Such a note may sound charming, but might be found a bit too flowery for many readers. The following annotation, which is somewhat more prosaic, still conveys information concerning the poetic quality of the book: "A philosophy of life essentially happy in its conception, centering in the thought that destiny cannot utterly destroy the wise. Somewhat mystical and elusive, but full of poetic beauty." The reader's note is usually brief, consisting of not more than one or two sentences.

Use of Annotations

The librarian's note is an aid to the librarian in deciding whether or not a certain book will be added to the collection and to what types of readers it will appeal. It is frequently clipped to printed reviews and kept on file. If unfavorable, it is convenient to refer to in explaining to a patron why the book has not been bought. The reader's note should be used to inform readers, either as brief notes in newspapers or in book lists prepared for distribution by the library. In some libraries, the notes are placed in the catalogs or in the books themselves.

Oral Book Reviewing

The oral book review is used in the evaluation of a book for library selection purposes and also as a means of interesting prospective readers. Ability to talk about books is an essential part of the librarian's professional equipment. It is important to organize the review to achieve a clear and effective result. Notes can be used as a guide in the presentation but it is generally inadvisable to read the review unless one is a very skilled reader. It is wise to talk to the person farthest back in the room and to watch his/her face to see if he/she hears you.

Timing the review before it is given and keeping within the time limit is a basic rule. Do not talk too quickly, or much of the presentation will be lost; good planning will enable you to speak at a reasonable pace. Try to avoid mannerisms which may distract from what is being said, such as fiddling with your glasses, mumbling into the notes, fidgeting, "oh'ing" and "ah'ing" before each sentence. A few sessions with a tape recorder will reveal much about one's speech habits. It is usually advisable to repeat the author and title several times during the talk to fix it in the minds of the audience, and to have a copy of the book on display. The best results can be obtained by being sincerely interested in the book and presenting the review with honest enthusiasm.

Uses of Oral Book Reviews

Some of the larger public libraries have book selection meetings, usually held at regular intervals, in which oral book reviewing is a part of the selection process. The point of view of the librarian's book review is the same as the librarian's book note: the review is critical and evaluates the book for possible inclusion in the library. The points to be covered in such a review include the following: (1) information about the author; (2) date of publication; (3) what the author is trying to do in this book, what has actually been done, and how it has been done; (4) comparison with other books of the same type or in the same subject field; (5) reviews and criticisms of the book; (6) type of library for which the book is suited; (7) type of borrower to which it will appeal.

When oral book reviews for public consumption are planned, the librarian should adjust the type of treatment to the intended audience, remembering that the backgrounds and interests of various groups differ, and that what might be a successful review for one group would not be satisfactory for another. The aim of a review for the general public is to try to interest those who hear it in reading a certain book, or group of books. The preference in public library reviewing is to talk about groups of books, thus differentiating the library-oriented review from the "literary club" review, which has been characterized as an attempt to substitute hearing about the book for reading it. The primary purpose of any library book review is to draw attention to books, not to substitute the review for a more substantial first-hand knowledge of the book.

The technique for doing this involves piqueing the curiosity, arousing the interest, catching the attention of the group and making them feel that a book is worth reading because of content, type, or timeliness. If the reviewer becomes sufficiently involved in the book himself, he/she can usually interest the reader in it.

Book reviews are given by librarians to community groups of all kinds and also over the radio and television. It is well to remember that reviewing is time-consuming and should not be undertaken unless time for preparation is provided. Radio is a particularly good medium for book reviewing. Radio reviews may be given by a single person reviewing several books, or by several people, with one acting as a moderator. A formal script or an ad lib program can be used. Usually an informal atmosphere is more easily created by using notes and talking from them in the same way as is done before a live audience.

Both radio and television programs improve with professional direction, which is frequently provided by the station. Station time for educational programs is generally provided free of charge. Many of the larger libraries cooperate with the radio and television stations in their communities to produce effective book reviewing programs. Such programs should be linked with the library's name as a means of promoting more and better reading.

BOOK SELECTION AIDS

Guides to Reviews and Selection Aids

1) **Book Review Digest.** New York, Wilson, 1905–

Recent books published or distributed in the U.S. may have reviews cited and excerpted here if enough reviews (generally, two or more for non-fiction and four or more for fiction) appear in the selected periodicals within eighteen months after publication of the book. Coverage per year is now running around 6,000 books. Each book is entered under author, with full bibliographic data, followed by a brief descriptive note and the excerpts, which are limited to three for fiction and four for non-fiction. Other reviews are cited bibliographically. A list of more than 70 periodicals from which reviews are taken is given, and the student of book selection should study this list carefully as a clue to the types of books which will be reviewed by *Book Review Digest*. It is published monthly except in February and July, with cumulations three times a year and an annual bound cumulation. An author and title index covering 1905–1974 in a single alphabet was published in 1976 in four volumes.

2) **Book Review Index.** Detroit, Gale Research, 1965–

Cites reviews from about 325 periodicals and newspapers and arranges the citations alphabetically by the author of the book reviewed. Unlike the *Book Review Digest* it provides no descriptive notes or excerpts from reviews but only the citation to the review (periodical, reviewer, volume, date and page). It does provide, however, greater speed, more diversity of sources, and a larger number of citations than *BRD*. Publisher claimed to have cited reviews of 40,000 new books during 1977. Frequency of publication has varied since 1965, but current publication is bimonthly with annual cumulations.

3) **Children's Book Review Index.** Detroit, Gale Research, 1975–

Excerpts from *Book Review Index* citations to all reviews of books intended for pre-school to junior high readers. Arranged alphabetically by author. Published three times a year with annual cumulations.

4) **Current Book Review Citations.** New York, Wilson, 1976–

Although published by the same company as *Book Review Digest,* this tool is more like *Book Review Index* in its approach to the indexing of reviews. Reviews are indexed selectively from more than 1,200 reviewing sources and arranged alphabetically by author or main entry. Bibliographical citations only are given for the reviews included. Publication is monthly with annual cumulations.

5) **Index to Book Reviews in the Humanities.** Detroit, Philip Thomson, 1960–

Originally a quarterly, it has been published annually since 1963. Beginning with the 1971 volume the policy of selectively indexing reviews from a wide range of popular and scholarly periodicals that might occasionally review a book in the "humanities" (broadly interpreted) was dropped in favor of indexing all reviews in a specified list of about 160 humanities periodicals. It is arranged alphabetically by author of the title reviewed.

6) Technical Book Review Index. Pittsburgh, JAAD Publishing Co., 1935–   .

Originally, the primary purpose of this index was to identify reviews in current scientific, technical, and trade journals. With the January 1973 issue the coverage was broadened to cite and briefly quote reviews from periodicals in all scientific, technical, and medical (except clinical) subjects. Special Libraries Association published *TBRI* from 1935 to 1976, when the present publisher assumed responsibility. Claims to cover more than 3,000 reviews each year. Publication is monthly.

7) Aids to Media Selection for Students and Teachers. Compiled by Kathlyn J. Moses and Lois B. Watt. Rev. Washington, D.C., U.S. Dept. of Health, Education and Welfare, 1976. 128p.

Selected and annotated list of review sources for materials "of relevance for elementary and secondary school instructional programs." Emphasizes tools published since 1970. Three sections: (1) book selection sources; (2) sources of audiovisual materials; (3) sources of multiethnic materials.

8) Hart, Thomas L. and others. *Multi-Media Indexes, Lists and Review Sources: A Bibliographic Guide.* New York, Dekker, 1975, 273p.

Includes more than 400 reviewing sources, covering both print and non-print media. Structured annotations give bibliographic information, scope, arrangement, special features, etc. for each entry. Sample pages are included to illustrate many of the sources.

9) Multi-Ethnic Media: Selected Bibliographies in Print. Compiled by Task Force on Ethnic Materials Information Exchange, Social Responsibilities Round Table; David Cohen, coordinator. Chicago, American Library Association, Office for Library Service to the Disadvantaged, 1975. 33p.

Annotated listing of in-print bibliographic essays and bibliographies dealing with most ethnic groups. Covers publications for children and young adults.

Current Reviewing Sources

10) Booklist. Chicago, American Library Association, 1905–   (Semimonthly)

Each issue contains longer reviews of 10–20 reference books (prepared by ALA's Reference and Subscription Books Review Committee), 100–130 shorter reviews of adult fiction and non-fiction, as well as books for children and young people, films, other non-book media and selected government publications. All items listed are recommended for library purchase and are intended to represent the best judgment of library subject specialists, who are familiar with the new books in their respective fields.

11) British Book News. London, British Council, 1940–   . (Monthly)

Reviews British publications on all subjects (excludes textbooks and most juvenile fiction). It is divided into three parts: 1) a general article or two dealing with some aspect of the library, literary, or artistic world; 2) signed evaluative reviews of recommended books (about 200 an issue), with full bibliographic information; 3) a selected list of forthcoming books, not annotated.

12) **Bulletin of the Center for Children's Books.** Chicago, University of Chicago, 1947– . (Monthly)

Each issue contains 60 to 80 reviews of current trade books for children. Unsigned reviews by specialists are critical, and grade levels, reading level difficulty, and literary quality are always evaluated. The *Bulletin* is noted for its inclusion of reviews of new books that are not recommended.

13) **Choice.** Chicago, American Library Association, Association of College and Research Libraries, 1964– . (Monthly)

Evaluates current books of a scholarly or academic nature considered to be of interest to an undergraduate library. Unsigned reviews of about 500–600 titles are provided in each issue. These are prepared by the editor and a large roster of subject specialists. Primarily intended to assist the selection of books for college libraries, this tool is useful in many other types of libraries: public, junior college, secondary school, special and foreign libraries. Special features include the "Opening Day Collection" which began in July 1965 and is now in its third edition (separately published in 1974) and regular subject-centered bibliographic articles. There is also a "reviews-on-cards" service, which supplies the reviews reprinted individually on 3 × 5 cards. A classified cumulation of all reviews from the first ten years of *Choice* (nearly 60,000 books) is currently being published (Rowman and Littlefield, 1976–) in nine volumes, including an index.

14) **Kirkus Reviews.** New York, Kirkus Service, 1933– . (Semimonthly)

Makes available to booksellers, librarians, and interested individuals informal and informative reviews of books, including children's books, with particular emphasis on coverage of fiction. Although not all publishers are represented, reviews are given about six weeks before date of publication, a feature which librarians have found very useful, as they can order and receive books by the time they are published and reviews for them appear in the general reviewing media, leading to a demand by patrons for the books. Widely used by public librarians as a primary selection tool, although the reviews are not presented from the library viewpoint alone.

15) **Library Journal.** New York, Bowker, 1876– . (Semimonthly)

Book review section, which is arranged by broad subject areas, contains signed reviews written by librarians and educators, giving practical evaluations of current titles. Many of the reviews appear prior to the date of publication of the book. These reviews are also available on 3 × 5 cards. In 1977, approximately 6,000 adult books were reviewed. Special features include spring and fall announcement issues and special issues on business, technical, medical, and scientific books, reference books, and small presses.

16) **New York Times Book Review.** 1896– . (Weekly)

Published weekly as part of the Sunday edition. (Daily editions also carry reviews of books, not by the *Book Review* staff.) Informative reviews, often written by authorities in the subject field, sometimes written by staff members. This is a standard selection tool for many librarians. In 1973, a cumulative index (1896-1970) was published in five volumes to serve as the index to a 125-volume reprint of all the reviews. The index allows an approach to earlier reviews by author, title, reviewer, subject, and genre.

17) Publishers Weekly. New York, Bowker, 1872– . (Weekly)

The standard American book trade journal; carries "Forecasts," a section of descriptive annotations of non-fiction, fiction, and children's books to be published in the next month or two. Special issues include Spring, Summer, and Fall announcement numbers (including books to be published in the near future) as well as a children's book number, etc.

18) School Library Journal. New York, Bowker, 1947– . (Monthly)

Supplies review coverage of juvenile books similar to that given adult books in *Library Journal*. Total number of signed reviews appearing in a year usually exceeds that of any other single reviewing service covering books published for children and young adults. Special features include semiannual "best books" lists. Formerly published as a part of *Library Journal*.

19) Times Literary Supplement. London, 1902– . (Weekly)

Weekly supplement to the *Times,* including reviews of books in English and foreign languages, as well as historical and literary articles. Spring and Autumn supplements discuss in some detail the literary activities in the book trade of the world.

Retrospective Selection Aids

20) Reader's Adviser. 12th ed. New York, Bowker, 1974–77. 3v.

Subtitled "A Layman's Guide to Literature," this basic selection tool (which has been published since early in this century) supplies bibliographic information and annotations on thousands of best books. *Reader's Adviser* has traditionally supplied considerable information about author, editions, translators and price. The three volumes cover 1) fiction, poetry, literary biography, bibliography and reference; 2) drama, world literature in English translation; 3) non-literary subjects (religion, science, communications, history, etc.).

21) Library Journal Book Review. New York, Bowker, 1967– .

An annual reprinting of all the reviews that have appeared in *Library Journal,* arranged by subject and indexed by author and title. Since several thousands of reviews are included for each year, this is a convenient place to search for reviews of books published in the U.S. during the years covered. Author and title index.

22) Canadian Book Review Annual. Toronto, Peter Martin Associates, 1975– .

Attempting to be an "annual evaluative guide to Canadian English-language trade books," *CBRA* provides concise reviews (200–400 words) of new Canadian titles published during the year. As more volumes of this source are published, it will serve as a useful tool for retrospective selection. Annual volumes are arranged by broad subject categories and have author, title, and subject indexes.

23) Fiction Catalog. New York, Wilson, 1908–

A guide to adult fiction found most useful in public libraries, it is published periodically, with annual supplements. The ninth edition, containing more than 4,700 titles in the basic volume, with 2,000 more to be covered in the four annual supplements, was published in 1975. The arrangement is alphabetical by author, with full bibliographic information and annotations. The second part is a subject and title index, followed by a directory of publishers and distributors. It is intended for use by medium-sized and small public libraries, but many high schools also find it useful.

24) Public Library Catalog. New York, Wilson, 1934–

Formerly known as the *Standard Catalog for Public Libraries,* the seventh edition of this work, published in 1978, is a selected, classified list of over 8,500 non-fiction titles which have been suggested by practicing librarians because of their usefulness in public library collections. Part 1 is a classified list (by Dewey) with brief annotations; part 2 is an author, title, and subject index, with analytical entries for parts of books; part 3 is a directory of publishers and distributors. Annual supplements will update the work with approximately 3,200 additional titles.

25) Books for College Libraries; A Core Collection of 40,000 Titles. 2d ed. Chicago, American Library Association. 1975. 6v.

The first edition of this tool (1967) was a one-volume work prepared under the direction of Melvin J. Voigt and Joseph H. Treyz and intended as a successor to Charles B. Shaw's *Books for College Libraries.* It listed 53,410 titles, carefully selected to support basic undergraduate studies and restricted to those published before 1964 (which was the beginning date for *Choice*). The second edition appeared as six paperbound volumes—five volumes divided by broad subject classes (humanities, language and literature, history, social science, and psychology, science, technology, and bibliography) with the sixth being an index. Each entry includes a complete catalog record (author, title, edition, collation, subject and added entries, L.C. class number, L.C. card number, and ISBN).

26) Senior High School Library Catalog. New York, Wilson, 1926–

Formerly the *Standard Catalog for High School Libraries,* this list emphasizes material for students in the tenth through twelfth grades. The eleventh edition, published in 1977, includes over 5,200 titles. The first part is a classified catalog, arranged according to the Dewey Decimal Classification, with an annotation for each title. The second part is an author, subject, and analytical index, while the third part is a directory of publishers and distributors. Annual supplements. Useful for basic, traditional titles.

27) Junior High School Library Catalog. New York, Wilson, 1965–

The 1975 edition includes over 3,500 titles selected for grades seven through nine; annual supplements add approximately 2,200 additional titles. As with other volumes in the Wilson Standard Catalog Series, part I is a classified list with full bibliographic information and a descriptive or critical annotation; part II is an author, title, subject index, with analytical entries for stories and plays in collections; and part III is a directory of publishers and distributors.

28) Children's Catalog. New York, Wilson, 1909–

The thirteenth edition of this work appeared in 1976, containing over 5,400 titles selected for their usefulness in school libraries and public library work with children. The books are arranged in classified order, using the latest abridged Dewey. An author, title, subject and analytic index follows the classified order, and a directory of publishers is appended. The catalog is supplemented annually between editions, adding approximately 2,200 new titles. Entry gives full bibliographical data, including subject headings and aids to cataloging, with an evaluative annotation quoted from reviews.

29) Elementary School Library Collection. New Brunswick, N.J., Bro-Dart Foundation, 1965–

The tenth edition appeared in 1976 and included approximately 9,500 recommended books, periodicals, filmstrips, transparencies, etc. The basic arrangement is a classified one, but there are index approaches by author, title, and subject. Annotations are included and there is a system of indicating which titles are considered most basic to a beginning collection. Updated regularly.

SELECTED SUPPLEMENTARY AIDS

Current Reviewing Sources

Appraisal; Children's Science Books. Cambridge, Mass., Children's Science Book Review Committee, 1967– . (3 issues per year)

Reviews of juvenile science books.

Aslib Book List. London, Aslib, 1935– . (Monthly)

Selected, classified list of new British publications in science and engineering. Annotations by specialists indicate the level of reader suitability.

Books in Canada. Toronto, Canadian Review of Books, Ltd., 1971– . (10 issues per year)

Each issue includes 30–50 signed reviews of varying length on selected new Canadian publications in a variety of fields. Includes general articles on Canadian writing and publishing. Aimed at the bookstore trade.

BooksWest; A National Journal of the Book Trade. Los Angeles, Books-West Magazine and Book Fair, Inc., 1976– . (Monthly)

General articles on books and publishing and a number of signed reviews and short notices of new books.

Canadian Materials; An Annotated Critical Bibliography for Canadian Schools and Libraries. Ottawa, Canadian Library Association, 1971– . (3 issues per year)

Signed annotations by librarians and teachers of "material in all media formats produced in Canada for elementary and secondary schools."

Children's Book Review Service. Brooklyn, Children's Book Review Service, 1972– . (Monthly)

Brief, signed reviews of books for pre-school through eighth grade. Looseleaf format.

Horn Book Magazine. Boston, 1924– . (Bimonthly)
Detailed reviews of children's books, along with many articles by and about authors and illustrators. A well-established source for information about children's books and reading.

In Review; Canadian Books for Children. Toronto, Provincial Library Service, Ontario Ministry of College and Universities, 1967– . (Quarterly)
Signed, critical reviews of recent books. Includes titles not recommended or only recommended with reservations. General articles on children's books.

Interracial Books for Children. New York, Council on Interracial Books for Children, 1967– . (8 issues per year)
Articles on the writing and publishing of children's books which treat racial minorities. Lists of recommended books.

Kliatt Paperback Book Guide. Newton, Mass., Kliatt Paperback Book Guide, 1967– . (3 issues per year with 5 interim supplements)
Reviews paperback originals, reprints, and new editions suitable for young adults. Covers approximately 1,200 titles a year with signed reviews by librarians and other educators.

New Technical Books. New York, New York Public Library, 1915– (Monthly)
Selected, classified list of new technical books, mostly published in the U.S. Descriptive annotations. Over 1,800 reviews were included in 1977.

New York Review of Books. New York, 1963– . (Semimonthly)
Each issue contains approximately a dozen very long reviews by a variety of reviewers.

Quill and Quire. Toronto, Greey de Pencier, 1935– . (17 issues per year)
Covers all aspects of Canadian publishing. Includes 30–40 reviews in a typical issue. Fall and spring announcement issues provide descriptions, arranged by subject, of new Canadian books. Regular education issues cover textbooks and non-book materials.

Saturday Review. New York, 1924– . (Weekly)
Book reviews and articles of general interest on literature, arts, and publishing.

School Librarian. London, School Library Association, 1913– . (Quarterly)
Short book reviews of new British children's books.

Science Books and Films; The Quarterly Review. Washington, D.C., American Association for the Advancement of Science, 1975– . (Quarterly)
Critical reviews of books and 16mm films on pure and applied sciences aimed at students (elementary, secondary, junior college) and general readers.

Replaces AAAS' earlier publication: *Science Books; A Quarterly Review* (1965–1975).

Small Press Review. Paradise, Calif., Dustbooks, 1966–   . (Monthly)
Lists new publications of small presses and little magazines and includes reviews (200 words or less) of small press titles.

Top of the News. Chicago, American Library Association, 1942–   . (Quarterly)
Occasionally includes lists of best books, best films, and subject lists; regularly includes a variety of articles about library service to young adults and children.

West Coast Review of Books. Hollywood, Rapport Publishing Co., 1974–   . (Bimonthly)
Carries "Books in Review" section in each issue with short, signed reviews of 100 or so new books; articles on books and publishing.

World Literature Today. Norman, University of Oklahoma, 1977–
(Quarterly)
Each issue contains several short studies of foreign literature and foreign writers, chiefly European, followed by brief reviews of current publications from many foreign countries. Reviews are thorough, yet compact and usually descriptive. Continues *Books Abroad; An International Literary Quarterly* (1927–1976).

Retrospective Selection Aids

Alternatives in Print: Catalog of Social Change Publications. San Francisco, Glide Publications, 1971–   .
Offers a subject and producer approach to movement publications of all varieties except serial publications. Annual.

Bertalan, Frank. *Junior College Library Collection.* 1970 ed. Newark, N.J., Bro-Dart Foundation, 1970. 503p.
In a 1970 revised edition, this selected list of more than 22,000 books for junior and community college libraries aims to assist in the selection of titles, in all subject areas, that should be provided by new institutions and by established schools that are expanding their facilities. Scope attempts to reflect the curriculum trends in junior and community colleges. Arranged by the Library of Congress classification with full bibliographic information. Libraries that had used the first edition of the collection contributed suggestions for the revision.

Deason, Hilary J. *The AAAS Science Book List; A Selected and Annotated List of Science and Mathematics Books for Secondary School Students, College Undergraduates and Nonspecialists.* 3d ed. Washington, D.C., American Association for the Advancement of Science, 1970. 439p. Supplement, 1977.
Annotated and classified list of nearly 2,500 recommended titles. Supplement covers 1969–1977 and includes 2,600 titles.

Harvard University. *Harvard List of Books in Pyschology.* 4th ed. Cambridge, Mass., Harvard University Press, 1971. 108p.

Harvard psychologists compiled and annotated this classified list of about 750 titles.

Information for Everyday Survival: What You Need and Where to Get It. Compiled by Priscilla Gotsick and others. Chicago, American Library Association, 1976. 403p.

Annotations of free and inexpensive materials are arranged under thirteen categories such as aging, children, etc.

Jarvi, Edith and others. *Canadian Selection: Books and Periodicals for Libraries.* Toronto, University of Toronto Press, 1978.

Selected, annotated list of approximately 4,300 English-language books and periodicals "about Canada, published in Canada, or written by Canadians at home and abroad." Includes wide range of subjects.

Leamer, Laurence E. and George G. Dawson. *Suggestions for a Basic Economics Library: A Guide to the Building of an Economics Library for School, Classroom, or Individual.* 5th ed. New York, Joint Council on Economic Education, 1973. 72p.

Annotated, classified list of 250–300 works chosen because they are considered to be "understandable to most secondary school students" and "acceptable from an academic standpoint." Indexed by priority for purchase, author, and publisher.

Memphis/Shelby County Public Library and Information Center. Library/ABE Project. *Bibliography of Easy Reading, Coping Skills Materials for Adults.* Memphis, 1975. 71p.

Annotated list of adult materials written at an eighth-grade (or lower) reading level. Arranged under eleven "coping skills categories" (e.g., "Legal Rights," "Money Management").

Philadelphia Free Library. Reader Development Program. *Reader Development Bibliography.* Syracuse, N.Y., New Readers Press, 1974. 75p. Supplement, 1975–76.

Materials for adults with a reading level of eighth grade or below.

Philbrook, Marilyn M. *Medical Books for the Layperson: An Annotated Bibliography.* Boston, Boston Public Library, 1976. 113p.

Pirie, James. *Books for Junior College Libraries.* Chicago, American Library Association, 1969. 452p.

Lists nearly 20,000 titles that have been selected as a basic collection for junior and community colleges, particularly for the liberal arts and transfer programs. Selection was based on the collections of several established junior colleges. Arrangement is by subject, with author and subject indexes, and full bibliographic information.

Public Library Association. Starter List for New Branch and New Libraries Collection Committee. *Books for Public Libraries: Nonfiction for Small Collections.* 2d ed. New York, Bowker, 1975. 220p.

Lists in classified order with no annotations, about 5,000 non-fiction titles which have been suggested as a beginning collection for the smallest unit of a public library. In general, the list is limited to a circulation collection for adults.

Reinhart, Bruce. *Vocational-Technical Learning Materials.* 2d ed. Williamsport, Pa., Bro-Dart, 1974, 307p.

Annotated subject list of more than 5,000 books and nearly 400 journals recommended for high school and college collections serving occupational education programs. Indicates if item is recommended for instructional, professional, or journal library and whether the title is considered essential, supplementary, or special interest.

Schuman, Patricia. *Materials for Occupational Education; An Annotated Source Guide.* New York, Bowker, 1971. 201p.

Describes professional and trade associations, government agencies, and private businesses that produce occupational training materials suitable for two-year colleges. Arranged by occupational groups.

Science and Technology: A Purchase Guide for Branch and Public Libraries. Pittsburgh, Carnegie Library of Pittsburgh, 1963. Supplements, 1964–

Basic volume is supplemented each year by a classified and briefly annotated list of recommended recent science and technology books of general interest to adults.

Weber, J. Sherwood. *Good Reading: A Guide for Serious Readers.* 21st ed. New York, Bowker, 1978.

Annotated list of approximately 2,500 books.

Children and Young Adults—General Aids

U.S. Library of Congress. Children's Book Section. *Children's Literature: A Guide to Reference Sources.* Washington, 1966. 341p. First Supplement, 1972. 316p. Second supplement, 1977. 413p.

Basic volume and supplements contain sections which list and annotate selection aids and other tools for the study of children's literature. Includes some international coverage.

American Library Association. Children's Service Division. Notable Children's Books Committee. *Notable Children's Books, 1940–1970.* Chicago, American Library Association, 1977. 84p.

Represents a reevaluation of the annual "Notable Children's Books" from 1940 to 1970 with annotations of "those children's books that have proved to be of enduring value from the perspective of today."

American Library Association. Young Adult Services Division. *Best Books for Young Adults.* Chicago, American Library Association.

Annual annotated list of outstanding young adult books selected by a committee of YASD.

Arbuthnot, May Hill. *Children's Books Too Good to Miss.* 6th ed. Cleveland, Case Western University Press, 1971. 97p.

About 230 recommended titles are annotated and classified by age groupings. Also includes information on a selected group of illustrators.

Best Books for Children. 15th ed. Edited by John T. Gillespie and Christine Gilbert. New York, Bowker, 1978.

Annotated list of approximately 5,500 in-print books, selected for grade levels K-6.

Child Study Association of America. *Children's Books of the Year.* New York, Child Study Press.

Represents committee's annual choice of several hundred books from among the more than 2,000 titles published each year for grades K-8.

Child Study Association of America. Children's Book Committee. *Reading with Your Child Through Age 5.* Rev. ed. New York, Child Study Press, 1972. 40p.

Selected list aimed at parents and staffs of nursery and day-care programs.

Children's Books of the Year. London, Hamish Hamilton, 1970–

Children's Book Officer of the National Book League (London) annually selects approximately 300 books from the year's output of children's books for a traveling exhibit. This is a listing of those books.

Cianciolo, Patricia J. and others. *Picture Books for Children.* Chicago, American Library Association, 1973. 174p.

Nearly 400 titles for preschoolers on up. Annotated.

Crosby, Muriel. *Reading Ladders for Human Relations.* 5th ed. Washington, D.C., American Council on Education, 1972. 346p.

Annotated list of recommended books, grouped around themes in human development and arranged according to reading difficulty. Selections for primary through mature readers.

Gillespie, John T. *Paperback Books for Young People: An Annotated Guide to Publishers and Distributors.* 2d ed. Chicago, American Library Association, 1977. 223p.

Discusses U.S. publishers and distributors of paperbacks and includes an annotated list of selection aids for paperback books.

Haviland, Virginia. *Children's Books of International Interest.* 2d ed. Chicago, American Library Association, 1978.

Annotated selection of fiction and non-fiction books "that present most vividly and dramatically the qualities of experience that will excite interest of children throughout the world."

Jacob, Gale Sypher. *Independent Reading Grades One Through Three: An Annotated Bibliography with Reading Levels.* Williamsport, Pa., Bro-Dart Foundation, 1975. 86p.

Lists more than 800 books, most published since 1970.

Munich. Internationale Jugendbibliothek. *The Best of the Best: Picture, Children's and Youth Books from 110 Countries or Languages.* 2d ed. Munich, Verlag Dokumentation, 1976. 342p.

Unannotated list, selected by librarians at the International Youth Library and other specialists in children's books.

National Association of Independent Schools. Library Committee. *Books for Secondary School Libraries.* 5th ed. New York, Bowker, 1976. 526p.

Classified list of about 6,000 titles, prepared for use in private schools with high academic requirements.

National Council of Teachers of English. *Adventuring with Books; A Book List for Preschool to Grade 8,* 2d ed. New York, Citation Press, 1973. 395p.

Selected subject list (with annotations) of more than 2,400 books that "combine the qualities of entertaining reading with literary merit."

National Council of Teachers of English. Committee on the High Interest— Easy Reading Booklist. *High Interest—Easy Reading for Junior High and Senior High School Students.* 2d ed. New York, Citation Press, 1972. 140p.

Subject list of 400–500 books selected for the reluctant reader. Emphasis is on "High Interest." Annotated.

National Council of Teachers of English. Committee on the Senior High School Booklist. *Books for You: A Booklist for Senior High Students.* 6th ed. Urbana, Ill., National Council of Teachers of English, 1976, 482p.

Classified and annotated list of over 2,500 recommended titles.

Spache, George D. *Good Reading for Poor Readers.* 10th ed. Champaign, Ill., Garrard, 1978. 284p.

Classified and annotated lists of recommended books accompany discussion of reading guidance with children.

Withrow, Dorothy and others. *Gateways to Readable Books.* 5th ed. New York, Wilson, 1975. 229p.

Subtitle: "An Annotated Graded List of Books in Many Fields." Classified list of over 1,000 titles.

Children and Young Adults—Special Topics

American Library Association. Children's Services Division. Library Service to the Disadvantaged Child Committee. *I Read . . . I See . . . I Hear . . . I Learn. . . .* Chicago, American Library Association, 1971. 112p.

Under four broad age level categories are annotations of recommended books, poems, stories, films, and recordings. Developed from a list done for the U.S. Office of Economic Opportunity.

Bernstein, Joanne E. *Books to Help Children Cope with Separation and Loss.* New York, Bowker, 1977. 255p.

Detailed annotations of nearly 1,500 books, arranged under broad headings (e.g., death of parents, divorce).

Buttlar, Lois and Lubomyr R. Wynar. *Building Ethnic Collections: An Annotated Guide for School Media Centers and Public Libraries.* Littleton, Colo., Libraries Unlimited, 1977. 434p.

Includes nearly 2,300 books and nonprint items on more than 40 ethnic groups.

Deason, Hilary J. *The AAAS Science Book List for Children; A Selected and Annotated List of Science and Mathematics Books for Children in Elementary Schools, and for Children's Collections in Public Libraries.* 3rd ed. Washington, D.C., American Association for the Advancement of Science, 1972. 253p.

Over 1,500 titles have been annotated and classified. Levels of difficulty are indicated.

Hardgrove, Clarence F. and Herbert F. Miller. *Mathematics Library— Elementary and Junior High School.* 3rd ed. Washington, D.C., National Council of Teachers of Mathematics, 1973. 70p.

Annotated selection of titles "to enrich the instructional program." Three sections: primary grades, intermediate grades, junior high school.

Hotchkiss, Jeannette. *African-Asian Reading Guide for Children and Young Adults.* Metuchen, N.J., Scarecrow Press, 1976. 269p.

Annotations of more than 1,200 books on Africa, Asia, Australia, and the South Seas. Reading and interest levels range from primary to adult.

McDonough, Irma K. *Canadian Books for Children/Livres canadiens pour enfants.* Toronto, University of Toronto Press, 1976. 112p.

Approximately 1,400 in-print books and magazines; short descriptive annotations. Revised edition announced for publication in 1978.

Mills, Joyce White. *The Black World in Literature for Children: A Bibliography of Print and Non-Print Materials.* Atlanta, Atlanta University, School of Library Service, 1975. 42p.

Short annotations of approximately 140 books and 60 non-print items published in 1974–75.

New York Public Library. *Libros en Español; An Annotated List of Children's Books in Spanish.* New York, 1971. 52p.

About 200 books are arranged in nine categories and annotated in both English and Spanish. Includes both U.S. and foreign publications; based on the collections of the NYPL.

Rabban, Elana. *Books from Other Countries, 1968–1971; A Bibliography of Translations of Books for Young People Available in the United States.* Chicago, American Association of School Librarians, 1972. 48p.

Almost 200 recommended translations of children's books are annotated and arranged by country.

Rollock, Barbara. *The Black Experience in Children's Books.* New York, New York Public Library, 1974. 122p.

Annotated list of recommended books for K–12. Earlier editions compiled by Augusta Baker.

Schaaf, William L. *High School Mathematics Library.* 6th ed. Reston, Va., National Council of Teachers of Mathematics, 1976. 74p.

Classified list with some brief annotations of approximately 925 titles, one-fourth published 1970–1975. Starred titles are suggested for a basic collection.

Schmidt, Nancy. *Children's Books on Africa and Their Authors: An Annotated Bibliography.* New York, Africana Publishing Co., 1975. 291p.

Includes books from elementary through secondary levels.

Snow, Kathleen M. and Philomena Hauck. *Canadian Materials for Schools.* Toronto, Macmillan and Stewart, 1970. 200p.

Concentrates on English-language materials and includes trade books, government publications, newspapers and magazines, and films. Discussion in bibliographic essay form.

Reference Books

American Library Association. Reference Services Division. Ad Hoc Reference Books Review Committee. *Reference Books for Small and Medium-Sized Libraries.* 2d ed. rev. Chicago, American Library Association, 1973. 146p.

Aimed at public libraries serving populations of 10,000–75,000. Nearly 800 annotations.

American Reference Books Annual. Littleton, Colo., Libraries Unlimited, 1970–

Signed, evaluative reviews of new reference books. Each annual list contains approximately 1,500 entries. A cumulative index for 1970–74, edited by Joseph Sprug, is available.

Best Reference Books: Titles of Lasting Value Selected from American Reference Books Annual, 1970–1976. Edited by Bohdan S. Wynar. Littleton, Colo., 1976. 448p.

Reprints more than 800 reviews chosen by the editor from the first seven volumes of *ARBA.*

Encyclopedia Buying Guide; A Consumer Guide to General Encyclopedias in Print. Edited by Kenneth F. Kister. New York, Bowker, 1975/76–

Detailed descriptions and evaluations of nonspecialized adult, school, popular and one-volume encyclopedias.

Henderson, Diane. *Guide to Basic Reference Materials for Canadian Libraries.* 5th ed. Toronto, University of Toronto Press, 1978. 250p.

Prepared for use in the Faculty of Library Science, University of Toronto. Contains "basic and representative works" under four broad headings. Some annotations. Looseleaf.

Kister, Kenneth F. *Dictionary Buying Guide: A Consumer Guide to General English-Language Wordbooks in Print.* New York, Bowker, 1977. 358p.

Evaluates 58 adult and 61 juvenile dictionaries, as well as a number of general and research dictionaries and wordbooks.

Peterson, Carolyn Sue. *Reference Books for Elementary and Junior High School Libraries.* 2d ed. Metuchen, N.J., Scarecrow Press, 1975. 314p.
Annotations of approximately 900 books.

Reference and Subscription Books Reviews. Chicago, American Library Association, 1956/60–   .
Reprints from *Booklist* reviews of reference books prepared by members of ALA's Reference and Subscription Books Review Committee. Formerly biennial, now annual. The 1976–77 volume (published in 1978) includes 101 reviews and 249 notes and comments. The 1975–76 volume contained a ten-year cumulative index. Quarterly.

Reference Services Review. Ann Arbor, Mich., Pierian Press, 1973–
"Reference Sources," a regular feature, carries bibliographic information, cataloging information, citations of reviews and quotations from them for new reference works (approximately 4,000 per year). Annual, hardcover cumulations of "Reference Sources" have been announced, beginning with 1977 coverage. RSR also carries state-of-the-art surveys on reference works in a variety of subject areas.

Ryder, Dorothy E. *Canadian Reference Sources: A Selective Guide.* Ottawa, Canadian Library Association, 1973. 185p. Supplement, 1975. 121p.
Basic volume includes a selection of over 1,200 Canadian reference materials. Supplement adds new works and editions published up to December 1973.

Sheehy, Eugene P. *Guide to Reference Books.* 9th ed. Chicago, American Library Association, 1976. 1015p.
Classified, annotated list of approximately 10,000 titles recommended for large, general reference collections. Arranged under five major subject areas, subdivided by subject and form. (Previous edition was edited by Constance M. Winchell.)

Walford, A. J. *Guide to Reference Material.* 3rd ed. London, Library Association, 1973–1977. 3v.
Classified, annotated list of important reference books. International with some emphasis on British publications. First volume covers science and technology; second covers social science, history, philosophy and religion; third covers literature, languages, arts, etc.

Wynar, Bohdan S. *Reference Books in Paperback: An Annotated Guide.* 2d ed. Littleton, Colo., Libraries Unlimited, 1976. 317p.
Second edition emphasizes books published since 1972. Arranged by subject.

Wynar, Christine L. *Guide to Reference Books for School Media Centers.* Littleton, Colo., Libraries Unlimited, 1973. 131p. Supplement, 1976.
Basic volume annotates more than 2,500 titles; supplement adds more

than 500. Selections are chosen because of suitability for grades K–12 and junior colleges.

Government Publications

Government Reference Books: A Biennial Guide to U.S. Government Publications. Littleton, Colo., Libraries Unlimited, 1968/69–
Biennial, annotated subject guide to reference books published by the U.S. Government Publishing Office. Serves to update Wynkoop's *Subject Guide to Government Reference Books* (1972), which lists over one thousand major government reference books published before 1968.

Municipal Government Reference Sources: Publications and Collections. Prepared by Local Government Task Force, Government Documents Round Table, American Library Association. New York, Bowker, 1978.
Identifies and annotates several thousand current reference publications of 200 municipalities and associations such as the League of Women Voters.

Parish, David W. *State Government Reference Publications: An Annotated Bibliography.* Littleton, Colo., Libraries Unlimited, 1974. 237p.
Selective guide to approximately 800 documents issued by states and territories. Arranged by state.

Pohle, Linda C. *A Guide to Popular Government Publications: For Libraries and Home Reference.* Littleton, Colo., Libraries Unlimited, 1972. 213p.
Approximately 2,000 books and periodicals on such subjects as consumer education, environment, etc.

"Selection Guide to High Interest Government Publications." *Government Publications Review,* 3:305–317, Winter 1976.
Special annotated list started with this issue and continued in later issues.

Van Zandt, Nancy Patton. *Selected U.S. Government Series; A Guide for Public and Academic Libraries.* Chicago, American Library Association, 1978. 172p.
Annotations of approximately 600 depository series titles considered useful for small and medium-sized libraries.

Wynkoop, Sally. *Subject Guide to Government Reference Books.* Littleton, Colo., Libraries Unlimited, 1972. 276p.
See *Government Reference Books.*

BIBLIOGRAPHY

Avant, John Alfred. "Slouching Toward Criticism." *Library Journal,* 96:4055–4059, December 15, 1971. Critical comments on popular reviewing tools.
Bone, Larry E. "Choosing the Best: A Review of Selection Aids for the Selection of Reference Books." *Reference Services Review,* 4:81–83, July 1976.
Boyer, Jean W. "Selection Tools—What's Available?" *Catholic Library World,* 47:420–422, May–June 1976. Brief review.
"Canadian Book and Periodical Selection Tools." *Ontario Library Review,* 60:249–250, December 1976.

Chen, Ching-Chih and Arthuree M. Wright. "Current Status of Biomedical Book Reviewing." *Medical Library Association Bulletin*, 62:105–119, April 1974. Results of a study; lists journals with reviews and gives information on time lag.

Cohen, David. "Multiethnic Media; Selected Bibliographies." *Library Journal*, 98:1352–1358, April 15, 1973. Annotated list.

Combs, Richard E. "Surging Behind in Print; or, Where, Oh Where Has My Little Book Gone?" *Wilson Library Bulletin*, 48:307–309, December 1973. Author's reaction to reviews of his book.

Doughty, Frances. "Responsibilities of Reviewers." *Library Trends*, 22:443–451, April 1974. Reviewing of science books for children.

Eshelman, Larry. "French Adult Book Selection." *Ontario Library Review*, 59:91–96, June 1975. Annotated list of selection tools.

Ettelt, Harold. *Book Reviews in Periodicals*. Brockport, N.Y., State University of New York at Brockport, 1971. 17p. Subject listing of periodicals that include book reviews more or less regularly.

Evans, Moira. "Selection Tools for Building a Children's Literature Collection." *Texas Libraries*, 37:73–79, Summer 1975.

Fry, Thomas K. *Use of Selection Tools*. Sacramento, Calif., California Library Association, 1974. 14p. (ED 104 332) Summarizes responses from a survey of academic libraries.

Goffman, William and Thomas G. Morris. "Bradford's Law and Library Acquisitions." *Nature*, 226:922–923, June 6, 1970. Suggests an acquisition policy for journals.

Gold, Herbert. "Reviewmanship and the I-Wrote-a-Book Disease." *Atlantic*, 225:114–117, June 1970.

Green, Alan. "Book Business." *Saturday Review*, 55:57–58, August 5, 1972. Brief comments on *Kirkus, Publishers Weekly,* and *Library Journal*.

Haines, Helen. *Living with Books*. 2d ed. New York, Columbia University Press, 1950. 610p. See Chapters 7 ("Book Evaluation and Reviewing by Libraries") and 8 ("The Art of the Annotation").

Heins, Paul. "Out on a Limb with the Critics: Some Random Thoughts on the Present State of the Criticism of Children's Literature." *Hornbook*, 46:264–273, June 1970.

Hernon, Peter. "State Publications: A Bibliographic Guide for Reference Collections." *Library Journal*, 99:2810–2819, November 1, 1974. State-by-state listing.

Hollander, John. "Some Animadversions on Current Reviewing." *Daedalus*, 92:145–155, Winter 1963.

Katz, Bill. "Best Titles of 1977; LJ's Small Press Roundup." *Library Journal*, 102:2467–2476, December 15, 1977. Includes list of publishers and review sources.

Kluger, Richard. "Such Good Friends?" *American Libraries*, 4:20–25, January 1973. Relationship between publishers and reviewers.

Kluger, Richard. "What I Did to Books and Vice Verse." *Harper's Magazine*, December 1966, pp. 69–74. How the author operated when editor of *Book Week*.

Kolins, Bill. "London Notebook." *Publishers Weekly*, 200:163–165, September 27, 1971. Brief comments on British book reviewers.

Kosa, G. A. "Book Selection Tools for Subject Specialists in a Large Research Library: An Analysis." *Library Resources and Technical Services*, 19:13–18, Winter 1975.

Lehman, James O. "*Choice* as a Selection Tool." *Wilson Library Bulletin*, 44:957–961, May 1970.

Lehman, Lola D. and Jeanne Osborn. "Fiction Recommendations in Two Popular Book Selection Tools." *School Libraries*, 20:21–24, Winter 1971.

"Looking Inside NYRB." *Publishers Weekly*, 205:36–40, March 11, 1974. How the *New York Review of Books* operates.

McCanse, Ralph A. *The Art of the Book Review*. Madison, University of Wisconsin, University Extension Division, 1963. 23p. Subtitle: "A Comprehensive Working Outline."

Milton, Joyce. "Unanswered Questions on Reviewing for YA's." *School Library Journal,* 23:127, March 1977. What is the role of a YA book reviewer?

Moore, Julie L. "Bibliographic Control of American Doctoral Dissertations." *Special Libraries,* 63:227–230, May–June 1972; 63:285–291, July 1972. Part one reviews history; part two analyzes control.

Nobile, Philip. *Intellectual Skywriting.* New York, Charterhouse, 1974. 312p. History of the *New York Review of Books.*

Peyre, Henri. "What's Wrong with American Book Reviewing." *Daedalus,* 92:128–144, Winter 1963.

Rawles, Beverly. *Materials Selection for Disadvantaged Adults.* Morehead, Ky., Morehead State University, Appalachian Adult Education Center, 1974. 28p. (Public Library Training Institutes, Library Service Guide No. 1) Discusses types of materials which are useful and sources.

Regnery, Henry. "Bias in Book Reviewing and Book Selection." *ALA Bulletin,* 60:57–62, January 1966.

"Reviewers Debate the Function of Reviewing." *Publishers Weekly,* 193:30–33, March 18, 1968.

Reviews in Library Book Selection. LeRoy C. Merritt, Martha T. Boaz, and Kenneth S. Tisdel. Detroit, Wayne State University Press, 1958. 188p.

Robbins, Jane. "Two in 'The Movement'; A Review of *Booklegger,* and *Emergency Librarian.*" *Library Journal,* 101:2010–2014, October 1, 1976.

Sadow, Arnold. "Book Reviewing Media for Technical Libraries." *Special Libraries,* 61:194–198, April 1970.

Samore, Ted. "TLS or NYTBR: Does It Matter?" *Choice,* 6:473–477, June 1969.

Sarton, George. "Notes on the Reviewing of Learned Books." *Science,* 131:1182–1187, April 22, 1960. Outlines techniques for writing a good review.

Schuman, Patricia. "Concerned Criticism or Casual Cop-Outs?" *Library Journal* 97:245–248, January 15, 1972.

"Selection Policy Statement of the *Booklist.*" *Booklist.* Usually appears in the first issue (September 1) of each volume.

Sheed, Wilfrid. "The Good Word: The Politics of Reviewing." *New York Times Book Review,* February 7, 1971, p. 2;16.

Shockley, Ann Allen. "Black Book Reviewing: A Case for Library Action." *College and Research Libraries,* 35:16–20, January 1974. Notes black journals which have reviews.

Sissman, L. E. "Confessions of a Second Class Citizen." *Atlantic,* 229:26–27, June 1972. Comments on certain popular, general reviewing tools.

Smith, Alice G. "The *Hornbook* Magazine." *Serials Review,* 2:7–14, July–September 1976. Historical review.

Smith, Maurice H. "Commentary on Book Reviewing Media." *Special Libraries,* 61:515–516, November 1970.

Sutherland, Zena. "Current Reviewing of Children's Books." *Library Quarterly,* 37:110–118, January 1967.

"They Love It in Boston, or How the *Globe*'s Book Section Works." *Publishers Weekly,* 199:69–70, May 31, 1971.

Weyr, Thomas. "The Making of the *New York Times Book Review.*" *Publishers Weekly,* 202:36–50, July 31, 1972.

Whittemore, Reed. "On Living in Glass Houses." *New Republic,* 162:21–24, May 2, 1970.

Young, Arthur P. "Scholarly Book Reviewing in America." *Libri,* 25:174–182, 1975.

CHAPTER 6

The Selector and Non-Book Materials

Libraries have always collected some types of non-book materials, such as pamphlets, maps, periodicals, and clippings. In the last two decades there has been growing emphasis on such items as films, musical and spoken recordings, microfilms, and microfiche. As video and audio cassettes have become widely used to package a large variety of instructional and research information, university and research libraries have begun to include statements on audiovisual materials in their collection development policies. The increased acquisition of such materials has brought with it a greater concern with problems of selecting the non-book forms, sources of information about and methods of acquisition of the various types, and problems of handling them once they are acquired. This field is so extensive that full treatment of the problem in all its aspects would require several separate volumes. In the present context, only the briefest introduction can be attempted.

The selection of non-book materials is, of course, based ultimately on the same principles as for the selection of books: one seeks the best material available in terms of authority, accuracy, effectiveness of presentation, usefulness to the community, etc. A key question is whether or not the medium used is the most effective one for presenting the chosen topic. As with books, selection will be affected by the type of library, its size, the community in which it functions, and the librarian's conception of the purposes of the institution. The library will try to have selection done by people who are informed about the subject matter presented in the non-book form, and it will employ sources of reviewing for evaluation of each item, just as it would for a book.

In addition to the general principles which one would apply in selecting non-book materials, there are special matters to be taken into consideration in selecting the various forms, especially technical matters involved in the production of films or records or microforms. One may be interested in the quality of the recording in a musical performance, in the lighting and cutting of a movie; but these are also like the judgments of the quality of the printing and binding job in a book. To judge these special materials adequately, a librarian needs additional

125

skills (which, of course, is also true as the librarian moves from judging books in one subject field to evaluating those in another subject field). Lacking a knowledge of film sound tracks, of orchestral balance, of all the myriad technical matters involved in films and recordings, the librarian again can turn to the judgments of those who have such knowledge published in reviewing and selection media, just as he/she does when selecting in a subject field in which he/she feels the need of assistance because of lack of subject knowledge.

The major problems involved in the non-book field are really not selection problems, but administrative ones. Many librarians have boggled at the tasks involved in checking films for damage, splicing broken film, keeping motion picture projectors in order. The problems involved in cataloging, storing, and preserving recordings in decent condition have weakened the resolve of some librarians to be modern and progressive in their acquisition of this medium. Limited financial resources may cause some libraries to hesitate about extensive acquisition of non-book media. Some of these media are expensive and require the purchase and maintenance of costly equipment if they are to be properly exploited.

Films, Filmstrips, Slides

Several of the non-book media collected by libraries are film formats. Libraries are most likely to acquire 16mm, 8mm, or super 8mm films. These films come with or without sound and are generally stored on reels, though they are sometimes available in cartridges. Filmstrips—lengths of 35mm film containing a series of still pictures— are fairly inexpensive, require uncomplicated projection equipment, and are popular in some libraries. They may be silent, with captions on the pictures, or accompanied by a tape or disc recording, sometimes with an inaudible signal which automatically advances the filmstrip one frame or an audible signal which cues the projector operator. The disadvantages of filmstrips are the lack of motion accompanied by the rigidity of the sequencing and, in the case of those filmstrips accompanied by sound, of the timing. Slides (single frames of 35mm film secured in a 2″ × 2″ or 2¼″ × 2½″ mounting) share with filmstrips the advantages of low initial cost and projection equipment which is relatively easy to operate. In addition, they are more flexible, can be arranged in any sequence and viewed at any speed, with or without sound accompaniment.

Problems arise in the selection of some of the non-book materials because they add facets not found in books. A pamphlet, after all, is only an abbreviated book. One can judge the effectiveness of the organization and style, one can evaluate the facts presented, one can compare it with other written materials with some ease. But a film presents its ideas with some additional factors which influence the effect of the presentation. Words spoken in the film are susceptible of shading by the tone of voice, the inflection of certain words, the facial expressions of the speaker. The film may be accompanied by background music, which can be employed to heighten the emotional impact of some scene or idea. There is, therefore, an emotional meaning built into films which is not found in books, and this emotional meaning may be as important as the explicit dialogue. To some extent, of course, the manner of presentation in a book functions in the same way, but most Americans are conditioned to think of movies as a source of pleasure, and they may not react as critically to the presentation of a film as they would to the same biased presentation in a book.

Thus selectors must consider the manner of presentation, which involves a wide variety of different factors. They must also consider, of course, the technical aspects of the film's production: lighting, quality of photography and sound, transitions between scenes, quality of the narration, etc. Two general guides are that the content should be more effectively presented through the film than it could be presented in a less expensive format and that the purchase cost of a film should be balanced against the potential quantity and variety of use. Since a film often involves the expenditure of a considerable sum of money, no library will want to purchase a film without first viewing it.

The sources of information about films, their producers, and their printed evaluations do not present as neat a pattern as the sources of information about books and their publishers. Most libraries are probably interested in films in the 16mm, 8mm, or super 8mm formats. (The 8mm film is not generally suitable for large audiences, but serves a small group satisfactorily.) Library collections generally emphasize the educational film, although some do not exclude the commercial film produced for entertainment. It must be admitted that, although there are some excellent educational films, there are many which have little to recommend them, that are fairly uninspired, sometimes downright distorted (especially those produced for free distribution by organizations interested in promoting their own interests), or at best merely passable. The annotation in the producer's or distributor's catalogue may not be a fair summary of the film, so that the librarian should be sure to have the film viewed before purchase.

The field of reviewing media presents a plethora of riches. There are many magazines devoted to the motion picture world, and, although not all are concerned with educational motion pictures, there are enough of those to present a wide spread. Filmstrips and slide sets are also being reviewed more often than in the past. (Examples of specific reviewing tools may be found at the end of this chapter.) In fact, educational films, filmstrips, and slides are now so widely reviewed that indexes to the reviews are being published. In addition to studying the journals that review films, the librarian who selects films should be familiar with the publications of the Educational Film Library Association (EFLA), including their film evaluation cards.

Librarians should also keep in mind the film services offered by universities, state libraries, and some other libraries in providing films for loan. Even the library which cannot afford to embark on the purchase of a film collection can borrow films or can join a film circuit in its state. In addition, the catalogues of such organizations as a university or state library can be an added source of suggestions for purchase. Individual public libraries also issue catalogues of their films, which have met the selection standards of the library concerned and may thus furnish other librarians with valuable guidance.

In summary: the librarian interested in films will keep up with the field by reading the reviews in current periodicals, by getting on the mailing list of distributors and producers, by seeing as many educational films as possible, in order to develop a sense of discrimination, and by viewing all films before purchase or use.

Audio Recordings

Audio recordings come on either disc or tape. The discs are the familiar phonodisc or phonograph records. Although there have been a variety of diameters, the typical disc today is 12″ in diameter and runs at a speed of 33⅓ r.p.m. The amount of recorded sound on a side may vary from ten minutes to more than thirty minutes. With the phonodisc, specific parts of a recording can be retrieved. The format is less expensive than tape, but it is easily scratched and warped and the quality of the sound tends to deteriorate with use.

A popular form of audio recording is the magnetic tape, which comes in ¼″ or ⅛″ and plays at 1⅞, 3¾, or 7½ i.p.s. (The faster speeds generally mean better quality sound.) Tapes may be single monaural, 4-track stereo, or 8-track stereo. Cassettes are now more popular than reel-to-reel. They are typically produced with ⅛″ tape and played at 1⅞ i.p.s., but they vary in amount of tape per cassette and in playing time. (Some are as short as ten minutes and others run as long as 120 minutes.) With tape recordings, it is difficult to locate specific parts of the recorded material. However, cassettes in particular are convenient to play and not particularly easy to damage.

The library which has elected to add audio recordings to its collection faces a bewildering variety of types of material recorded, of types of recording and reproducing systems, of performances of a given work (especially in the so-called "standard repertory" of the classics), of sources of information concerning the choices available. The bibliographical network for nonbook materials does not exhibit the same degree of organization as that for books. Perhaps this only means that selection is less routine—and hence more interesting?—than book selection.

The materials available on sound recordings encompass a wide scope. Predominant in terms of bulk is music, of course, ranging from medieval and renaissance works to the latest compositions of our contemporaries. In addition to the standard composers, audio recordings allow one to hear the music of very minor figures, some of whose music has not been performed in public concert for hundreds of years, but which can now be heard on recordings.

In deciding to build an audio collection, one must first decide how far the standard composers—and the standard works by each of them—will dominate the collection of musical works. One can see the general principles entering into consideration as the question of "completeness" is raised. How delightful to have *all* the works of Beethoven in the collection. Opera, symphony, concerti, chamber works, songs—a full representation of the great man! And—consider the joy—a glorious collection which would have, not only each work, but each work in every performance ever recorded! For most libraries, such a collection would be burdensomely expensive, to say nothing of being somewhat overbalanced in Beethoven's direction. To buy all of Beethoven, one would have to forego buying other composers. The selection of a good, basic representation of the standard classical repertory demands, naturally, some acquaintance with composers and the history of music.

In addition to the collecting of the standard classics, the library may add non-western classics, and collect extensively in light classical works, folk music, jazz, Broadway musicals, popular singers and contemporary musical groups.

In addition to this vast array of musical material, the library can also add non-musical recordings. There are anthologies of recorded poetry, some read by well-known actors and including the works of one or more poets, some read by the poet and being restricted to his/her own works. Plays have been recorded in considerable quantity. The library might elect to attempt a collection of all Shakespeare's plays on recordings, to be checked out along with the text. Instructional materials (as, for example, foreign language courses) seem a reasonable choice for a library which stresses its educational role, and there are now many lectures, interviews, etc. of an educational nature available on cassette.

To the variety of materials available one must add the variety of forms in which recording is done. A library may still have a formidable collection of the old 78 r.p.m. recordings. (One hopes that some of the great performances available only on the old 78s will have been put on tape by a library owning them before the records were worn out.) Currently, 33⅓ r.p.m. is the vogue in discs and cassettes are the most popular form for the packaging of tape. Other variations in disc and tape recording formats were mentioned earlier. The different systems require different machines, and although this is not a materials selection problem, it raises the whole new area of equipment selection problems.

Variety is introduced at another level by the recording of a given work by different artists or groups. The library may desire not merely to have a recording of the Beethoven Fifth Symphony, but to have the best performances of it, so those who are being introduced to it will hear it at its most stunning. Many of the most famous works are available in at least a dozen versions—and the selector may even have the joy of choosing from as many as thirty versions. Conversely, of course, a less familiar, less popular, more remote work may be available in only one performance, and that not a stellar one, perhaps also recorded with less than standard technical excellence. The library may want this particular work as an example of a period or a type, and it might be forced to buy this product, just as it sometimes has to buy a book in less than perfect physical shape if no other edition is available.

As with books, selectors will be interested in reading reviews of new recordings. Such reviews appear in *Booklist* and *Previews* and in a host of magazines devoted to records, such as *American Record Guide, High Fidelity, Stereo Review, Gramophone, Rolling Stone,* etc. A quarterly "Index of Record Reviews" appears in the Music Library Association's *Notes,* and record reviews are also indexed in multi-media review indexes (see examples at end of the chapter). The Schwann catalogues are the *PTLA-BIP* of the record business, listing records available from a variety of producers, including all types of materials, musical and non-musical. The catalogues of individual companies are also useful in furnishing a full listing of their production.

Video Recordings

Many libraries (and even individuals) now own video tape recording and playing equipment. Such systems are based on magnetic tape, usually ½″ or ¾″ in width, and many now use the popular and convenient video cassette to house the tape. These video systems can be used to record programs off-air, to plan and record original programs, or to play commercially-produced tapes. Material which was formerly put on film is now being distributed on video tape. Since video recordings are the newest format to be collected widely in libraries, bibliographic control and evaluation sources are less well-developed. Video recordings are listed in some of the multi-media series such as those compiled by Educators' Progress Service and the National Information Center for

Educational Media (NICEM Index Series). They are also sometimes reviewed in other multi-media selection tools.

Experts are predicting that video recordings will soon become an important part of most libraries' collections and services. The development and marketing of low cost, portable equipment is helping to bring this about. Experimental programs already undertaken in a number of libraries have shown some of the variety of ways in which video can be used to package and distribute informational and recreational content. Not only are some libraries collecting commercial video tapes, producing their own recordings, using video recordings for in-library programs and lending video tapes for home viewing, but they are assisting their users in planning and developing video tape presentations. To librarians working with this medium, the possibilities seem limitless.

Maps and Globes

Maps and globes, as visual representations of areas of the world, are an important reference source in libraries of all types. Maps may be physical, emphasizing natural features of the land; political, showing boundaries of governmental units; or special topic, showing such information as historical events, manufacturing, crop production, weather patterns, religious movements, etc. Most libraries have little trouble with maps which come collected in book form as atlases, but some small libraries do have problems with the collection of individual sheet maps and sometimes resist them altogether. Because of the special acquisition, storage, and reference requirements associated with individual sheet maps, large research libraries tend to house them in special map collections.

Many maps are produced by government agencies and others are published by commercial firms specializing in that type of material. Information about new maps and atlases may be found in geographical journals, some of which list maps of specified areas and occasionally review atlases. Acquisition lists of large map libraries and certain national bibliographies also furnish a convenient way to find out what has been published. (Several articles cited in the bibliography at the end of this chapter give details on specific bibliographical sources and distributors for new maps.)

For the average small or medium-sized general library, which collects maps but does not maintain a special collection, the following selection criteria might be useful. Any map, atlas, or globe added to the collection ought, at the very least, to be as accurate as possible. Accuracy may be partly determined by the reputation of the publisher or producer of the map, the type of projection and scale used, and the date of production. Maps, atlases, or globes should be easy to read. The amount of detail presented ought to be appropriate for the size and design of the map and for the intended purpose or audience. Finally, of course, librarians must be concerned with the potential durability of the new acquisition. Atlases should be on suitable paper and well-bound; individual sheet maps should be on paper appropriate for their intended use and in some cases ought to have a cloth backing or a plastic finish. In all cases, of course, the collection plan of the library and the potential use of the materials will influence decisions about format.

Microforms

Microforms come in three basic formats—microfilm, microfiche, and micro-opaque—each of which has several variations. Microfilm is generally produced from high contrast photographic film, 16mm or 35mm, usually in black and white, although some materials are now available in color microfilm. A single roll of film, typically stored on a reel but sometimes available in a cartridge or cassette, may be rather short (enough to contain a 200-page thesis) or up to 100 feet long (common for long newspaper or journal runs). Microfiche resembles microfilm in that it contains a series of microimages on film, but instead of the images appearing in a row on a roll of film, they are arranged in a grid pattern on a sheet of film. The standard size for microfiche is approximately 4" × 6" (105mm × 148mm), but other sizes are still available. Library materials are also produced on two kinds of micro-opaques, each of which uses a different process for transferring microimages to opaque cards. Microprint is the trade name for the form (stiff 6" × 9" sheets) produced by Readex Microprint Company, and Microcard (3" × 5" opaque cards) is the form owned and produced by Microcard Corporation. Each microform has its own advantages and disadvantages and each requires its own equipment for reading and viewing.

Microforms have greatly enlarged the scope of materials from which the library can select. Many libraries which never could have hoped to build up, for example, a collection of early printed English books in original editions can subscribe to a microform series covering them. This means that it is possible to purchase at a fairly reasonable price copies of items which in the original could not be bought at any price, since they are simply not available, or, if available, could cost a fortune. A whole universe of books is now added to the current trade and ordinary o.p. market.

The traditional principles of selection apply very directly to microforms, since most microform materials acquired by libraries are simply direct copies of printed originals (an exception to this is Computer Output Microform [COM] which is produced directly from machine-readable files without an intermediate printing step). Some of the decisions relating to the purchase of microforms involve broad questions of collection development policy: Will microform be chosen only as a last resort or will it be the favored medium (when available) for certain categories of materials (such as newspapers and back files of journals)? A library's collection development policy ought to help the librarian make decisions about when to buy hard copy and when to acquire microforms. Assuming that a given item is available in both forms, the selector may first consider potential use of the material. How would it probably be used? By whom? For what purpose? For how long? Where? How often? If expected use patterns seem consistent with purchasing in microform, the selector may also consider the questions of storage space, equipment for reading and printing, and relative costs of various formats.

The selector who considers microform purchases must learn a new set of terms. Knowing whether the microform in question comes as a sheet (film or opaque) or a roll and what its overall dimensions are in terms of size and number of cards or width and length of roll is only the beginning. The librarian ought also to be aware of the image size and placement on the roll or sheet and the reduction ratio. Reduction ratios (the ratio between the size of the original and the size of the microimage) vary widely from one microform project to another, but ought to bear some relationship to the size of type and general condition of the material being reduced. Reduction ratios of 1/12, 1/14, or 1/16 have been typical when the originals were average monographs or journals; 1/16, 1/18, 1/20, when the originals were newspapers or other oversized publications. Microfiche tend to have somewhat higher reduction ratios than microfilm; ultrafiche, for example, is available at reduction ratios greater than 1/100. Higher reduction ratios are being used today because more sophisticated equipment is now available for reducing and enlarging the images.

Another term which the microform selector should add to his/her vocabulary is polarity (whether the image is black on a white background or white on a black background). Positive film reproduces the relationship of black and white found on the original. Negative polarity reverses that relationship, but, of course, a paper copy made from a negative film on a reader-printer will appear as a positive copy. Sometimes microforms are available in both positive and negative forms, so selectors should always specify which is preferred.

Before spending thousands of dollars on a set of microform materials, the selector will also want to investigate the quality of the reproduction, its generation, and the type of film on which the set has been produced. Quality of a microform depends heavily on the density of the images (extent to which dark parts of the image are really opaque), the contrast (extent of difference between dark areas and light areas of the image), and resolution (extent to which fine lines, closely spaced, can be distinguished). A factor which may affect quality of image is the generation of the film—that is, how many copying steps separate the film in question from the original copy. The original negative, called the master negative, is referred to as the first generation. A copy made from that is second generation, and so on. Librarians are generally advised to look for second or third generation films; later generations are too far removed from the original. The most common film types used in microform projects are silver halide, diazo, and vesicular. Of these three, only silver halide is considered to be of archival quality, and many librarians prefer to buy large or important microform collections on that type of film only.

In addition to the special technical problems relating to the physical characteristics of microforms, librarians encounter selection problems because of the way producers organize their microform projects. Much microform publishing involves long series or large sets, many of which are made up of out-of-print materials. Selectors have some of the same problems here that they have with hard-copy reprint series, with added complications caused by the microformat which makes inspection difficult. Questions arise on the level of individual selection decisions. Does the library really need that expensive microform set? How many of the titles in the series does the library already have? Did the producer furnish enough information about the contents of the series so that it is even possible to answer the previous question? Will the producer agree to supply only part of the set? If not, is the material in the series which the library does not now own important enough to justify taking unwanted duplicates along with it? Is another producer offering a similar set for sale? How much duplication is there between the two sets? Does physical quality appear to be comparable? Which of the two sets is the better buy? Does the series in question come with a manufacturer's guarantee of the content and quality? Does the set come with cataloging copy supplied? (The library's collection development policy may furnish guidelines on whether or not to buy sets that can not be verified or sets with no cataloging available.) Because many microform sets cost hundreds and even thousands of dollars, the time spent avoiding unwise selection decisions is worth the cost.

In the past, librarians often had trouble discovering what existed in microform and locating evaluations of these materials. That situation has been improving in recent years. *Guide to Microforms in Print*, started in 1961, appears annually and originally attempted to list all types of microforms (except theses and dissertations) which were available from U.S. publishers. For similar coverage of microforms issued by foreign publishers, the *International Microforms in Print: A Guide to Microforms of Non-United States Micropublishers* was started in

1974, but it has now been incorporated into *Guide to Microforms in Print*. (There is also a *Subject Guide to Microforms in Print*.) The Library of Congress has, since 1965, issued an annual, non-cumulative *National Register of Microform Masters*, which may be used to determine whether another library has a particular item on a master microfilm from which duplicates can be made. Since 1975, micropublishing has had its own version of *PTLA—MTLA: Micropublishers Trade List Annual*—with, appropriately enough, the publishers' catalogues reproduced on microfiche. There are microform acquisition tools limited by format—*Dissertation Abstracts International* for doctoral theses, *Newspapers on Microform*, a Library of Congress publication, *Resources in Education* for ERIC documents, etc.—and by subject. *Microform Review*, published since 1972, is a likely place to find evaluations of newly-available microform sets. There are other sources of information on microforms; several are listed at the end of this chapter.

Serials

Serials represent a type of publication which is usually distinguished from monographs (separately-published works, usually called books). In general, a serial is considered to be a publication which is issued in successive parts with numbering or chronological designation and intended to be continued indefinitely. The term includes magazines, periodicals, and journals, as well as other kinds of serials such as annual reports, association proceedings, certain kinds of directories, etc. "Magazine," "periodical," or "journal" tend to be used interchangeably, although some prefer to make distinctions among the terms. To these persons, "magazine" seems generally to refer to more popular publications, while "journal" is reserved for scholarly titles; "periodical" seems to be used for either category.

The selection of serials, of whatever variety, presents problems that book selection does not. The decision to buy a book is usually a one-time commitment of money—purchase price and processing cost. The decision to buy a serial represents a continuing commitment of money—a renewed subscription for an indefinite number of years, undoubtedly at a higher price each year, processing costs for each issue, and possible binding costs for each volume. A new serial subscription also means that staff time will be spent on additional decisions concerning that one serial title. Should the serial be bound? When and how? Instead of being bound, should it be purchased in microform for preservation of back files? If the library's subscription does not begin with the first issue of volume one, should back files be obtained? Should they be in original paper format or in microform? None of these decisions is easy and many of them affect sizeable amounts of the library's limited materials budget. The answers to the questions will vary with the purpose of the library and even with individual titles within a collection.

Libraries buy periodicals to cover the most current events or the most recent developments in subject fields (which will not get into book form for some time), to provide reference materials, and for general reading. The type of library involved will strongly affect the original selection of titles and the choice of those for binding and retention. A very small library may buy only a few general magazines and bind only the *Reader's Digest*. The large university library may buy and preserve tens of thousands of titles and may spend a large percentage of its materials budget on serial publications.

Serial selection means first finding out that a serial publication exists and then attempting to obtain the information needed to evaluate it. In a library which attempts to build general rather than research collections, the first step is not difficult and the second will be easier than for a research collection. In a library serving primarily non-specialist users, the choice of titles may be based partly on the indexes which the library can afford to buy and keep. If one purchases *Readers' Guide,* it seems desirable to try to buy as many of the magazines indexed in it as one can afford, to get the maximum use out of both the indexes and the magazines. In the area of coverage of current events, the library should strive to represent a variety of viewpoints, as it does in selection of other kinds of materials. Since commitment to subscribe represents a potential continuing annual charge, as well as possible annual binding costs and a constantly expanding storage space, periodicals should be selected carefully even in the smallest library, and only after they have demonstrated that they make a solid contribution to the collection. Selecting a periodical for binding reflects the judgment that it will have continuing reference use.

Research libraries face special problems with their serials collections. In many fields, especially scientific disciplines, serials are the major form of publication. This means that most university and many special libraries buy heavily in scientific serials. In recent years serial prices have risen drastically and the number of serial publications has also increased. A survey published in 1977 showed that in 1969 large academic libraries were spending about $2 for books to every $1 on serials. By 1973, the expenditures for the two types of materials were almost even. In some libraries, serials expenditures now easily exceed book expenditures. Costs of serial publications are not the only problem for research collections. Finding out that a new serial exists and verifying its title and publisher are not easy, since the percentage of non-trade, or otherwise elusive, serial publications has been estimated to be as high as eighty per cent of the total. A general collection may appropriately concentrate its purchases in the 20–25 per cent of serials which are easy to locate, but a research collection can not.

A number of factors arise when an academic or research library considers starting a new serial subscription. Obviously, the courses offered in the institution or the research programs carried on will be an early consideration. Even if the serial appears to be within the scope of the library's collection, the selector may hesitate because of the price, the lack of indexing for the new title, the language of the text, the availability of back files (if the serial has appeared in more than one or two issues), or the fact that another library in the area already has a subscription.

Both qualitative and quantitative criteria are used in making a selection decision. The influence of the individual making the request, the reputation of a new journal's editors, referees, and initial authors, the opinion of local experts, or appearance on a recommended basic list are examples of qualitative factors which might influence the decision. Among quantitative criteria are statistics showing usage of the title through interlibrary loan or in a comparable library and various kinds of measures of numbers of articles published within a specified period of time, frequency and speed with which the journal is cited by other important journals in the field, or frequency and speed with which the journal is cited in abstracting and indexing services. For most decisions, a selector would not want to rely only on one or two of the above indices of possible relevance and importance, but would want to gather and consider as much information about the title as is practical.

Sources of information about serials are growing in number, but they never seem to equal librarians' needs for information. Reviews of new journals tend to be slow for the obvious reason that most people are reluctant to judge a new journal publication on the basis of one, or even two, issues. *Serials Review,* a quarterly publication started in 1975, attempts to give some review coverage and so do *Library Journal* and *Choice* in regular features. The series of directories published by Bowker, beginning with *Ulrich's International Periodicals Directory,* are standard tools for serials acquisition. Another important source is *New Serial Titles* and its various supplements and cumulations. Recommended lists of periodicals for various kinds of libraries or on various subjects have been published for many years. A few examples of this kind of selection tool may be found at the end of the chapter. A relatively new form of serial selection tool is the journal citation study, which attempts to identify the most important journals in a field by determining which ones have been cited most often in the professional literature of that field. Selected examples of this type of study are also listed at the end of the chapter.

Pamphlets

The pamphlet collection can form an important adjunct to the book collection by providing up-to-date material which supplements or illustrates subjects covered elsewhere and by furnishing a variety of viewpoints on controversial issues. Pamphlets offer the added advantage of appealing to some library users who really do not want to read or skim an entire book on a subject of interest.

The problems of selecting are complicated by the almost incredible number of producers of pamphlet material, much of it intended for free distribution. The producers are often engaged in distributing the pamphlets to present some point of view which is connected with their business, and the librarian will want to ensure that the materials are factual and unbiased. Obtaining the material involves writing to many different sources, and this in itself can be a very time-consuming task. In addition, the usefulness of a pamphlet file can be much reduced unless there is a program of continuous weeding, to eliminate those materials which have become out-dated. There are a number of guides which are of real service in helping the librarian through the flood of pamphlet materials. Among the major ones are the *Vertical File Index* and the guides (to free materials, curriculum materials, etc.) of the Educators' Progress Service. But hundreds of organizations issue lists of free and inexpensive materials available on almost every subject imaginable, and some popular magazines do a good job of alerting their readers to useful pamphlets on topics covered by the magazine.

SELECTION AIDS

General Guides

Audiovisual Market Place. New York, Bowker, 1969–   . (Annual)
Directory information for producers of nonprint materials, listing under name of producer, medium/media produced, and subject. Also includes associations, annotated list of reference publications, review services, and other information of interest to the purchaser of audiovisual materials.

Educational Media Yearbook. New York, Bowker, 1973–   . (Annual)
Annual review of important developments in educational media field. Useful in selection for section on "Mediagraphy: Print and Non-Print Resources." Claims to do for the field of education what the *Bowker Annual* does for librarianship and the book trade.

Hart, Thomas L. and others. *Multi-Media Indexes, Lists, and Review Sources: A Bibliographic Guide*. New York, Dekker, 1975. 273p.
Includes more than 400 reviewing sources, covering both print and nonprint media. Structured annotations give bibliographic information, scope,

arrangement, special features for each entry. Sample pages are included to illustrate many of the sources.

Index to Instructional Media Catalogs. New York, Bowker, 1974. 272p.

Subject index to instructional materials, listing by media, grade level, etc. with information on producers and publishers.

Media Review Digest. Ann Arbor, Mich., Pierian Press, 1973/74 . (Annual)

Indexes reviews from a variety of journals (about 150 journals were represented in the 1977 volume) of films, filmstrips, tapes, and miscellaneous media forms. Bibliographic citation is accompanied by a symbol "assigned to indicate the general nature or overall trend of the evaluations of the author of the review." Published annually in a hardbound volume with paperbound supplements. Claims to provide 50–60,000 review citations annually. Successor to *Multi-Media Review Index* (1970–72).

Rosenberg, Kenyon C. and John S. Doskey, *Media Equipment: A Guide and Dictionary.* Littleton, Colo., Libraries Unlimited, 1976. 190p.

Thorough coverage of media equipment terminology.

Rufsvold, Margaret I. *Guides to Educational Media.* 4th ed. Chicago, American Library Association, 1977. 159p.

Annotated guide to published catalogues of films, filmstrips, records, slides, transparencies, etc.

Sive, Mary Robinson. *Selecting Instructional Media: A Guide to Audiovisual and Other Instructional Media Lists.* Littleton, Colo., Libraries Unlimited, 1978.

Classified list of 428 bibliographies of audiovisual materials, free materials, government documents, etc. on various subjects. (The 1975 edition was titled: *Educators' Guide to Media Lists.*)

Aids to Media Selection for Students and Teachers. Compiled by Kathlyn J. Moses and Lois B. Watt. Rev. Washington, D.C., U.S. Dept. of Health, Education and Welfare, 1976. 128p.

Selected and annotated list of review sources for materials "of relevance for elementary and secondary school instructional programs." Emphasizes tools published since 1970. Three sections: (1) book selection sources; (2) sources of audiovisual materials; (3) sources of multiethnic materials.

Multi-Media Guides

Audiovisual Instruction. Washington, D.C., Association for Educational Communications and Technology, 1956– . (10 issues per year)

Articles and bibliographies of special interest to those doing media selection in schools.

Booklist. Chicago, American Library Association, 1905– . (Semimonthly)

Started reviewing non-print materials in 1969 and now regularly includes selective coverage of recommended 16mm films, filmstrips, spoken-word recordings, multimedia kits, etc.

Brown, Lucy Gregor. *Core Media Collection for Secondary Schools.* New York, Bowker, 1975. 221p.

Selection of 2,000 recommended audiovisual items released 1965–1974. Some annotations. Notes items recommended for early purchase.

Canadian Materials; An Annotated Critical Bibliography for Canadian Schools and Libraries. Ottawa, Canadian Library Association, 1971–
(3 issues per year)

Signed annotations by librarians and teachers of "material in all media formats produced in Canada for elementary and secondary schools."

Educators' Guide Series.

Educators' Progress Service of Randolph, Wisconsin, publishes annual multi-media guides with annotated listings of free films, filmstrips, tapes, scripts, transcriptions, pamphlets and chart and poster material in the subject areas designated in the titles of the guides. Guides are produced for guidance materials, social studies materials, science materials, and health, physical education, and recreation materials.

Elementary School Library Collection. New Brunswick, N.J., Bro-Dart Foundation, 1965–

The tenth edition appeared in 1976 and included approximately 9,500 recommended books, periodicals, filmstrips, transparencies, etc. About 1,500 of the items were non-print. Annotations are included and there is a system for indicating which titles are considered to be necessary in a beginning elementary school collection. Revised and up-dated regularly.

Greene, Ellin and Madalynne Schoenfeld. *Multimedia Approach to Children's Literature.* 2d ed. Chicago, American Library Association, 1977. 206p.

Annotates more than 500 children's books and lists 16mm films, filmstrips, and audio recordings based on the books.

Johnson, Harry A. *Ethnic American Minorities: A Guide to Media and Materials.* New York, Bowker, 1976. 304p.

Covers all kinds of non-book media "relevant to the needs of minority groups." Four chapters on major ethnic groups and one on all other groups include essays and bibliographies.

Learning Directory. New York, Westinghouse Learning Corporation. 1970/71–

The seven volumes of the first edition indexed over 200,000 instructional items in all media; included materials for all audience levels and for a wide variety of educational applications. Supplement (1972–73) added about 24,000 items produced in 1971 and 1972.

NICEM Index Series.

The National Information Center for Educational Media of the University of Southern California publishes several multimedia indexes which list and describe a variety of nonbook media falling within the subject area of concern. The following titles are published.

NICEM Index to Psychology.
NICEM Index to Health and Safety Education.

NICEM Index to Vocational and Technical Education.
NICEM Index to Black History and Studies.
NICEM Index to Ecology.
The *NICEM Update of Nonbook Media* (1973/74–   ) is a multi-subject update service.

Previews. New York, Bowker, 1972–   . (9 issues per year)
Started in September 1972, in an effort to include and expand upon *LJ*'s and *SLJ*'s coverage of non-print news and reviews; attempts to review new examples of 16mm films, filmstrips, videocassettes, slides, prints, kits, and spoken recordings.

Films, Filmstrips, Slides

AAAS Science Film Catalog. Washington, D.C., American Association for the Advancement of Science, 1975.
Includes annotations of 5,600 films (16mm) on physical and social sciences. Elementary to adult level.

College Film Library Collection. Editor-in-chief: Emily S. Jones. Williamsport, Pa., Bro-Dart, 1972. 2v.
Recommended films for undergraduate use. Arranged by subject and annotated. First volume (16mm films) includes about 1,900 films and the second describes about 600 filmstrips and 5,700 8mm films.

EFLA Evaluation Cards. New York, Educational Film Library Association, 1946–   . (bimonthly)
New nontheatrical films are evaluated and annotated by committees from around the country and the results are furnished to EFLA members on 3 × 5 cards.

Educators' Guide Series.
In addition to the previously-mentioned multi-media guides, Educators' Progress Service of Randolph, Wisconsin, also publishes annual guides to free films and filmstrips.

Film Library Quarterly. New York, Film Library Information Council, 1967–   . (Quarterly)
Articles about film and film-makers and reviews of films and books about film.

Film News. New York, Film News Co., 1939–   . (Bimonthly)
An important source for information about new non-theatrical films. Regularly reviews, in some detail, new films and filmstrips.

Film Review Digest. Millwood, N.Y., Kraus-Thomson, 1975–   . (Quarterly)
Cites reviews from more than 20 American, Canadian, and British publications of "300–400 feature films that open in the United States each year." Basic information on films and quotations from reviews. Alphabetical by title.

Gaffney, Maureen. *More Films Kids Like.* Chicago, American Library Association, 1977. 159p.

Annotates 200 films. Companion volume to Susan Rice's *Films Kids Like.*

Landers Film Reviews. Los Angeles, Landers Associates, 1956–   (9 issues per year)

Reviews new 16mm films and lists new filmstrips and slides. In format and audience this publication is similar to *Kirkus Reviews* for books.

Limbacher, James L. *Feature Films on 8mm and 16mm; A Directory of Feature Films Available for Rental, Sale, and Lease in the United States.* 5th ed. New York, Bowker, 1977.

Films (both silent and sound) of more than 45 minutes duration (or more than one reel) are included. Includes more than 15,000 films and compiler estimates that nearly 95 per cent of all feature films generally available in this country are listed.

New York Library Association. *Films for Young Adults: A Selected List and Guide to Programming.* New York, 1970. 54p.

Selected and annotated list of films that have been used and accepted by young adults.

New York Library Association. Children's and Young Adult Services Section. *Films for Children: A Selected List.* 3d ed. New York, 1972. 32p.

Annotated list of films "which children have seen and enjoyed over a period of years." Subject index.

NICEM Index Series.

The National Information Center for Educational Media of the University of Southern California publishes several indexes which list and describe media in film format. These indexes claim to include more entries for each of the formats covered than any of the other tools discussed here, but not all of the items listed in the NICEM indexes are still easily available. Distributors must be contacted for the latest information and prices. The following indexes are published.

NICEM Index to 16mm Educational Films.
NICEM Index to 35 mm Filmstrips.
NICEM Index to 8mm Motion Cartridges.
NICEM Index to Overhead Transparencies.
NICEM Index to Educational Slides.

The *NICEM Update of Nonbook Media.* (1973/74–   ) is a multi-subject update service.

Rice, Susan. *Films Kids Like.* Chicago, American Library Association, 1973. 150p.

Annotates 200 films selected for ages 2–12.

Science Books and Films; The Quarterly Review. Washington, D.C., American Association for the Advancement of Science, 1975–   . (Quarterly)

Critical reviews of books and 16mm films on pure and applied sciences, aimed at the student—elementary, secondary, junior college—and the adult nonspecialist. Annual author and film source index.

Sightlines. New York, Educational Film Library Association, 1967–
(Bimonthly)
Often has subject-oriented groupings of critical annotations. Also carries general articles on new developments in educational uses of film.

Recordings

American Record Guide. New York, 1935–   (Monthly)
Detailed reviews of new records, stereo tapes and books on music. Tends to emphasize classical music. Indexed in *Notes*.

Annual Index to Popular Music Record Reviews. Metuchen, N.J., Scarecrow Press, 1972–   . (Annual)
Indexes reviews in approximately 60 American, Canadian, and British journals. The 1976 volume carried more than 12,000 reviews of 5,586 individual records.

Educators Guide to Free Audio and Video Materials. Randolph, Wis.,
Educators' Progress Service, 1955–
Annual annotated listing, aimed at the needs of teachers.

Gray, Michael and Gerald Gibson. *Bibliography of Discographies.* New
York, Bowker, 1977–
Volume one covers classical music and lists more than 3,000 "discographies appearing in American, European, and Russian publications from 1925 through 1975." Four additional volumes, to cover jazz, popular music, ethnic music, etc., have been announced.

Halsey, Richard S. *Classical Music Recordings for Home and Library.* Chicago, American Library Association, 1976. 340p.
Approximately 4,000 entries, coded by listening level.

High Fidelity. *Records in Review.* Great Barrington, Mass., Wyeth Press,
1955–
Annual compilation of the reviews of new recordings of classical and semiclassical music which appeared in the previous year's edition of *High Fidelity*.

NICEM Index Series.
Multimedia and film indexes published by the National Information Center for Educational Media of the University of Southern California have been listed previously. The NICEM series also includes the following titles:
NICEM Index to Educational Audio Tapes.
NICEM Index to Educational Video Tapes.
NICEM Index to Educational Records.
Similar to the other NICEM Indexes in scope and format, the above indexes are also updated by the *NICEM Update of Nonbook Media*.

National Center for Audio Tapes. *Catalog.* Boulder, Colo., 1970–
   Annotated subject list of available tapes suitable for curriculum use.

New York Library Association. Children and Young Adult Services Section.
   Recordings for Children; A Selected List of Records and Cassettes. 3d ed.
   New York, 1972. 40p.
   Annotated, recommended list of about 200 non-musical and about 300
musical recordings.

Notes. Music Library Association, 1947–   . (Quarterly)
   In addition to general articles on music librarianship, reviews of books
about music, and reviews of scores, this journal regularly contains an index to
current record reviews found in 18 U.S. and British publications.

Schwann-1 Record and Tape Guide. Boston, 1949–   . (Monthly)
   Furnishes "in-print" information for about 45,000 stereo LP records,
8-track cartridge tapes and cassette tapes. Covers the range of music from
classical to electronic. *Schwann-2 Record and Tape Guide* (semiannual) lists
monaural records, as well as imports and a few other low-demand categories.
There is also a special (annual since 1965) guide for children's records and
tapes.

Stereo Review. Chicago, Ziff-Davis, 1958–   . (Monthly)
   Reviews new records and tapes and new equipment; also contains articles on compositions and performers. Indexed in *Notes.*

Microforms

Dodson, Suzanne. *Microform Research Collections: A Guide.* Westport, Conn.,
   Microform Review, 1977.
   Describes contents and indexes of 200 microform collections; interna-
tional coverage.

Guide to Microforms in Print. Westport, Conn., Microform Review,
   1961–   .
   Annual alphabetical listing of microform publications offered for sale.
Now incorporates *International Microforms in Print.*

Microform Review. Westport, Conn., Microform Review, 1972–   (Bimonthly)
   Contains critical and detailed reviews of new microform projects, as
well as reviews of new books and citations to recent articles on the subject of
micropublishing. Index to first five volumes (1972–1976) has been published,
with a special subject index to reviews.

Micrographics Equipment Review. Westport, Conn., Microform Review,
   1976–   . (Quarterly)
   Thorough reviews of micrographics equipment.

Microlist. Westport, Conn., Microform Review, 1977   (Quarterly)
   International listing of new micropublications.

Micropublishers' Trade List Annual. Westport, Conn., Microform Review, 1975–
    Catalogues of micropublishers (on microfiche in a looseleaf binder). International coverage. Annual.

Subject Guide to Microforms in Print. Westport, Conn., Microform Review, 1962/63–
    Annual subject listing of publications in *Guide to Microforms in Print.*

Maps

International Maps and Atlases in Print. 2d ed. New York, Bowker, 1976. 866p.
    Complete information on more than 15,000 maps and atlases.

Wise, Donald A. "Selected Geographical and Cartographical Serials Containing Lists and/or Reviews of Current Maps and Atlases." SLA Geography and Map Division *Bulletin,* no. 102:42–45, December 1975.
    Brief annotations.

Serials

Association of College and Research Libraries. Community and Junior College Libraries Section. *Vocational-Technical Periodicals for Community College Libraries.* Rev. ed. Middletown, Conn., Choice, 1976. 44p.
    List represents the combined holdings of nearly 100 community college libraries; arranged under seven broad subject areas.

Ayer Directory of Publications. Philadelphia, Ayer Press, 1880–   .
    Subtitle: "The Professional's Directory of Print Media Published in the U.S.; Puerto Rico; Dominion of Canada; Bahamas; Bermuda; the Republics of Panama and the Philippines." This standard directory covers daily and weekly newspapers, college and university newspapers, religious newspapers and magazines, trade journals, etc.

Canadian Serials Directory/Répertoire des publications seriées canadiennes. 2d ed. Toronto, University of Toronto Press, 1977.
    Provides bibliographic information on more than 4,000 English and French language Canadian periodicals.

Current Australian Serials. Canberra, National Library of Australia. 1963–
    Annotated selection of "serials currently published in or relating to Australia, its Territories and Papua New Guinea." Ninth edition (1975) lists more than 3,500 entries.

Farber, Evan Ira. *Classified List of Periodicals for the College Library.* 5th ed. Westwood, Mass., Faxon, 1972. 449p.
    Detailed annotations of over one thousand periodical titles (published before 1969) considered to be important for a liberal arts college collection.

Farber, Evan Ira and others. "Periodicals for College Libraries." *Choice.*
Most issues of *Choice* carry this column which reviews new periodicals of possible interest to academic libraries.

International Directory of Little Magazines and Small Presses. Paradise, Calif., Dustbooks, 1965–   .
Detailed descriptions of both presses and magazines. Annual. Supplemented by the same publisher's annual *Directory of Small Magazines/Press Editors and Publishers.*

Irregular Serials and Annuals; An International Directory. New York, Bowker, 1967–   .
Bibliographic information on "serials, annuals, continuations, conference proceedings, and other publications from all over the world issued irregularly or less frequently than twice a year." Fifth edition (1978–1979) covered approximately 32,000 entries.

Katz, William. "Magazines." *Library Journal.*
Critical reviews of a wide variety of new periodicals have appeared once a month since this column became a regular *LJ* feature in January 1967. An index to the titles reviewed in the column during its first five years was published in the first issue of *Reference Services Review,* January/March 1973.

Katz, William and Berry Gargal. *Magazines for Libraries.* 2d ed. New York, Bowker, 1972. 822p. Supplement, 1974, 328p.
Annotated list of approximately 4,500 periodicals considered suitable for the general reader. Comments on the value of each periodical for a particular type of library are usually included. Supplement adds approximately 1,800 periodicals. A third edition was announced for publication in late 1978.

Muller, Robert H. and others. *From Radical Left to Extreme Right; A Bibliography of Current Periodicals of Protest, Controversy, Advocacy, or Dissent, with Dispassionate Content—Summaries to Guide Librarians and Other Educators through the Polemic Fringe.* 2d ed. Vol. 1: Ann Arbor, Mich., Campus Publishers, 1970. 510p. Vol. 2: Metuchen, N.J., Scarecrow Press, 1972. 504p. Vol. 3: Metuchen, N.J., Scarecrow Press, 1976. 762p.
Detailed annotations (incorporating much information from the editors of the individual publications) of more than a thousand often controversial periodicals (per volume).

New Serial Titles 1950–1970; Subject Guide. New York, Bowker, 1975. 2v.
Approximately 220,000 titles are arranged under 250 subject headings, with 1,200 cross references.

Richardson, Selma K. *Periodicals for School Media Programs.* 2d ed. Chicago, American Library Association, 1978. 397p.
Annotations of more than 500 periodicals for grades K–12. Includes foreign and ethnic publications.

Serials Review. Ann Arbor, Mich., Pierian Press, 1975–   . (Quarterly)
Reviews of new serials, as well as articles and columns on various aspects of serial librarianship.

Small Press Review. Paradise, Calif., Dustbooks, 1966–   . (Monthly)
Lists new publications of small presses and little magazines and includes reviews (200 words or less) of small press titles.

Sources of Serials: An International Publisher and Corporate Author Directory. New York, Bowker, 1977–
Covers all serials listed in *Ulrich's International Periodicals Directory, Irregular Serials and Annuals,* and *Ulrich's Quarterly.* Arranged first by country and then alphabetically by publisher or corporate author.

Ulrich's International Periodicals Directory. New York, Bowker, 1932–
The seventeenth edition (1977–78) furnished a subject approach, with bibliographic information and some information on circulation, indexing, etc., to about 60,000 publications issued more often than once a year. For serials issued irregularly or not more than twice a year, see *Irregular Serials and Annuals; An International Directory.*

Ulrich's Quarterly; A Supplement to Ulrich's International Periodicals Directory and Irregular Serials and Annuals. New York, Bowker, 1977–   . (Quarterly)
Updated information on new serial titles, title changes and cessations.

Woodworth, David P. *Guide to Current British Journals.* 2d ed. London, Library Association, 1973. 2v.
Subject arrangement with complete descriptions of more than 4,500 journals.

Yannarella, Philip A. and Rao Aluri. *U.S. Government Scientific and Technical Periodicals,* Metuchen, N.J., Scarecrow Press, 1976, 263p.
Describes more than 250 scientific and technical periodicals published by U.S. government agencies or federal contractors and grantees. Includes primary journals, review serials, indexing and abstracting services, and newsletters. Emphasizes such topics as oceanography, meteorology, public health, and conservation of natural resources.

Pamphlets

Bulletin of the Public Affairs Information Service. New York, 1915–
(Weekly)
Index to information on economic, social, and political affairs selected from periodicals, papers, books, government documents, and typewritten and mimeographed materials, published in English throughout the world. Often includes items suitable for the pamphlet collection.

Elementary Teachers' Guide to Free Curriculum Materials. Randolph, Wis., Educators' Progress Service, 1944–
Annual revisions keep this source of free printed material for teachers and librarians up to date. See Educators' Progress Service's multi-media subject guides for another approach to free pamphlets.

Free and Inexpensive Learning Materials. Nashville, George Peabody College for Teachers, 1941–   .

Biennial, annotated listing of current, factual materials available on subjects generally taught in elementary and secondary schools.

Information for Everyday Survival: What You Need and Where to Get It. Edited by Priscilla Gotsick and others. Chicago, American Library Association, 1976. 403p.

Annotations of free and inexpensive materials are arranged under thirteen categories such as aging, children, etc.

Vertical File Index. New York, Wilson, 1932/34–   . (Monthly)

Subject listing of new pamphlets, leaflets, etc. considered to be of possible interest in school, college, public, and business libraries. Title index follows the subject index.

BIBLIOGRAPHY

American Library Association. Children's Services Division. Toys, Games, and Realia Evaluation Committee. "Realia in the Library." *Booklist,* 73:671–674, January 1, 1977. Rationale and examples.

Anderson, Ronald H. *Selecting and Developing Media for Instruction.* New York, Van Nostrand Reinhold, 1976. 138p.

Andrew, J. R. *Non-Book Materials and the Librarian: A Select Bibliography.* 3d ed. rev. London, Aslib, 1972. 59p.

Aungle, Ann. "Non-Print Media." In *Libraries in Higher Education: The User Approach to Service,* edited by John Cowley, pp. 65–82. London, Clive Bingley, 1975.

Boyle, Deirdre. *Expanding Media.* Phoenix, Ariz., Oryx Press, 1977. 343p. Reprints more than forty articles published since 1969 on nonprint media in libraries.

Brown, James W. *New Media in Public Libraries: A Survey of Current Practice.* New York, Jeffrey Norton; Syracuse, N.Y., Gaylord, 1976. 218p.

Brown, James W. *Public Libraries and New Media: A Review and References.* ERIC Clearinghouse on Information Resources, 1975. 39p. Arranged by medium and annotated.

Cabeceiras, James. *The Multimedia Library; Materials Selection and Use.* New York, Academic Press, 1978. 275p. Covers most forms of media; intended for all types of libraries.

Cassata, Mary B. "Selected References on the Acquisition, Organization, and Dissemination of Nonprint Media in Academic Libraries." In *Nonprint Media in Academic Libraries,* edited by Pearce S. Grove, pp. 189–213. Chicago, American Library Association, 1975. (ACRL Publications in Librarianship No. 34)

Chisholm, Margaret. *Media Indexes and Review Sources.* College Park, University of Maryland, School of Library and Information Services, 1972. 84p.

Differentiating the Media. Edited by Lester Asheim and Sara I. Fenwick. Chicago, University of Chicago Press, 1975. 74p. Papers from the 37th Annual Conference of the Graduate Library School, 1974. Originally published in *Library Quarterly,* January 1975.

Eason, Tracy. "A Selected Bibliography of A-V Media in Library Literature, 1958–69." *Wilson Library Bulletin,* 44:312–319, November 1969.

Enright, Brian J. "New Media and the Library." In *The Art of the Librarian; A Collection of Original Papers from the Library of the University of Newcastle upon Tyne,* edited by Alan Jeffreys, pp. 14–32. London, Oriel Press, 1973. Essay on problems and opportunities for libraries.

Evans, Hilary and others. *Picture Researcher's Handbook; An International Guide to*

Picture Sources and How to Use Them. New York, Scribners, 1974. 365p. First section gives hints on procedures; second lists sources.

Foster, Donald L. *Prints in the Public Library.* Metuchen, N.J., Scarecrow Press, 1973. 124p. Includes information on selecting and acquiring.

French, Janet. "The Evaluation Gap." *Library Journal,* 95:1162–1166, March 15, 1970.

Gillespie, John T. and Diana L. Spirt. *Creating a School Media Program.* New York, Bowker, 1973. 236p. Appendix III (pp. 189–214) discusses "Specific Criteria for Selecting Educational Media."

Grove, Pearce S. *Nonprint Media in Academic Libraries.* Chicago, American Library Association, 1975. 239p. (ACRL Publications in Librarianship No. 34) Includes chapters on various formats (by different authors) and on selection and acquisition.

Grove, Pearce S. and Herman L. Totten. "Bibliographic Control of Media: The Librarian's Excedrin Headache." *Wilson Library Bulletin,* 44:299–311, November 1969.

Hektoen, Faith B. and Jeanne R. Rinehard. *Toys to Go: A Guide to the Use of Realia in Public Libraries.* Chicago, American Library Association, 1976. 24p. Includes criteria for selection.

Hicks, Warren B. and Alma M. Tillin. *Developing Multi-Media Libraries.* New York, Bowker, 1970. 199p. Covers selection and acquisition.

Hill, Donna. *The Picture File; A Manual and Curriculum-Related Subject Heading List.* Hamden, Conn., Linnet Books, 1975. 140p.

Hingers, Edward J. "The Audiovisual Supplier: Dealing with Dealers and Distributors." *Library Trends,* 24:737–748, April 1976. Includes both hardware and software distributors.

Kane, Leslie. "An Index to Non-Print Media Indexes." *Serials Review,* 2:73–83, July–September 1976. Annotates 14 indexes and gives alphabetical list of many of the journals covered by those indexes.

Krummel, Donald W. "Musical Editions: A Basic Collection." *Choice,* 13:177–195, April 1976. Selection of various kinds of musical scores.

Lasher, Edward B. "Evaluative Criteria of Non-Print Materials: A Compromise." *Audiovisual Instruction,* 20:16–17, April 1975. Alternative to a checklist.

LeClercq, Angie. "Collecting Non-Print Media in Academic Libraries." *Tennessee Librarian,* 27:84–87, Summer 1975. Review of a survey.

LeClercq, Anne. "Organizing and Collecting Nonprint Materials in Academic Libraries." *North Carolina Libraries,* 33:21–28, Spring 1975. Results of a survey.

LeClercq, Angie. "Why Non-Print Media?" *Catholic Library World,* 47:430–431, May–June 1976.

McLean, Isabel K. "Non-Print Materials in Ontario's Public Libraries." *Ontario Library Review,* 59:242–246, December 1975. Report of a survey.

Mill, Joy K. and Patricia Hermann. "Evaluation and Selection of Toys, Games, and Puzzles: Manipulative Materials in Library Collections." *Top of the News,* 31:86–89, November 1974. Includes selected list of producers and distributors.

Nadler, Myra. *How to Start an Audiovisual Collection.* Metuchen, N.J., Scarecrow Press, 1978. 165p. Essays by seven experts.

Prostano, Emanuel T. *Audiovisual Media and Libraries: Selected Readings.* Littleton, Colo., Libraries Unlimited, 1972. 276p. Reprints articles dealing with a variety of topics.

Public Library Association. Audiovisual Committee. *Guidelines for Audiovisual Materials and Services for Large Public Libraries.* Chicago, American Library Association, 1975. 35p.

Public Library Association. Audiovisual Committee. *Recommendations for Audiovisual Materials and Services for Small and Medium-Sized Public Libraries.* Chicago, American Library Association, 1975. 28p. Includes quantitative recommendations.

Reader in Media, Technology, and Libraries. Edited by Margaret Chisholm. Englewood, Colo., Microcard Editions, 1975. 530p.

Romiszowski, A. J. *Selection and Use of Instructional Media*. New York, Wiley, 1974. 350p.

Rufsvold, Margaret I. and Carolyn Guss. "Software: Bibliographic Control and the NICEM Indexes." *School Libraries*, 20:11–20, Winter 1971.

Shapiro, Cecile and Laurie Mason. *Fine Prints; Collecting, Buying, and Selling*. New York, Harper, 1976. 256p.

Shaw, Renata V. "Picture Organization: Practices and Procedures." *Special Libraries*, 63:448–456, October 1972 (Part I): 63:502–506, November 1972 (Part II).

Shaw, Renata V. "Picture Searching." *Special Libraries*, 62:524–528, December 1971 (Part I); 63:13–24, January 1972 (Part II). Part I: Techniques; Part II: Tools.

Shaw, Renata V. *Picture Searching: Techniques and Tools*. New York, Special Libraries Association, 1973. 65p. Bibliography of sources arranged by subject.

Teo, Elizabeth A. "Audiovisual Materials in the College and Community College Library; The Basics of Collection Building." *Choice*, 14:487–501, June 1977; 14:633–645, July–August 1977. Thorough discussion of why and how. Notes selection aids.

Topper, Louis. "Imponderable? Evaluating AV Materials for the Library." *Canadian Library Journal*, 30:487–488, November 1973. Suggests a procedure.

Wellisch, Hanan. *Nonbook Materials: A Bibliography of Recent Publications*. College Park, University of Maryland, College of Library and Information Services, 1975. 131p. (Student Contribution Series No. 6) Annotated.

Wittich, Walter A. *Audiovisual Materials: Their Nature and Use*. 4th ed. New York, Harper and Row, 1967. 554p.

Films, Filmstrips, Slides

Bukalski, Peter J. "Collecting Classic Films." *American Libraries*, 2:475–479, May 1971. What's available and who distributes it.

Harrison, Helen P. *Film Library Techniques; Principles of Administration*. New York, Hastings House, 1973. 277p. Includes chapter on selection.

Iarusso, Marilyn B. "Films for Children: Selection and Programming." *Connecticut Libraries*, 19:16–21, 1977.

Irvine, Betty Jo. "Slide Collections in Art Libraries." *College and Research Libraries*, 30:443–445, September 1969.

Irvine, Betty Jo. *Slide Libraries: A Guide for Academic Institutions and Museums*. Littleton, Colo., Libraries Unlimited, 1974. 219p. Chapter 4 covers acquisitions.

Jones, Emily S. *Manual on Film Evaluation*. New York, Educational Film Library Association, 1967. 32p.

Lennox, Tom. "Slides Acquisitions; A Media Librarian's Problem." *Previews*, 1:5–11, November 1972. Examples of what's available and who produces it.

Palmer, Joseph W. "Widely Owned Films in Public Libraries." *Illinois Libraries*, 56:221–226, March 1974. Lists films and where they were reviewed.

Rehrauer, George. *Film User's Handbook: A Basic Manual for Managing Library Film Services*. New York, Bowker, 1975. 301p.

Spehr, Paul. "Feature Films in Your Library." *Wilson Library Bulletin*, 44:848–855, April 1970.

Spirt, Diana L. "Criteria, Choices, and Other Concerns About Filmstrips." *Previews*, 1:5–7, January 1973.

Audio Recordings

Boss, Richard W. "Audio Materials in Academic Research Libraries." *College and Research Libraries*, 33:463–466, November 1972. Survey of 68 ARL libraries.

Doebler, Paul. "Audio Tapes Seek a Place in Bookstores, Libraries." *Publishers Weekly*, 203:65–68, February 19, 1973. Growth of the market for non-musical recordings.

Egan, Carol M. *Establishing a Cassette Program for a Public Library*. Hinsdale, Ill., Suburban Library System, 1974. 6p (ED 100 398)

Egan, Carol M. "Tape Cassette and Framed Art Print Collections in the Public Library." *Catholic Library World*, 46:52–57, September 1974.

Noble, Valerie. "Business Information Audio Cassettes: Their Care and Feeding." *Special Libraries*, 64:419–422, October 1973.

Poulos, Arthur. "Audio and Video Cassettes: Friend or Foe of the Librarian?" *Special Libraries*, 63:222–226, May/June 1972. Readable account of technical developments.

Rosenberg, Kenyon C. "Look Before You Leap. Tape Recorders: Open Reel vs. Cassettes." *Previews*, 1:5–11, October 1972. Explains basic specifications and technical terms.

Shaffer, Dale E. *The Audio-Tape Collection*. n.p., 1973. 32p. Subtitle: "A Library Manual on Sources, Processing, and Organization."

Stevenson, Gordon. "Sound Recordings." In *Advances in Librarianship*, Vol. 5, pp. 279–320. New York, Academic Press, 1975. Comprehensive review of the literature.

Video Recordings

Avon, Paul and others. "Video—An Information Resource." *Ontario Library Review*, 61:196–201, September 1977. Brief review of how Ontario libraries are using video.

Boyle, Deirde. "Video Art: Not for Visionaries Only." *American Libraries*, 8:349–350, June 1977. What it is and how it is distributed.

Boyle, Deirde. "Video: What Librarians Do with a Recycle Medium." *American Libraries*, 7:584–586, October 1976. Includes citations to other sources.

Boyle, Deirde. "Whatever Happened to Videodisc?" *American Libraries*, 8:97–98, February 1977. Characteristics and possible uses.

Feldman, Seth. "Programming Video: The Hardware, the Software, and Some Directions." *Film Library Quarterly*, 7:91–102, 1974.

Goldstein, Seth. *Video in Libraries: A Status Report, 1977–78*. White Plains, N.Y., Knowledge Industry Publications, 1977. 104p.

Gray, Robert A. "Videodisc Technology: Its Potential for Libraries." *School Library Journal*, 24:22–24, January 1978. Discusses systems available and possible uses.

Harrelson, Larry E. "Cable Television and Libraries: The Promise, the Present, and Some Problems." *RQ*, 14:321–333, Summer 1975.

Kenney, Brigitte L. "The Future of Cable Communication in Libraries." *Journal of Library Automation*, 9:299–317, December 1976. State-of-the-art.

Kiersky, Loretta J. "Videotape—A Library Communications Tool." *Special Libraries*, 66:383–385, August 1975.

LaComb, Denis J. "Video Technology: Its Future in Libraries." *Library Journal*, 101:2003–2009, October 1, 1976. Describes several projects.

LeClercq, Angie. "The Video Industry: Equipment, Software, and Library Applications." *Library Technology Reports*, 12:217–243, March 1976. Emphasizes equipment specifications and sources of software.

May, Jill P. "Copyright Clearance Problems in Educational Television: Children's Materials." *Journal of Education for Librarianship*, 17:149–160, Winter 1977. Experiences of one university in trying to obtain permission to use published material on video tapes.

Murray, Alice and Stuart A. Brody. "Videotape in the Law Library." *Law Library Journal*, 68:171–175, May 1975. Examples of library use.

Rice, James, Jr. "There's a Videodisc in Your Future." *Library Journal*, 103:143–144, January 15, 1978. Brief discussion of characteristics and advantages.

Simmons, Beatrice and Karl Stock. "Peter Piper Picked a Porta-Pak." *Catholic Library World*, 47:432–436, May–June 1976.
Thorne, Tom. "Videotapes for Home Viewing." *Ontario Library Review*, 59:88–90, June 1975. Brief report on an experimental lending service.
Vasilakis, Mary, "Video as a Service in Special Libraries." *Special Libraries*, 64:351–354, September 1973.

Maps

Cobb, David A. "Selection and Acquisition of Materials for the Map Library." *Drexel Library Quarterly*, 9:15–25, October 1973. Entire issue is devoted to map librarianship.
Current, Charles E. "The Acquisition of Maps for School (and Other Small) Libraries." *Wilson Library Bulletin*, 45:578–583, Fall 1971.
Drazniowsky, Roman. *Map Librarianship: Readings*. Metuchen, N.J., Scarecrow Press, 1975. 548p. Reprints of 48 articles.
Fetros, John G. "Developing the Map Collection in Smaller Libraries." *SLA Geography and Map Division Bulletin*, no. 85:24–28, September 1971.
Galneder, Mary. "Acquisition Tools and Sources of Maps." *Illinois Libraries*, 56:342–349, May 1974.
Galneder, Mary. "Equipment for Map Libraries." *Special Libraries*, 61:271–274, July–August 1970.
Hébert, John R. "Panoramic Maps of American Cities." *Special Libraries*, 63:554–562, December 1972.
Koerner, Alberta G. "Acquisition Philosophy and Cataloging Priorities for University Map Libraries." *Special Libraries*, 63:511–516, November 1972. Argues for a written acquisition statement.
Koerner, Alberta G. "The Map Room at the University of Michigan Library." *SLA Geography and Map Division Bulletin*, no. 85:33–38, September 1971.
Larsgaard, Mary. *Map Librarianship*. Littleton, Colo., Libraries Unlimited, 1978. 332p. Basic introduction; covers selection and acquisition.
Low, Jane Grant-Mackay. *The Acquisition of Maps and Charts Published by the United States Government*. Urbana, University of Illinois, Graduate School of Library Science, 1976. 36p. (Occasional Papers No. 125)
Nichols, Harold. *Map Librarianship*. London, Clive Bingley, 1976. 298p. Includes guidelines for identifying and acquiring maps.
Prescott, Dorothy F. "Problems of a University Map Collection." *Australian Library Journal*, 22:303–308, September 1973. Selection and acquisition problems are included.
Schorr, Alan Edward. "Map Librarianship, Map Libraries, and Maps: A Bibliography, 1921–73." *SLA Geography and Map Division Bulletin*, no. 95:2–35, March 1974. Classified and indexed by author; unannotated.
Schorr, Alan Edward. "Written Map Acquisition Policies in Academic Libraries." *SLA Geography and Map Division Bulletin*, no. 98:28–30, December 1974. Results of a survey of 45 larger academic libraries.
Stephenson, Richard W. "Published Sources of Information About Maps and Atlases." *Special Libraries*, 61:87–98; 110, February 1970. Describes types of sources.
Stevens, Stanley D. "Planning a Map Library? Create a Master Plan!" *Special Libraries*, 63:172–176, April 1972.
Treude, Mai. "Maps and Atlases: Basic Reference Bibliography." *SLA Geography and Map Division Bulletin*, no. 111:32–37, March 1978. Annotated.
Wise, Donald A. "Cartographic Sources and Procurement Problems." *Special Libraries*, 68:198–205, May–June 1977. Emphasizes government map sources.

Wise, Donald A. "Cartographic Sources and Procurement Problems; Appendices." *SLA Geography and Map Division Bulletin*, no. 112:19-26, June 1978. Additional appendices to the author's article that appeared in *Special Libraries*, May/June 1977. Brief annotations.

Microforms

Boner, Marian D. "Acquisition of Microforms in Law Libraries." *Law Library Journal*, 63:66-69, February 1970.

Darling, Pamela W. "Developing a Preservation Microfilming Program." *Library Journal*, 99:2803-2809, November 1, 1974.

Darling, Pamela W. "Microforms in Libraries: Preservation and Storage." *Microform Review*, 5(2):93-100, April 1976. Methods for storing and preserving microforms.

Diaz, Albert J. "Microform Information Sources: Publications and Hardware." *Microform Review*, 4:250-261, October 1975.

Dranov, Paula. *Microfilm: The Librarians' View, 1976-77*. White Plains, N.Y., Knowledge Industry Pubs., 1976. 101p. Survey of librarians conducted in 1975-76.

Folcarelli, Ralph J. and Ralph C. Ferragamo. "Microform Publications: Hardware and Suppliers." *Library Trends*, 24:711-725, April 1976. Defines terms; lists guides and sources.

Gregory, Roma S. "Acquisitions of Microforms." *Library Trends*, 18:373-384, January 1970. Brief survey of sources, procedures, etc.

Hawken, William R. "Systems Instead of Standards." *Library Journal*, 98: 2515-2525, September 15, 1973. Describes development of the "Microbook" ultrafiche system used to produce *Encyclopaedia Britannica*'s 20,000-volume *Library of American Civilization*. Emphasizes technical problems and steps taken to solve them.

Hernon, Peter. "The Use of Microforms in Academic Reference Collections and Services." *Microform Review*, 6:15-18, January 1977.

Hernon, Peter and George W. Whitbeck. "Government Publications and Commercial Microform Publishers: A Survey of Federal Depository Libraries." *Microform Review*, 6:272-284, September 1977.

Hsia, Gloria. "Library of Congress' Contribution to the Bibliographic Control of Microforms." *Microform Review*, 6:11-14, January 1977.

LaHood, Charles G. "Selecting and Evaluating Microform Reading Equipment for Libraries." *Microform Review*, 6:79, March 1977. Checklist of factors to consider.

Lynden, Frederick C. "Replacement of Hard Copy by Microforms." *Microform Review*, 4:15-24, January 1975. Emphasizes practical aspects.

Microfilm Technology Primer on Scholarly Journals. Princeton, N.J., Princeton Microfilm Corporation, 1969. 32p. Simple explanation of types of microforms—characteristics, advantages, etc.

Reichmann, Felix and Josephine M. Tharpe. *Bibliographic Control of Microforms*. Washington, D.C., Association of Research Libraries, 1972. 256p.

Rice, E. Stevens. *Fiche and Reel*. Rev. Ann Arbor, Mich., University Microfilms, 1976. 20p. Basic explanation of technical terms and points to consider when selecting microforms and their equipment.

Saffady, William. *Micrographics*. Littleton, Colo., Libraries Unlimited, 1978. 240p. Covers microforms from several angles.

Spigai, Frances G. *The Invisible Medium: The State of the Art of Microform and a Guide to the Literature*. Washington, D.C., American Society for Information Science and the ERIC Clearinghouse on Media and Technology, 1973. 38p. (ED 075 029) Focuses on microfilm and microfiche.

Sullivan, Robert C. "The Acquisition of Library Microforms." *Microform Review*, 6:136-144, May 1977; 6:205-211, July 1977. Covers tools and procedures.

Teague, Sydney J. *Microform Librarianship*. London, Butterworths, 1977. 117p. Administrative aspects of acquiring and using microforms.

Veaner, Allen B. *The Evaluation of Micropublications: A Handbook for Librarians*. Chicago, American Library Association, 1971. 72p. (LTP Publication No. 17) Practical guidelines and procedures.

Veaner, Allen B. *Studies in Micropublishing: A Reader*. Westport, Conn., Microform Review, 1976. 489p.

What Is Microprint? A Guide for Scholars and Librarians. New York, Readex Microprint Corporation, n.d. 12p.

Yerburgh, Mark R. "Academic Libraries and the Evaluation of Microform Collections." *Microform Review*, 7:14–19, January 1978. Problems and practical suggestions on selecting sets.

Serials

Abell, D. F. "Guidelines in Recommending Back Numbers of Scientific Journals for Purchase." *Illinois Libraries*, 54:231–233, March 1972.

Allerton Park Institute, 16th, 1969. *Serial Publications in Large Libraries*. Edited by Walter C. Allen. Urbana, University of Illinois, Graduate School of Library Science, 1970. 194p. Contains eleven papers.

Bell, Jo Ann. "The Academic Health Sciences Library and Serial Selection." *Medical Library Association Bulletin*, 62:281–290, July 1974. Reviews literature on ways in which core lists can be compiled.

Bolgiano, Christina E. and Mary Kathryn King. "Profiling a Periodicals Collection." *College and Research Libraries*, 39:99–104, March 1978. Methods used to gather information about a collection and its use.

Bourne, Charles P. and Dorothy Gregor. "Planning Serials Cancellations and Cooperative Collection Development in the Health Sciences: Methodology and Background Information." *Medical Library Association Bulletin*, 63:366–377, October 1975.

Brown, Clara D. *Serials Acquisition and Maintenance*. Birmingham, Ala., EBSCO Industries, 1972. 201p. Practical suggestions.

Brown, Norman B. "Price Indexes: U.S. Periodicals and Serial Services." *Library Journal*, 103:1356–1361, July 1978. Results of the annual survey of subscription prices.

Carson, Doris M. "What Is a Serial Publication?" *Journal of Academic Librarianship*, 3:206–209, September 1977. Analyzes various published definitions.

Coffman, R. J. "Microform Serials Collections: A Systems Analysis." *Serials Librarian*, 1:45–50, Fall 1976. Issues in selection of microform serials.

"Current Issues in Serials Librarianship." *Drexel Library Quarterly*, 11:1–83, July 1975. Collection of papers.

Cylke, Frank Kurt and Catherine Wires. "Periodicals for the Blind and Physically Handicapped." *Serials Librarian*, 2:29–65, Fall 1977.

Davinson, D. E. *The Periodicals Collection; Its Purpose and Uses in Libraries*. London, Andre Deutsch, 1969. 212p. British viewpoint.

Dobroski, Charles H. and Donald D. Hendricks. "Mobilization of Duplicates in a Regional Medical Library Program." *Medical Library Association Bulletin*, 63:309–318, July 1975. Operation of a duplicate journal exchange.

Durey, Peter. "Weeding Serials Subscriptions in a University Library." *Collection Management*, 1:91–94, Fall–Winter 1976–77. Cancellation project at the University of Auckland (N.Z.).

Dym, Eleanor D. and Donald L. Shirey. "A Statistical Decision Model for Periodical Selection for a Specialized Information Center." *Journal of the American Society for Information Science*, 24:110–119, March–April 1973.

Fowler, Jane E. "Managing Periodicals by Committee." *Journal of Academic Librarianship*, 2:230–234, November 1976. Selection and cancellation procedures at Bates College.

Fry, Bernard and Herbert S. White. *Publishers and Libraries*. Lexington, Mass., Heath/Lexington Books, 1976. 166p. Report of a survey of serials publication and purchase. For shorter version, see White (1976).

Gabriel, Michael. "Surging Serial Costs: The Microfiche Solution." *Library Journal*, 99:2450–2453, October 1, 1974.

Gellatly, Peter. "Cancelling Duplicate Serials: The University of Washington Experience." *Serials Librarian*, 1:399–402, Summer 1977.

Hafner, Arthur W. "Primary Journal Selection Using Citations from an Indexing Service Journal: A Method and Example from Nursing Literature." *Medical Library Association Bulletin*, 64:392–401, October 1976.

Hansen, Harlen S. "Magazines: Acquisition and Use." *Wisconsin Library Bulletin*, 67:155–157, May–June 1971. Survey of a small group of Wisconsin schools.

Hendricks, Donald D. "Interuniversity Council Cooperative Acquisitions of Journals." *Texas Library Journal*, 47:269–270; 293–296, November 1971. Procedures for eliminating duplicate subscriptions.

Holland, Maurita Peterson. "Serial Cuts vs. Public Service: A Formula." *College and Research Libraries*, 37:543–548, November 1976. Using serial use data to plan cancellations.

Huff, William H. "The Acquisition of Serial Publications." *Library Trends*, 18:294–315, January 1970. From the research library perspective.

James, John R. "Serials in 1976." *Library Resources and Technical Services*, 21:216–231, Summer 1977. Review of trends and publications.

Kamenoff, Lovisa. "Journal Usage at a Community Hospital Library." *Medical Library Association Bulletin*, 65:58–61, January 1977. Lists most-used titles.

Katz, William. *Magazine Selection: How to Build a Community-Oriented Collection*. New York, Bowker, 1971. 158p. Emphasizes selection for the public library.

Kraft, Donald H. "The Journal Selection Problem in a University Library System." (Ph.D. Thesis, Purdue University, 1971). 286p. Linear programming approach to journal selection.

Kraft, Donald H. and others. "Journal Selection Decisions: A Biomedical Library Operations Research Model." *Medical Library Association Bulletin*, 64:255–264, July 1976. Also reviews previously-developed selection models.

Mark, Linda. "Serial Review Index." *Serials Review*, 2:37–72, July–September 1976. Indexes reviews of serial publications found in other periodicals and four monographs.

Matarazzo, James M. *The Serials Librarians: Acquisition Case Studies*. Boston, F. W. Faxon, 1975. 60p. Eight serial acquisition problems.

Maxim, Jacqueline A. "Weeding Journals with Informal Use Statistics." *De-Acquisition Librarian*, 1:9–11, Summer 1976.

Osborn, Andrew D. *Serial Publications; Their Place and Treatment in Libraries*. 2d ed. rev. Chicago, American Library Association, 1973. 434p. Thorough coverage of theoretical and practical aspects.

Perk, Lawrence J. and Noelle Van Pulis. "Periodical Usage in an Education-Psychology Library." *College and Research Libraries*, 38:304–308, July 1977. Project at Ohio State University.

Perkins, David. "Periodicals Weeding, or Weed It and Reap." *California Librarian*, 38:32–37, April 1977. Cancellation project at California State University at Northridge.

Reed, Jutta R. "Cost Comparison of Periodicals in Hard Copy and or Microform." *Microform Review*, 5:185–192, July 1976.

Robertson, S. E. and Dandr Hensman. "Journal Acquisition by Libraries: Scatter and Cost-Effectiveness." *Journal of Documentation,* 31:273–282, December 1975.

Rush, Barbara and others. "Journal Disposition Decision Policies." *Journal of the American Society for Information Science,* 25:213–217, July–August 1974.

Scales, Pauline A. "Citation Analyses as Indicators of the Use of Serials: A Comparison of Ranked Title Lists Produced by Citation Counting and from Use Data." *Journal of Documentation,* 32:17–25, March 1976.

Subramanyam, K. "Criteria for Journal Selection." *Special Libraries,* 66:367–371, August 1975. Reviews pros and cons of several objective techniques for determining journal significance.

Swartz, Linda J. "Serials Cancellations and Reinstatements at the University of Illinois Library." *Serial Librarian,* 2:171–180, Winter 1977.

Tatum, G. Marvin and Marcia Jebb. "Olin Serials Selection Committee." *Cornell University Library Bulletin,* no. 200:27–29, April 1976.

Wenger, Charles B. and Judith Childress. "Journal Evaluation in a Large Research Library." *Journal of American Society for Information Science,* 28:293–299, September 1977. Study done at the National Oceanic and Atmospheric Administration Library in Boulder, Colo.

White, Herbert S. "Publishers, Libraries, and Costs of Journal Subscriptions in Times of Funding Retrenchment." *Library Quarterly,* 46:359–377, October 1976. Report of a survey. For more complete version, see Fry and White (1976).

Williamson, Marilyn L. "Serials Evaluation at the Georgia Institute of Technology Library." *Serials Librarian,* 2:181–191, Winter 1977.

Windsor, Donald A. "Core Versus Field Journals: A Method for Weeding During Changes in Research Needs." *De-Acquisition Librarian,* 1:1,5–6, Summer 1976.

Windsor, Donald A. "De-Acquisitioning Journals Using Productivity/Cost Rankings." *De-Acquisition Librarian,* 1:1;8–10, Spring 1976.

Windsor, Donald A. "Rational Selection of Primary Journals for a Biomedical Research Library: The Use of Secondary Journal Citations." *Special Libraries,* 64:446–451, October 1973.

Woodward, W. B. "The Management of Periodical Subscriptions in the Science Section of the University Library, Durham." *Aslib Proceedings,* 27:385–388, September 1975. System uses an advisory committee.

Wright, Geraldine Murphy. "Current Trends in Periodical Collections." *College and Research Libraries,* 38:234–240, May 1977. Survey of nearly 150 medium-sized academic libraries.

Pamphlets

Berner, Richard C. "On Ephemera: Their Collection and Use." *Library Resources and Technical Services,* 7:335–339, Fall 1963. Experiences at the University of Washington Library.

King, Jack. "The Pamphlet in the University Library." *Library Resources and Technical Services,* 10:51–56, Winter 1966. Pamphlet collection at the University of Iowa.

Miller, Shirley. *The Vertical File and Its Satellites; A Handbook of Acquisition, Processing, and Organization.* Littleton, Colo., Libraries Unlimited, 1971. 220p.

CHAPTER 7

Censorship and Selection

A Fundamental Problem

The basic cause of attempts at censorship of library collections derives from the very nature of our society. Democratic societies are characterized by constant tension between the freedom of the individual and the demands of organized living. It is clear that in a free society, no matter how much liberty to differ people may have, there must be some areas of general agreement or community life could not continue. We have agreed to accept many limitations of our God-given right to liberty: we patiently apply for drivers' licenses; we submit to limitations on the number of deer we may shoot or the number of fish we may catch; we accept the prescribed times allotted to the hunting and fishing seasons; we allow the government to withhold our income tax in advance; and we accept a great many similar restrictions. However much we may be irked by one or another of these curbs on our actions, we are quite passive in accepting most of them.

American society has always believed that in the area of intellectual life, as opposed to the series of actions which make up our social life, such restrictions are abominable. The concept of thought control is abhorrent to us. We shrink from the idea of subliminal advertising to sell us a product. We submit to the curtailment of our actions but rebel at the curtailment of thought. Here at least we will be free!

Libraries represent the embodiment of human thought which we respect so highly. Our feeling for the sacredness of living thought adheres to these artifacts which preserve the record of past thought. The burning of a book strikes the lover of freedom with something like the same horror as the burning of its author. Attacks on library collections for their inclusion of one book or another, or of one film or another, seem attacks on the human intellect itself. And certainly, as a general principle of life, librarians ought to stand strongly for the freedom of communication, for the freedom of intellectual activity, for the freedom of thought which their institutions represent. They ought to resist all attempts to limit the use of libraries in the search for wisdom, knowledge, peace of mind, or entertainment.

However, there is a difference between freedom of thought and freedom of expression. Society may be willing to allow us to think what we please, but it does not allow us complete freedom to communicate whatever we think. The moment thought moves out of the mind in written or spoken form it becomes action and encounters licenses and rules, seasons and withholding taxes. The law restrains us from uttering libels and slanders, from false reports of crimes and fires; it limits and restricts the products of our fertile imaginations from finding unlimited propagation.

Graphic records are thoughts put into concrete form. Society has laid restrictions on the freedom of those records to communicate, just as it has restricted the individual's freedom to communicate. The problem which confronts society eternally is simply this: at what point does a communication in graphic form become dangerous and thus subject to suppression?

This question implies that there is someone who can decide when that point has been reached and that there are measures which can be applied; that there is a calculus of sedition, a yardstick of moral decay. Unfortunately for the easy application of this necessary social regulation, democratic societies are not homogeneous. The very nature of the principles underlying freedom gives rise to a certain degree of dissimilarity among the citizens. Even in mass-production, robotized cultures, the assembly line worker is not a carbon copy of all his/her fellows; he/she is an individual. He/she may be less varied in attitudes than another type of worker might be (the researcher in pure mathematics, perhaps, building unthought-of geometries), but he/she still retains the stamp of individual humanity.

The existence of this variety leads to complications in attempting to protect the people from evil. Attitudes toward what is evil are not uniform. The old admonition that one man's meat is another man's poison certainly applies in this area of attitudes. To attempt to determine the median attitude or to attempt to measure the sum of total attitudes in a large population and then strike an average attitude appears to be quite difficult and not a little silly. Would-be censors have to fall back on guesses as to what the community feels, or they rely on their own shocked attitudes and extrapolate from them. "What dismays me," they are forced to say, "must necessarily dismay thee."

If the censor is delicate and tender of mind, he/she may restrict long before the danger point is reached. And, in any case, there will be different points of danger for different readers in the community. The censor may hit on the solution of shutting out all materials which might offend the most sensitive or the least mature mind. The basic fact which must be faced is that all the people do not conceive of evil in the same way, and that even among those who do, the thresholds of titillation or sedition vary. This is the inevitable conundrum for the censor in a free society, for the free society does not require such uniformity of attitudes as the censor must have for the easy operation of his/her rules.

There is another variation which arises. The line marking off the socially permissible from the socially dangerous is not fixed; it shifts from time to time and from place to place within the same period. What shocked or horrified the reader of 1910 may seem innocuous today. What shocks or horrifies the reader in the rural hamlet today may leave his/her big-city contemporary unshaken.

This shifting in what is considered permissible is amply demonstrated in the efforts of the courts to find some stable definition of obscenity. For some 90 years, the United States Supreme Court followed the doctrine set down by British Chief Justice Cockburn in *Regina v. Hicklin* (1868). Judge Cockburn defined obscenity as follows: "... whether the tendency of the matter charged is to deprave and corrupt those whose minds are open to such immoral influences, and into whose hands a publication of this sort may fall." The Lord Chief Justice maintained that even if the purpose of the work were honest and laudable, it did not matter: what is obscene (by his test) is obscene—and there's an end to it!

In 1933, however, enough time had marched on past great Victoria's heyday so that the Cockburn definition could be refined. In the case of the *United States v. Ulysses,* District Judge John M. Woolsey found that theretofore infamous novel not pornographic, if frank. He noted that the legal definition of obscenity is "that which tends to stir the sex impulses or to lead to sexually impure and lustful thoughts." But, he pointed out, the law is concerned only with the normal person, and thus the court must attempt to assess the effect of a particular book upon a person of average sexual instincts. Judge Woolsey borrowed a French phrase to describe this hypothetical normal man which the court would use as a test—*"l'homme moyen sensuel."* His decision was upheld by Circuit Judge Augustus N. Hand. (Both decisions make excellent reading. They are reproduced in Robert Downs' *First Freedom.*)

Thus the doctrine that all reading must be safe for the weakest, most susceptible mind was set aside. In 1957, the Supreme Court gave its endorsement to the view that the stable adult mind must be the governing factor when it struck down the state of Michigan's censorship law in *Butler v. Michigan.* Justice Felix Frankfurter remarked: "[Michigan] insists that, by thus quarantining the general reading public against books not too rugged for grown men and women *in order to shield juvenile innocence* [italics added] it is exercising its power to promote the general welfare. Surely this is to burn the house to roast the pig . . . [This reduces] the adult population of Michigan to reading only what is fit for children.''

The Court had second thoughts in 1968, at least to a limited extent, when it sustained a New York law which makes it a punishable offense to sell certain types of materials to young people, even though their sale to adults would be legal. This decision followed a decade of court decisions which seemed to be widening the area of permissible publications.

On January 1, 1968, President Johnson named 18 members to a Commission on Obscenity and Pornography, which had been authorized by Public Law 90-100. The Commission was to conduct a thorough study of the effect of obscenity and pornography upon the public and of the relationship of pornography to anti-social behavior. It was charged with analyzing the laws pertaining to the control of obscenity and pornography; recommending definitions of obscenity and pornography; investigating the methods employed in the distribution of obscene and pornographic materials as well as the nature and volume of the traffic; and to recommend actions to control that traffic without in any way interfering with constitutional rights. Frederick H. Wagman, Director of the University of Michigan Library, was the only librarian appointed to the Commission. To carry out its work, the Commission was empowered to ''make contracts with universities, research institutions, foundations, laboratories, hospitals, and other competent public or private agencies to conduct research.''

That report was released in 1970 but the results were in no way comforting. President Nixon soundly denounced it, while the Senate of the United States distinguished itself by voting to condemn it before (it has been maintained) they could have read it. It seems highly unlikely, at the very least, that any of the national figures who help guide policy ever read, or will read, the six volumes of the technical report. The hope that the Commission would cast some firmer light on the relationship of pornography to delinquency—or to general social decay—was a vain hope. The national picture remains uncertain.

At the state level, the uncertainties have been even greater, and the states have certainly not been as permissive. Many state laws are more restrictive than the Supreme Court and not all those laws have been challenged and brought before the high tribunal. Until the decision in *Miller v. California,* the Supreme Court seemed to judge obscenity by the effect of a book taken as a whole (not merely basing judgment upon passages taken in isolation) upon a mature, intelligent, and fairly sophisticated adult. Even when the book seemed pretty far out on the scale, the Court refused to condemn it if it had any redeeming social significance or artistic merit. But state courts—and certainly many local magistrates and police forces—have been less ready to depart from Cockburn's century-old definition. Thus the same old variations in judgment, feeling, and opinion arise to create continuing difficulties at the local level. The local law has now become more important than ever because of the Supreme Court's decision in *Miller v. California*.

In June of 1973, the Supreme Court handed down a decision (by a vote of 5–4) in the case of *Miller v. the State of California*. The Court announced that it was no longer necessary to prove that an alleged pornographic work had to be "utterly without" any redeeming social value. It also stated that the "community standards" by which a work was to be judged were to be the local community standards, and not some artificial "national" standard. That decision has already resulted in further lawsuits, as states and communities have attempted to re-write their obscenity laws to follow the Court's guidelines.

This case is the latest in the series which have tried to meet the problem of imposing some control on obscene materials, while at the same time securing the rights guaranteed under the First and Fourth Amendments. Because of its importance as the last major decision in this area, we are introducing the text as an appendix to this chapter.

Although it announced in October 1977 that it would clarify its meaning of "community" standards, the Supreme Court has not yet issued any clarification—as far as the authors can tell. In the meantime, state legislatures have been busy passing new laws against pornography and obscenity. Local community councils have also been passing ordinances restricting materials, assuming that as "communities" they now had the right to legislate their own local standards into law. Several state supreme courts, including Michigan's, have declared such city ordinances unconstitutional, since the state legislature had already passed legislation in that area, thus pre-empting it from local invasion. With our usual luck, we will probably have just sent the manuscript off when the Court will issue its anxiously-awaited declaration. We suggest that library school students watch the actions of the Court closely to see how it reacts to the rulings of those state supreme courts which make the entire state the "community" whose standards must be applied.

With the new stress on local community standards, all the past variations in judgment, feeling, and opinion characterizing states in the various parts of the United States will become more important for the publisher. It will still be difficult to decide what the "contemporary community standards" of a given state—a given city?—really are. The question of who defines the standards, the question of deciding whether that definition is indeed a fact, will remain to plague courts as they have plagued them before. The fact that these difficulties are real and do exist does not mean that censors will abandon their efforts. They might say—to cite the classic case, which is so often advanced in this argument—that we all know it is dangerous to cry "Fire!" in a crowded building. Similarly, we know it is dangerous to issue a book which cries its own version of "Fire!" for all to hear. It may be that panic does not ensue every time someone falsely raises the alarm in a theater. Does it then follow that laws against such an action are unnecessary or undesirable? A wicked or seditious book may not lead to social upheaval in every case, but does it therefore follow that no attempt should be made to protect society against evil and sedition?

Such a question is legitimate and is very difficult to answer. For the problem is not simple, however much we might wish it were. No matter how strong our conviction in the ideal of a free press, there is a realization in every one of us that there is a line beyond which we do not believe it is right for a publisher to go. There are films which each of us would find too disgusting, too vile, to countenance (although some of us might be far out along the scale before we rebelled). Somewhere there is a book which even the most trusting of us might consider so devilishly clever in its treason as to constitute a threat to the security of the State.

The central weakness of all demands for censorship can be put simply: the censor is sure that *he* or *she* can recognize evil—but that the people cannot. The desire for censorship arises from a simple lack of faith in the powers of judgment and discrimination of others. Other people must be protected from evil, we say, but what we are really saying is that they are not bright enough, not good enough, not trustworthy enough to protect themselves. They cannot see what we see so clearly; so we must not allow them to look upon the book whose evil is so obvious to us.

In any other area, such an attitude would be characterized as the most blatant arrogance. And for a member of a democratic society, in which the sovereign power resides with the people, such a lack of faith in the people's judgment is strange indeed. If the people cannot be trusted to read books intelligently and react sensibly to other media, what can they be trusted with? If the censor is honest, he/she just might perforce reply that, of course, they cannot really be trusted at all; they must be shepherded and guided along the right ways. This is by no means a new idea in the world, but it is truly, fundamentally, and completely anti-democratic. If we are to be truly free to choose what we wish, we must be allowed the luxurious freedom of choosing wrongly. To take the view of democracy that the people are free to believe whatever they choose, *so long as what they believe is right,* is to confess oneself no believer in freedom.

The people do not need to be protected from evil by any self-appointed or official vigilante group, because most people will not be utterly corrupted by any reading experience. Even the most normal and balanced person has moments and areas of undesirable desires, but this fact does not warp the whole personality. To say that because a person occasionally enjoys a book that is not all it should be, is only to say that we are all human. But to say that such occasional reading demonstrates complete rottenness and unreliability of the mind is too extreme a statement. The reader must make moral choices, and, while we believe that in the long run he/she will be a responsible and stable citizen, we cannot deny the basic human right to make one's own mistakes. Broadening one's horizons is not only a matter of going always onward and upward— it includes also the experience of sinking downward and backward. These regressions are a normal part of life, and the human right to err, to slip, to sin, to stumble—and to recover oneself—must be insisted upon.

A special problem arises, of course, in dealing with minds which are not wholly normal, which are particularly weak or susceptible, which are inclined to corruption. But who is qualified to pick out these minds? It must be assumed that an adult is responsible for carrying the burden of his/her own adulthood. The psychiatric or psycho-analytic treatment of the non-normal mind must be left to those qualified to deal with it. The library is not a mental hospital, and society cannot tolerate that its activities should be limited by the restrictions necessary in a hospital ward in order to give treatment to the few who are unbalanced. To restrict all sound and intelligent adults to the reading safe for the near-insane is as unsound a procedure as to restrict all sound and intelligent adults to the reading considered safe for children.

A Contemporary Problem

In addition to this general problem, arising out of the very nature of democracy, there is a further current problem caused by a change in the understanding—by some people, at least—of the meaning of democracy. There has been a tendency in mid-twentieth century America toward a more restricted view of democratic life, which might be described as a belief in the freedom to conform. We all recognize that the library is a social institution whose characteristics have been determined by the nature of the society in which it developed. What we sometimes forget is the additional truism that society is not static and that as society alters the institutions which it supports also change.

Perhaps the simplest definition of democracy which one could make would be that it is a system in which every person is equal before the law. One cannot be arrested without due process, cannot be condemned without a trial, one's house cannot be invaded without a warrant, one's speech cannot be limited except by the libel and slander laws, one's religion remains a matter of private conscience. By a simple extension of that idea of equality, one moves out of the realm of democracy into something which is really quite different, and which has been ponderously described as conformitarian equalitarianism. In its most extreme form, this point of view holds that a person is not only equal before the law, but that he/she is intellectually, socially, spiritually, esthetically, and morally equal to all other persons. Equal, in a democratic society, means entitled to the same treatment; in an equalitarian society, equal means alike.

The argument behind this system of thought is simple. Nature is a uniform mechanism; its laws are everywhere and at all times the same; the minds of people are part of that natural machinery; they too—everywhere and in all ages, like all natural things—have been alike. Why do all people not think alike, if this is true? Because of a faulty system of social training and education. If one could only reform this faulty system, all people would think alike.

The development of mass-production economies has added impetus to the belief that all people are fundamentally alike. We eat the same prepared cereals, hear the same broadcasts, enjoy the same sports, drive the same kinds of cars, wear the same kind of clothing, talk about the same scandals, value the same goods, are buried in the same way.

If this point of view continues to extend itself unchecked, the library as we have known it will not be able to survive. One of the unique features of the library collection was the fact that the reader could find books there of every complexion, could find ideas aired there which would not be disseminated through the agencies of mass communication. This function makes the library most suspect in the eyes of equalitarians, for this diversity is dangerously subversive of their conception. Censorship becomes much more understandable if one accepts this view. It is the aim of the equalitarian to discourage controversy and discussion in order to preserve essential community uniformity. To talk of presenting trustworthy information on all sides of a subject, to think of furnishing people with evidence which can broaden their understanding of a problem, to try to present contemporary issues in their full complexity violates their cardinal principle—that all issues are really very simple.

Selection in the equalitarian framework becomes a simple matter: one selects those things which are general enough and harmless enough to be handed out to the least intelligent, the least capable, the least discriminating. There is always the possibility that if one chose materials in any other manner, one of the less capable might stumble on something which would disorganize his/her simplified thinking, and so the collection must be directed at the lowest level of comprehension.

In the struggle between equalitarianism and democracy, librarians may feel few and weak. They may feel that the library as an institution makes no great impact upon the community. Let the less optimistic librarians never underestimate the power of a book; let them reflect on the fact that one of the first acts of the tyrant is to destroy books, those dangerous purveyors of freedom.

The library was conceived as a democratic institution—that is, one to which individuals with widely-differing capabilities and ambitions could come for a variety of books on every subject. To attempt to make it an equalitarian institution is folly, for it cannot survive under such a system. It could make its peace with such a master only at the price of surrendering all those attitudes which have made it what it is.

Librarians must decide whether they will set their institutions' force—whatever it may be—against the tide of equalitarianism, or whether they will permit their libraries to serve the forces of robotization. They must decide whether they will work to preserve individual thought, or help to obliterate all independent thinking. They must decide whether they will help to carry the gospel of individual freedom or sink back inactive.

The library is a social institution whose nature is determined by the society which supports it. There is nothing in this commonplace which dictates that the library must play a passive role in society. As a social institution, it has the potentiality—and librarians have the moral responsibility—to use the force of the institution to help preserve free access to reliable and unbiased information.

Some Pragmatic Considerations

In discussing the principles of selection, a distinction was made between the ideal library and the actual library in any given community. Thus far in this chapter, discussion has consisted of prescriptions for the ideal attitude toward censorship. It is easy to give assent to these principles as long as the discussion remains general. What happens to this easy assent when the discussion begins to involve an actual library, trying to function in a real community?

It has been enunciated as one of the guiding principles of selection that a librarian should know the community and select for its needs. Let us suppose that a librarian has selected something which he/she judged the community wanted, or needed, and is then faced with vehement, angry, impassioned criticism for having chosen it. Does not the very existence of this principle justify removing the item post haste? After all, if the librarian is supposed to select for a particular community, it is implied that he/she is not to select things which are of no interest to that community. Is it not obvious that the librarian has even less right to select something to which the community is opposed?

The librarian does indeed select for the community. But if this means the whole community (whether conceived of as the community of actual library users, or the community of non-users as well, who are all potential users), then one can ask, is it the whole community which objects to a given item? Does such objection not usually start, at least, with some individual or group? Is the librarian justified in removing a book or film to which only part of the community objects? Even if a majority of the users object, does not the minority have a right to find it in the library?

One could, of course, raise the legal question as to who has the ultimate responsibility for selection. An objecting individual or group could be told that the library board has legal responsibility for selecting, that the job is one to be done by those trained in this area, that the board will not surrender its prerogatives, that it will insist upon buying what it considers good. This may all be true enough, if the current law so states, but it may not be the best way of meeting the situation. Will financial support be forthcoming if the library acts in an autocratic and high-handed manner, no matter how legally correct its stand may be? Such a position might well engender greater hostility toward the library than the presence of the controversial materials themselves.

Once the issue has been joined the problem moves out of the realm of selection into that of library administration, but the fear of such a situation can be intimately connected with selection. A librarian may attempt to avoid any such turn of events simply by not purchasing a potentially controversial item, even though it might be of interest to part of the community. This might be called, not materials selection, but material evasion. That such a procedure is sometimes followed has been demonstrated in *Book Selection and Censorship* by Marjorie Fiske. A sampling of librarians in California revealed that although the librarians interviewed believed that the controversial nature of the book should not enter into selection, about one-fifth actually omitted such books. In other cases restricted circulation of these books was substituted for refusal to purchase. Fiske found that professionally trained librarians with professional association affiliations were less restrictive, although the longer such a librarian had worked in a community, the more cautious he/she became in the selection of controversial materials. Without similar studies of a number of other states, it is not possible to generalize these findings. It seems reasonable to assume, however, that avoidance of controversy would be found to some degree in other places.

Another problem is the danger of censorship by the librarian because of the librarian's own personal disapproval of materials. How can librarians maintain impartiality when they have their own strong convictions and see them violated by a book? Will the librarian who disapproved of a political demagogue buy books defending him/her? If a novel outrages the librarian's personal standards of morality and decency—assuming, for the sake of argument, that those standards were more rigid than those of the library's readers—would there not be a temptation to pass it over in silence? If the librarian is firmly convinced that America stands in dire peril of Communist subversion, would he/she not be very loath to buy films representing the Communist point of view?

When the discussion moves from the general principles to a specific item in a particular library in a real town inhabited by actual people, the problem gets harder and harder to solve easily and comfortably.

Once again, it can only be concluded that there are no general prescriptions which will enable us to achieve desired results without judgment. But the problems raised here suggest (and this moves once more into the realm of administration) that one of the constant activities of the library must be that of explaining its role in a democracy. The library has the responsibility for making clear to the community that it represents the democratic ideal of tolerance, that it has the duty to be many-sided, to give service to all of the citizens, and not just those of one particular shade of opinion. That this task will not always be easy, that on occasions it may be impossible, that sometimes it may not be worldly wise, is beyond doubt.

There is at least the comfort that the proponents of censorship remain convinced that libraries are important enough to be concerned about. They firmly believe that libraries make a difference, that they can lead to actions in the real world, and that the work done in this world by librarians is important enough to demand watching.

Realizing that the librarian cannot evade the responsibility for making decisions in this difficult matter, one begins to see clearly that the personal characteristics of the librarian acting as selector are very important in determining how he/she will react to the problems of censorship. The personality, convictions, honesty, and courage of the librarian will influence the course of action taken when groups or individuals outside the library attempt to also figure in the librarian's own attempt to select impartially.

APPENDIX TO CHAPTER 7

Marvin Miller, Appellant,
v.
State of California

[June 21, 1973]

Syllabus

Appellant was convicted of mailing unsolicited sexually explicit material in violation of a California statute that approximately incorporated the obscenity test formulated in *Memoirs v. Massachusetts,* 383 U.S. 413, 418 (plurality opinion). The trial court instructed the jury to evaluate the materials *by the contemporary community standards of California.* [Italics added by authors of *Bldg. Lib. Coll.*] Appellant's conviction was affirmed on appeal. In lieu of the obscenity criteria enunciated by the *Memoirs* plurality, it is held by the Court:

1. Obscene material is not protected by the First Amendment. *Roth v. United States,* 354 U.S. 476, reaffirmed. A work may be subject to state regulation where that work, taken as a whole, appeals to the prurient interest in sex: portrays, in a patently offensive way, sexual conduct specifically defined by the applicable state law; and taken as a whole, *does not have serious* literary, artistic, political, or scientific value. [Italics added]

2. The basic guidelines for the trier of fact must be: (a) whether "the average person, applying contemporary community standards" would find that the work, taken as a whole, appeals to the prurient interest, *Roth supra* at 489, (b) whether the work depicts or describes, in a patently offensive way, sexual conduct specifically defined by the applicable state law, and (c) whether the work, taken as a whole, lacks serious literary, artistic, political or scientific value. If a state obscenity law is thus limited, First Amendment values are adequately protected by ultimate independent appellate review of constitutional claims when necessary.

3. The test of *"utterly* without redeeming social value" articulated in *Memoirs, supra,* is rejected as a constitutional standard.

4. The jury may measure the essentially factual issues of prurient appeal and patent offensiveness by the standard that prevails in the forum community, and *need not employ a "national standard."* [Italics added]
Vacated and remanded.

BURGER, C. J., delivered the opinion of the Court, in which WHITE, BLACKMUN, POWELL, AND REHNQUIST, JJ., joined. DOUGLAS, J., filed a dissenting opinion. BRENNAN, J., filed a dissenting opinion, in which STEWART and MARSHALL, JJ. joined.

MR CHIEF JUSTICE BURGER delivered the opinnion of the Court.

This is one of a group of "obscenity-pornography" cases being reviewed by the Court in a re-examination of standards enunciated in earlier cases involving what Mr. Justice Harlan called "the intractable obscenity problem." *Interstate Circuit, Inc., v. Dallas,* 390 U.S. 676, 704 (concurring and dissenting opinion) (1968).

Appellant conducted a mass mailing campaign to advertise the sale of illustrated books, euphemistically called "adult" material. After a jury trial, he was convicted of violating California Penal Code par. 311.2, a misdemeanor, by knowingly distributing obscene matter, and the Appellate Department, Superior Court of California, County of Orange, summarily affirmed the judgment without opinion. Appellant's conviction was specifically based on his conduct in causing five unsolicited advertising brochures to be sent through the mail in an envelope addressed to a restaurant in Newport Beach, California. The envelope was opened by the manager of the restaurant and his mother. They had not requested the brochures; they complained to the police.

The brochures advertise four books entitled "Intercourse," "Man-Woman," "Sex Orgies Illustrated," and "An Illustrated History of Pornography,'' and a film entitled ''Marital Intercourse.'' While the brochures contain some descriptive printed material, primarily they consist of pictures and drawings very explicitly depicting men and woman in groups of two or more engaging in a variety of sexual activities, with genitals often prominently displayed.

I

This case involves the application of a State's criminal obscenity statute to a situation in which sexually explicit materials have been thrust by aggressive sales action upon unwilling recipients who had in no way indicated any desire to receive such materials. This Court has recognized that the States have a legitimate interest in prohibiting dissemination or exhibition of obscene material[2] when the mode of dissemination carries with it a significant danger of offending the sensibilities of unwilling recipients or of exposure to juveniles.

[At this point the authors of this text wish to introduce footnote 2, for its interesting discussion of obscene versus pornographic.—Footnote two thus follows this up-coming colon:

This Court has defined ''obscene material'' as ''material which deals with sex in a manner appealing to prurient interest,'' *Roth v. United States* 354 U.S. 476, 487 (1957), but the Roth definition does not reflect the precise meaning of ''obscene'' as traditionally used in the English language. Derived from the Latin *obscaenus, ob,* to, plus *caenum,* filth, ''obscene'' is defined in the Webster's New International Dictionary (Unabridged, 3d ed, 1969) as 1a: disgusting to the senses . . . b: grossly repugnant to the generally accepted notions of what is appropriate . . . 2: offensive or revolting as countering or violating some ideal or principle.'' The *Oxford English Dictionary* (1933 ed.) gives a similar definition, ''offensive to the senses, or to taste or refinement; disgusting, repulsive, filthy, foul, abominable, loathsome.''

The material we are discussing in this case is more accurately defined as ''pornography'' or ''pornographic material.'' ''Pornography'' derives from the Greek (porne, harlot, and graphos, writing). The word now means ''1: a description of prostitutes or prostitution. 2: a depiction (as in writing or painting) of licentiousness or lewdness; a portrayal of erotic behavior designed to cause sexual excitement''; *Webster's New International Dictionary, supra.* Pornographic material which is obscene forms a sub-group of all ''obscene'' expression, but not the whole, at least as the word ''obscene'' is now used in our language. We note, therefore, that the words ''obscene material,'' as used in this case, have a specific judicial meaning which derives from the Roth case, i.e., obscene material ''which deals with sex.''] (end of the footnote—and return to the main text of the opinion)

It is in this context that we are called on to define the standards which must be used to identify obscene material that a State may regulate without infringing the First Amendment as applicable to the States through the Fourteenth Amendment.

The dissent of MR. JUSTICE BRENNAN reviews the background of the obscenity problem, but since the Court now undertakes to formulate standards more concrete than those in the past, it is useful for us to focus on two of the landmark cases in the somewhat tortured history of the Court's obscenity decisions. In *Roth v. United States,* 354 U.S. 476 (1957), the Court sustained a conviction under a federal statute punishing the mailing of "obscene, lewd, lascivious or filthy... materials." The key to that holding was the Court's rejection of the claim that obscene materials were protected by the First Amendment. Five Justices joined in the opinion stating:

> "All ideas having even the slightest redeeming social importance—unorthodox ideas, controversial ideas, even ideas hateful to the prevailing climate of opinion—have full protection of the [First Amendment] guarantees, unless excludable because they encroach upon the limited area of more important interests. But implicit in the history of the First Amendment is the rejection of obscenity as utterly without redeeming social importance... This is the same judgment expressed by this Court in *Chaplinsky v. New Hampshire,* 315 U.S. 568, 571-72.

> " '... There are certain well-defined and narrowly limited classes of speech, the prevention and punishment of which have never been thought to raise any Constitutional problem. *These include the lewd and obscene... It has been well observed that such utterances are no essential part of any exposition of ideas, and are of such slight social value as a step to truth that any benefit that may be derived from them is clearly outweighed by the social interest in order and morality....'* [Emphasis by Court in Roth opinion.]
> "*We hold that obscenity is not within the area of constitutionally* protected speech or press." 354 U.S. at 484-485 (footnotes omitted).

Nine years later in *Memoirs v. Massachusetts,* 383 U.S. 413 (1966), the Court veered sharply away from the Roth concept and with only three Justices in the plurality opinion, articulated a new test of obscenity. The plurality held that under the Roth definition:

> "... as elaborated in subsequent cases, three elements must coalesce: it must be established that (a) the dominant theme of the material taken as a whole appeals to a prurient interest in sex; (b) the material is patently offensive because it affronts contemporary community standards relating to the description or representation of sexual matters; and (c) the material is utterly without redeeming social value." *Id,* 383 U.S. at 418.

The sharpness of the break with Roth, represented by the third element of the *Memoirs* test, and emphasized by JUSTICE WHITE's dissent, *id.,* 383 U.S. at 460-462, was further underscored when the *Memoirs* plurality went on to state:

> "The Supreme Judicial Court erred in holding that a book need not be 'unqualifiedly worthless before it can be deemed obscene.' A book cannot be proscribed unless it is found to be *utterly* without redeeming social value." [Italics in original.] 383 U.S. at 419.

While *Roth* presumed "obscenity" to be "utterly without redeeming social value," *Memoirs* required that to prove obscenity it must be affirmatively established that the material is "*utterly* without redeeming social value." Thus, even as they repeated the words of *Roth,* the *Memoirs* plurality produced a drastically altered test that called on the prosecution to prove a negative, i.e., that the material was "utterly without redeeming social value"—a burden virtually impossible to discharge under our criminal standards of proof. Such considerations caused Justice Harlan to wonder if the *"utterly"* without redeeming social value" test had any meaning at all.

Apart from the initial formulation in the *Roth* case, no majority of the Court has at any given time been able to agree on a standard to determine what constitutes obscene, pornographic material subject to regulation under the States' police power. We have seen "a variety of views among the members of the Court unmatched in any other course of constitutional adjudication." [footnotes omitted]. This is not remarkable, for in the area of freedom of speech and press the courts must always remain sensitive to any infringement on genuinely serious literary, artistic, political, or scientific expression. This is an area in which there are few eternal verities.

The case we now review was tried on the theory that the California Penal Code paragraph 311 approximately incorporates the three-stage *Memoirs* test. But now the *Memoirs* test has been abandoned as unworkable by its author and no member of the Court today supports the *Memoirs* formulation.

II

This much has been categorically settled by the Court: that obscene material is unprotected by the First Amendment.... We acknowledge, however, the inherent dangers of undertaking to regulate any form of expression. State statutes designed to regulate obscene materials must be carefully limited. See *Interstate Circuit, Inc. v. Dallas, supra,* 390 U.S. at 682–683 (1968). As a result, we now confine the permissible scope of such regulation to works which depict or describe sexual conduct. That conduct must be specifically defined by the applicable state law, as written or authoritatively construed. A state offense must also be limited to works which, taken as a whole, appeal to the prurient interest in sex, which portray sexual conduct in a patently offensive way, and which, taken as a whole, do not have serious literary, artistic, political, or scientific value.

The basic guidelines for the trier of fact must be (a) whether "the average person, applying contemporary community standards" would find that the work, taken as a whole, appeals to the prurient interest; (b) whether the work depicts or describes, in a patently offensive way, sexual conduct specifically defined by the applicable state law, and (c) whether the work, taken as a whole, lacks serious literary, artistic, political, or scientific value. We do not adopt as a constitutional standard the *"utterly"* without redeeming social value" test of *Memoirs v. Massachusetts, supra,* 383 U.S. at 419 (1966); that concept has never commanded the adherence of more than three Justices at one time. If a state law that regulates obscene material is thus limited, as written or construed, the First Amendment values applicable to the States through the Fourteenth Amendment are adequately protected by the ultimate power of appellate courts to conduct an independent review of constitutional claims when necessary.

We emphasize that it is not our function to propose regulatory schemes for the States. That must await their concrete legislative efforts. It is possible, however, to give a few plain examples of what a state statute could define for regulation under the second part (b) of the standard announced in this opinion, *supra:*

(a) patently offensive representations or descriptions of ultimate sexual acts, normal or perverted, actual or simulated.

(b) patently offensive representations or descriptions of masturbation, excretory functions, and lewd exhibition of the genitals.

Sex and nudity may not be exploited without limit by films or pictures exhibited or sold in places of public accommodation any more than live sex and nudity can be exhibited or sold without limit in such places. At a minimum, prurient, patently offensive depiction or description of sexual conduct must have serious literary, artistic, political, or scientific value to merit First Amendment protection. For example, medical books for the education of physicians and related personnel necessarily use graphic illustrations and descriptions of human anatomy. In resolving the inevitably sensitive questions of fact and law, we must continue to rely on the jury system, accompanied by the safeguards that judges, rules of evidence, presumption of innocence and other protective features provide, as we do with rape, murder, and a host of other offenses against society and its individual members.

MR. JUSTICE BRENNAN, author of the opinions of the Court, or the plurality opinions, in *Roth v. United States, Jacobellis v. Ohio, Ginzburg v. United States, Mishkin v. New York,* and *Memoirs v. Massachusetts,* has abandoned his former positions and now maintains that no formulation of this Court, the Congress, or the States can adequately distinguish obscene material unprotected by the First Amendment from protected expression. (*Paris Adult Theatre v. Slaton,* 1973). Paradoxically, MR. JUSTICE BRENNAN indicates that suppression of unprotected obscene material is permissible to avoid exposure to unconsenting adults, as in this case, and to juveniles, although he gives no indication of how the division between protected and nonprotected materials may be drawn with greater precision for these purposes than for regulation of commercial exposure to consenting adults only. Nor does he indicate where in the Constitution he finds the authority to distinguish between a willing "adult" one month past the state law age of majority and a willing "juvenile" one month younger.

Under the holdings announced today, no one will be subject to prosecution for the sale or exposure of obscene materials unless these materials depict or describe patently offensive "hard core" sexual conduct specifically defined by the regulating state law, as written or construed. We are satisfied that these specific prerequisites will provide fair notice to a dealer in such materials that his public and commercial activities may bring prosecution. If the inability to define regulated materials with ultimate, god-like precision altogether removes the power of the States or the Congress to regulate, then "hard core" pornography may be exposed without limit to the juvenile, the passer-by, and the consenting adult alike, as, indeed, MR. JUSTICE DOUGLAS contends. . . . In this belief, however, MR. JUSTICE DOUGLAS now stands alone.

MR. JUSTICE BRENNAN also emphasizes "institutional stress" in justification of his change of view. Noting that "the number of obscenity cases on our docket gives ample testimony to the burden that has been placed upon this court," he quite rightly remarks that the examination of contested materials "is hardly a source of edification to members of this Court." He also notes, and we agree, that "uncertainty of the standards creates a continuing course of tension between state and federal courts. . . ." "The problem is . . . that one cannot say with certainty that material is obscene until at least five members of this Court, applying inevitable obscure standards, have pronounced it so."

It is certainly true that the absence, since *Roth*, of a single majority view of this Court as to proper standards for testing obscenity has placed a strain on both state and federal courts. But today, for the first time since *Roth* was decided in 1957, a majority of this Court has agreed on concrete guidelines to isolate "hard core" pornograph from expression protected by the First Amendment. Now we may abandon the casual practice of *Redrup v. New York* and attempt to provide positive guidance to the federal and state courts alike.

This may not be an easy road, free from difficulty. But no amount of "fatigue" should lead us to adopt a convenient "institutional" rationale—an absolutist, "anything goes" view of the First Amendment—because it will lighten our burdens. "Such an abnegation of judicial supervision in this field would be inconsistent with our duty to uphold the constitutional guarantees." (*Jacobellis v. Ohio*, opinion of BRENNAN, J.) Nor should we remedy "tension between state and federal courts" by arbitrarily depriving the States of a power reserved to them under the Constitution, a power which they have enjoyed and exercised continuously from before the adoption of the First Amendment to this day. "Our duty admits of no 'substitute for facing up to the tough individual problems of constitutional judgment involved in every obscenity case.'" (*Roth v. United States; Manual Enterprises Inc. v. Day.*)

III

Under a national Constitution, fundamental First Amendment limitations on the powers of the States do not vary from community to community, but this does not mean that there are, or should or can be, fixed, uniform national standards of precisely what appeals to the "prurient interest" or is "patently offensive." These are essentially questions of fact, and our nation is simply too big and too diverse for this Court to reasonably expect that such standards could be articulated for all 50 States in a single formulation, even assuming the prerequisite consensus exists. When triers of fact are asked to decide whether "the average person, applying contemporary community standards" would consider certain materials "prurient," it would be unrealistic to require that the answer be based on some abstract formulation. The adversary system, with law jurors as the usual ultimate factfinders in criminal prosecutions, has historically permitted triers-of-fact to draw on the standards of their community, guided always by limiting instructions on the law. To require a state to structure obscenity proceedings around evidence of a *national* "community standard" would be an exercise in futility.

As noted before, this case was tried on the theory that the California obscenity statute sought to incorporate the tripartite test of *Memoirs*. This, a "national" standard for First Amendment protection enumerated by a plurality of this Court, was correctly regarded at the time of trial as limiting state prosecution under the controlling case law. The jury, however, was explicitly instructed that, in determining whether the "dominant theme of the material as a whole . . . appeals to the prurient interest" and in determining whether the material "goes substantially beyond customary limits of candor and affronts contemporary community standards in the State of California."

During the trial, both the prosecution and the defense assumed that the relevant "community standards" in making the factual determination of obscenity were those of the State of California, not some hypothetical standard of the entire United States of America. Defense counsel at trial never objected to the testimony of the State's expert on community standards or to the instructions of the trial judge on "state-wide" standards. On appeal to the Appellate Department, Superior Court of California, County of Orange, appellant for the first time contended that application of state, rather than national, standards violated the First and Fourteenth Amendments.

We conclude that neither the State's alleged failure to offer evidence of "national standards," nor the trial court's charge that the jury consider state community standards, were constitutional errors. Nothing in the First Amendment requires that a jury must consider hypothetical and unascertainable "national standards" when attempting to determine whether certain materials are obscene as a matter of fact. Chief Justice Warren pointedly commented in his dissent in *Jacobellis v. Ohio,* 378 U.S. at 200.

> "It is my belief that when the Court said in Roth that obscenity is to be defined by reference to 'community standards,' it meant community standards—not a national standard, as is somtimes argued. I believe that there is no provable 'national standard'. . . At all events, this Court has not been able to enunciate one, and it would be unreasonable to expect local courts to divine one."

It is neither realistic nor constitutionally sound to read the First Amendment as requiring that the people of Maine or Mississippi accept public depiction of conduct found tolerable in Las Vegas, or New York City. . . . People in different States vary in their tastes and attitudes, and this diversity is not to be strangled by the absolutism of imposed uniformity. As the Court made clear in *Mishkin v. New York,* the primary concern with requiring a jury to apply the standard of "the average person, applying contemporary community standards" is to be certain that, so far as material is not aimed at a deviant group, it will be judged by its impact on an average person, rather than a particularly susceptible or sensitive person—or, indeed, a totally insensitive one. . . . We hold the requirement that the jury evaluate the materials with reference to "contemporary standards of the State of California" serves this protective purpose and is constitutionally adequate.

IV

The dissenting Justices sound the alarm of repression. But, in our view, to equate the free and robust exchange of ideas and political debate with commercial exploitation of obscene material demeans the grand conception of the First Amendment and its high purposes in the historic struggle for freedom. It is a "misuse of the great guarantees of free speech and free press. . . ." *Breard v. Alexandria,* 341 U.S. 622, 645 (1951). The First Amendment protects works which, taken as a whole, have serious literary, artistic, political or scientific value, regardless of whether the government or a majority of the people approve of the ideas these works represent. "The proection given speech and press was fashioned to assure unfettered interchange of *ideas* for the bringing about of political and social changes desired by the people," *Roth v. United States*, 354 U.S. at 484 (1957). But the public portrayal of hard core sexual conduct for its own sake, and for the ensuing commercial gain, is a different matter.

There is no evidence, empirical or historical, that the stern 19th century American censorship of public distribution and display of material relating to sex (see *Roth v. United States*, 354 U.S. at 484–485 [1957]) in any way limited or affected expression of serious literary, artistic, political, or scientific ideas. On the contrary, it is beyond any question that the era following Thomas Jefferson to Theodore Roosevelt was an "extraordinarily vigorous period" not just in economics and politics, but in belles lettres and in "the outlying fields of social and political philosophies." We do not see the harsh hand of censorship of ideas—good or bad, sound or unsound—and "repression of political liberty lurking in every state regulation of commercial or human interest in sex."

MR. JUSTICE BRENNAN finds "it is hard to see how state-ordered regimentation of our minds can ever be forestalled" (*Paris Adult Theatre I v. Slaton*). These doleful anticipations assume that courts cannot distinguish commerce in ideas, protected by the First Amendment, from commercial exploitation of obscene material. Moreover, state regulation of hard core pornography so as to make it unavailable to nonadults, a regulation which MR. JUSTICE BRENNAN finds constitutionally permissible, has all the elements of "censorship" of adults; indeed even more rigid enforcement techniques may be called for with such dichotomy of regulation. One can concede that the "sexual revolution" of recent years may have had useful byproducts in striking layers of prudery from a subject long irrationally kept from needed ventilation. But it does not follow that no regualtion of patently offensive "hard core" materials is needed or permissible; civilized people do not allow unregulated access to heroin because it is a derivative of medicinal morphine.

In sum we (a) reaffirm the *Roth* holding that obscene materials is not protected by the First Amendment, (b) hold that such material can be regulated by the States, subject to the specific safeguards enunciated above, without a showing that the material is *utterly* without redeeming social value," and (c) hold that obscenity is to be determined by applying "contemporary community standards," not "national standards."

The judgment of the Appellate Department of the Superior Court, Orange County, California, is vacated and the case remanded to that court for further proceedings not inconsistent with the First Amendment standards established by this opinion.

Vacated and remanded for further proceedings.

BIBLIOGRAPHY

See Appendix B for some of the official statements of the American Library Association on the subject of intellectual freedom.

Allain, Alex P. "The First and Fourteenth Amendment as They Support Libraries, Librarians, Library Systems, and Library Developments." *Illinois Libraries*, 56:3–14, January 1974. Statement by a lawyer.

American Library Association. Office for Intellectual Freedom. *Intellectual Freedom Manual.* Chicago, American Library Association, 1975. 192p. Brings together ALA documents, essays on intellectual freedom, etc.

Anastaplo, George. "Librarians and the Cause of Freedom." *Illinois Libraries,* 60:112–116, February 1978.

Anderson, A. J. *Problems in Intellectual Freedom and Censorship.* New York, Bowker, 1974. 195p. Thirty case studies.

Asheim, Lester. "Not Censorship But Selection." *Wilson Library Bulletin,* 28:63–67, September 1953. Classic essay.

Benemann, William E. "Tears and Ivory Towers: California Libraries During the McCarthy Era." *American Libraries,* 8:305–309, June 1977. How librarians faced censorship in the 1950s.

Berninghausen, David K. *Flight from Reason.* Chicago, American Library Association, 1975. 175p. Essays on intellectual freedom issues.

Berninghausen, David K. "Intellectual Freedom and the Press." *Library Journal,* 97:3960–3967, December 15, 1972.

Berninghausen, David K. "The Librarian's Commitment to *The Library Bill of Rights.*" *Library Trends,* 19:19–38, July 1970.

Berninghausen, David. "Social Responsibility *vs.* The Library Bill of Rights." *Library Journal,* 97:3675–3681, November 15, 1972.

Bosmajian, Haig A. *Obscenity and Freedom of Expression.* New York, Burt Franklin, 1976. 348p. Discusses important court cases dealing with obscenity.

Boyer, Paul S. *Purity in Print; The Vice-Society Movement and Book Censorship in America.* New York, Scribners, 1968. 362p. Historical review.

Bradley, Norman. "What Do You Care What I Read? Or What Do I Care What You Read?" *Tennessee Librarian,* 27:58–61, Spring 1975. Speech by a newspaper editor.

Burger, Robert H. "The Kanawha County Textbook Controversy: A Study of Communication and Power." *Library Quarterly,* 48:143–162, April 1978.

Busha, Charles H. *Freedom Versus Suppression and Censorship; With a Study of the Attitudes of Midwestern Public Librarians and a Bibliography of Censorship.* Littleton, Colo., Libraries Unlimited, 1973. 240p.

Busha, Charles H. *An Intellectual Freedom Primer.* Littleton, Colo., Libraries Unlimited, 1977. 221p. Essays by a number of authors on various aspects of censorship.

Carnovsky, Leon. "The Obligation and Responsibility of the Librarian Concerning Censorship." *Library Quarterly,* 20:21–32, January 1950.

Clapp, Jane. *Art Censorship: A Chronology of Proscribed and Prescribed Art.* Metuchen, N.J., Scarecrow Press, 1972. 582p.

Coughlan, Margaret. "Guardians of the Young...." *Top of the News,* 33:137–148, Winter 1977. Reviews history of censorship of children's reading.

Daily, Jay E. *Anatomy of Censorship.* New York, Dekker, 1973. 403p. Censorship of sexual materials.

Darling, Richard L. "Censorship: An Old Story." *Elementary English,* 51:691–696, May 1974. Historical review.

DeGrazia, Edward. *Censorship Landmarks.* New York, Bowker, 1969. 657p.

Donelson, Kenneth L. "Censorship in the 1970's: Some Ways to Handle It When It Comes (And It Will)." *English Journal,* 63:47–51, February 1974.

Donelson, Kenneth L. "White Walls and High Windows: Some Contemporary Censorship Problems." *English Journal,* 61:1191–1198, November 1972.

Downs, Robert B. *The First Freedom; Liberty and Justice in the World of Books and Reading.* Chicago, American Library Association, 1960. 469p.

Durbin, Ann B. "Pressure Groups and School Library Censorship: A Bibliography." *Catholic Library World,* 46:119–121, October 1974.

Edgar, Jerry A. "Obscenity Standards. What Is Obscenity? What Is a Community?" *Wisconsin Library Bulletin,* 70:203-204, September–October 1974.

Ellis, Ken. "Censorship: An Annotated Bibliography." *Moccasin Telegraph,* 19:13-17, Spring–Summer 1977. Long annotations of thirteen articles.

England, Claire. "Climate of Censorship in Ontario: An Investigation into Attitudes Toward Intellectual Freedom and the Perceptual Factors Affecting the Practice of Censorship in Public Libraries Serving Medium-Sized Populations." (Ph.D. Thesis, University of Toronto, 1974). 270p.

England, Claire. "Comments on Obscenity; A Review of Recent Law Reform Commissions." *Canadian Library Journal,* 30:415-419, September–October 1973.

Ernst, Morris L. *To The Pure; A Study of Obscenity and the Censor.* New York, Viking Press, 1928. 336p. (Reprinted by Kraus, 1969.)

Fiske, Marjorie. *Book Selection and Censorship; A Study of School and Public Libraries in California.* Berkeley, University of California Press, 1959. 145p. Classic research report.

Flanagan, Leo N. "Defending the Indefensible; The Limits of Intellectual Freedom." *Library Journal,* 100:1887-1891, October 15, 1975. Criticism of ALA's *Intellectual Freedom Manual.*

Gaddy, Wayne. "The Obscenity Muddle." *PNLA Quarterly,* 39:4-9, Summer 1975.

Geller, Evelyn. "Intellectual Freedom—Eternal Principle or Unanticipated Consequence?" *Library Journal,* 99:1364-1367, May 15, 1974. Reviews development of librarians' concern with intellectual freedom.

Gerhardt, Lillian N. "Who's In Charge of School Libraries?" *School Library Journal,* 23:27-28, November 1976. Comments on the Strongsville (Ohio) decision.

Glover, Virginia. "Censorship in Indiana Public Secondary School Media Centers 1970-75." (Ph.D. Thesis, Purdue University, 1975). 78p. Questionnaire survey of librarians and their experiences with censorship.

Golden, Lawrence. "How Free Is Our Freedom." *Illinois Libraries,* 60:123-124, February 1978.

Haight, Anne L. *Banned Books.* 3rd ed. New York, Bowker, 1970. 166p. Important examples of banned books, arranged chronologically. 4th ed., compiled by Chandler B. Grannis, was announced for 1978.

Hentoff, Nat. "Any Writer Who Follows Anyone Else's Guidelines Ought to Be in Advertising." *School Library Journal,* 24:27-29, November 1977. An author's comments on pressure groups watching children's publishing.

Hepburn, Mary A. "A Case of Creeping Censorship, Georgia Style." *Phi Delta Kappan,* 55:611-613, May 1974.

Horn, Steven. "Intellectual Freedom and the Canadian Library Association." *Canadian Library Journal,* 35:209-215, June 1978.

Horn, Zoia. "The Library Bill of Rights vs. The 'Racism and Sexism Awareness Resolution'." *Library Journal,* 102:1254-1255, June 1, 1977.

"Intellectual Freedom." Issue edited by Everett T. Moore. *Library Trends,* 19:2-168, July 1970. Collection of articles by various authors.

"Intellectual Freedom and School Libraries; An In-Depth Case Study." *School Media Quarterly,* 1:111-135, Winter 1973. Several articles review, from various perspectives, the 1971-72 challenges in Rochester, Michigan, to *Slaughterhouse Five.* Illustrates who may become involved and how, when a censorship controversy arises.

Krug, Judith F. "Censorship in School Libraries: National Overview." *Journal of Research and Development in Education,* 9:52-59, Spring 1976.

Krug, Judith F. "The Curse of Interesting Times." *PLA Bulletin,* 29:250-255; 289, November 1974. Address by director of ALA's Office for Intellectual Freedom to Pennsylvania Library Association.

Leon, S. T. "Survey of the Handling of Certain Controversial Adult Materials by Philadelphia Area Libraries." *Library Journal,* 98:1081–1089, April 1, 1973.

Lewis, Felice Flanery. *Literature, Obscenity, and Law.* Carbondale, Southern Illinois University Press, 1976. 297p. Censorship of fiction.

McCormick, John. *Versions of Censorship; An Anthology.* New York, Doubleday, 1962, 374p.

MacLeod, Lanette. "The Censorship History of *Catcher in the Rye.*" *PNLA Quarterly,* 39:10–13, Summer 1975.

Martin, Sandra. "Limits to Freedom? Oklahoma's Private Values and Public Policies on the Right to Read." *Oklahoma Librarian,* 26:6–28, January 1976.

Merritt, LeRoy Charles. *Book Selection and Intellectual Freedom.* New York, Wilson, 1970. 100p. From the public library perspective.

Molz, R. Kathleen. "The Public Custody of the High Pornography." *American Scholar,* 36:93–103, Winter 1966/67.

Moon, Eric. *Book Selection and Censorship in the Sixties.* New York, Bowker, 1969. 421p. Reprints 55 articles from *Library Journal.*

Moore, Everett T. "Threats to Intellectual Freedom." *Library Journal,* 96:3563–3567, November 1, 1971.

National Council of Teachers of English. Committee on the Right to Read. *The Students' Right to Read.* Urbana, Ill., 1972. 24p.

Nelson, Jack and Gene Rogers, Jr. *The Censor and the Schools.* New York, Little, Brown, 1963. 208p.

"New Selection Guidelines for NY Schools." *Wilson Library Bulletin,* 51:394, January 1977. Guidelines on selection of controversial books. See similar news note in *Library Journal,* 101:2417, December 1, 1976.

Newmyer, Jody. "Art, Libraries, and the Censor." *Library Quarterly,* 46:38–53, January 1976. Censorship of art works within libraries.

Newsletter on Intellectual Freedom. Chicago, American Library Association, 1952– (Bimonthly) Important source for current trends in censorship activity.

Norwick, Kenneth P. *Pornography: The Issues and the Law.* New York, Public Affairs Committee, 1972.

Oboler, Eli M. *The Fear of the Word; Censorship and Sex.* Metuchen, N.J., Scarecrow Press, 1974. 362p.

Oboler, Eli M. "The Free Mind: Intellectual Freedom's Perils and Prospects." *Library Journal,* 101:237–242, January 1, 1976.

Parrella, Gilda. "Threats to the First Amendment." *Illinois Libraries,* 60:116–119, February 1978.

Pilpel, Harriet F. "Libraries and the First Amendment." In *Libraries and the Life of the Mind in America,* pp. 87–106. Chicago, American Library Association, 1977. Lecture delivered at ALA Centennial Conference in 1976.

Pilpel, Harriet F. "Obscenity and the Constitution." *Publishers Weekly,* 204:24–28, December 10, 1973. Lawyer's reaction to Supreme Court rulings.

Pope, Michael. *Sex and the Undecided Librarian; A Study of Librarians' Opinions on Sexually Oriented Literature.* Metuchen, N.J., Scarecrow Press, 1974. 209p.

"Reality and Reason: Intellectual Freedom and Youth." *Top of the News,* 31:296–312, April 1975. Four speeches which were presented at a 1974 ALA Conference program session.

Rembar, Charles. *The End of Obscenity; the Trials of Lady Chatterley, Tropic of Cancer, and Fanny Hill.* New York, Random House, 1968. 528p.

Serebnick, Judith. "The 1973 Court Rulings on Obscenity: Have They Made a Difference?" *Wilson Library Bulletin,* 50:304–310, December 1975. Results of a survey in ten medium-sized cities.

Shapiro, Lionel. "Freedom to Read." *Canadian Library Journal,* 31:296–300, August 1974.

Simpson, Dick. "Restricting Pornography While Protecting First Amendment Rights." *Illinois Libraries,* 60:120–122, February 1978. Comments on Chicago's movie ordinance.

Simpson, Imogene. "A Survey: The Influence of Censorship on the Selection of Materials in the High School Libraries in the Third Education District in Kentucky." *Southeastern Librarian,* 24:29–31, Summer 1974.

Smith, Shirley A. "Crisis in Kanawha County: A Librarian Looks at the Textbook Controversy." *School Library Journal,* 21:34–35, January 1975.

" 'The Speaker': Step or Misstep Into Filmmaking?" *American Libraries,* 8:371–376, July–August 1977. Report of the controversial reaction to "The Speaker" at ALA's 1977 Conference in Detroit.

"The Strongsville Decision." *School Library Journal,* 23:23–26, November 1976. Court case in Ohio involving censorship of books in a high school.

Tedford, Thomas. "Freedom of Speech: The Students' Right to Read (and Speak): Sources for Help in Formulating Policy." *English Journal,* 63:14–16, December 1974.

Thompson, Anthony H. *Censorship in Public Libraries in the United Kingdom During the Twentieth Century.* Epping, Essex, England, Bowker, 1975. 236p. Chronological approach, highlighting well-known censorship cases.

Tribe, David H. *Questions of Censorship.* New York, St. Martin's Press, 1973. 362p. Censorship of all types of media. British viewpoint.

U.S. Commission on Obscenity and Pornography. *Report.* Washington, D.C., U.S. Government Printing Office, 1970. 646p. Report was also published in hardback and paperback by trade publishers.

U.S. Commission on Obscenity and Pornography. *Technical Reports.* Washington, D.C., U.S. Government Printing Office, 1971. 6v.

White, M. L. "Censorhip: Threat Over Children's Books." *Elementary School Journal,* 75:2–10, October 1974.

Williams, Patrick and Joan Thornton Pearce. "Censorship Redefined." *Library Journal,* 101:1494–1496, July 1976. Attempts to distinguish censorship from the controls required by library objectives.

Willis, Susan C. "Today's Child, Yesterday's Standard: A Brief Look at Censorship." *Kentucky Library Association Bulletin,* 38:2–10, Fall 1974.

CHAPTER 8

The Publishing Trade

The publishing trade is closely connected with library collection development in that it sets the limits within which the library selector must work. Libraries cannot select materials which are not published, and thus the willingness—or lack of it—on the part of publishers to risk producing a particular item will determine what the libraries find available to choose from. If publishers do not feel a responsibility to produce quality materials, libraries will not be able to select quality materials. If publishers find that the nature of their market limits the types of materials they can produce, libraries may find that a full representation of subjects and a wide range of treatments of subjects will not be made. It is not the purpose of this chapter to discuss in great detail the history and nature of the publishing trade, but to restrict the discussion to those aspects of the trade which have an impact on the materials available for library purchase.

The Structure of the Industry

The publishing trade is not one of the giant industries of the United States. Since 1958, total sales have exceeded $1 billion per year, reaching more than $4.5 billion in 1977. To put this figure in its proper perspective vis-à-vis our larger industries, one must remember that General Motors' reported gross income in 1977 was more than $55 billion. One spokesman for the publishing industry remarked that people spend more for dog food than for textbooks and more for caskets than for trade books.

The trade was characterized in the past—and is still primarily so today—by a large number of relatively small producers. The total number of American publishers has been estimated variously. There are certainly more than 1,000 trade publishers, but, if one includes publishing agencies outside the book trade, the number would reach several thousand. If one thinks of governmental units at all levels of government as publishers, then the count would soar impressively. Of the trade publishers, only 25 produced more than 100 titles in 1955; by 1971, the

180

total had reached 117; in 1976, the total was 128. In 1955, only 313 publishers issued over five new titles that year; by 1971, 672 were issuing at least five titles; and in 1976, 821 publishers reached that level. By way of contrast, one might invoke the automobile industry, which has substantially only three major producers. Over the years, however, this publishing industry, with its many independent and small producers, has been turning out more and more books.

One of the striking features of the book trade, beginning in the late 1950s, was a series of mergers, which is altering the former structure of the trade. In the past, librarians were admonished to become familiar with individual publishing firms, to learn their characteristics, to estimate their reliability—and firms had, by and large, individual and stable personalities. It is becoming increasingly difficult to make very definite statements about individual firms, because firms are merging, being bought out, buying out other firms in turn, and generally swirling around at a giddy pace which leaves the onlooker pretty thoroughly confused. When mergers reach the hundred mark—and push on beyond—it becomes difficult to remember just who has emerged with whom. Many of the mergers are of recent enough vintage so that it is difficult to estimate what the impact will be on the character of the old firms. The reason for this development can be found in the growing disparity between the inefficiencies of the small, independent companies and the steadily rising costs of a mass production economy. As costs have risen steadily, publishers have been forced to seek the economies implicit in large-scale operations. There has been a tendency for the general trade publisher to ally himself with a textbook publisher—anyone familiar with the statistics of the burgeoning school population in the 1960s can see the reasonableness of such a move.

In the 1960s, the mergers continued (between 1962 and 1967, for example, some 124 publishers were involved in some kind of merger). A second interesting development was the invasion of publishing by non-publishing corporations which bought up established firms. Xerox bought Bowker as well as University Microfilms; Columbia Broadcasting System bought Holt, Rinehart, and Winston, itself a product of mergers; Radio Corporation of America bought Random House; *Time* cast abroad to buy Editions Laffont (France), while it also bought the American firm, Silver-Burdett, and then joined with General Electric to turn Silver-Burdett into General Learning. By the end of 1971, the number of firms involved in some kind of merger since 1960 was about 400. Mergers slowed down somewhat in the 1970s, but even in 1977 there were at least ten merger negotiations reported. (In that year the Authors Guild asked the Justice Department and the Federal Trade Commission to investigate publishing mergers under the Clayton Anti-Trust Act.)

The name "General Learning" gives some clue as to the nature of the attraction of publishing firms to outside organizations. The level of education has been rising steadily, and every study of reading has shown that the amount of reading done rises as level of education rises, other things being equal. The book market is bound to increase if an ever-increasing percentage of a constantly-increasing population goes on to college. In addition, the federal programs of aid to schools, college, university, and public libraries for the purchase of materials have certainly made publishing more attractive as a source of earnings. In fiscal 1968, the money appropriated for purchase of materials under the Elementary and Secondary Education Act, the Library Services and Construction Act, the Higher Education Act, and the Medical Library Assistance Act amounted to more than 225 million dollars. In 1972 it amounted to roughly 206 million dollars. (These figures are approximations—not accurate to the dollar.)

Still another development in publishing was the great expansion, during the 1960s, of the reprint business, reflecting the growth in the number of new colleges and junior/community colleges; the evolution of teachers' colleges to universities (with a concomitant need to build up collections, including retrospective materials in order to support the expanded curricula); the development of new programs at universities (such as the area study programs) which also demand the purchase of retrospective materials; the availability in the 1960s of large amounts of government funds for the purchase of materials; the development of new methods of reproducing books, especially since the end of World War II. The number of firms engaged in reprinting has increased, as has the number of titles reprinted—whether in traditional type settings, facsimile, or reproduction from microfilm. A study published in 1971 identified 274 U.S. reprint publishers and estimated title output of these publishers to be in the vicinity of 100,000 titles. Lack of proper bibliographic control in such a rapidly-expanding sector of the publishing industry brought problems to both librarians and publishers. Publishers sometimes issue reprints under completely new titles, leading libraries to buy unwanted duplicates. Some titles were announced for reprint publication (really only as trial balloons, to see how many order responses would come in, as a means of deciding whether or not to actually publish) and never appeared, while others were reprinted by more than one publisher. Prices for reprints of the same title varied widely, and prices were sometimes higher than the price of the same title on the used-book market. However, the severe cut in federal support to libraries in the early 1970s has apparently had a dampening effect upon this segment of the publishing trade.

Although hardcopy reprinting seems to have reached the end of its growth period, micropublishing is on the rise. Micropublishing includes reproduction in the form of microfilm, microfiche, or micro-opaque. It is used for both reprinting and original publishing. Microfiche, particularly, has become popular for the kind of scholarly work whose audience is too small to make conventional publishing economical and is used, along with microfilm and micro-opaques, for reproducing important out-of-print works. (The large reprint sets produced by micropublishers present some of the same problems of bibliographic control and quality variation as did the sets of hardcover reprints.) An interesting current use of microfiche involves combination publications which have text in hardcopy and accompanying illustrations in microforms.

Another important trend in publishing has been the enormous growth of the paperback industry. Larger and larger quantities of copies are sold, with prices moving up as "quality" paperbacks appear. In the early 1960s, paperbacks reached a rate of sale of one million copies a day. Standard publishers moved into the publishing of paperbacks, drawing on their backlists, publishing classics in the public domain, and sometimes issuing original editions of new works. The paperback market came of age when it developed its own in-print list (Bowker's *Paperbound Books in Print*). Paperbound books are now not only distributed through the old magazine stand channels (as they had been for decades in the cheaper versions), but appear in bookstores, in direct competition with their hardcover cousins. Librarians have been mixed in their reaction to the paperback blessing, but the past two decades have seen steadily growing use of the paperback in libraries of all kinds.

An interesting development in publishing has been the burgeoning of the book clubs, which have turned out to be a marvelously successful way of distributing books, rather than through the high-cost bookstore route. It is essentially a mail order procedure, and its ease has tapped a very large audience, which will buy a book by mail but may never have patronized a bookstore. The clubs have expanded from the big, general reader type (Book-of-the-Month, Literary Guild, etc.) to smaller and more specialized clubs (history, mysteries, etc.), which appeal to narrower audiences. Membership varies in clubs, running from highs of a million or more members in general book clubs to several thousands or tens of thousands in specialized clubs. According to the 1977-78 issue of *Literary Market Place,* there were 170 adult book clubs operating and over 20 juvenile clubs. Some publishers operate their own book clubs. This seems to be more common with publishers of scientific-technical-professional books—McGraw-Hill had eight clubs listed in *Literary Market Place,* Macmillan had 15, and Prentice-Hall had 26. These clubs are often aimed at very specific groups of professionals and are typical of the trend for clubs to be established for well-defined hobbies or other special interests. Even Book-of-the-Month Club operates specialized book clubs, in addition to the original general-audience BOMC.

Problems of the Industry

What are the problems of this industry which may affect the kind of books which libraries will find on sale? Various spokesmen for the trade have all fairly well agreed that the dominant factor is the rise of the break-even point, i.e., the number of copies at which the publisher recovers his investment and begins to show a profit. Postwar costs have soared for the publisher as for others, with the result that publishers are finding it more and more important to discover books which will sell large numbers of copies. Even more unfortunate, several spokesmen for the industry have asserted that—particularly because of the high cost of distribution—publishers may suffer a small loss on each trade copy of a book sold. They must rely on the sale of subsidiary rights (to movies, TV, book clubs, paperback reprint publishers) to realize a profit. There is, as a result, an understandable tendency for publishers to search for some books, at least, which will achieve the kind of popularity which will create a demand for the title in Hollywood. The book which can appeal to such a wide audience as is represented by the movies, TV, and the book clubs must have some of the characteristics of the product of the mass media—that is, it must be enjoyable to millions and must not be offensive to any large group. It may tend to take on some of the colorlessness or lack of originality in presenting new or different ideas that are too often characteristic of the product of the mass media.

This trend could have unfortunate effects in the long run. Publishers used to be able to put out a book if they thought they could find an audience of a few thousand readers. A firm would not have to stake its whole investment on any departure from the expected pattern in its publishing. It could attempt to reach many different audiences with many different kinds of books, any one of which would not have to appeal to its total audience. Printed books were one of the few places where unpopular or unorthodox or untried ideas could get an airing; such a luxury cannot often be indulged in by the mass media.

One way of meeting these rising costs, as was remarked earlier, is to form larger firms, pooling resources and eliminating duplicating and inefficient facilities. This reduction of the cost would help to meet the problem of rising break-even points. In addition, book publishing firms have "gone public," that is, they have begun to sell stock on the open market in an effort to raise larger amounts of capital. Raising capital by stock sales, rather than borrowing, reduces interest charges, but this is of course offset to some degree by the need to issue dividends if the stock is to continue to sell. A general publisher that has consolidated shipping and billing operations by merging with another firm (or two, or three), or has raised capital by sale of stock, or has been wise enough to merge with a textbook firm with a good solid line of elementary and secondary textbooks may well find itself in the position of being able to publish some of the worthwhile books for which there will not be a large market. In this way publishers become less dependent on the need for the patronage of the mass media markets—movies, television, the book clubs. It is possible, of course, that the pressure of producing presentable returns on the stockholders' investment may lead publishers to seek fewer and fewer titles, all as mass-media-like as possible. Only time will decide whether the optimists or pessimists among the commentators on the recent changes in publishing are right.

A very common way of meeting rising costs in any business is to raise prices. The book publishing industry is no different from others in this regard. There has been a steady rise in prices since the 1940s, as a check of the annual figures compiled by *Publishers Weekly* will demonstrate. This particular solution has hit libraries especially hard, because in the last twenty years library salaries have had to be increased to attract staff, at a time when library budgets have not risen as fast as library needs. A larger and larger part of total budgets has had to go to salaries. Some libraries now spend less than 15 per cent of their budget on materials and binding. While the amount available for materials has been shrinking, the cost of the individual item has been rising, producing an intensified effect.

When one considers the special interests of libraries in the publishers' product, the question immediately arises as to how much influence library demands might have on the publishing trade. If libraries represent a large part of the publishers' business, the need of libraries would undoubtedly be given serious consideration. If, on the other hand, the bulk of sales go to other types of consumers, it is clear that their needs or desires must be given primary consideration. The estimated receipts for U.S. publishers for 1976 were about $4.5 billion. Libraries' expenditures for the products of these publishers were estimated to be about $400 million.

This over-all figure is somewhat misleading, however. Although the over-all percentage of total gross sales to libraries is low, university presses and publishers of business, technical, scientific, law, and high-priced juveniles depend rather heavily on the library market. Several well-known students of the publishing industry have expressed the opinion that the library market is of real importance. It is certainly true that publishers enjoyed the increases in federal funds for libraries which came in the 1960s.

In talking about the publishing trade in this chapter, especially in regard to the production of books which appeal to large audiences versus those which have a more limited appeal, the authors have been thinking largely of the "trade" book. They suspect that when public library selectors talk about the publishing trade they more or less automatically also think in terms of the kind of book that the former Knopf firm used to publish, or the former Harper Brothers. But adult and juvenile trade books, which figure so largely in public library selection, represented less than 19 per cent of the total dollar receipts of U.S. publishers in 1976. The bulk of commercial publishing is made up of textbooks, encyclopedias, professional books and mass market paperbacks. Some writers do not use the term "trade publishing" to include the textbook, encyclopedia and paperback publishers, but the present authors feel that they belong to the same publishing world as general publishers, and they would consider publishers like federal, state, local, and international governmental bodies as being "outside" the trade, along with such publishers as societies and institutions.

There is one type of publisher which began as a producer of works really "outside the trade," but many of whose present publications aim at trade sales. The university presses began as organizations dedicated to publishing those books which make a contribution to knowledge, even though they may not have a wide audience, and even though they may have to be published at a loss. Such a program requires subsidization, either by the parent educational institution, the author, or some foundation. This original aim has not been hewn to in all university presses, however. Some have had the fortune to issue a book which turned out to be a heavy seller. Having once experienced the financial joys of best-sellerdom, there appears to have been a temptation to look for other best-sellers, rather than to adhere to the original purpose of the press. However, the difficult financial conditions of many universities in the 1970s have brought many university presses back to a more limited publishing program, one which emphasizes serious scholarly and educational materials.

In summarizing the present state of the publishing trade, one needs to recall the various types of publishers, fitting each into the proper niche. The federal government in all its many branches publishes vast quantities of material, including books, pamphlets, periodicals, reports, research papers, and a wide variety of processed materials. The state governments, the counties, the townships, the municipalities, school districts, metropolitan authorities, sewage disposal districts, etc., etc.—there are a host of local governmental agencies that publish. Societies, fraternal organizations, business associations, committees, corporations—there are thousands of publishers of material never intended for sale in the book trade. Although the bulk of much of this publishing will not be of interest to the average public library, some of it will be of considerable importance to specialists who may have recourse to the large metropolitan public library's central collection, or to a university, or to a special library. For the purposes of library selection, all these extra-trade publishers must also be kept in mind, since selection is not limited to the choosing of general books for the general reader, but includes also the selection of highly specialized materials for the specialist or scholar. In the chapter on bibliography which follows later in this book, an attempt will be made to distinguish among the bibliographies, to point out which are substantially lists of trade books only, which run to more specialized materials, and which combine both.

BIBLIOGRAPHY

Altbach, Philip G. and Keith Smith. "Publishing in the Third World." *Library Trends*, 26:449–600, Spring 1978. Articles cover publishing in Africa, Russia, Canada, India, Egypt, Latin America, etc.

American Library Association. Washington Office. *Librarian's Guide to the New Copyright Law.* Chicago, American Library Association, 1977. 48p.

Bailey, Herbert S. *The Art and Science of Book Publishing.* New York, Harper and Row, 1970. 216p. Management science approach to publishing.

Benjamin, Curtis G. *A Candid Critique of Book Publishing.* New York, Bowker, 1977. 187p. Informal comments by former president of McGraw-Hill.

Bingley, Clive. *Business of Book Publishing.* Oxford, New York, Pergamon Press, 1972. 157p.

Book Publishers Directory; A Quarterly Information Service. Detroit, Mich., Gale Research, 1977– .

Bookseller. London, J. Whitaker, 1858– . Standard weekly journal of the British book trade.

Bowker Annual of Library and Book Trade Information. New York, Bowker, 1956– .

Bullard, Scott R. "The Language of the Marketplace." *American Libraries*, 9:365–366, June 1978. Short glossary.

Business of Publishing; A PW Anthology. New York, Bowker, 1976. 303p. Reprints 45 articles from *Publishers Weekly*.

Canada. Department of the Secretary of State. *The Publishing Industry in Canada.* Ottawa, 1977. 418p. Analysis of the problems.

Canfield, Cass. *Up and Down and Around: A Publisher Recollects the Time of His Life.* New York, Harper and Row, 1971. 272p. Emphasizes relationships with authors.

Cerf, Bennett. *At Random: The Reminiscences of Bennett Cerf.* New York, Random House, 1977. 306p. Informal recollections of the founder of Random House.

Chambers, Bradford and others. "Why Minority Publishing." *Publishers Weekly*, 199:35–50, March 5, 1971.

Dessauer, John P. *Book Publishing: What It Is, What It Does.* New York, Bowker, 1974. 231p. Basic introduction; covers most aspects.

Ernst and Ernst Management Consulting Services, Montreal. *The Book Publishing and Manufacturing Industry in Canada.* Ottawa, 1970. 172p.

Escarpit, Robert. *The Book Revolution.* New York, UNESCO, 1966. 160p.

Grannis, Chandler B. *What Happens in Book Publishing.* 2d ed. New York, Columbia University Press, 1967. 467p. Chapters cover a variety of topics; written by experts.

Greenfield, Howard. *Books from Writer to Reader.* New York, Crown, 1976. 211p. Basic introduction, with some emphasis on design and manufacturing aspects.

Gross, Gerald. *Publishers and Publishing.* New York, Grosset and Dunlap, 1962. 491p.

Holley, Edward G. "Copyright: The Librarian's View." *Illinois Libraries*, 60:128–133, February 1978.

International Literary Market Place. New York, Bowker, 1965– . Annual.

Johnston, Donald. *Copyright Handbook*. New York, Bowker, 1978. Guide to the copyright law which went into effect January 1, 1978.

Jovanovich, William. *Now, Barabbas*. New York, Harper and Row, 1963. 228p. Essays by a leading publisher.

Kujoth, Jean S. *Book Publishing—Inside Views*. Metuchen, N.J., Scarecrow Press, 1971. 519p. Reprints a collection of articles on the book industry.

Literary Market Place. New York, Bowker, 1940– . Annual.

Madison, Charles A. *Book Publishing in America*. New York, McGraw-Hill, 1966. 628p. History from colonial times.

Madison, Charles A. *Irving to Irving: Author-Publisher Relations 1800–1974*. New York, Bowker, 1974. 279p. Chapters on about thirty specific author-publisher relationships, beginning with Washington Irving.

Marke, Julius J. "United States Copyright Revision and Its Legislative History." *Law Library Journal*, 70:121–152, May 1977.

Morrisey, Marlene. "Copyright: An Overview of the Requirements of Revision." *Illinois Libraries*, 60:133–138, February 1978. Comments by the Special Assistant to the Register of Copyrights.

Mumby, Frank A. and Ian Norrie. *Publishing and Bookselling; A History from the Earliest Times to the Present Day*. New York, Bowker, 1974. 685p. Scholarly review of booktrade in Great Britain.

Mycue, David. "University Publishing and Scholarship: An American Confrontation." *Libri*, 27:31–35, 1977. Contemporary problems of university presses.

Myers, Robin. *The British Book Trade from Caxton to the Present Day*. London, Deutsch, 1973. 405p.

Nash, Mary. "British Micropublishing—A Survey 1975–76." *Microform Review*, 6:342–352, November 1977.

Nemeyer, Carol A. *Scholarly Reprint Publishing in the United States*. New York, Bowker, 1972. 262p. Hardcover reprint publishing.

Ontario. Royal Commission on Book Publishing. *Background Papers*. Toronto, Queen's Printer and Publisher, Province of Ontario, 1972. 395p. More than twenty authors have contributed papers on various aspects of Canadian publishing.

Ontario. Royal Commission on Book Publishing. *Canadian Publishers and Canadian Publishing*. Toronto, Ministry of Attorney General, Queen's Printer for Ontario, 1973. 371p. Report of the commission, covering wide range of topics.

Petersen, Clarence. *The Bantam Story: Thirty Years of Paperback Publishing*. New York, Bantam, 1975. 167p. Also covers American paperback publishing in general.

Publishers' International Directory, Munich, Verlag Dokumentation, 1964–

Publishers' Weekly. New York, Bowker, 1872– . Standard weekly journal of the U.S. book trade. Important source for current developments.

Roth, Harold L. "The Book Wholesaler: His Forms and Services." *Library Trends*, 24:673–682, April 1976. One aspect of the distribution of publications.

Smith, Datus C. *A Guide to Book Publishing*. New York, Bowker, 1967. 244p. Intended as a manual for new publishers in developing countries.

Smith, Roger H. *The American Reading Public; A Symposium*. New York, Bowker, 1963. 268p. Essays cover such topics as economics of publishing and problems of reviewing system.

Taubert, Sigfried. *The Book Trade of the World*. New York, Bowker, 1972– . Volume one (published 1972) covered Europe; volume two (published 1976) included the Americas, Australia, and New Zealand. Volume three (publication scheduled for 1979) will cover Africa and Asia.

Tebbel, John. *A History of Book Publishing in the United States*. New York, Bowker, 1972– . Four volumes have been announced.

U.S. Library of Congress. Copyright Office. *General Guide to the Copyright Act of 1976*. Washington, D.C., 1977. 134p. Includes a list of "Official Source Materials on Copyright Revision."

Unwin, Stanley. *The Truth About Publishing*. 7th ed. New York, Macmillan, 1960. 348p. Classic work on British publishing.

Wall, C. Edward. "Budget Stretching: Remainder Books for Libraries." *American Libraries*, 9:367–370, June 1978. Describes operations of remainder houses and lists a few that sell directly to libraries.

Wall, C. Edward. *Remainder Books: A Background Paper*. Ann Arbor, Mich., Pierian Press, 1978. 6p. (Public Service Brochure No. 1) Outlines why books are remaindered and how remainder companies operate.

Warburg, Frederic. *An Occupation for Gentlemen*. London, Hutchinson, 1959. 287p. Emphasizes relations with authors. British view.

White, Herbert S. *The Copyright Dilemma*. Chicago, American Library Association, 1978. 212p. Proceedings of a conference at Indiana University in 1977.

CHAPTER 9

Resource Sharing

In previous chapters we have talked primarily about collection building from the viewpoint of individual libraries—determining the objectives, clientele, collection needs, etc. for a specific library in a specific community. Now it is time to consider how a library's relationship to other libraries may affect its collection building activities. We have chosen to use the term "resource sharing" in this discussion, rather than "library cooperation," because resource sharing seems to be more descriptive of the activities we want to emphasize.

The term resource sharing now appears frequently in the professional literature of librarianship and through use has come to cover a number of diverse library activities. Libraries have many types of resources—collections of materials, staff members with special skills, bibliographic records of various kinds, physical facilities, special equipment, etc. Some libraries also have the somewhat less tangible resources of public goodwill, political influence, future plans, or efficient procedures for accomplishing specific library functions. When two or more libraries agree to share collections, personnel, facilities, planning activities, etc., they are engaged in resource sharing. Resource sharing covers a broad field of potential activities, but reciprocity is important in all these activities. Each participant in the resource-sharing agreement (which may be called a cooperative, consortium, or network and probably will be identified by a catchy acronym) ought to have something useful to contribute and ought to be willing and able to make that resource available to other participants in the organization.

Although resource sharing can have many specific objectives, the two which have received the most emphasis are the improvement of bibliographic access—the information needed to identify publications, varify their existence, location, etc.—and the improvement of physical (or textual) access—the delivery of the published item or a copy of it to the person who wants it. In most major resource-sharing schemes both objectives are pursued, and both have clear implications for collection development plans.

There is some disagreement about the most influential reasons behind the current interest in resource sharing in libraries. Do librarians only consider cooperative ventures when local funds are scarce, or has the improvement of communication technology simply made possible what librarians always knew was necessary and desirable? Such obvious conditions as the rapidly increasing volume of publication, cost of new publications, and cost of storing and servicing collections appear to be likely influences. For some libraries, pressures came from the need to offer something to previously unserved users who have requirements for highly specialized materials or unusual formats (Braille, talking books, etc.). Parallel to those demands from previously unserved members of the community are the rising expectations for service from others, such as college students, who have always used libraries to some extent. In many places the availability of federal funds or foundation grants apparently has encouraged cooperative arrangements. Whatever the true cause (or causes) leading to adoption of resource-sharing plans, many libraries are being pulled into such plans and librarians are learning to adapt policies and procedures to the situation.

Resource sharing is not a new idea. Influential librarians have acknowledged the need for cooperation among libraries for at least a hundred years, but earlier efforts tended to require no adjustment of local policies or procedures. Union catalogs such as the National Union Catalog, started at the beginning of this century, and ordinary interlibrary loan, which was practiced in isolated cases far back in library history but became common after World War I, are two examples of the kind of resource sharing which had little effect on collection development in the local library. Of course, some librarians contend that the most successful resource-sharing projects are the ones, such as union lists and reciprocal borrowing by individual library users, which do not require local adjustments.

Some fairly uncomplicated plans for cooperative acquisition, some of them very informal, have existed for a number of years in many cities and some regions. These plans were usually set up by dividing collecting responsibilities on the basis of easily defined categories, which frequently covered an expensive or bulky format—serials, government documents, dissertations, items costing more than $100, etc. Sharing of bibliographic information on these materials might or might not be a part of the plan, but interlibrary loan and reciprocal borrowing privileges usually were. Most of these resource-sharing arrangements required only minor adjustments by local libraries, since selection responsibilities were ordinarily assigned on the basis of collection strengths and assumed because of local needs.

Farmington Plan

The Farmington Plan was the first cooperative acquisition scheme to operate at a national level in the United States. It grew out of a concern for the inadequacy of our library resources, when viewed from a national perspective. During World War II, American librarians and scholars became acutely aware of the limitations of their collections of foreign materials, particularly those in languages other than English and from parts of the world other than Western Europe. Serious discussion of the problem and what large research libraries might do to alleviate it began in response to concern voiced at a conference of the Librarian of Congress' Librarian's Council held in Farmington, Connecticut in 1942. Following the conference, a group began working on plans for assigning collection responsibilities to research libraries throughout the country—responsibilities which would encourage subject specialization based on existing collection strengths.

The resulting project, sponsored by the Association of Research Libraries (ARL), became known as the Farmington Plan. Its goal was to ensure that at least one copy of every new foreign publication of research interest would be acquired by a U.S. library, cataloged promptly, reported to the National Union Catalog, and made available on interlibrary loan to other participants in the plan. Although that goal appears very comprehensive, in practice certain restrictions were observed from the beginning. For example, publications from the United Kingdom were excluded because it was assumed that these were already being adequately covered. Other restrictions were placed on the types of materials to be collected. Serials (except for first copies of new publications) were excluded, as were dissertations, government documents, music, maps, works costing over a specified amount, and certain other categories. Another limitation was the voluntary nature of the plan, which meant that libraries joined and withdrew as local circumstances influenced them. During most years of the plan's operation, 60–70 research libraries participated.

The Farmington Plan went into operation in 1948, beginning with coverage of France, Sweden, and Switzerland. The next year coverage was expanded to Belgium, Denmark, Italy, Mexico, the Netherlands, and Norway. During the next two years, the participants continued to add countries to the plan until, by 1952, most major publishing countries were covered. In 1952 a regional plan was added to cover publishing in Asia, Africa, Latin America, Eastern Europe, and the Near East. The plan for Western Europe and the new regional plan differed in several respects. The original Western European plan was based on subject responsibilities assigned according to divisions of the Library of Congress Classification, covered primarily current trade monographs and first issues of new serials, and involved blanket arrangements in each country with dealers selected by the coordinating committee. The regional plan was based on geographic assignments (a particular library would agree to buy on all subjects from an assigned country), covered most forms of publication (serials, government documents, retrospective materials, etc., as well as current monographs), and involved arrangements with dealers made individually by each library.

The Farmington Plan for Western Europe (meaning specifically the automatic supply by European dealers) was formally ended in December 1972, although the ARL's Farmington Plan office, which monitored and to some extent evaluated the plan, had closed earlier. Reasons offered for the demise of the plan centered around budget restrictions in participating libraries, unhappiness with the quality of service and materials sent by dealers, withdrawal of certain influential libraries, and redundancy of the plan in view of the increasing use of blanket orders by member libraries and the inception of the Library of Congress' National Program for Acquisitions and Cataloging (NPAC). Almost from the beginning, there had been complaints about the coverage of materials by the Farmington Plan. Some participants thought the scope was too limited—that periodicals, particularly, ought to be included; others worried about the amount of ephemeral material which came through on the plan. (In 1959, a study had been made of the operation of the plan and certain recommendations made for improving coverage.) Availability of funds in member libraries had an effect on participation in the Farmington Plan. In the beginning, some libraries had accepted subject assignments out of a sense of national responsibility rather than a real collection need, and there was no strong academic program as a base for the voluntarily accepted subject assignment. Such outside commitments were likely to be among the first to be dropped when budget cutting occured. During the 1960s, many large libraries had started blanket orders for foreign materials, often duplicating and even exceeding the Farmington Plan assignments accepted by other libraries. This appeared to make the Farmington Plan commitments unnecessary, although later budget problems often curtailed the foreign blanket plans. NPAC too, although not a cooperative acquisition plan, seemed to some people to meet the objectives of the Farmington Plan in a more efficient way.

PL-480 and the National Program for Acquisitions and Cataloging

Even before the Farmington Plan officially ended, it had begun to be overshadowed by foreign acquisitions activities originating at the Library of Congress. The older of two major activities at LC was a program operated under Public Law 480. Beginning in 1961, PL-480 allowed selected research libraries in the United States to acquire current publications from some of the developing countries. (The legal base for the program was a 1958 amendment to the Agricultural Trade Development and Assistance Act of 1954 which permitted the U.S. to accept foreign currency in exchange for agricultural products and to spend the foreign currency in that country, for such materials as books and periodicals.) PL-480 first started operation in India, Pakistan, and the United Arab Republic and later expanded to other countries, including Indonesia, Israel, Yugoslavia, Poland, and Iran. Since the program depended on the availability of surplus foreign currencies in a given country, the list of countries covered by the plan changed regularly— some dropped out as funds were exhausted, and others were added. In some ways, PL-480 served as a pilot project for the National Program for Acquisitions and Cataloging and has now been coordinated with it.

The National Program for Acquisitions and Cataloging of the Library of Congress originated in provisions of the Higher Education Act of 1965. Title IIC of that act authorized appropriations to the Library of Congress "for the purpose of (1) acquiring, as far as possible, all library materials currently published throughout the world which are of value to scholarship; and (2) providing catalog information for those materials promptly after receipt, and distributing bibliographic information by printing catalog cards and by other means, and enabling the Library of Congress to use for exchange and other purposes such of these materials as are not needed for its own collections." The coverage of the acquisitions program has been more comprehensive than that of the Farmington Plan in that most types of materials other than periodicals and non-book materials have been included. Other libraries have benefited from NPAC in a number of ways, primarily through improved access to bibliographic information concerning foreign materials.

Cooperative Storage

The cooperative storage library is another form of resource sharing. Storage libraries became popular after World War II as a result of the rapid rate of increase in the size of research libraries. They relieve the cooperating member libraries of the pressure of constantly increasing holdings, and they provide a central collection upon which all members may draw for more extended research materials than any one could hold.

Cooperative storage libraries were first proposed about 1900 by William Coolidge Lane, librarian of Harvard. His proposal was supported by President Eliot but opposed by the faculty. (It has been suggested that part of its failure must be attributed to an unfortunate choice of terms: the storage facility was proposed as a place for "dead" books.) Although discussed from time to time, it was not until the 1940s that the New England Deposit Library was opened as "a regional bibliographic research center for little used books." (Which, one must admit, sounds more impressive than a storage warehouse for dead books.) Charter members included the Massachusetts State Library, Boston Public Library, Boston Athenaeum, Boston College, Boston University, Massachusetts Historical Society, Massachusetts Institute of Technology, and Harvard University.

Center for Research Libraries

The Center for Research Libraries, organized in 1949 under the name "Midwest Inter-Library Center" and located in Chicago, was established to supply midwestern universities with storage space for little-used materials. While its general purpose is similar to that of the New England Deposit Library, the midwestern project placed more emphasis on cooperative storage as a way to share infrequently used research materials. The report which led to the establishment of the Center listed four general areas of activity, three of which were concerned with cooperative purchase of materials and coordination of acquisitions to avoid unwanted duplication. In its early years the Center attempted to eliminate duplication of storage holdings by discard and to fill in gaps in the collections of member libraries by purchase, thus providing a centralized location for new acquisitions not held by any of the member libraries.

A survey of the Center's operation, authorized in 1963 and published in 1965, led to the opening of membership to libraries on a national basis, a change in name and governance to reflect these national responsibilities, and an expansion of acquisition programs. The influence of CRL has grown steadily since its broadening of membership and programs. As a central storage and lending agency, it has become an essential adjunct for most libraries attempting to meet extensive research needs.

The collections of CRL, which are available by fairly rapid loan procedures to member libraries, include such materials as foreign dissertations (if the Center does not own a requested title, it will attempt to acquire it), foreign government documents, state government documents, foreign and U.S. newspapers (another type of material which the Center attempts to supply comprehensively), university and college catalogues, and microfilms of archival materials, both foreign and U.S. Its extensive runs of serial publications form perhaps the most important feature of CRL's collections. Since 1956, the Center has attempted to maintain subscriptions to all titles indexed in *Chemical Abstracts* and *Biological Abstracts* that are not readily available elsewhere in the country. In 1973, working with a grant from the Carnegie Corporation, the Center began an "Expanded Journals Project" which provides access either directly or through the British Library Lending Division to all journals published since 1970 in the sciences (except medicine) and the social sciences (except history). The Center is also the depository for several ARL-sponsored cooperative microfilm projects.

Other Examples of Resource Sharing

The Farmington Plan and the Center for Research Libraries have involved large groups of libraries drawn from all regions, but that is not the only way that academic libraries have banded together. Examples of cooperation in collection development by small groups of academic libraries include such projects as the Hampshire Inter-Library Center (HILC), established in 1951 by Amherst, Mt. Holyoke, and Smith Colleges (joined later by others, including the University of Massachusetts) to provide for acquisition and storage of infrequently used serials and expensive sets. Ten liberal arts colleges belonging to the Associated Colleges of the Midwest (ACM) founded, in 1968, a central periodical collection which provides both joint storage and joint acquisition for this type of material. The Five Associated University Libraries (FAUL), made up of Syracuse, Rochester, Cornell, SUNY at Binghamton and SUNY at Buffalo, sponsored a study on cooperative resource development in 1970. The latest prominent addition to this list of small groups of libraries banding together for resource sharing are the Research Libraries Group (RLG), established in 1974 by the New York Public Library and Columbia, Harvard, and Yale universities, and the cooperative program announced in 1977 by Stanford University and the University of California at Berkeley.

While some of the better-publicized resource-sharing arrangements involve primarily large research or other academic libraries, public libraries were active in the development of systems during the late 1950s and the 1960s. The patterns of federal funding for libraries and the establishment, in many places, of state library plans encouraged the trend toward cooperation. By the 1970s, libraries of all sizes and types were being drawn into systems, networks, consortia, etc. Some of these cooperative schemes were single-function (meaning only one library operation, such as cataloging), but others involved cooperating in a variety of activities. Many arrangements for cooperative acquisition and improved interlibrary loan delivery joined only libraries of a single type—public libraries, for example—which had similar patterns of operation, funding, governance, and service. (An example of a well-established network limited to one type of library is the Regional Medical Library Program of the National Library of Medicine.) By the mid-1970s the multitype cooperative pattern, mixing libraries of different types and sizes, was firmly established.

Some resource-sharing arrangements involving libraries of various types have been limited to a city or state; more recent organizations have crossed state boundaries. The cooperative acquisition, storage, and lending programs of METRO (the New York Metropolitan Reference and Research Library Agency) indicate what can be accomplished in a large metropolitan area. The state networks of New York (NYSILL), Illinois (ILLINET), and Washington (WLN) have been cited as examples of how statewide plans can draw more than one type of library into resource-sharing schemes. Many other states have networks, particularly of public and academic libraries, which have encouraged the trend toward viewing all state-supported library collections as a state resource.

Interstate cooperatives involving the sharing, in some form, of bibliographic and/or physical access to library materials and admitting to membership more than one type of library became quite common in the 1970s. Among the better-publicized examples are NELINET (New England Library Network), which includes some academic and public libraries from the six New England states; SOLINET (Southeastern Library Network), open to academic, public, special, and state libraries in ten southeastern states; SLICE (Southwest Library Interstate Cooperative Endeavor), covering interested libraries in the six-state area of the Southwest Library Association; the Denver Bibliographic Center, serving 11 states between the Mississippi River and the West Coast; PNBC (Pacific Northwest Bibliographic Center), open to all libraries in five U.S. states and some libraries in British Columbia; and MINITEX-WILS, a cooperative arrangement available to all types of libraries in Minnesota and Wisconsin. OCLC (Ohio College Library Center) may also be included in this group since its on-line cataloging and card reproduction services are now available to and used by various types of libraries in a number of states.

National Commission on Libraries and Information Science

As librarians began to experiment with a variety of cooperative patterns for sharing library resources and as federal funding to libraries increased in the 1960s, it was natural that many would begin to advocate planning on a national level. The movement in this direction began in 1966 when President Lyndon Johnson appointed a National Advisory Commission on Libraries. The Commission contracted for research studies on a number of information transfer issues and problems bothering libraries. In 1968 the Commission issued its report. (For the Commission's report and summaries of many of the research reports, see *Libraries at Large,* published by R. R. Bowker Co. in 1969.) A major recommendation of the National Advisory Commission was that a permanent agency be established to advise the President and Congress on matters relating to library and infor~~~~tion needs. Following the recommendation, the National Commi sion on Libraries and Information Science (NCLIS) was created as an independent agency in 1970, one of its charges being the development of a plan for meeting library and information needs on a national level, involving coordinating efforts at all levels of government and considering all available library and information resources. After a two-year process of drafting, review, feedback, and reconsideration, NCLIS issued, in May 1975, its outlined plan (*Toward a National Program for Library and Information Services. Goals for Action,* U.S. Government Printing Office, 106p.). The proposed national plan had eight objectives, but the one given the most emphasis in the report was Objective 8: "Plan, develop and implement a nationwide network of library and information service."

As part of its planning effort, NCLIS had commissioned a research firm to study the present distribution of library collections and bibliographic centers around the country and to make recommendations on how such centers might in the future be developed into a national network (*Resources and Bibliographic Support for a Nationwide Library Program; Final Report to the National Commission for Library and Information Science,* 1974, 267p.). This comprehensive study covered a wide range of issues related to developing collections which can guarantee "access to recorded materials of all types in all languages" and providing rapid and accurate bibliographic identification and location of library materials. In the introduction, the writers of the report observed: "Poor and uncoordinated bibliographic access has limited the potential for locating materials not widely held; and collection policies of individual libraries, necessarily aimed at the needs of their own borrowers, leave gaps and deficiencies in the overall holdings." If the objectives of a national library network should be actively pursued in the future, collection development in individual libraries clearly will be affected.

National Periodicals Center

Although a comprehensive national library network would include all types of library materials, a national plan for access to periodicals is drawing the most attention currently. Because they are expensive to acquire and bulky to store, but relatively easy to keep under bibliographic control (as compared to individual monographs), periodicals are often a focus for cooperative schemes. No library can afford to maintain all the periodical subscriptions demanded by its users, so the sharing of periodical resources has appeal for all sizes and types of libraries. NCLIS appointed a task force in 1976 to make recommendations concerning a national periodical system. The report (*Effective Access to the*

Periodical Literature: A National Program, U.S. National Commission on Libraries and Information Science, 92p.), which was issued in 1977, recommended a three-level scheme, with local, state, and regional library systems being made responsible for meeting routine needs (estimated at 80 per cent of the total) for periodicals. The second level would be a comprehensive periodicals collection reserved for lending and photocopying, and the third level would be the unique holdings of national, university, and special libraries. This plan is (at the time of this writing) being debated, restudied, and reformulated. Librarians with responsibilities for developing local collections are eagerly awaiting the outcome of this process.

One of the complications which may have delayed plans for a periodical center (as well as other resource-sharing plans) is the uncertainty about how the new U.S. copyright law, which went into effect in 1978, will affect any resource-sharing scheme that relies heavily on photocopying. A 1975 study of interlibrary loan activity by large research libraries (ARL members) estimated that 50 per cent of the interlibrary requests were for periodical articles and that 80 per cent of those requests were filled with photocopies. How the new copyright regulations may affect this activity is not yet known.

Conclusion

Resource sharing has never been considered a solution to all collection development problems, but it is now being recognized as a form of library organization which may be here to stay. In its more recent manifestations resource sharing has tended to be formally structured (many cooperatives are established as non-profit corporations), to cover all types of libraries and a variety of activities, and to require more of an institutional commitment—in terms of membership fees, staff time, policy adjustments, etc.—than did earlier examples of library cooperation. (Another interesting sign of commitment is the number of network or consortia memberships which may be held by a single library.)

There are still questions in the minds of some librarians as to how well large-scale resource sharing can work. Both large and small libraries fear being overwhelmed—the large ones by the number of requests which may come from poorer collections, the smaller ones by the influence of the larger libraries in setting and establishing procedures. There is always a fear that too much concern for resource sharing will cause librarians to overlook the needs of a library's primary constituency. Library users are not always pleased, either, by their library's participation in resource sharing. Some can not understand why needs (especially their own needs for library materials) can not be met locally. There are still some legal and administrative barriers to resource sharing, but many of these have been removed in recent years. However, physical and geographical problems still pose difficulties in areas where great distances make the rapid exchange of library materials nearly impossible. Funding problems are likely to arise if federal, state, or foundation grants to cooperative projects begin to decline. Many networks have membership fees, but most of them also rely heavily on other financial sources. Nevertheless, there are bright spots in the pattern of resource-sharing activities.

Some librarians are convinced that resource sharing is an essential part of modern library service. Projects reported as successful by their participants exhibit certain key characteristics: quick and accurate sharing of information on holdings; rapid delivery of materials from one participating library to another; good communication among staff members at all levels of the hierarchy in all participating libraries; and careful planning and research activities. As more research is conducted on the structure and operation of cooperatives, it is likely that the causes for success or failure in resource sharing can be identified and used as a basis for planning and review of present operations. When resource-sharing projects achieve a stable and satisfactory pattern of operation, collection building at every level of the network will be affected.

BIBLIOGRAPHY

Association of Caribbean University and Research Libraries. *Research Library Cooperation in the Caribbean; Papers of the First and Second Conferences of the Association of Caribbean University and Research Libraries.* Edited by Alma Jordan. Chicago, American Library Association, 1973. 145p. Contains twelve papers.

Association of Research Libraries. *Farmington Plan Survey; Final Report.* Directed by Robert Vosper and Robert Talmadge. 1959. unpaged.

Association of Research Libraries. Office of University Library Management Studies. *SPEC Kit on Resource Sharing in ARL Libraries.* Washington, D.C., 1978. 108p. Includes examples of resource-sharing plans, manuals, etc.

Association of State Library Agencies. Interlibrary Cooperation Subcommittee. *The ASLA Report on Interlibrary Cooperation.* 2d ed. Chicago, 1978. 446p. Attempts to give basic information on cooperative activities within each state and territory.

Balliot, Robert L. *A Program for the Cooperative Acquisition and Use of Library Materials of Seven New England Liberal Arts Colleges (CONVAL) Based on an Analysis of Their Collections.* Cullowhee, N.C., Western Carolina College, 1970. 82p. (ED 047 711)

Butler, Brett. "State of the Nation in Networking." *Journal of Library Automation,* 8:200–220, September 1975. Describes current networking organizations.

Canadian Library Systems and Networks; Their Planning and Development. Papers Presented at a Symposium on Library Systems and Networks at the Canadian Library Association Conference, Winnipeg, 25 June 1974. Ottawa, Canadian Library Association, 1974. 50p.

Carter, Harriet and Raymond A. Palmer. "Operation of a Rational Acquisitions Committee." *Medical Library Association Bulletin,* 65:61–63, January 1977. Cooperative collection development in several health sciences libraries.

Center for Research Libraries. *Report of a Survey with an Outline of Programs and Policies.* Chicago, 1965. 24p.

Chandler, George. "Proposed Development of Resource Sharing Networks (UNISIST, NATIS, ALBIS)." *International Library Review,* 8:237–264, 1976. Reviews efforts of National Library of Australia.

Chang, Diana M. "Academic Library Cooperation: A Selective Annotated Bibliography." *Library Resources and Technical Services,* 20:270–286, Summer 1976.

Clinic on Library Applications of Data Processing, University of Illinois, 1973. *Proceedings of the 1973 Clinic on Library Applications of Data Processing: Networking and Other Forms of Cooperation.* Edited by F. Wilfred Lancaster. Urbana, University of Illinois, Graduate School of Library Science, 1973. 185p.

Cooke, Michael. "Future Library Network Automation." *Journal of the American Society for Information Science,* 28:254–258, September 1977. Discusses issues of concern in networking.

Corbin, John. "Library Networks." *Library Journal,* 101:203–207, January 1, 1976. Review of developments and predictions for the future.

De Gennaro, Richard. "Austerity, Technology, and Resource Sharing: Research Libraries Face the Future." *Library Journal,* 100:917–923, May 15, 1975. Argues for emphasis on access to materials rather than size of holdings.

Directory of Academic Library Consortia. 2d ed. Edited by Donald V. Black and Carlos A. Cuadra. Santa Monica, Calif., System Development Corp., 1975. 437p. Information on 264 consortia.

Dougherty, Richard M. "The Impact of Networking on Library Management." *College and Research Libraries,* 39:15–19, January 1978.

Downs, Robert B. "Future Prospects of Library Acquisitions." *Library Trends,* 18:412–421, January 1970. Brief review of research library cooperation.

Downs, Robert B. "The Significance of Foreign Materials for U.S. Collections: Problems of Acquisition." *Foreign Acquisitions Newsletter,* No. 34:1–7, Fall 1971. Brief review of cooperative projects for foreign acquisitions.

Edelman, Hendrik. "The Death of the Farmington Plan." *Library Journal,* 98:1251–1253, April 15, 1973. Discusses several questions related to cooperative acquisitions programs.

El-Erian, Tahany Said. "The Public Law 480 Program in American Libraries." (D.L.S. Thesis, Columbia University, 1972). 278p.

Franckowiak, Bernard. "Networks, Data Bases, and Media Programs: An Overview." *School Media Quarterly,* 6:15–20, Fall 1977. Networks from a school point of view.

Goderich, Mario. "Cooperative Acquisitions: The Experience of General Libraries and Prospects for Law Libraries." *Law Library Journal,* 63:57–61, February 1970.

Gregor, Dorothy. *Feasibility of Cooperative Collecting of Exotic Foreign Language Serial Titles Among Health Sciences Libraries in California.* Berkeley, Calif., University of California, Institute of Library Research, 1974. 50p. (ED 104 407)

Gribbin, J.H. "Interlibrary Cooperation and Collection Building." In *Academic Library: Essays In Honor of Guy R. Lyle,* pp. 105–117. Metuchen, N.J., Scarecrow Press, 1974.

Hamilton, Beth A. and William B. Ernst, Jr. *Multitype Library Cooperation.* New York, Bowker, 1977. 216p. Most of the twenty-one essays printed here were presented at the ALA Centennial Conference in Chicago in 1976.

Hayes, Robert M. "Distributed Library Networks: Programs and Problems." In *The Responsibility of the University Library Collection in Meeting the Needs of Its Campus and Local Community; A Symposium in Honor of Melvin J. Voigt Upon His Retirement as University Librarian of The University of California, San Diego, Friday, September 17, 1976,* pp. 32–39. La Jolla, Calif., Friends of the UCSD Library, 1976.

Heard, J. Norman. "Suggested Procedures for Sharing Acquisitions in Academic Libraries." *Louisiana Library Association Bulletin*, 35:17-21, Spring 1972. Specific suggestions for Louisiana libraries.

Hendricks, Donald D. *A Report on Library Networks*. Urbana, University of Illinois, Graduate School of Library Science, 1973. 23p. (Occasional Papers No. 108) Covers types of network activities and some specific examples.

Hewitt, Joe A. "The Impact of OCLC." *American Libraries*, 7:268-275, May 1976.

Hopkins, Judith. "The Ohio College Library Center." *Library Resources and Technical Services*, 17:308-319, Summer 1973. Outlines development and describes operation.

Houze, Robert A. "The Council of Research and Academic Libraries, San Antonio, Texas." *Texas Library Journal*, 47:263-268, November 1971. Example of a local cooperative project.

Impact of the Public Law 480 Program on Overseas Acquisitions by American Libraries; Proceedings of a Conference Held May 12, 1967. Edited by William L. Williamson. Madison, University of Wisconsin-Madison, Library School, 1967. 41p.

"Introducing ILLINET . . . The Beginnings of a Statewide Network." *Illinois Libraries*, 57:364-370, June 1975.

Jay, Donald F. and Frank M. McGowan. "The Library of Congress PL-480 Program." *DC Libraries*, 40:29-33, Spring 1969. Concise overview of the program.

Jefferson, George. *Library Co-operation*. 2d ed. London, Deutsch, 1977. 189p. Reviews cooperative projects of various kinds. Emphasis is on cooperation in the United Kingdom, but several U.S. projects are covered in detail. Includes classified bibliography (pp. 169-182).

Jones, C. Lee. "A Cooperative Serial Acquisition Program: Thoughts on a Response to Mounting Fiscal Pressures." *Medical Library Association Bulletin*, 62:120-123, April 1974. Outlines way to set up a cooperative acquisitions program.

Kaplan, Louis. "Midwest Inter-Library Center, 1949-1964." *Journal of Library History*, 10:291-310, October 1975. MILC was the predecessor of Center for Research Libraries.

Kilgour, Frederick G. "Ohio College Library Center: A User-Oriented System." In *New Dimensions for Academic Library Service*, edited by E.J. Josey, pp. 250-255. Metuchen, N.J., Scarecrow Press, 1975.

Klieman, Janet and Cathleen Costello. "Cooperation Between Types of Libraries; An Annotated Bibliography, 1973 Supplement." *Illinois Libraries*, 56:250-258, March 1974.

Knightly, John J. "Cooperative Collections Development in Academic Libraries: The Relationship of Book Collections to Curricula of Cooperating Institutions." (Ph.D. Thesis, University of Texas at Austin, 1973). 175p.

Knightly, John J. "Library Collections and Academic Curricula: Quantitative Relationships." *College and Research Libraries*, 36:295-301, July 1975. Discusses implications for cooperative acquisition.

Kolb, Audrey. "Development and Potential of a Multitype Library Network." *School Media Quarterly*, 6:21-27, Fall 1977. Describes Washington Library Network.

Kolb, Audrey and Jo Morse. "Initiating School Participation in Networking." *School Media Quarterly*, 6:52-59, Fall 1977. Step-by-step approach.

Lehman, James O. "Cooperation Among Small Academic Libraries." *College and Research Libraries*, 30:491-497, November 1969. Brief survey of small college consortia.

"Library Cooperation." Issue edited by Pearce S. Grove. *Library Trends*, 24:157-423, October 1975. Includes articles on various aspects of cooperation.

Library Resource Sharing; Proceedings of the 1976 Conference on Resource Sharing in Libraries, Pittsburgh, Pennsylvania. Edited by Allen Kent and Thomas J. Galvin.

New York, Dekker, 1977. 356p. Six major papers and a number of reaction statements.

Line, Maurice. "Access to Resources Through the British Library Lending Division." *Aslib Proceedings,* 27:8–15, January 1975.

Line, Maurice. "The Developing National Network in Great Britain." *Library Resources and Technical Services,* 16:61–73, Winter 1972. Brief description of the British Library.

Lucht, Irma and Blair Stewart. "The ACM Periodical Bank and the British National Lending Library: Contrasts and Similarities." In *Management Problems in Serials Work,* pp. 3–18. Edited by Peter Spyers-Duran and Daniel Gore. Westport, Conn., Greenwood Press, 1974.

McDonald, John P. "Interlibrary Cooperation in the U.S." In *Issues in Library Administration,* edited by Warren M. Tsuneishi and others, pp. 125–137. New York, Columbia University Press, 1974. General review.

Markuson, Barbara Evans. "Library Network Planning: Problems to Consider, Decisions to Make." *Wisconsin Library Bulletin,* 71:98–102, May–June 1975.

Martin, Susan K. *Library Networks 1976–77.* White Plains, N.Y., Knowledge Industry Publications, 1978. Reviews extent of networking and describes major U.S. networks.

Miller, Ronald F. and Ruth L. Tighe. "Library and Information Networks." In *Annual Review of Information Science and Technology,* Vol. 9, pp. 173–219. Washington, D.C., American Society for Information Science, 1974. Review article with extensive bibliography.

Orne, Jerrold. "Newspaper Resources of the Southeastern Region: An Experiment in Coordinated Resource Development." *Southeastern Librarian,* 21:226–235, Winter 1971.

Palmour, Vernon E. *Resources and Bibliographic Support for a Nationwide Library Program; Final Report.* Washington, D.C., National Commission for Libraries and Information Science, 1974. 267p.

Palmour, Vernon E. and others. *Access to Periodical Resources: A National Plan.* Washington, D.C., Association of Research Libraries, 1974. 222p.

Parker, Thomas F. "Resource Sharing from the Inside Out: Reflections on the Organizational Nature of Library Networks." *Library Resources and Technical Services,* 19:349–355, Fall 1975. Theoretical approach.

Quick, Richard C. "Coordination of Collection Building by Academic Libraries." In *New Dimensions for Academic Library Service,* edited by E.J. Josey, pp. 100–120. Metuchen, N.J., Scarecrow Press, 1975. Reviews trends in a few consortia.

Resource Sharing in Libraries: Why, How, When, Next Action Steps. Edited by Allen Kent. New York, Dekker, 1974. 393p. Papers presented at a 1973 conference in Pittsburgh.

Reynolds, Maryan E. and others. *A Study of Library Network Alternatives for the State of Washington.* Olympia, 1970. 317p. (ED 045 862)

Reynolds, Michael. *Reader in Library Cooperation.* Washington, D.C., NCR/Microcard Editions, 1972. 398p. Contains several articles on cooperative acquisition and storage.

Rouse, William B. "A Library Network Model." *Journal of the American Society for Information Science,* 27:88–99, March–April 1976. Operations research approach to evaluating networks.

Savary, M.J. *The Latin American Cooperative Acquisitions Program; An Imaginative Venture.* New York, Hafner, 1968. 144p.

Selective Annotated Bibliography on Library Networking. ERIC Clearinghouse on Information Resources, Stanford University, 1975. 27p. (ED 115 219)

Shank, Russell. "The Locus for Cooperation in Collection Sharing." In *The Responsibility of the University Library Collection in Meeting the Needs of Its Campus and Local Community;* A Symposium in Honor of Melvin J. Voight Upon His Retirement as University Librarian of The University of California, San Diego, Friday, September 17, 1976, pp. 27–31. La Jolla, Calif., Friends of the UCSD Library, 1976.

Shepard, Marietta Daniels. "Cooperative Acquisitions of Latin American Materials." *Library Resources and Technical Services,* 13:347–360, Summer 1969. Reviews history of U.S. efforts.

Shepard, Marietta Daniels. *Seminars on the Acquisition of Latin American Library Materials; A Seven Year Report, 1956 to 1962.* Washington, D.C., Pan American Union, 1962. 100p. Reviews efforts at cooperative acquisitions.

Simkin, Faye. *Cooperative Resources Development; A Report on a Shared Acquisitions and Retention System for Metro Libraries.* New York, New York Metropolitan Reference and Research Library Agency, 1970. 69p. (ED 039 903) Describes early phases of SHARES.

Sinclair, Michael P. "A Typology of Library Cooperatives." *Special Libraries,* 64:181–186, April 1973. Describes four cooperative library system models.

"Stanford University's BALLOTS System." *Journal of Library Automation,* 8:31–50, March 1975. Background and overview of system operation.

Stevens, Robert D. "The Library of Congress Public Law 480 Program." *Library Resources and Technical Services,* 7:176–188, Spring 1963. Reviews early activities of PL-480.

Stewart, Blair. "Periodicals and the Liberal Arts College Library." *College and Research Libraries,* 36:371–378, September 1975. Describes operations of ACM Periodical Bank.

Stuart-Stubbs, Basil. "An Historical Look at Resource Sharing." *Library Trends,* 23:649–664, April 1975.

Stuart-Stubbs, Basil and others. *A Survey and Interpretation of the Literature of Interlibrary Loan.* Vancouver, University of British Columbia Library, 1975. 158p. Comprehensive study of Canadian ILL.

Sullivan, Harry A. "Ten Years After: The Joint Acquisition Committee in Detroit." *Stechert-Hafner Book News,* 23:129–131, May 1969. Cooperative procedures of Detroit Public Library and Wayne State University.

Sylvestre, Guy. "Co-operative Acquisition Plan for Canada." *Canadian Library Journal,* 26:433–438, November 1969. Statement by the National Librarian.

Thomas, Lawrence E. "Tri-University Libraries." *Canadian Library Journal,* 35:27–33, February 1978. Describes consortium including three British Columbian universities.

Trezza, Alphonse F. "Toward a National Program for Library and Information Services: Progress and Problems." *Aslib Proceedings,* 30:72–87, February 1978. Reviews history of National Advisory Committee on Libraries and National Commission on Libraries and Information Science.

U.S. National Commission on Libraries and Information Science. *Toward a National Program for Library and Information Services: Goals for Action.* Washington, D.C., 1975. 106p.

U.S. National Commission on Libraries and Information Science. Task Force on a National Periodicals System. *Effective Access to the Periodical Literature: A National Program.* Washington, D.C., 1977. 91p.

Vosper, Robert G. *Farmington Plan Survey; A Summary of the Separate Studies of 1957–1961.* Urbana, University of Illinois, Graduate School of Library Science, 1965. 46p. (Occasional Papers No. 77) For related report, see Association of Research Libraries (1959).

Weber, David C. "A Century of Cooperative Programs Among Academic Libraries." *College and Research Libraries,* 37:205–221, May 1976.

Wilden-Hart, Marion. *Cooperative Resource Development in the Five Associated University Libraries; A Study with Recommendations.* Syracuse, N.Y., Five Associated University Libraries, 1970. 84p. (ED 049 768) Discusses problems, objectives, importance of acquisition policy statements, as well as recommendations.

Williams, Edwin E. *Farmington Plan Handbook.* Bloomington, Ind., Association of Research Libraries, 1953. 170p. Includes description of the plan and review of its early history.

Williams, Edwin E. *Farmington Plan Handbook; Revised to 1961 and Abridged.* Ithaca, N.Y., Association of Research Libraries, 1961. Updates history and bibliography, but does not repeat everything in earlier edition.

Williams, Gordon R. "Center for Research Libraries: Its New Organizations and Programs." *Library Journal,* 90:2947-2951, July 1965. Includes brief review of early history.

Wright, Gordon H. "The Canadian Mosiac—Planning for Shared Partnership in a National Network." *Aslib Proceedings,* 30:88-102, February 1978.

PART II

ACQUISITIONS

CHAPTER 10

National and Trade Bibliography

Introduction

An ideal national bibliography would attempt to record all materials published in a given country, whether available through the regular book trade or not, whether copyrighted or not, and regardless of format. It would include books, pamphlets, films, printed music, phonorecords, government publications, theses, newspapers, periodicals, prints and engravings, microforms—and any other form. This happy ideal would enter each item under author, under title, and under subject, with additional entries where appropriate for series, joint author, editor, compiler, translator, etc. It would, of course, be freely supplied with all necessary cross references. Since the ideal is being described, let a descriptive annotation be added to the full bibliographical information which would be given.

Trade bibliography is one part of national bibliography, but of more restricted scope. It attempts to record those materials which are available through the regular trade channels. Most large encyclopedias and government publications, for example, are not ordinarily sold through bookstores—they are "outside the trade." Doctoral dissertations are not to be found on the shelves of the ordinary bookstore. The serial publications issued by business and industry as house organs, the publications of fraternal societies, of many learned societies, the research reports of laboratories and institutes, etc.—all these are not "trade items."

In studying a country's bibliography, it is desirable to try to see the pattern that exists among the various pieces, which, if put together, make up the total national bibliography. In the United States, for example, we have such bits and pieces as the *Catalog of Copyright Entries,* the Library of Congress catalogs, the *Monthly Checklist of State Publications,* the *Monthly Catalog of U.S. Government Publications, Comprehensive Dissertation Index, Vertical File Index, CBI, Publishers' Trade List Annual, American Book Publishing Record,* etc. But we have no single source containing all types of materials, and the manner of presentation in the sources that we do have is not uniform. In addition, there is no assurance that even this variety of sources will pick up everything. Furthermore, the frequency with which these several parts of the American bibliography are published varies as much as the sources. This factor must be kept in mind in attempting to estimate the speed with which the national output is recorded (especially if one is concerned with early identification of current but obscure non-trade items). It is suggested that the student use American bibliography as the standard and compare it with British, Canadian, Australian, French, and German national bibliographies, noting essential differences in an attempt to decide which country's method seems most useful.

Although all of the bibliographies discussed in this chapter appear in a printed form, the student should be aware that the recent trend toward building extensive bibliographic files in machine-readable form has had a great influence on the compilation of national and trade bibliographies—and on the way they are used by searchers to verify order requests. One of the most important innovations has been the MARC (*MA*chine-*R*eadable *C*ataloging) Project of the Library of Congress. MARC, which was developed and used on a pilot basis beginning in 1966, is a standard format for recording bibliographic data on magnetic tape. Through the MARC Distribution Service, which became operational in 1969, the Library of Congress puts most of its new cataloging into the MARC format and distributes those catalog records on tape to subscribers. The subscribers include commercial firms, such as the publishers of trade bibliographies, individual libraries, and library cooperatives such as OCLC, Inc. (formerly Ohio College Library Center) and similar shared cataloging networks. This means that in many large libraries most bibliographic searching and verification can now be done on-line, with no reference to a printed source. Even when a printed bibliography is used, the searcher expects to find quicker coverage of new publications and a more standard entry. American bibliography is not the only area to be affected by MARC. Other countries, including most of those represented in this chapter, either have or are planning their own versions of MARC.

Another development leading to changes in national and trade bibliographies is the International Standard Bibliographic Description (ISBD). First issued in a draft version in 1971, ISBD is now widely used as a method of providing a standard description of a monograph (ISBD's for other forms of publications have also been developed). This description comprises a standard set of descriptive elements in a standard order with specified punctuation marks to separate the various elements. Anyone who wishes to see how this has changed the appearance of a trade bibliography should look at a current issue of *American Book Publishing Record* and an issue of ten years ago. Though the type of information given in the bibliographic entries in the two issues will probably be similar, punctuation and arrangement of the elements will be different. One effect of ISBD has been to make foreign bibliographies a little easier to read. Elements of the entries can be recognized by their position and the punctuation which precedes them.

One other development which should be mentioned is the CIP (Cataloging in Publication) Project of the Library of Congress. Under CIP, the Library of Congress makes arrangements with individual publishers to receive galleys of new publications. LC then proceeds to create basic catalog information, which is supplied to the cooperating publisher so that it may be printed on the verso of the title page when the publication appears in its final form. These CIP records also become a part of the MARC data base (each CIP record is updated to a full MARC record after the item is actually published). The wide distribution of CIP data means that publications tend to appear in on-line files and printed bibliographies quicker than in the past—sometimes the entry is incomplete (since CIP is based on pre-publication data) and occasionally it may even appear before the official publication date. Other countries have also developed schemes similar to CIP for their new publications, a move which should have an effect on their national and trade bibliographies.

AMERICAN BIBLIOGRAPHY

Variety appears in the retrospective coverage of American publishing due to the fact that different periods have been covered by different individuals or organizations with varying degrees of skill, time available for the undertaking, and differing convictions concerning what ought to be done and how material should be presented. Thus Sabin attempted to list not only books published in the Americas, but those about the Americas published elsewhere, and he presented the results alphabetically by author and anonymous title (largely). Evans restricted himself to books published in the United States and chose to arrange the titles chronologically by year of publication, with author-anonymous title and subject indexes. While both of these gentlemen provided considerable information about individual titles (Sabin's bibliographical notes are sometimes quite extensive), Roorbach and Kelly present a minimum of information, occasionally abbreviating the amount given to the point of near-uselessness. Shaw and Shoemaker attempted to fill the 1801–19 gap left as a result of Evans' death. They based their compilation on secondary sources as did Evans and Roorbach and Kelly. Shoemaker, using the same method of compilation, began moving beyond 1819 in an effort to provide more satisfactory coverage than that of Roorbach. Since his death, the project has been carried forward by others.

In addition to these bibliographies, one must remember the catalogs of out-of-print dealers, which are of great importance in retrospective searching (aimed at the purchase of out-of-print books). If the standard bibliographies represent infinite variety, these catalogs can only be described as "infinitest" variety. In arrangement, accuracy of entry and of information, care in description of items, extensiveness, adequacy of reproduction, and usefulness to librarians, these catalogs display a truly remarkable spread.

The field of current bibliography also displays a variety of approaches. *Weekly Record* tries to list American titles published that week by trade publishers; the *Cumulative Book Index* provides a monthly approach to all English-language publications in the United States and to all books in the English language published abroad; *Publishers' Trade List Annual, Books in Print* and *Subject Guide to Books in Print* give another approach to American trade publications still in print, regardless of date of publication. The government lists its publications in the *Monthly Catalog* (not all of them), and paperbound books are represented in *Paperbound Books in Print.* Serial publications are listed in the Library of Congress' *New Serial Titles* as well as in the *National Union Catalog.* There is overlapping of coverage among these various titles and varying manners of presenting the material, but the identification of currently issued trade books published in the United States (by reasonably active publishers) is not generally a major problem.

What all of this variety may detract from the efficiency of the librarian's efforts is certainly compensated for by the excitement, the mystery—sometimes, alas, the frustration—which is generated in trying to track down and identify some bibliographical culprit. The detective work going into the hunt is sometimes of a high order, and the ultimate discovery of the truth about a book sometimes approaches the kind of excitement and satisfaction which Balboa must have felt when he first viewed the Pacific. In the discussion of the individual bibliographies which follows, some of the surprises, puzzles, and eccentricities which lie in wait for the searcher will be detailed at greater length. Greater emphasis has been placed on current American bibliography because it is most used by most librarians in the United States; briefer treatment is given other types.

CURRENT AMERICAN BIBLIOGRAPHY

For library selection and acquisitions purposes, coverage of current publishing actually begins before the publication of many of the titles which will eventually be recorded in the bibliographies. The librarian will have his/her attention called to forthcoming items by publishers' announcements sent to the library. These individual, scattered, and ephemeral broadsides, pamphlets, odd-sized sheets (arrayed in all the colors of the advertising psychologist's rainbow) are of great temporary utility. Once having served their purposes, however, they are disposed of expeditiously, disappearing from recorded bibliographic history via the wastebasket route. The selector's current bibliography begins at this point. An additional record of books to be published may be found in the announcement issues of such magazines as *Library Journal,* or such publications as *Forthcoming Books.*

(1)   Forthcoming Books, v.1 - Jan. 1966– . New York, Bowker.

Supersedes the *Publishers' Weekly Interim Index,* which was a quarterly supplement to *Publishers' Weekly,* being issued some two months after the announcement numbers of that magazine, revising and updating the information given in the announcement numbers and providing an index to books about to be published.

Forthcoming Books, currently being issued six times a year (as of summer 1978), attempts also to serve as a supplement to the annual edition of *Books in Print,* giving books which have been published since the last edition of that work. Thus the July 1978 issue, for example, listed books which had been published in the United States since summer 1977, while at the same time listing and updating information about books to be published in the following five months.

Each bi-monthly issue updates and expands the preceding issue and includes all categories of titles. (Since *Webster's Third* has permitted a muddying of the waters concerning the meaning of "bi-monthly," let it be noted that it here means "every two months," not "twice a month.")

FROM THE AUTHOR INDEX:

Francesi, W. Crowds of Power. (Studies in Political History, No. 85)
  Repr. of the 1870 ed. lib. bdg. 18.95. (ISBN 0-985-90906-9)
  Tripleday.

FROM THE TITLE INDEX:

Crowds of Power. Francesi, W. (Studies in Political History, No. 85)
  Repr. of the 1870 ed. lib. bdg. 18.95 (ISBN 0-985-90906-9)
  Tripleday

When one shifts one's attention to the record of books which have actually been published, one will find the most current and timely title is *Weekly Record,* the first step in the permanent record of published titles in American bibliography.

(2)   Weekly Record. New York, Bowker, 1974–   .

Scope: Weekly Record is "the American bibliographic weekly journal which conscientiously lists current American books and foreign books distributed in the United States"—to use *WR*'s own statement. This description of its scope is modified by a listing of the kinds of materials not included: federal and state government publications, subscription books, dissertations, successive printings or impressions, pamphlets under 49 pages, and publications of a transitory character, e.g., telephone books, calendars, etc.

Arrangement: The list is arranged alphabetically by author or title (where there is no author—as, for example, *World Almanac and Book of Facts*). At the risk of appearing to underestimate the capacities of the reader, may the authors point out that one cannot expect to find a book listed under both author and title. This is—to use another term—a listing by *main entry.* For those not familiar with cataloging terminology, this may not seem helpful, but for initiates it should fix the arrangement clearly and specifically. This particular point is being belabored here because it will reappear under subsequent titles. The reader will be expected to distinguish among various arrangements: author list; author and title; author and title and subject; title list only; etc. Sometimes a bibliography will be praised for listing under both main and added entries. This implied comparison with the dictionary card catalog should enable the reader to apprehend immediately the kinds of approaches afforded to individual items.

Information Given for Each Entry: WR uses the ISBD and gives author, title, publisher, place, date (publisher, place and date will frequently be condensed in subsequent descriptions to one term: *imprint*), paging or volumes, size, whether illustrated or equipped with maps, tables, bibliographies, etc. (These will sometimes be condensed to *collation,* or the statement "full collation given.") A series statement appears, if appropriate. LC card number, International Standard Book Number (ISBN), price, and frequently LC tracings (both Arabic and Roman numerals) are given. The author entry and descriptive cataloging information are taken from records supplied by the Library of Congress, although the *Weekly Record* staff attempts to complete CIP entries and sometimes produces cataloging copy for publishers that do not submit their works to L.C. (Occasionally publishers are omitted from *WR* because new publications have not been submitted to the Library of Congress for cataloging.) Dewey classification numbers are given at the upper right-hand corner of the entry. Note that mass market paperbacks are given separate treatment.

Sample Entry:

FRANCESI, Wolfgang Ludwig, 1999-   301.158
Crowds of power / Tr. from French by Starol Smith. NY:
Imaginary Books Co., c2049. 612p. : illus. ; 24cm.
[HM141.F7] 49-8426 ISBN 0-998989-01-X : 6.95
1. *Political Science I. Smith, Starol, tr. II. Title.*

Comment: There are two uses of *Weekly Record* especially appropriate to our purposes. It is widely used as a selection device, and it is used for verification of titles requested for purchase. *WR* is frequently circulated to heads of subject divisions in a public library (departmental, college, or other subdivisions of a university library system), who check each weekly number for publications in their subject area. For their purposes, of course, it would be more convenient to have the weekly list arranged by subject, rather than by author. (The subject arrangement is accomplished each month in the *American Book Publishing Record,* the next title to be discussed.) But it is not an overwhelming task to read down the classification number at the upper right-hand corner of each entry to pick out those books in the subject area for which one is responsible. Many of the titles may have been ordered before publication on the basis of publishers' announcements or review in *Kirkus Reviews,* but weekly reading of *WR* provides a check against possible oversights. The student who is alarmed at the thought of using *Weekly Record* for selection is referred to that part of Chapter 2 in which "block buying" is discussed. The second use is in the process of verification of order requests (described at length in Chapter 11). For this particular purpose, of course, the alphabetical arrangement by author is most satisfactory.

A brief comment on the scope: we remind the reader that the reference to "current American books and foreign books distributed in the United States" quoted above really must be modified. A more accurate description would be: "*Weekly Record* aims at including every *trade* book published in the United States." Trade bibliography is well covered, then, by *WR* on a weekly basis. Nothing so current exists for the recording of the total national publishing output.

(3)   American Book Publishing Record. New York, R. R. Bowker, Feb. 1, 1960– .

Scope: A monthly cumulation and updating of the *Weekly Record.* Thus it is primarily a list of current American trade books.

Arrangement: The titles which had appeared in alphabetical order by author are now re-arranged under Dewey Decimal Classification numbers (by the Dewey number in the upper right hand corner). Following the classed order, there are two lists—fiction and juvenile— for such titles as could not be categorized by subject. (Please note the shortened form "classed arrangement." Wherever this appears in de- scription of subsequent bibliographies, the authors mean that the titles included are classified by subject—although not necessarily by the Dewey Classification.) An index of authors and titles is also given, so that individual items can be located for verification. The information given in the entry and its format are identical with the entries in *Weekly Record*. There are annual and quinquennial cumulations. In 1977, about 34,000 books were listed in the cumulated annual volume.

Entries are similar to those in *Weekly Record,* sometimes includ- ing updating.

(4)   Cumulative Book Index. New York, Wilson, 1898–

Scope: CBI attempts to be an international bibliography of books in the English language. It records the following two groups of publications: (1) all books published in the United States which include some English; (2) books published abroad which include some English. Works wholly in a foreign language are not listed. Dictionaries, grammars, phrase-books, readers, editions of foreign classics and other aids to language learning are included if they include some English.

Omissions: two very large and important categories are not in- cluded in CBI—government documents and periodicals. Both of these categories are, of course, listed in other bibliographies. Other excluded categories include maps, sheet music, pamphlets, cheap and pa- perbound books (not *all* paperbounds), tracts, propaganda, and what *CBI* describes as local, fugitive, and ephemeral materials. *CBI*'s term "Periodicals" includes newspapers as well as magazines. Note that films and phonorecords are also excluded. *CBI* is, therefore, adhering pretty well to the root meaning of bibliography—it is a list of books.

Arrangement: CBI lists books in a dictionary arrangement, with entries under author, subject, title, and where appropriate, such additional entries as editor, translator, joint author, illustrator, series, etc. There is one essential fact to bear in mind concerning these entries: full information is found under the *main entry* (usually author). This particular practice applies to many other bibliographies, and the librar- ian might well begin early to make an iron-bound habit of always consulting the main entry for any item located first under added entry. Much of the material found under main entry in *CBI* will be duplicated under all other entries, but such an important piece of information as series may not be given except under main entry. This is of great importance in order work to avoid duplication of items purchased on standing order for series, and the whole problem is discussed at greater length in the next chapter.

CBI is published monthly except August and cumulates quarterly, with annual bound cumulations.

Information Given: Under main entry, one will find author, title, edition statement where appropriate, price, publisher, date, LC card number, collation, and indication of the availability of Wilson cards. For titles in English appearing abroad, price is given in the currency of the country (25 kr, 66s, 12s6d, Rs7.50 etc.). Where appropriate, price will be given for both British and American editions of the same title, affording an interesting opportunity for some trans-Atlantic bargain hunting. Generally speaking, full cataloging information is given (except size and place of publication).

Sample Entries:

> (A) Francesi, Wolfgang, 1964–1984.
> *Crowds of power;* first translated into English in accordance with the original French ms. by T. L. Williams; with an introd. by the translator. 612p. $4.95 '84 Imaginary Books ISBN 0-998989-01-X LC-84-493
> (B) Williams, Trevor Loper, 1954–1984.
> (tr) See Francesi, Wolfgang, *Crowds of power*
> (C) Crowds of power. Francesi, W. L. $4.95 Imaginary Books
> (D) Political Science
> Francesi, W. L. *Crowds of power.* $4.95 '84 Imaginary Books

History: CBI began publication in 1898. It was intended to be the current, continuing supplement to the *United States Catalog,* which appeared at intervals, cumulating *CBI* for those works still in print at the time of the publication of *U.S. Cat.* The last edition of the *U.S. Cat.* appeared in 1929, including books in print at that time. That edition also included those foreign titles which were regular importations of U.S. publishers and Canadian books in English not published in the U.S. It was with the 1928/29 volume (published 1930) that *CBI* expanded its coverage to all English language books published abroad.

Comment: CBI does attempt to record books outside the regular trade—publications of societies and institutions, as well as privately printed books, and therefore its scope is wider than *Weekly Record* and *American Book Publishing Record.* It has for many years been a major bibliographical tool for American librarians and the standard tool for many who cannot afford the very costly LC catalogs. However, *CBI* has recently been overtaken in libraries which can afford to buy the more comprehensive bibliographies such as the *National Union Catalog* (to be discussed later) and by the on-line cataloging data bases mentioned earlier.

(5)   Publishers' Trade List Annual. New York, Bowker, 1873– .

Scope: PTLA is a bibliography of American trade books, including only those publishers who cooperate in the venture by furnishing their catalogues. (The 1977 *PTLA* carried the catalogues of about 1,400 publishers.) It is, further, an in-print list, that is, it contains not only the titles published in a given year, but any titles published previously which are still in stock at the publisher (and which may have been published years earlier). Its scope is more restricted than *CBI,* resembling more closely the range of *PW* and *BPR.*

Omissions: books published outside the trade, periodicals, government documents, and non-book forms are largely excluded, unless a publisher includes them in his catalog, as in the case with some periodicals. The major content, however, consists of books, and one should not think of *PTLA* as attempting a comprehensive coverage of periodical publishing in the United States.

Arrangement: PTLA is a collection of publishers' catalogues and lists, in two sections. There is the large alphabet of uniform-size catalogues, arranged by name of publisher, occupying most of the bulk of each edition. There is also a section on colored pages at the front of the first volume containing lists by publishers of smaller compass. An index to both lists heads the volumes. If one checks the name in the regular alphabet of catalogues and does not find a catalogue for that publisher, one ought to check the index before concluding that the publisher is not represented—the particular list sought may be in the colored section.

Within the catalogues of individual publishers, arrangement is not uniform. Some catalogues are arranged alphabetically by author; some by author and title; some by subject. Some include out-of-print titles; some list titles in a series; some include advance listings. It is fruitless, therefore, to study one of the catalogues and hope to use it as a model of arrangement for other publishers. It seems most useful to fix in mind the fact that the catalogues vary in arrangement, and, when using a given catalogue, to take a few moments to check on its arrangement.

Sample Entries:

(A) *Crowds of Power.* Wolfgang L. Francesi. 2050 $6.95
This interesting book contains a discussion of the application of political power through mob action.

(B) Francesi, Wolfgang L. *Crowds of Power.* $6.95

(C) Francesi, Wolfgang Ludwig.
Crowds of Power. (c.2049) 612p. 49-9426 $6.95
This book contains a discussion of the application of political power through mob action.

The amount of information given in these three samples varies considerably, with B not even indicating the date of publication. Entry A gives the publication date, but C actually gives copyright date, as well as LC card number.

Comment: PTLA began in 1873, but there were no indexes to the catalogues until 1948 when *Books in Print* was begun, so that one would have to know the name of the publisher to locate an item in the volumes before that date. It does not serve, therefore, as a very useful retrospective national bibliography. (For studies of the output of a given publisher, of course, it is invaluable.) Its lack of indexes is not a serious blow to bibliography, for it is highly unlikely that the titles listed there would not be in the Library of Congress catalogs and—for the 20th century—also in *CBI,* since *PTLA* lists standard copyrighted trade items.

PTLA's major use is as an order department tool, rather than as a part of national bibliography in its broad sense. It enables the library to find out what is available and forthcoming, as well as how much it costs—pragmatic details needed in ordering.

The statement made above—that *PTLA* will show prices and what is available—must be qualified in the interests of accuracy. Between the time that the catalogues are printed and *PTLA* is received in libraries, prices sometimes change and books are remaindered by the publishers. This is not a fault to be laid at the feet of the publisher of *PTLA.* One can only hope that eventually most publishers will keep titles in print for a reasonable length of time, and that they will hold to the prices listed in their catalogue for at least the year covered by the catalogue.

In using *PTLA* the librarian should keep in mind that the entries do not follow the ALA rules for author entry. This is a book trade list, and authors are given as they appear on the title page—and hence as the books will be asked for in bookstores. A book published under the pseudonym of John Garnett (who is really our wondrous Wolfgang Francesi, let us say) will be listed under Garnett. If a librarian recognizes that a name is a pseudonym and hopes to save a trip on the cross reference merry-go-round by going directly to the real name, he/she will be disappointed.

PTLA is undoubtedly a tool of the greatest utility. Armed with it and *Books in Print,* the librarian can successfully dispatch much current American order work (for trade books). With the addition of the *Subject Guide, PTLA* begins to resemble *CBI,* affording author, title, and subject approaches to the material. Certain differences still exist, however: *PTLA* does not include coverage of as many American publishers; it does not attempt to pick up all books in the English language published outside the U.S.; the amount of information given for each title—and the number of approaches to it—are not identical with *CBI*.

(6)   Books in Print. New York, Bowker, 1948– .

Scope: In the past, *Books in Print* was an index to the *Publishers' Trade List Annual*. Beginning with 1973, it became more than just an index to that collection, since it is now compiled from a variety of sources and not just from the annual collection of publishers' catalogues. An attempt is being made to keep it as close to current as possible (including the publication of a supplement each six months, as well as the publication of new titles every two months in *Forthcoming Books*. Bowker has pointed out that its administration of the International Standard Book Numbering Agency has provided greatly increased access to publisher information, and the availability of MARC tapes served to enlarge the master file. It is this file of information which forms a data base from which Bowker has been able to create several specialized in-print lists: *Children's Books in Print, Subject Guide to Children's Books in Print, Medical Books and Serials in Print, Scientific and Technical Books and Serials in Print, Business Books and Serials in Print, Religious Books and Serials in Print*. In addition, older titles continue: *El-Hi Textbooks in Print* and *Paperbound Books in Print*. In 1970, Bowker also published the first edition of *Large Type Books in Print* (2d ed: 1976).

Arrangement: BIP consists of two parts: (1) an alphabetical list by author; (2) an alphabetical list by title (including titles of monographic series, as well as any other serial publications carried in the publishers' catalogs).

Sample Entry:

> (1) From the author index:
> Francesi, Wolfgang L. *Crowds of power.* 2050 (ISBN 9-9999-9999-9). $6.95 Imaginary Books
> (2) From the title index:
> *Crowds of power.* Wolfgang L. Francesi. (ISBN 9-9999-9999-9). $6.95 Imaginary Books

Subject Guide to Books in Print. New York, Bowker, 1957– .

Arrangement: Entries are arranged under thousands of subject headings, consisting generally of regular Library of Congress headings (with some compression of highly complicated subdivisions).

Sample Entry:

> POLITICAL SCIENCE:
> *Francesi, Wolfgang L. Crowds of power.* 2050. (ISBN 0-9990-9990-9). $6.95 Imaginary Books

(7)   Paperbound Books in Print. New York, Bowker, 1955– .

Scope: An in-print and forecast list for American paperbacks. Each succeeding issue has seen the number of publishers represented increase, with the number of titles listed also increasing. It is issued three times a year (a "base" volume in December; supplements in May and September) and each issue is divided into three parts: (1) title listing; (2) by author; (3) by subject. Examples of entry:

> (1) Title: *Crowds of Power.* Wolfgang Francesi. 1.50 (ISBN 0-999-99000-9). Thoth Paperbounds.
> (2) Author: Francesi, Wolfgang. *Crowds of Power.* 1.50 (ISBN 0-999-99000-9). Thoth Paperbacks (369) [The 369 is a subject key]
> (3) Subject: SOCIOLOGY, ANTHROPOLOGY AND ARCHAE-OLOGY—SOCIOLOGY GENERAL. *Crowds of power,* Wolfgang Francesi, 1.50 (ISBN 0-999-99000-9). Thoth Paperbacks.

Comments: One of the past complaints about the paperback trade was the difficulty of obtaining a book you wanted, once its short day on the newsstands had passed. With this in-print list, there is assurance that titles will be held in stock to a greater degree than was true when the paperback trade was tied too completely to the system of magazine distribution. The growing use of paperbacks—as in education—will be facilitated by the continuance of this work. At the same time, *Paperbound Books in Print* may also stimulate that use further by allowing adequate access to desired works.

(8)   Monthly Catalog of United States Government Publications. Washington, Govt. Printing Office, 1895–

Scope: The *Monthly Catalog* attempts to list all government publications offered for sale by the Superintendent of Documents or available from the various issuing agencies (even if not sold through the Superintendent's office). Current estimates indicate that 1,500–3,000 new publications are listed in each issue.

Arrangement: The *Monthly Catalog* has experienced a number of changes in the past few years. In fact, the Government Printing Office speaks of it as "an evolving publication." Since July 1976 the format has been larger and the arrangement and indexing have been changed. The basic arrangement is by Superintendent of Documents number, which groups publications together by issuing agency. There are now four indexes: *author,* which includes personal authors, editors, co-authors, corporate authors, and conferences; *title,* which lists titles, series titles, and sub- or alternate titles; *subject,* based on *Library of*

Congress Subject Headings (8th ed.); and *series/report*, which is an alphabetical list of report numbers and series statements. Since July 1976 the indexes have cumulated semiannually and annually. Decennial indexes cover 1941–1950 and 1951–1960. There is a quinquennial index for 1961–65. Carrollton Press has published a 15-volume *Cumulative Subject Index to the Monthly Catalog of the United States Government Publications, 1900–1979.* (Anyone using older issues of *Monthly Catalog* should note that the author and title indexes were not included until 1974 and the series/report index did not start until July 1976.)

Information given: Before the major changes in format, the *Monthly Catalog* used its own particular form of entry, which included most bibliographical information. It has now joined the movement toward bibliographical standardization and uses MARC format, AACR, and LC subject headings.

Comment: Although most librarians would regard the *Monthly Catalog* as the basic tool for U.S. government documents, there are other bibliographies which give information on documents. The Superintendent of Documents lists all of the publications for sale (about 25,000 titles) in a series of more than 250 subject bibliographies. The documents judged to have the most popular appeal are listed ten times a year in *Selected U.S. Government Publications.* Coverage in this publication runs 150–200 documents per issue. In 1977, the Superintendent of Documents started issuing *GPO Sales Publications Reference File (PRF),* a bimonthly "in-print" list of documents. *PRF* appears on microfiche and in its first edition included about 19,000 documents in stock at GPO, about 2,000 documents still in the printing stage, and about 6,000 exhausted or superseded documents (kept on file for one year). The documents in this file are arranged in three sequences: by GPO stock number, by Superintendent of Documents class number, and alphabetically by "subjects, titles, agency series and report numbers, keywords and phrases, and personal authors."

(9)   Dissertation Abstracts International. 1938–

Known as *Microfilm Abstracts* for its first eleven volumes and *Dissertation Abstracts* for the next eighteen (v.12–29), this is a monthly compilation of abstracts of doctoral dissertations which have been deposited for microfilming with University Microfilms International. More than 400 institutions (primarily in the United States and Canada) cooperate, but all institutions do not send every dissertation.

Dissertation Abstracts International is published in two parts: Section A, which includes humanities and social sciences, and Section B, which covers the sciences. There are author and subject indexes for both sections.

(10)   **Comprehensive Dissertation Index, 1861–1972. 1973. 37v.**

     A computer-produced author and keyword index to all (or as close to that as the editors could come) dissertations accepted by U.S. universities during the dates indicated in the title. Many Canadian and other foreign dissertations are also included.

     Arrangement is by seventeen broad subject groupings (for example, volumes 1–4 cover chemistry; volume 5, mathematics and statistics; volumes 6–7, astronomy and physics, etc.) and alphabetical within volumes. Full citations appear in all listings. Updated annually.

BIBLIOGRAPHIC ACTIVITIES OF
THE LIBRARY OF CONGRESS

     The several catalogs of the Library of Congress form an excellent bridge between current and retrospective bibliography, since even the most current issues of the "author catalog" are simultaneously current and retrospective. They also furnish a good contrast between trade bibliography and the far-ranging national bibliography. For the purposes of this discussion, the bibliographic separateness of the LC series of catalogs will be ignored at first: they will be considered as parts of one large bibliography. Having surveyed the forest in this manner, we shall then turn our attention to the individual trees in the LC jungle.

     Scope: The Library of Congress catalogs are a universal list covering materials issued anywhere in the world, at any time. They are therefore, both current and retrospective in coverage. One part (the *National Union Catalog*) includes entries cataloged by the Library of Congress and those libraries which participated in its original cooperative cataloging, as well as about 1,100 North American libraries (LC's estimate) reporting publications issued in 1956 and afterward, which are not represented by LC printed cards. The *NUC* shows locations for at least one library holding the publication, and serves, for those imprints, as a North American union catalog.

     The Library of Congress catalogs currently contain entries for books, pamphlets, maps, atlases, periodicals and other serials—regardless of date of publication. Entries for reproductions of such materials are also included. The catalogs include materials written and published in a wide variety of languages: Arabic, Cyrillic, Gaelic, Greek, Hebraic, Roman, the various Indic alphabets, and in Chinese, Japanese, and Korean characters. (In listing materials cataloged by other libraries, but not held by LC, those in Greek and Gaelic are given in transliteration, as are those materials printed in the Cyrillic or Hebraic alphabets.) Entries for librettos, books about music and musicians, and nonmusical sound recordings appear in both the music catalog and in *NUC,* but entries for printed music and musical sound recordings are found only in *Music, Books on Music, and Sound Recordings*. LC entries for motion pictures and filmstrips appear in *Films and Other Materials for Projection*.

Entries prepared by reporting libraries for U.S. federal or state documents are included only when there are no LC entries for these titles. Masters' theses accepted by U.S. colleges and universities are excluded (except honors theses and those in library science). American doctoral dissertations (which are included in *Dissertation Abstracts International*) are not cataloged by LC, and, therefore, are not generally represented in *NUC*. If a reporting library submits a catalog entry for any doctoral dissertation in its own collections, however, it will be included. LC entries for serials are included, while serial titles reported by other libraries are excluded—but see *New Serial Titles*, which lists serials first published in 1950 or later, cataloged either by LC or the cooperating libraries.

The *NUC* is printed in nine monthly issues, three quarterly cumulations (January–March, April–June, July–September), and annual and quinquennial cumulations. In the last year of a quinquennial cumulation, no annual cumulation is published. The monthly issues contain only the cards prepared for publications of the current and preceding two years. The quarterly, annual, and quinquennial cumulations contain all cards currently printed, regardless of the date of publication represented. For the publishing frequency of the other parts of the Library of Congress catalogs, see the individual titles discussed later.

Very useful additions to the catalogs are the LC *see, see also,* and explanatory references, which are included only in quarterly and larger cumulations, and only if the heading referred to appears in that issue. The quarterly and larger cumulations include LC information cards, giving information about changes of names, mergers, etc., and the special cards for acronyms. Those information cards are added whether or not there are entries in the issue under the headings for which these cards are prepared. (A full record of LC cross references for new or newly revised headings can be found in *Library of Congress Name Headings with References,* publication of which began in 1974.)

History: Before describing the individual parts, a brief resumé of the development of this set of catalogs may be useful (or thoroughly confusing and demoralizing). The changes in title which have occurred in the original "main entry only" catalog reflected LC's expansion of its catalogs. Each part will receive its own description later, but perhaps it can be better understood with the history of the whole series in mind.

The catalogs began with *A Catalog of Books Represented by Library of Congress Printed Cards (Cards Issued from August 1898 through July 1942),* consisting of 167 volumes of photographically reproduced LC cards. This catalog listed all items only once—under main entry. It was primarily a book, pamphlet, and periodical list. The first supplement cumulated the years 1942–47 under the title *A Catalog of Books Represented by Library of Congress Printed Cards. Supplement. (Cards Issued from August 1942 through December 1947)*. Like the basic set, this was a "main entry only" catalog.

Between this cumulation and the next 5-yearly supplement to the basic set, a change of title occurred (with the annual cumulation for 1949). This change was made because LC was about to begin issuing an addition to the catalog series, entitled *Library of Congress Catalog. A Cumulative List of Works Represented by Library of Congress Cards. Books: Subjects*. To distinguish between the two sets, the author catalog was renamed *The Library of Congress Author Catalog* for the duration of the current volumes, appearing in a more expanded form with the next cumulation: *The Library of Congress Author Catalog. A Cumulative List of Works Represented by Library of Congress Cards 1948–1952*.

Before the appearance of the third 5-yearly cumulation (1953–57), two changes of title took place in the current supplements, reflecting a reorganization of the catalog. The first change altered the name from *The Library of Congress Author Catalog* to *The Library of Congress Catalog—Books: Authors*. (This change was made in January, 1953). The title was changed because three new parts of the catalog series had begun publication: (1) *Films;* (2) *Maps and Atlases;* (3) *Music and Phonorecords*. It was in 1953 that LC also began issuing *New Serial Titles*, which can be thought of as another "form" catalog to be added to the music and film sets. *Maps and Atlases* was short-lived, lasting only from 1953 to 1955.

In July of 1956, the title of the current volumes changed a second time, reflecting an expansion of the union catalog coverage of the author set. The third 5-yearly cumulation appeared as *The National Union Catalog; A Cumulative Author List Representing Library of Congress Printed Cards and Titles Reported by Other American Libraries, 1953–57*.

In 1973, a new catalog—*Newspapers in Microform*—began appearing, while two of the older parts had name changes: from *Music and Phonorecords* to *Music, Books on Music, and Sound Recordings;* and from *Motion Pictures and Filmstrips* to *Films and Other Materials for Projection*. In 1974, LC began issuing the Monographic Series.

The Library of Congress catalogs will continue to evolve. LC has announced that it hopes to have all of its cataloging in machine-readable form by the end of 1981. As those plans are being made, LC is also looking for better ways to produce and distribute the *National Union Catalog*. A new pattern for *NUC* has been offered to the library world for discussion. The proposed pattern would be based on a series of Master Registers "which will provide full bibliographic records for all items cataloged, that is, all of the information which now appears on LC printed catalog cards." These Master Registers would be published at regular, but as yet unspecified, intervals. They would not cumulate, but would be permanent records of the full bibliographic data published during the year. Accompanying the Master Registers would be a series of cumulative indexes. These indexes might offer access points by names, titles, subjects, monographic series, LC card numbers, locations, or ISBN/ISSN. These indexes would actually be brief entry catalogs and would probably contain enough information to satisfy most reference needs. An entry in an index would refer to the corresponding entry in the Master Register by a unique reference number. Students can follow the progress of these proposals in, among other places, the pages of the *Library of Congress Information Bulletin.*

At the present time, the Library of Congress catalogs contain the following parts:

    I. *The National Union Catalog*
        a. the "pre-1956 Imprints" (in progress—but very far along)
        b. the "basic set" and its supplements ("Basic set" is a brief way of referring to some very long titles, and a series of title changes.)
    II. *Subject Catalog*
    III. *Monographic Series*
    IV. *Films and Other Materials for Projection*
    V. *Music, Books on Music, and Sound Recordings*
    VI. *New Serial Titles*
    VII. *National Union Catalog of Manuscript Collections*
    VIII. *Newspapers in Microform*
    IX. *National Register of Microform Masters.*

National Union Catalogs

(11)   Pre-1956 Imprints. (in progress)

At the beginning of August 1973, when the final push on the re-writing of the Fourth Edition of this book was under way, over 260 volumes of the projected 610 volumes of the *National Union Catalog. Pre-1956 Imprints* were off the press. As of August 4, 1973, Volume 269 was on the shelves of the University of Michigan Library. By June 1, 1978, volume 554 (SOC-SOE) was on the shelves of that library. On August 24, 1978, the head of the book purchasing division reported by phone that they had just received volume 579. The price for that volume was $38.50, compared to the price of $15.68 for the first volumes.

Estimating an average cost per volume of $30.00, the whole set (675 volumes are now projected) will cost in the range of $20,000. The printing task is the largest print order executed to date.

The catalog will contain entries for all LC titles with printed cards, in addition to the titles held by other libraries. It is based on the original National Union Catalog in card form, which dates from the beginning of the twentieth century.

Herbert Putnam, Librarian of Congress, wrote the following in his annual report for the fiscal year ending June 30, 1901:

> It is fully recognized by the Library of Congress that next in importance to an adequate exhibit of its own resources, comes the ability to supply information as to the resources of other libraries. As [a step] in this direction [the Library plans] a catalogue of books in some of the more important libraries outside of Washington. The Library of Congress ... hopes to receive a copy of every card printed by the New York Public Library, the Boston Library, the Harvard University Library, the John Crerar Library, and several others. These it will arrange and preserve in a card catalogue of great collections outside of Washington.

By 1926, there were almost 2,000,000 cards in the catalog, but unfilled requests for the location of titles indicated clearly that a more comprehensive coverage of research library holdings was needed (although libraries like Newberry, the University of Illinois, and the University of Chicago had joined in sending cards). John D. Rockfeller, Jr. gave LC a gift of $250,000 ($50,000 per year for five years for the period 1927–32) for the extension of the holdings of the Union Catalog. At the end of the period, LC established a permanent Union Catalog Division. Between 1932 and 1945, the Library added another 3,350,000 cards. Later additions included the holdings of the regional union catalogs in Cleveland and Philadelphia, the entire catalogs of the libraries of Yale and the University of California (Berkeley), as well as the North Carolina Union Catalog. By the time volume I of this current catalog was printed, the union catalog held more than 16 million cards, recording about 10 million titles and editions.

This Mansell edition of the pre-1956 imprints will supersede the following parts of the author series:

1) *A Catalog of Books Represented by Library of Congress Printed Cards (Cards Issued from August 1898 through July 1942).*
2) *A Catalog of Books Represented by Library of Congress Cards. Supplement (Cards issued from August 1942 through December 1947).*
3) *The Library of Congress Author Catalog, 1948–1952.*

4) *The National Union Catalog, 1952–1955 Imprints.*
5) *The National Union Catalog, A Cumulative Author List, 1953–1957.*

To summarize the contents of the *Pre-1956 Imprints:* it reports the cataloged holdings of works published before 1956 in the Library of Congress and in major research libraries of the United States. It includes the more rarely held items in the collections of selected smaller and specialized libraries. The materials included consist of books, pamphlets, maps, atlases, and music. Periodicals and serials are included if catalogued by LC or reported by other libraries, but because of the special union lists of periodicals, such as the *Union Lost of Serials, New Serial Titles,* etc., the reporting of holdings to LC by other libraries has not been systematically done, and thus one cannot expect the set to be a complete record of serial holdings for other libraries. Manuscript collections are listed in the *National Union Catalog of Manuscripts,* but individual manuscripts will be in the *Pre-1956 Imprints* if reported to LC.

The following materials are not included, even if represented by LC cards or cards prepared by other libraries: phonorecords; motion pictures and filmstrips; and cards for books for the blind (in Braille, raised type, etc.). Masters theses of American colleges have also generally been excluded, since they are usually available only from the institution granting the degree. Masters theses represented by LC printed cards, by cards of the National Library of Medicine, and by cards for commercially available microforms have been included—as have Harvard honors theses.

Only works printed or written in languages in the Roman alphabet, Greek, and Gaelic are included. Works in the Cyrillic, Arabic, Hebrew, Chinese, Japanese, Korean, and various Indic alphabets, and all other non-Roman characters are included only if represented by LC cards, since transliteration in such cases has been uniform. Works in these languages represented in the National Union Catalog on cards (the original one, that is, not the currently published one) are not included due to lack of uniform transliteration.

The catalog is primarily a catalog of *main entries,* with needed cross references and selected added entries. It is important to note that the form of both main and added entries is the American Library Association's *Cataloging Rules for Author and Title Entries,* 1949 edition. Changing all entries to conform to the *Anglo-American Cataloging Rules* of 1967 would have been an impossible task. The new rules are used in those cases which represent the first reporting of that particular entry in the new form (a cross reference is made from the old form). The editors tried to standardize all entries to conform to the 1949 rules, and to collect all the works of one author together under one form of entry. But because of the variant forms of names used by one author, because of differing library practices in the reporting libraries—or in the Library of Congress over time—because of typographic errors in transcribing the author's name, different copies of the same work, or different works by the same author may be found under different main entries. In the special case of music, conventional titles have been ignored, and the music has been alphabetized under composer by the titles used on the title page. Johannes Dewton, Head of the National Union Catalog Publication Project at LC, reminds us that one should keep in mind that this catalog attempted to record the results of more than a hundred years of cataloging at LC and at the hundreds of libraries represented. Variation was inevitable, but the editors tried to get all main entries under the Library of Congress entry (if there was more than one entry for an author); under a form called for by the 1949 rules, if there were no LC entry. But the editors accepted entries from other libraries, if it were not obvious from the entry itself that it deviated from the 1949 rules. Cross references were made from other entries to that chosen for this work.

Added entries were included for joint authors, editors, and the like; for titles of works published anonymously that have been given a main entry under the actual author; and for instances in which a choice of main entry was possible.

Dewton's introduction in the first volume gives a key to explanations of marks and symbols used on LC printed cards, and also those used on cards contributed by other libraries. Some examples may be suggestive of the helpful information given:

A Maltese cross with call number, enclosed in parentheses, indicates that the publication has been withdrawn from the library's collections (i.e., LC's collection).

Alternative Dewey numbers (on cards for those titles which have had Dewey numbers assigned by LC, i.e., publications of general interest) are shown in square brackets; Decimal numbers in parentheses indicate the number assigned to a monographic series, as opposed to the number of the individual monograph.

An asterisk after the card number indicates that it was cataloged between July 1947 and December 1949 by the then new *Rules for Descriptive Cataloging*. A double dagger indicates cataloging done under the rules for limited cataloging (used at LC between April 1951 and September 1963).

When the set is completed, it will constitute an extraordinarily useful resource for covering the human record since Gutenberg. Scholars from this time onward will have recourse to the set to learn not only what has been produced, but where copies of material their own libraries do not hold can be found. (The authors have waited long for LC

and all those others who have struggled long to bring this project to
fruition—they cannot pass by this first opportunity they have to urge
students to appreciate this matchless set. We are swept away into the
hortative: treasure it!)

(12)   **A Catalog of Books Represented by Library of Congress
        Printed Cards (Cards Issued from August 1898 through July
        1942). 167v.**

   Scope: includes books, pamphlets, periodicals and other serials,
but not motion pictures or filmstrips, since LC did not begin to issue
cards for such materials until 1951. Music is not strongly represented
(i.e., sheet music and music scores—one does find books on music or
anthologies of music). The total number of items runs to about
4,250,000, with about 250,000 representing titles not held by LC, but
for which copy was supplied by those libraries participating in LC's
cooperative cataloging program. (Thus, even in this first catalog, a
union catalog feature is present.) Inclusion is not restricted to materials
produced in the United States, but includes work published
anywhere—and at any time.
   Arrangement: Listing is alphabetical *by main entry only,* that is,
by personal or corporate author where there is one, or under title for
serials, anonymous works, or wherever else appropriate under the ALA
rules. This means, of course, that an item is listed only once, and one
must have the correct main entry to find it.
   Sample Entry: (for book cataloged by LC)

> Francesi, Wolfgang Ludwig, 1999–
> > *Crowds of power.* Trans. from the French by Starol
> Smith. New York, Imaginary Books, 2050 [c.2049]
> > 612p. illus.
> > Most of the above material first appeared in *Madder
> Magazine.*
> > 1. Political Science I. Title
> Library of Congress HQ 9875.F6   A49-8426

   Sample Entry: (for book cataloged by another library)

> Francesi, Wolfgang Ludwig, 1999–
> > *Crowds of power.* Trans. from the French by Starol
> Smith. New York, Imaginary Books, 2050 [2049]
> > 612p. illus.
> > Most of the above material first appeared in *Madder
> Magazine.*
> > 1. Political Science I. Title
> New York. Public Library
> > for Library of Congress   A49-8426

(13)   A Catalog of Books Represented by Library of Congress Printed Cards. Supplement. (Cards Issued from August 1942 through December 1947). 42v.

Scope: This is the first 5-yearly supplement to the basic set, and there are no significant changes in scope, format, or arrangement, beyond the expansion of coverage of all forms of printed music. In 1943, LC began a more comprehensive cataloging program for music—although some cards had always been issued. One minor but interesting feature is the re-printing from the basic set of about 26,000 anonymous and pseudonymous titles, which had been listed in the basic set under author, but which are here realphabetized under title (identifiable by the black line drawn through the author entry).

Since there was no change in form of entry, no sample will be given here—it would be identical with the preceding entries.

(14)   The Library of Congress Author Catalog. A Cumulative List of Works Represented by Library of Congress Cards, 1948–52. 24v.

Scope: This was expanded to include motion pictures and filmstrips, when LC began issuing cards for such materials. This change began in the current supplements in 1951. The last two volumes of this set cumulated *Music and Phonorecords* entries and *Films,* whose arrangement will be described below, after the author set is finished.

Arrangement: a significant change was made in the former main entry listing. Beginning with this supplement, entries were made for essential added entries (editor, joint author, corporate body which might be thought to be the author of a book entered under personal author—and vice versa), which enables one to locate material more easily. These added entries are prepared especially for the catalogs and give only the more important bibliographical data.

(15)   The National Union Catalog; a Cumulative Author List Representing Library of Congress Printed Cards and Titles Reported by Other American Libraries, 1953–57. 28v.

Scope: With the beginning of the National Union Catalog, the scope of coverage of titles cataloged by other libraries was very greatly increased. Whereas in the basic set only about one-seventeenth of the titles were those of cooperative libraries, in this first set over one-half are. About 500 libraries are represented. The coverage of this country's holdings are thus enormously increased. One special case: all serials included are those cataloged by LC; serial titles held by other libraries are reported in *New Serial Titles*. It is most important to note that a uniform cut-off date was employed. (It is really a uniform "start-off" date, but that term has never turned up in the authors' experience!) LC accepted cards for listing for all items published in *1956* or later. It did *not* print cards for older materials which might have just been purchased and cataloged by a cooperating library. If, for example, a library cataloged a 1475 title, this incunabulum would not have been reported in the *National Union Catalog*. Unfortunately, life can seem complicated at first glance, because, of course, this date does not apply to LC's own titles. Older works bought and cataloged by LC will appear in the *National Union Catalog*.

Arrangement: remains unchanged. But the information given now shows holdings of more than one library.

Sample Entry:

Francesi, Wolfgang Ludwig, 1999–
    Crowds of power. Trans. from the
French by Starol Smith. New York, Imaginary Books, 2050.
        612p. illus.
        Most of the above material first appeared in *Madder Magazine.*
        1. Political science   I. Title
    HQ9875.F6   301.158   A49-8426
    NNG IU CMiC MoSU MiU NN IaU InU

(16)   1952–1955 Imprints. 30v.

Although this title is out of chronological order of coverage, it has been put in at this point because it was issued after the preceding title. It is an extension backwards in coverage of date of publication, but is no different in scope or arrangement from the 1953–57 volumes, with one major qualification: it is restricted to monographs. There is some difference in appearance, since many of the cards are typed and the letters showing libraries holding copies are often at the side—but these are hardly major matters, since they in no way affect the content.

(17)   1958–1962 Imprints . . . 54v.

A 54-volume set, with no change in system of entry or in inclusions. Volumes 1–50 comprise the author list; volumes 51–52, the cumulation of *Music and Phonorecords;* volumes 53–54, the cumulation of *Motion Pictures and Filmstrips*.

(18)   1963–1967 Imprints. 72v.

This cumulation lists 1,210,000 entries, including the music and motion picture additions at the end of the cumulation.

(19)   1968–1972 Imprints. 128v.

Volumes 1–104 make up the author list; 105–119, the *Register of Additional Locations;* and five additional volumes are devoted to *Music and Phonorecords* and *Motion Pictures and Filmstrips.*

(20)   1973–1977 Imprints.

The 1978 catalog of Library of Congress publications in print announced that this was being published by Rowman and Littlefield in about 150 volumes.

(21)   Current Volumes.

As of June 1, 1978, the following volumes were on the shelves of the University of Michigan Graduate Library:
1. *The National Union Catalog 1973.* 16v. (plus 2v. of additional locations)
2. _____. 1974. 18v. (plus 2v. of additional locations)
3. _____. 1975. 18v. (plus 2v. of additional locations)
4. _____. 1976. 16v.
5. _____. 1977—January–March. 3 paperbound volumes
6. _____. 1977—April–June. 3 paperbound volumes
7. _____. 1977—July–September. 4 paperbound volumes
8. _____. 1977—October. 1 paperbound volume
9. _____. 1977—November. 1 paperbound volume
10. _____. 1977—December. 1 paperbound volume
11. _____. 1978—January. 1 paperbound volume
12. _____. 1978—February. 1 paperbound volume

No further volumes were on the shelves on August 31, 1978. The February volume was received by the University Library on May 17, 1978. (The March volume will be a three-month cumulation [January/February/March], whose printing and preparation takes longer than a single month's catalog.)

Thus a searcher in August 1978, looking for a title published, let us say, in 1830, but not acquired and cataloged by the Library of Congress until this year—a fact unknown to our searcher—would probably search in twenty different alphabets before finding it, assuming he/she started with the basic set, as is reasonable and logical for such an early title. For a recently published book, of course, this problem would not arise.

Other Book Catalogs

(22)   Subject Catalog. (1950–1954; 1955–1959; etc.)

Scope: Includes those titles for which the Library of Congress has printed cards, covering books, pamphlets, periodicals and other serials, and maps, motion pictures, and music scores *through 1952.* (Motion pictures and music scores have their own subject indexes in their separate catalogs beginning with 1953. Maps were out for the brief span of the life of that separate catalog, and then were re-introduced into the subject catalog.) There is one very important limitation to keep in mind: only those items are included whose imprint date is 1945 or later.

Arrangement: LC cards (slightly abridged by omission of notes and tracings) are re-arranged under LC subject headings. Continued by quarterly and annual supplements, followed by quinquennial cumulations. Quarterly issues exclude belles-letters and imprints issued before the current year being recorded. Annual cumulations include titles with imprint dates of 1945 or later if they were currently cataloged by LC.

(23)   Monographic Series. 1974–

Scope: A listing of all monographs appearing as parts of series which have been cataloged by LC. It thus includes complete LC cataloging information, including LC card numbers, which makes it a useful acquisition tool, in addition to its bibliographic uses. It gives materials in all languages in which LC catalogs. Series in non-Roman alphabets are recorded in the LC system of transliteration.

Arrangement: It is a listing by both series titles and corporate bodies responsible for a monographic series. Individual authors are listed under the series entry. Cross references are made from short or popular names of the series to the complete form used in cataloging and from variant names of corporate authors of series to the form established in the LC catalogs.

Exclusions: Those series issued by publishers in which the series title is purely promotional (''or esthetic,'' LC says) and series which form the completed works of personal authors. In addition, it does not list those government documents which have been numbered only for the purposes of identification.

·   *Frequency:* Appears in three quarterly paperbound issues and a bound annual cumulation. If quinquennial cumulations are planned, 1978 should see the beginning of work on the first cumulation, with publication perhaps late in 1979.

Films

(24)   Films and Other Materials for Projection. 1953–

Formerly *Motion Pictures and Filmstrips,* the title was changed
with the January/March 1973 quarterly issue to its present form, signal-
ing an expansion of its coverage of forms. The new catalog has the
following characteristics:

Scope: Films and Other Materials for Projection tries to catalog
all motion pictures, filmstrips, sets of transparencies and slide sets
released in the United States or Canada which have instructional value.
Presently, video recordings are restricted to those distributed by the
National Audiovisual Center. The material needed for catalog entries is
supplied largely by producers, manufacturers, film libraries, or distributing agencies. The National Audiovisual Center provides information
for United States government materials, including video recordings. In
most cases, cataloging is done from the information thus provided,
without actual viewing of the material itself.

From 1951 through April 1957, cards were printed for almost all
the motion pictures and filmstrips registered for copyright during that
period. From May 1957 through 1971, cards were printed only for those
copyrighted films which were added to the collections of the Library of
Congress. Starting with 1972, cards have been printed almost completely from data supplied by producing or distributing agencies.

Frequency: It appears in three quarterly issues (January/March,
April/June, and July/September), with annual and quinquennial cumulations.

Arrangement: Entries are made under main and added entries,
and under subject headings and cross-references. The 1976 annual issue
also contained catalog entries by personal and corporate author (although the major part of the entries are still under title). It was the first
LC catalog to be produced entirely by computer processing, and "the
techniques and procedures that required definition and implementation
at every stage of the publication process involved a greater number of
people from a greater variety of positions than has ever been the case
with any of the library's other book catalogs" (LC). This forced the
delay in the appearance of the 1976 annual and the 1977 quarterlies, so
that LC issued a January/June semiannual cumulation in lieu of the first
two quarterlies. Some of the delay resulted from quite unexpected problems which the Government Printing Office had in finding a subcontrac-
tor to do the photocomposition.

Sample Entry:

Crowds of power. (Motion Picture) Futuristic Films, 2050.
   3 hrs., sd., color, 35 mm.

Cinemascope. Color by Colortronics.
Based on the study of the same title by Wolfgang L. Francesi.
Credits: Producer, John Smith; director, Frank Smith; screenplay, John Smith, Jr.; music, Frank Smith, Jr.; film editor, John Smith III. *Cast:* Adele Smith, Robert Smith, Kipp Smith, Douglas Smith, John Smith IV.
1. Political science. I. Francesi, Wolfgang L. Crowds of power.

Added Entries:

Futuristic Films.
  see
    Crowds of power

Entry from the Subject Index:

POLITICAL SCIENCE
  Crowds of power

Music

(25)   Music, Books on Music, and Sound Recordings. 1953–

Once again, the change of title signals a change in the catalog. Until 1973, this catalog contained only Library of Congress printed cards. In that year the Music Library Association recommended the inclusion of material from seven college and university libraries (Toronto, Stanford, Chicago, Illinois, Harvard, North Carolina, Bowling Green, Ohio State, Oberlin), and the character of the catalog became "quasi-national" (LC's term).

Scope: Includes actual music scores of all kinds, sheet music, libretti, and books about music and musicians, as well as sound recordings of all kinds, whether musical, educational, literary, or political, representing LC catalog cards and the materials supplied by the seven cooperating libraries. Literature on music and such related materials as libretti and music textbooks are also included in the *National Union Catalog* and the *Subject Catalog*.

Frequency: It is published semiannually, one issue containing materials received between January and June, and the other being an annual cumulation. In the last year of a quinquennial cumulation no annual cumulation is published.

Arrangement: Alphabetical, with references from variant forms of personal names and titles. Added entries are provided for Library of Congress cards.

Sample Entry:

Francesi, Wolfgang Ludwig, 1999–
  Crowds of power, a secular oratorio, with special ob-
ligato by Elias Jones.
  New York, Imaginary Music Co., 2050.
  295p. 36 cm.
    1. Oratorios—since 1950—Scores. I. Jones, Elias. II. Title
M2050.F25C7   Music 256

Entry from the Subject Index:

ORATORIOS
  Francesi, Wolfgang Ludwig, 1999–   *Crowds of power*
  English

Serials

(26)   New Serial Titles.

Scope: Includes serials which began publication in 1950 or later.
The term "serial" includes monographic series as well as magazines
and journals. Certain types of serial publications are omitted: newspapers, looseleaf publications, municipal government serial documents,
and publishers' series. It is published in eight monthly issues, four
quarterly issues, and an annual supplement. Cumulations appeared for
1950–1960; 1961–1965; 1966–1969, but these were all superseded by
the 20-year cumulation issued by Bowker in 1973, which covers the
period 1950–1970. There is also a cumulation for 1971–75.

Arrangement: An alphabetical list by main entry (most often by
title, but sometimes by issuing body), showing which libraries hold
runs, and indicating by symbols the completeness of the holdings in a
general way (but not with the specificity of the *Union List of Serials*).

Sample Entry:

Crowds of Power. A quarterly devoted to political affairs.
  New York. v. 1, 2050–
    DLC 1-MiU 1–

Subject guide: All entries in the regular issues of *New Serial
Titles* are arranged into subject sequence and are published in *New
Serial Titles—Classed Subject Arrangement.* This appears in twelve
monthly issues, but does not often cumulate. *New Serial Titles, 1950–
1970, Subject Catalog* is the most comprehensive cumulation.

Manuscripts

(27)   National Union Catalog of Manuscript Collections. 1959–

This collection is based on reports from American manuscript depositories, in addition to those of the Library of Congress, and thus it also shares the union catalog feature of the National Union Catalog.

The following criteria for admission were laid down in the introductory volume's introduction:

> A large group of papers (manuscript or typescript, diaries, originals (or copies) of letters, memoranda, accounts, log books, drafts, etc., including associated printed or near-print materials), usually having a common source and formed by or around an individual, a family, or corporate entity, or devoted to a single theme.
>
> Small groups consisting of a highly limited number of pieces should not be reported as collections in themselves but should be taken care of by more inclusive reports covering many such groups, either by an entry under an appropriate theme, if possible, or by a general entry for the miscellaneous (residual) collections of the repository.
>
> A collection must be located in a public or quasi-public repository that regularly admits researchers.

The 1976 volume of *NUCMC* noted that the catalog had, since its beginnings, published information on approximately 37,600 collections held in 990 different depositories. *NUCMC* has also provided indexing by approximately 382,000 entries to topical subjects and personal, family, corporate, and geographical names.

Microforms

(28)   Newspapers in Microform. 1973–

In 1973, the Library of Congress published *Newpapers in Microform: United States, 1948–1972* and *Newspapers in Microform: Foreign Countries, 1948–1972*. *Newspapers in Microform* (1973–) was planned to be the annual supplement to those basic volumes.

Scope: The preface to the first basic volume described it as part of "a continuing cumulative series designed to bring under bibliographic control United States newspapers that have been reduced to microform and are housed permanently in United States, Canadian and other foreign libraries as well as in the vaults of domestic and foreign commercial producers of microforms." The other volume did the same for foreign papers. The annual supplements contain reports of titles newly reduced to microform, additional holdings of titles previously reported, and corrections and revisions to earlier entries. They combine coverage of U.S. and foreign newspapers. The 1976 annual volume included information from 190 U.S. and 78 foreign institutions.

Arrangement: Foreign newspapers are listed in the first section and U.S. in the second. Within those sections, the arrangement is alphabetical by geographical location. A third section provides a combined title index to both U.S. and foreign papers.

Sample entry:

```
Worcester magazine. Ap 1786-Mr 1788.              w
    Replaces Thomas's Massachusetts spy, or Worcester
    gazette.
    AuCNL smp 1786-1788
    AuSU smp 1786-1788
    NPotU s 1786-1788
```

(29)   National Register of Microform Masters. 1965–

Scope: This annual publication now lists microform masters of foreign and U.S. books, pamphlets, serials, and foreign doctoral dissertations. It excludes technical reports, typescript translations, foreign or U.S. archival manuscript collections, U.S. doctoral dissertations, masters' theses, and newspapers. (A microform master is one which exists solely for the purpose of making other copies. They are usually negatives, although occasionally a positive microform may serve as a master.)

Entries are based on reports made to the Library of Congress by the institutions, associations, publishing companies, etc. which own the microform masters.

Arrangement: Although arrangement (as well as scope) has varied through the years, the first eleven years of the *Register* have been cumulated into a single alphabet, in a six-volume set. The annual supplements now appear in one alphabetical arrangement by main entry.

Sample entry:

```
Francesi, Wolfgang, 1939-  ed. Crowds of power. New
    York, Imaginery Books, 1984.
    xi, 612p. 2v.
    MiUS m mf                              84-0909
```

RETROSPECTIVE AMERICAN BIBLIOGRAPHY

(3))   **Sabin, Joseph. Dictionary of Books Relating to America, from its Discovery to the Present Time. New York, Sabin, 1868–92; Bibliographical Society of America, 1928–36. 29 vols.**

Sabin's work is one of the very important retrospective American bibliographies, listing about 250,000 editions (including those mentioned in the notes). As its title suggests, it is not limited to books published in America, but includes any dealing with America. The period covered and the materials included are not uniform throughout the set. Sabin tried to include materials up to the date of publication of each volume. The twenty-first volume (1929) restricted titles listed to those published not later than 1876. In 1932, the cut-off date became 1860, and sermons, government publications, and much local material were omitted. After 1933, the date of inclusion dropped back to 1840.

Arrangement is primarily alphabetical by author. Anonymous works, however, are listed alphabetically under title, under subject, or under place if they deal with a geographic entity (for example, there are 582 items listed under New York). The information given for each title includes full title, publisher, place, date, format, paging, and often contents. There are frequent bibliographical notes, which are sometimes extensive. Other titles by the author may be presented in the notes, references to a description or review of the item in some other work may be given, and, in many cases, the names of libraries having copies are listed.

In consulting Sabin, it is important to remember that his work cannot be used with the same ease as the *CBI*. Many irregularities would have to be forgiven an author undertaking so mammoth a task single-handedly. Sabin himself remarked in volume one: "Had the magnitude and extreme difficulty of the undertaking been presented to my mind in full proportions at the outset, I should never have attempted it; and, indeed, I may remark that I have more than once almost determined upon its abandonment."

With this by way of introduction, consider some of the following examples of non-uniform presentation of material. Sabin enters under the letter "A" the title *Abrégé de la révolution,* with the cross-reference: "see Buisson." Under Buisson, one can find the title listed, with fuller information as to what was on the title page: *Abrégé de la révolution de l'Amérique* . . . Par M.***, Américaine. If one looks under the pseudonym "M.***", one will find a cross-reference to Buisson. Thus two expectations are aroused by this example: (1) cross-references will be made from the titles of pseudonymous works to the real author; (2) cross-references will be made from the pseudonym to the real author.

But, under Buisson, Sabin lists another title published by him under another pseudonym: *Nouvelles considérations* . . . par M.D.B.*** If one looks under the title *Nouvelles considérations* or under the pseudonym, one will find no cross-references to Buisson. Thus two titles by the same author are not treated in the same way.

Sabin also lists under title *Battle of New Orleans,* by a Citizen of Baltimore. If—on the basis of other examples of his procedure—one looks for a cross-reference from ''Citizen of Baltimore'' to this particular title, none will be found. Yet Sabin gives many cross-references under other pseudonyms beginning with the words ''Citizen of.''

He will also occasionally bury potentially interesting material under fairly useless entries. Under the title of a periodical, *Bulletin de la Société Philomatique,* he informs the reader that the volume for 1817 contains ''Note sur une nouvelle espèce d'ours de l'Amérique du Nord, 'Ursus griseus,' and Note sur le Wapité, espèce de cerf de l'Amérique septentrionale, by H. M. Ducrotay de Blainville.'' It might easily happen that a researcher would know the titles of these articles or even the author's name. If one looks under ''Ducrotay de Blainville,'' ''Blainville,'' ''Note sur une . . . , '' ''ours,'' ''ursus,'' ''Wapité,'' one will find nothing that leads to the entry for the name of the periodical.

Admiral Vernon's *A New Ballad on the Taking of Porto-Bello,* issued with Vernon's name on the title page, is entered under title, not under Vernon nor under the place Porto Bello. It is true that the title can be found under Vernon's name; not, however, among the regular list of titles, but buried some 50 lines into the notes.

These examples are not given in an attempt to discredit or belittle Sabin's monumental work. They are intended, however, to caution the user of Sabin not to assume that an item is not in Sabin because it was not found in the place in which similar titles had been listed. As is the case with the British Museum *Catalogue,* if you don't find it in the first place you look, try four or five other approaches.

Sample Entry:

> FRANCESI (W.) *Crowds of Power.* An Oration. Pronounced July 4, 1808. At the request of a number of the Inhabitants of the Town of Dedham and its Vicinity. In Commemoration of the Anniversary of American Independence. By Wolfgang Francesi. . . . Dedham: Printed by the Imaginary Press. July 8, 1808. 8vo., pp. 16.
>
> One hundred and twenty-five copies printed for Mr. J. Carson Francesi. Ten copies were printed on large paper for distribution to the friends of Mr. Francesi. M. +Another edition. Same title. *Philadelphia. Printed and Sold by William Metz, in Plymouth Alley,* 1810. 12mo., pp. 24. The editor of the Bibliography of Americana calls this the second edition. I think it is the third.

The twenty-ninth volume of Sabin contains a paragraph near the close of the introduction which we have decided should be included, as a general comment on all bibliographic work:

Sabin is finished and, as did the monks writing in their scriptoria during the Middle Ages, we have placed after the last entry of our manuscript a fervent "Laus Deo." On the title page of each volume of "Sabin" you will find the following quotation from the preface of Anthony a Wood's History of Oxford of 1674:
"A painfull work it is I'll assure you, and more than difficult, wherein what toyle hath been taken, as no man thinketh so no man believeth, but he hath made the triall."

Two bibliographic projects of the 1970s have used Sabin as a base. John E. Molnar's three-volume *Author-Title Index to Joseph Sabin's Dictionary of Books Relating to America* was published in 1974 by Scarecrow Press. That was the same year that Lawrence S. Thompson's *The New Sabin: Books Described by Joseph Sabin and His Successors, Now Described Again on the Basis of Examination of Originals, and Fully Indexed by Title, Subject, Joint Authors, and Institutions and Agencies* began to appear to mixed reviews. Contents of this latter work are at least partially based on certain microform reprint collections and appear to be only loosely tied to Sabin. The publication is planned as a long-term project. (The first three volumes, for example, included a total of only about 8,400 entries.)

(3)　**Evans, Charles. American Bibliography; a Chronological Dictionary of All Books, Pamphlets, and Periodical Publications Printed in the United States of America from the Genesis of Printing in 1639 down to and including the Year 1820; with Bibliographical and Biographical Notes. Chicago, 1903–34. 12 vols. Vol. 13, 1799–1800, Worcester, Am. Antiq. Soc., 1955.**

As Evans' title indicates, this is a year-by-year listing of publications printed in the United States. The date in the title is misleading, however, since he did not complete the task he had assigned himself and had reached only the letter "M" for the year 1799 at the time of his death. The volume finishing 1799 and carrying the work through 1800 appeared in 1955. The chronological arrangement results in quite a different presentation from that of Sabin's alphabetical one. Evans believed that the chronological arrangement had proven "its perfect adaptability and superiority for reference" to an alphabetical one. That all those interested in tracing information about a particular title would agree with this judgment is doubtful. Some of the difficulties involved will be discussed in a moment, but at this point these remarks can be confined to the effect that this method of presentation has on the physical make-up of the individual volumes. If one arranges chronologically, it becomes imperative that some key be given for the searcher who is seeking a particular author's works. Evans was therefore forced to include an index of authors and anonymous titles in each volume. He further included a subject index, which enables one to gather the titles published in a given field. The subject approach is not afforded by Sabin (except, of course, to the degree that his listing under place and his listing of some anonymous titles under subject affords a subject analysis of his titles). Evans also furnished an index of printers and publishers in each volume.

For each title, he gives the standard information: author's full name, full title, place, date, publisher or printer, paging, size, and—in many cases—the names of libraries possessing copies.

A cumulated author and title index to all the volumes was published in 1959. It does afford a limited subject approach, since entries have been made for people, ships, and Indian tribes named in titles. But no systematic subject approach was attempted, so that it may still be necessary on occasion to use the subject index found in each volume. In using the subject indexes, it must be kept in mind that Evans was not employing a standard list of subject headings. In addition to the occasional scattering of materials which results from the lack of a standard list, there are other mysteries and difficulties to be encountered. Take, as a case in point, the following example: let us assume that a searcher is attempting to locate a certain title, which he/she assumes has been transcribed correctly. The title, as the inquirer transmitted it, is Offers Made by the Sachems of the Three Maquas Castles, to the Mayor . . . of Albany. Boston. What the searcher does not know is that the title really begins, not with the word ''Offers'' but with the word ''Propositions.'' Not knowing the date, he/she dutifully searches through all the volumes under the title in the author-anonymous title indexes. He/she finds nothing. Being resourceful and reflective, he/she concludes that the title is suspect and probably garbled, and decides to use the subject indexes to locate the volume. But under what subject will he/she search? The word ''castles'' might well turn his/her mind entirely away from the personages concerned in making the offer, for who would associate castles with Indians? But the subject entry is ''Indians,'' and, once located, it is clear that the keyword in the title for suggesting Evans' subject is ''Sachems.'' But even here, one might assume that the sachems meant were politicians of the Tammany Society, doing business with a politician in Albany, rather than the chiefs of Indian tribes. Detective ability and careful thought might enable one to locate the item eventually, but the approach through Evans would not be an easy or a quick one. If one lacks the author's name, accurate title, or the date of publication, Evans should not be used until other sources had failed. But he lists titles which cannot be located elsewhere, and the bibliographic searcher will sooner or later either get accustomed to Evans' vagaries, or at least resigned to them.

There are certain other problems which arise in part from his method in compiling. He began his compilation of the early volumes from dealers' catalogs upon which he placed considerable reliance. As a result, he describes many volumes which never existed, ascribes titles to the wrong authors, and makes many minor errors, as in matters of pagination.

These errors have been eradicated—and many titles not known to Evans added—in the new microform edition of Evans which has been undertaken by the American Antiquarian Society and the Readex Microprint Corporation (The Early American Imprints Project). This project filmed the actual text of all of the non-serial titles represented in Evans.

In 1969, Clifford K. Shipton and James E. Mooney's *National Index of American Imprints through 1800—the Short-Title Evans* appeared in two volumes. It incorporates the tens of thousands of corrections in Evans entries turned up by the staff of the American Antiquarian Society in the course of 50 years of work. It contains a total of 49,197 entries (of which 10,035 are additional to the titles listed by Evans). The publication of this list marks a most important contribution to American bibliography.

The American Antiquarian Society has purchased thousands of titles with the express purpose of supporting this bibliographical effort, since it was convinced of the dangers involved in describing an item without having seen it (a problem which produced a sizeable crop of bibliographic ghosts in Evans). In their work. Shipton and Mooney became closely aware of some of the problems in Evans. There were hundreds of errors in the identity of authors (often a book ascribed to a person with same name, but different dates, as the real author). Evans did not like to enter anonymous works under title, so he made great efforts to locate authors, without indicating his contribution of ascription of authorship by bracketing the names (not always correct) which he listed the item under. Shipton and Mooney have estimated that taking the 39,162 Evans items, about one in ten contains a serious bibliographical error, or was never printed. This was not by any means because of stupidity or lack of diligence on Evans' part (he was a prodigiously dedicated worker—at cost to his own income), but due to the fact that he used sources like newspapers or other catalogs when he could not find the originals.

The preface to the 13th volume of Sabin (written by Clifford Shipton for the 1955 publication of this final section of the chronological period covered) gives an excellent brief sketch of Evans' life and his work on the bibliography, which occupied 35 years of his life, as well as that of his wife. (It was of considerable interest to learn that, for the sake of mobility and economy, he wrote his notes with a very fine pen on the backs of 3×5 library cards which had been cut in half, and which he stored in *corset boxes!* When manufacturing costs rose, he met the costs by hiring five printers and serving as their foreman, as well as compiler, office boy, and messenger. It has just occurred to us that Edward G. Holley has written *Charles Evans, American Bibliographer,* published in 1963 by the University of Illinois. If you are interested in "humanizing" your study of his bibliography, you might want to read this splendid biography.)

A second work ancillary to Evans' original list of titles is the *Supplement to Charles Evans' American Bibliography* by Roger P. Bristol (published in 1970 by the University Press of Virginia for the Bibliographical Society of America and the Bibliographical Society of the University of Virginia). It includes over 11,000 items not listed by Evans, constituting an increase of nearly 30% over the original 13-volume set. Together, Evans-Shipton-Bristol total more than 50,000 titles. Frederick R. Goff, Chief of the Rare Book Division of the Library of Congress, remarked in his introduction to the Bristol title: "These are the blood and fabric of America's formative years. These books and pamphlets, newspapers and journal, broadsides and other ephemera, are the basic source materials which historians must read and understand if our early history is to be properly appraised and accurately written."

Bristol also published his Index of *Printers, Publishers, and Booksellers Indicated by Charles Evans in His American Bibliography,* which is an excellent tool for those concerned with American Printing and publishing history.

The presentation of the problems involved in certain kinds of searches in Evans and the knowledge that there are errors in his work might lead one to conclude that Evans is not of much value. This impression—if it has been given—must be corrected. For most searching, in which one knows author, title, and date, and in which one is only attempting to verify the information, Evans will present no major difficulties and remains a bibliographical tool of utmost value.

Sample Entries:

```
AD                                          VALUES
4700  FRANCESI, Wolfgang
          Crowds of Power. An oration, pronounced July 4,
      1808. At the request of a number of the Twon of Ded-
      ham and its Vicinity. In Commemoration of the An-
      niversary of American Independence. Dedham:
      Printed by the Imaginary Press. 1808. pp. 16    $45
```

From the Index of Authors:
    FRANCESI, WOLFGANG
        Crowds of power.   4700

From the classified subject index:
                POLITICAL SCIENCE
        Patriotism   4700, 5706, 6512

(32)   **Shaw, Ralph R. and Shoemaker, Richard H. American Bibliography, a Preliminary Checklist, 1801–1819.**

This work closes a major gap in the chronological coverage of American publishing, which was left because Evans was unable to complete the task he had set himself. The bibliography was compiled from secondary sources, with the hope that libraries would report corrections and additions after the appearance of this preliminary edition. It consists of a series of annual volumes, arranged alphabetically by main entry. The entries are brief, with long subtitles omitted, main title sometimes shortened, and both imprint and collation abbreviated. Holdings are shown.

Sample Entry:

Francesi, Wolfgang
    Crowds of power. An oration... pronounced July 4,
    1808. Dedham, Pr. by The Imaginary Press, 1808. 16p. DLC;
    MWA; NN   15031

Comment: In 1965, Scarecrow Press issued a title index to the 20 volumes, giving references to the item numbers as the key. In 1966, Scarecrow issued a volume of corrections and an author index.

The Early American Imprints series of Readex Microprint Corporation and the American Antiquarian Society, which was mentioned earlier in connection with Evans, has been extended into a second series, which will cover every non-serial title published in the United States from 1801 to 1819, based on the twenty volumes of Shaw and Shoemaker.

(33)   **A Checklist of American Imprints. [For 1820–].**

The first volume of this set (for 1820), announced that Shoemaker had projected a bibliography covering the years 1820–25, and planned coverage has since been extended. He noted that most of the material for the later volumes was already on hand, and that work on them was in progress at the time of publication of the 1820 volume. The method of publication is identical with that of the Shaw and Shoemaker (Item no. 32). The volumes covering 1824 and 1825 were issued in 1969. The 1820–25 list does not include periodicals or newspapers.

Shoemaker died in 1970; the volume covering 1829 appeared in 1971 and is the last volume to have his name on the title page. The 1830 volume (published 1972) was compiled by Gayle Cooper, who had assisted on earlier volumes. A title index for the 1820–1829 volumes was published in 1972; an author index for the same volumes (which also included a list of sources and a list of corrections) was published in

1973. Both indexes were compiled by M. Frances Cooper. Volumes for 1831 (published 1975), 1832 (published 1977), and 1833 imprints (published 1979) were compiled by Scott and Carol Bruntjen. (Catalogers have tended to enter this work under the name of whomever was compiling it at the moment, which may make finding all parts of it on the shelves a bit tricky.)

Plans have been announced to extend coverage of this series through 1875.

(34)   **Roorbach, Orville. Bibliotheca Americana, 1820–61. New York, Roorbach, 1852–61. 4 vols.**

Roorbach's list begins with the year to which Evans intended to come. It is by no means as full in its treatment of titles as Sabin or Evans, nor is it always accurate. It is, in the main, an alphabetical list of authors, with titles also given in the alphabet. Not all titles are entered, however. Under "Abbess, The," one finds the entry "by Mrs. Trollope. 2 v. 12mo. cl. 0 90 Harper & Bros." Under the entry "Trollope," the information is cited again, not quite as fully. "Trollope, Mrs. Abbess. 2 v. cl. 0 90 Harper & Bros." However, under "Abbott, Jacob," his *Elements of Astronomy* is listed, but the title is not given under either "Elements" or "Astronomy, Elements of." Once again we are faced with a lack of uniform practice. It is noteworthy that for the Trollope and the Abbott items, no dates of publication are given. Roorbach does not omit all dates but they cannot be counted upon. His rule was to give dates for history, voyages, and travel. As one can see from the entry for Mrs. Trollope's *Abbess,* the amount of bibliographical information given is minimal, even to the failure to give authors' full names. Roorbach also gives a list of periodicals published in the United States. One peculiarity of arrangement to be kept in mind is that he enters biography of individuals under the name of the biographee, not under the name of the biographers.

Sample Entries:

(A) Author entry:
Francesi, W. L. *Crowds of Power.* 8 mo cl 0 75 Stringer '49
(B) Title entry:
Crowds of power. By Francesi 9 75 Stringer

(35)   **Kelly, James. American Catalogue of Books Published in the United States from Jan. 1861 to Jan. 1871. New York, Wiley, 1866–71. 2 v.**

Kelly continues the recording of American publishing from Roorbach's closing date and gives much the same kind of brief information, with the difference that he regularly gives the year of publication. In addition to the main alphabetical author-title list, he supplies a valuable list of pamphlets, sermons, and addresses on the Civil War. He also appends to each volume a list of learned societies and literary associations with their publications. His two volumes include about 11,300 titles, excluding the appendix. He picked up some books published before 1861 which had been missed by Roorbach.

The extreme brevity of the statement of title page information occasionally leads to puzzles. Kelly gives the following cross-reference: "Abbot, Ezra see Alger." When one consults the entry "Alger," he finds that two Algers are listed: H. Alger, Jr., and W. R. Alger. There is nothing in the two title entries under each to connect either with Ezra Abbot. One might suspect that Ezra Abbot was a pseudonym used by Horatio Alger, Jr., or by W. R. Alger. Checking in other sources, however, will reveal that W. R. Alger's *A Critical History of the Doctrine of the Future Life* (which is all the information that Kelly gives) had an appendix written by Ezra Abbot (an extensive bibliography which was also published separately). The shortening of the title-page information leads into a blind cross-reference.

Both Roorbach and Kelly do not cover their periods completely, and they are often inaccurate and incomplete in presenting bibliographical data, but they represent the fullest lists for their periods and will list some titles not easily found elsewhere.

Sample Entry:

Francesi, W. L. *Crowds of Power.* 8vo. pap., 10cts. N.Y. Carters.... 1864

(36) American Catalogue of Books, 1876–1910. New York, Publishers' Weekly, 1876–1910. 15 vols.

The first volume of the *American Catalogue* intended to list all books in print and on sale to the general public as of July 1, 1876. The record included all reprints, importations kept in stock, those publications of learned societies which were for general sale, important government publications, and the law reports of the courts of the several states. The list excluded periodicals, sheet music, unbound maps, tracts and other low-priced pamphlets, local directories, and books composed largely of blank pages.

This catalog represents cumulations of the *Annual American Catalogue,* which was an annual cumulation of the titles appearing weekly in *Publishers' Weekly.* The annual volumes are largely but not entirely superseded by the cumulations. The cumulated volumes employed three different arrangements of the material: (1) through the

1890–95 volume, there were two volumes issued for each edition; one contained author and title entries, the other, subject entries; (2) the 1895–1900 cumulation bound both sections in one volume, but as separate parts; (3) the three succeeding cumulations combined authors, titles, and subjects in one alphabet.

In presenting the information, the author's full name is often not given, but initials are employed for first name and middle name. Title entries are usually restricted to novels, plays, poems, and juveniles, although some series titles, with contents given, are listed for those sets which were commonly quoted by title. The subject list is made up of catch-words from the titles, rather than being a standard list.

Sample Entries:

> Francesi, Wolfgang L. *Crowds of power.* Phil., Penn Pub.
> Co., 1899. c. 19p. S (Dramatic lib., v. 1, no. 188) pap.,
> 15¢

> From the Author and Title Index:
> Francesi, Wolfgang L. *Crowds of power.* '99 c. (D2) S.
> (Dramatic Lib., v. 1, no. 188) pap., 15¢ . . . Penn Pub.
> Co.
> *Crowds of power.* Francesi, W. L. 15¢ Penn

> From the Subject Index:
> Power.
> Francesi, W. L. *Crowds of power.* '99 15¢ Penn

(37)   American Book Prices Current. 1895–

This list of books, periodicals, manuscripts, autographs, broadsides, maps, and charts sold at auction in England, the United States and Canada is presented here as part of the retrospective bibliography because: (1) it will enable the librarian to arrive at some judgment concerning the prices at which desired out-of-print titles are offered. If a dealer offers a book for $100 which sold recently at auction for $20.00, the buyer might well beware. (2) The auction lists also serve as a supplement to the national and trade bibliographies for bibliographic details of an occasional title which may have slipped through the bibliographic net. It would certainly not be a place of first resort for the search, but may occasionally enable one to verify a title not listed elsewhere. Each entry gives author, title, edition, place, date, size, binding condition, date of sale, lot number, and price. Publication is annual and there is a cumulative index every five years. The title has been selected as a sample of a type of compilation—*Guide to Reference Books* may be consulted for other American or British auction records.

Sample Entry:

FRANCESI, WOLFGANG LUDWIG
—*Crowds of power.* London, 1818. Sm 4to, 19th century
   mor. S
Nov 17 (51) $50
Anr copy. In 19th century lev mor, extra. S June 5 (97)
£170
Anr copy. Lacking the title leaf. In old calf, worn. Sold
w.a.f.
S June 5 (98) £6

(38)   Bookman's Price Index. 1964–

This is not a listing of prices of books sold at auction, but a list
of the prices given in dealers' catalogs, furnishing some idea of the
value of out-of-print books even if they have not appeared at auction.
The more than 420,000 entries listed in the first ten volumes give an
indication of the extent of coverage.
Sample Entry:

FRANCESI, WOLFGANG L. *Crowds of Power.* Detroit,
   Makeshift Press, 2041. 8vo, frontis, 2 maps, cloth. Zilch
   4821. $800.00

BRITISH BIBLIOGRAPHY

In the field of British bibliography, as in that of American bibliography, only a few of the major titles have been selected for consideration. The retrospective field is represented here by the general bibliographies of the British Museum's *Catalogue of Printed Books*, Watt,
Lowndes, and Allibone. The short-title catalogs of Pollard and Wing are
listed as examples of period bibliographies, while current bibliography is
represented by the Whitaker series and the *British National Bibliography*.

**(39)   British Museum. Dept. of Printed Books. General Catalogue
          of Printed Books, Photolithographic Edition to 1955.**

Scope: Like the Library of Congress catalog, it is a universal
bibliography, but it represents the pre-1800 period more thoroughly
than the LC catalogs do. It is a major tool for European retrospective
searching, in addition to its paramount importance for British works.
Arrangement: It is primarily an alphabetical list by author. Subject approaches are afforded in several areas: (1) works about a person
appear under his/her name; (2) many items are located under place

name—see London, for example; (3) in treating anonymous titles, an effort is made to bring out the subject expressed in the title. Ordinary subjects (e.g., coal, war, health, etc.) are represented in the separate *Subject Index of the Modern Works Added to the Library,* which is not included in our list of titles for acquisition purposes.

History: The *Catalogue of Printed Books* was published from 1881–1900, and a *Supplement* was published from 1900–05. These catalogs represented accessions to about 1899. The catalogs were so heavily used that agitation led to a reprint of both (the *Catalogue* in 1946 and the *Supplement* in 1950).

In 1931, a new edition was begun, entitled *General Catalogue of Printed Books,* adding about 30 years' accessions. By 1954, the work had reached the letters DEZW- when mounting costs forced its discontinuance. The Museum announced that it would continue the alphabet by photocopying the reading room sheaf catalogue, and it entitled the new enterprise *General Catalogue of Printed Books. Photolithographic Edition to 1955.* When the alphabet was completed, the Museum swung round to the head of the alphabet and redid the A-Dezw volumes in the same manner. Production began in 1959, and the catalog was completed in 1966, running to some 263 volumes and containing over 4 million entries. An edition of 750 sets was published.

It is planned to keep the catalog current with annual supplements, which will cumulate into polyennial sets. These *Additions* began with 1963. No annual volumes were published for the period 1959–63 since cumulative supplements will be published. So far, supplements covering 1955–65 and 1966–70 have appeared.

Comment: For librarians accustomed to searching the LC catalog, the BMC may seem difficult and may generate a sense of insecurity when a title cannot be located. The major difficulty in using the BMC arises from the fact that it uses rules of entry which do not always coincide with American library usage. If an author—take as an example a woman—has published anonymously under three pseudonyms, under three different married names, as well as under her maiden name, all these works will usually be gathered together by American catalogers under the latest form of her name, with cross-references from alternative forms. American cataloging has long been convinced of the usefulness of the uniform author entry, whether for persons or corporate bodies. The BMC, on the other hand, prefers to take the book in hand as the ultimate source of main entry, rather than any information gathered from sources extraneous to the book. From the American point of view, the application of this rule can lead to a dismaying scattering of an author's work. Various titles by a given author, or even various editions of the same title, may have been published under the author's real name, under a pseudonym, and anonymously. Entry in the BMC would be made in three different places, sometimes without cross-references to tie the various entries together.

An inspection of the works of some of the famous English authors will reveal that this rule has been adhered to. Under Alexander Pope's name, a number of the editions of the *Essay on Criticism* will be found. Not all of the editions are listed here, for cross-references will send one to the entry "Essay," where the editions issued without Pope's name on the title page will be found. Similarly, the novels of Sir Walter Scott issued with his name on the title page are listed under Scott; those issued without his name on the title page are entered under title.

A second major difference arises in the treatment of anonymous titles. In standard American use, the entry for anonymous title is the first word of the title not an article. BM practice centers around catchwords, i.e., content revealed by the title, and there is a sequence of preferences for choice of catch-word. Any book naming or adequately describing a person, place, or object is cataloged under that name. If the book lacks such a person, place, or object, the first noun in the title is chosen as entry. Such a title as *Of and pertaining to the lately described and minutely analyzed perturbations* . . . would be entered under "Perturbations." This rule, of course, requires that the cataloger recognize the different parts of speech, which some might consider a most unreasonable requirement.

When the title contains no noun, BM will surrender and enter it under the first word not an article.

A third major difference arises from the definition distinguishing pseudonymous from anonymous works. According to BM usage, many items are treated as anonymous works which would be entered under pseudonym in American cataloging. The meaning of pseudonym is sharply restricted. Any book signed by a pseudonym of more than one word, which is (1) not made up like a real name; (2) not composed of a Christian name and an epithet; and (3) which is descriptive of the author, is treated as an anonymous work. Thus, a book whose title page gives "Farmer" as author would be entered under the pseudonym "Farmer." If the title page gives "Northern Farmer"—ah! more than one word; not made up like a real name; not a Christian name plus epithet; descriptive of the author: treat as anonymous.

There are various refinements and subdivisions of these rules, but this general statement may suffice to warn the reader using the BMC not to think in LC terms. In addition to the above, it is well to remember that BM uses form entries freely: congresses, periodical publications, ephemerides, dictionaries, encyclopedias, hymnals, etc. Another important practice is the habit of listing works about a person under his/her name.

The importance of this catalog, representing as it does the splendid collection of the British Museum, warrants effort on the part of the American librarian to become familiar with its procedures and practices. Perhaps, however, an anecdote will illustrate the unhappy truth that even long acquaintance with the BMC will not always produce intimate knowledge in every case. One of the authors went to consult the BMC recently and noticed a cataloger of some 25 years' experience paging through the BMC, looking somewhat disconsolate. Upon being asked what was wrong, the cataloger explained that he had had to check up on a rather difficult pamphlet, had searched BMC long and hard, had finally located it. Some hours later, when preparing his final catalog copy, he noted that he had neglected to take down an item in the collation. Unfortunately, he had also failed to record the entry in the BMC under which he had located the title, and, on coming back to BMC, he could not find it again. Of course, it must be remembered that these difficulties occur only with certain types of titles, and that when one has the author, locating the title desired is simple.

Sample Entries:

FRANCESI (WOLFGANG L.)
—*Crowds of Power.* An inquiry into their origin, growth, functions and future. pp. x. 282. Imaginary Books: New York and London, [1984.] 8°   08230.h.47

—[Another copy.] R.75.(6.)
—[Another edition.] pp. 305. J. Teulon: London, 2084. 12°
                                                                   3455.b.75

(40)   British Museum. Dept. of Printed Books. General Catalogue of Printed Books. Additions. 1963–

Scope: Shows holdings added to the library each year. Universal bibliography. A ten-year supplement (1956–65) of 50 volumes and a 5-year supplement (1966–70) of 26 volumes are available.
Arrangement and Entries: Same as the general catalog.

(41)   Watt, Robert. Bibliotheca Britannica; or, A General Index to British and Foreign Literature. Edinburgh, Constable, 1824. 4 vols.

Scope: Includes some 40,000 authors. Although he includes non-British writers, this is most useful as a supplement to the British Museum *Catalogue.* At the serious risk of belaboring the obvious, one may add that this work is not useful for works published after the 1820s. Like Allibone and Lowndes (to be discussed below), Watt is not a first place to go for anything. But if LC, and then BMC, fail—try Watt.

Arrangement: Watt's general bibliography is divided into two sections: an author list containing about 40,000 authors, which gives biographical notes, a chronological listing of the author's works, and brief bibliographical details of each title. The second part is a list of subjects, with the various titles grouped chronologically. The subjects are catch-words from the titles—not a standardized list of subject headings. Anonymous works are listed in this part of the bibliography only. In the subject list, only brief title and date are given, with full title in the author section. A number and letter following the citation indicate the page of the author section on which the title will be found, with the letter indicating the section of the page.

In addition to books, Watt analyzed the more important periodicals on art and science, such as the *Transactions* of the Royal Society of London and of Edinburgh, the Linnaean Society, Horticultural Society, etc. His list is wider in scope than Lowndes, which will be described below. Like both Allibone and Lowndes, Watt is not the place to begin a search, but he will list titles not found elsewhere, so that one may have recourse to him if the British Museum *Catalogue* fails. Allibone's own comment on Watt is perhaps an adequate summary: ''Some late writers have affected to depreciate the value of this work, because inaccuracies have not escaped the eye of the critic. Errors there are, and some glaring ones, which can readily be excused in a work of such vast compass, yet [it] will always deserve to be valued as one of the most stupendous literary monuments.''

Sample Entries:

FRANCESI, WOLFGANG L., a learned Latin Philosopher; was born in Rome, in the year 455, beheaded in prison, at Pavia, October 23, 555, by order of Theodore, King of the Goths. He wrote an Epic Poem, the hero of which was Noah, under the title of the Noachides. Printed at Zurich, 1752, 1765, 1766. Translated into English, by Jos. Collyer. Lond. 1767, 2 vols. 12mo.—His Other Works were, *Crowds of Power.* Zurich, 1796.—*Of Homer.* 1799.—*Of Apollonius Rhodius.* 1799.

From the Subject Index:
POWER, CIVIL.—1796.   *Crowds of Power.*   384k

(42)   **Allibone, Samuel Austin. A Critical Dictionary of English Literature and British and American Authors, Living and Deceased, from the Earliest Accounts to the Latter Half of the 19th Century. Containing over 46,000 articles (Authors) with 40 Indexes of Subjects. Philadelphia, Lippincott, 1858. 3 vols. (Supplement, 1891. 2 vols.)**
Scope: As the title indicates, Allibone included some 46,000 authors, with another 37,000 included in the supplement. The authors

are largely British and American. His work was based on Watt (and thus some of Watt's errors were perpetuated).

Chronological coverage extends (via the supplement) to about the 1880's, but it is irregular, varying with the letter of the alphabet. The supplement also picks up earlier works missed by Allibone. As with Watt and Lowndes, its usefulness derives from the fact that the out-of-the-way title, not listed by BM or LC, may sometimes be found here.

Arrangement: An alphabetical author list, supplemented by the various subject indexes. Includes biographical information, a list of the works, and often quotations from criticism of the author's work. The 2-volume supplement was done by J. F. Kirk.

Sample Entry:

> Francesi, Wolfgang L., b. in Jamaica, where his father was island secretary; educated in England, returned to Jamaica in 1850; afterwards served in the Crimean War and the Indian Mutiny and was K.C.B. After his return to England, he entered upon a successful literary career, writing books which have been very popular. He was superintendent of the Kensington School 1874–75 and has since resided in the colonies where he has held appointments. Some of his works, having become rare, command high prices with collectors. 1. *Songs of the Governing Classes,* Lon., 1874, 18mo. 2. *Station Life in Jamaica,* Lon., 1869, 8vo; new eds., 1871, 1874, 1878, 1833.
> "If grown-up people can be tempted as doutless they can, to run off to the colonies in the way that school-boys are tempted by stirring narratives of adventure to run off to sea, this must be a very dangerous book. Mr. Francesi gives some express cautions on the subject, but the whole book is very exhilarating ... We find it full of singular interest and charm."—*Spectator,* xii, 591.
> 3. *Crowds of Power,* 1860.
> "It can make no pretence of being a finished study. Nor, for lack of material, can it claim to be exhaustive. It may, however, be described as trustworthy and straightforward."—*Sat. Rev.,* lv, 289.

(43) Lowndes, William Thomas. Bibliographer's Manual of English Literature, Containing an Account of Rare, Curious, and Useful Books, Published in or Relating to Great Britain and Ireland, from the Invention of Printing, with Bibliographical and Critical Notices, Collations of the Rarer Articles, and the Prices at Which They have been Sold. (4 vol., 1871, Bohn edition.)

Scope: About 50,000 titles are recorded, including only those Lowndes considered to be the principal works in their subject fields.

Arrangement: Alphabetical by author; also includes titles and catch-word subject entries. Often records prices at 19th century sales (which must not be confused with current value!). Like Watt and Allibone, supplements BMC.

Sample Entry:

FRANCESI, Rev. Wolfgang L. *Crowds of Power;* from the
remotest Period to the Present Time. Felper, 1811. 2 vols. 8
mo.
This work has certain incidents not mentioned by the Duke of
Chalfont in his *Arts of War.* An appendix contains charts and various notes by Capt. Basil Hall and a vocabulary of the Loo Choo
language. An interesting and pleasing work, extremely valuable in
its field.

**(44)   Pollard, Alfred W., and Redgrave, G. R. Short-title
Catalogue of Books Printed in England, Scotland, and Ire-
land, and of English Books Printed Abroad, 1475–1640.
London, Bibliographical Society, 1926.**

Scope: Attempts to include all books published in England during its period (although it does not list books known to have been
published, but for which no copies could be found). Its 26,500 titles
have been estimated to include about 90% of extant titles and about 80%
of extant editions.

Arrangement: Entry is alphabetical by main entry, giving brief
title, size, printer, date, reference to entry in the *Stationers' Register,*
and indication of libraries owning a copy. The first words of the title
were accorded great respect in transcription, but following the opening
words, extensive omissions might be made without indication. An
Index to the Printers, Publishers and Booksellers was prepared by Paul
G. Morrison and published in 1950.

Comment: The most comprehensive list for the period, and the
bibliographer can only rejoice when comparing the ease of using the
STC with the problems involved in attempting to do bibliographic work
in such a title as the *Stationers' Register.*

University Microfilms (Ann Arbor, Michigan) has been engaged
in filming STC items since 1937. Catalog cards have been prepared for
each filmed item by the Catalog Department of the University of Michigan Library.

In addition to the STC, there are a number of supplementary
bibliographies, which grew out of STC, covering this period. Various
libraries printed their holdings for the STC period, showing corrections
to titles listed in STC and additional titles not shown in STC. The late
Dr. William Warner Bishop published a *Checklist of American Copies
of "Short Title Catalogue" Books,* which showed holdings in about 120
libraries. A corrected and enlarged edition was published in 1950.

In 1976, the Bibliographical Society of London published the
second volume (I–Z) of the second revised and enlarged edition of the
STC. Work on this revision had been under way since about 1950. The

first volume (A–H) of the new edition is projected for publication in 1980.

Sample Entry:

> Francesi, Wolfgang L. *Crowds of power,* etc. 4°. [Cambridge,] C. Legge, 1484. LC

(45) Wing, Donald Goddard. Short-Title Catalogue of Books Printed in England, Scotland, Ireland, Wales, and British America and of English Books Printed in Other Countries, 1641–1700. New York, Index Society, 1945–51. 3 vols.

Scope: A continuation of Pollard & Redgrave, bringing the coverage down to 1700. About 90,000 titles are listed, representing the holdings of more than 200 libraries.

Arrangement: Similar to Pollard & Redgrave. An *Index to the Printers, Publishers, and Booksellers* was prepared by Paul G. Morrison and published in 1955.

Comment: The first volume of the second revised and enlarged edition appeared in 1972. This edition adds titles discovered since publication of the original edition and also increases the number of libraries where locations of copies are noted.

(46) Allison, Antony F. and Goldsmith, Valentine F. Titles of English Books (and of Foreign Books Printed in England); an Alphabetical Finding-List by Title of Books Published under the Author's Name, Pseudonym or Initials. 1976–1977. 2v.

Planned as a title index to the two previous bibliographies—Pollard and Redgrave, and Wing—this publication gives an alphabetical arrangement of titles, accompanied by authors' names, pseudonyms, or whatever will enable the user to find the full entry in either Pollard and Redgrave or Wing. Volume one covers 1475–1640 and volume two completes the index for 1641–1700.

CURRENT BRITISH BIBLIOGRAPHY

Current British bibliography is covered by two major works—*Whitaker's Cumulative Book List* and the *British National Bibliography.*

(47) The Whitaker series

Whitaker's bibliographies begin with *The Bookseller,* a weekly trade magazine, containing articles on the book trade, news, etc. Its bibliographic part consists of a list of publications for the week. Whitaker's also issues a monthly *Whitaker's Books of the Month and Books to Come* (which began January 1970). It provides a list of books published during the past month, along with listings of those scheduled to be published within the next two months. *Whitaker's Cumulative Book List* appears quarterly, the fourth issue each year turning into *Whitaker's Cumulative Book List Annual Volume*—a complete cumulation for the entire year. Polyennial cumulations complete the series.

In addition to this record of current publication, Whitaker also issues an annual in-print list—*British Books in Print*, subtitled "The Reference Catalogue of Current Literature." Originally, this was issued as a collection of publishers' catalogues. In 1936, however, it abandoned the catalog format and issued two parts: author and title lists. The 1977 edition recorded over 276,000 in-print titles in a single alphabetical sequence—author, title, and subject. Annual editions appear in November.

(48) The British National Bibliography. 1950–

Material listed in the *BNB* is based upon those titles received at the British Library for copyright purposes, but its editors have tried to expand its coverage beyond copyright items. Because of British publishers' arrangements with non-British publishers, the list includes publications issued in non-English-speaking countries, and some American books simultaneously published in Britain. Cheap novelettes, music, maps, publications of the government of Eire, and most British government publications are omitted. Periodicals are listed at the time of their first issue and also on the first issue of a change of title.

Full bibliographical information is given, with many happy bonuses (translations are listed with a note of their original title, publisher, and date of publication; new editions have the date of the original or previous editions; series are listed; titles are identified as parts of series).

BNB appears weekly, with monthly and quarterly indexes (each quarterly index cumulates all entries preceding its publication), an annual volume, and polyennial indexes. Arrangement is classified by Dewey, which makes the weekly issues useful to the selector responsible for given areas. The fullness of the indexes enables the searcher to find a given author or title easily. (There is one difference from American practice which is worth remembering: pseudonymous works are listed under the title-page pseudonym, according to the rules for cataloging of the British Library.) Cumulated subject catalogs have been published to cover the period from 1951 through 1970. Five cumulations cover this period, although all cumulations do not cover the same number of years.

Sample entry:

320 - Politics. General works.
   Francesi, Wolfgang L. *Crowds of Power* / by Wolfgang L.
   Francesi. - New York: Imaginary Books, 1984. - xii,
   591p.: maps, tables; 24 cm.
   ISBN 0-898989-01-X : £1.50

                                                    (B84-21350)

From the index:
   Crowds of power. (Wolfgang L. Francesi).
      Imaginary £1.50 320 (B84-21350)
                                    ISBN 0-898989-01-X

CANADIAN BIBLIOGRAPHY

Although there are a number of bibliographies, checklists, in-
ventories, short title catalogs, etc. covering Canadiana for various time
periods—some of these bibliographies even list publications dating
from the earliest days of settlement—there does not appear to be anything which is regarded as *the* standard retrospective Canadian bibliography. An indication of this is the fact that the National Library of
Canada is currently engaged in compiling a retrospective national bibliography which will cover the period before 1950 (*Canadiana,* to be
discussed later, began in 1950). Collections and files of other libraries,
associations, and individuals will be searched to locate pre-1950 publications. The first phase of the retrospective project covers monographs
published from 1867 (the date of Confederation) to 1900. The 1977/78
Annual Report of the National Librarian announced that data collection
for phase one was complete (approximately 30,000 titles have been
included in this phase) and that editing of entries, adding locations, and
completing and coding worksheets would begin. Files are being created
in machine-readable form, and the printed version will be published in
installments.

**(49)   Canadiana; Publications of Canadian Interest Received by
         the National Library. 1950–**

Scope: Current Canadian publishing is well-covered by this successor to the *Canadian Catalogue of Books (1921–1949)*. Published
monthly by the National Library, *Canadiana* includes material published in Canada, received through legal deposit, or published in other
countries if either the author or the subject is Canadian.

The first part of the bibliography lists monographs, classified
according to Dewey, with full cataloging information. The sections
which follow include other formats—theses in microform, serials, pam-

phlets, sound recordings, and provincial and federal government publications—in a similar arrangement. (Films were included from 1964 through 1976, but are now covered in *Film Canadiana*, prepared by the Canadian Film Institute.)

Coverage of *Canadiana* has expanded considerably through the years. When the first cumulation of *Canadiana* appeared in 1950–51, it contained only 2,951 entries. In 1967, the centennial of Confederation, the coverage was slightly over 12,000 entries. The following statistics from the 1977/78 report of the National Librarian give an indication of how much material is now covered:

	1976 entries	1977 entries
Pt.I. Monographs	7,803	10,104
Pt.II. Theses in Microform	3,130	3,730
Pt.III. Serials	3,277	2,756
Pt.IV. Pamphlet File Material	588	641
Pt.V. Sound Recordings	1,428	1,291
Pt.VI. Films and Filmstrips	1,172	not included
Pt.VII. Federal Government Publications	4,467	5,213
Pt.VIII. Provincial Government Publications	3,272	4,777
Total	25,137	28,512

(The above figures can not be taken to represent individual publications. Since many Canadian publications are bilingual and are therefore listed twice [see below], a total count of Canadian publishing output for a year would probably be less than the total number of entries in the national bibliography.)

Treatment: English- and French-language publications are cataloged in their respective languages. Bilingual publications receive two entries—one in French and one in English. Cataloging information is complete and follows the ISBD format.

Indexing: In addition to the subject approach through the classified arrangement, *Canadiana* includes indexing entries for personal and corporate authors, titles, added entries, and series. Several cumulative indexes have been published. The latest was a ten-volume cumulated author index for 1968–1976, published in 1978.

Comment: In January, 1968, the National Library began distributing *Canadiana. Microfiche.*—an edition made available on computer-output microfiche. Since this version is produced from proof copy, the text has entries which appear 6–8 weeks later in the printed edition.

Sample entry:

320   HM141
Francesi, Wolfgang, 1999–
   Crowds of power / Wolfgang Francesi.-Toronto: Imaginary Books, c2049.

612p. : ill. ; 24cm.
Includes index.
ISBN 0 998989 01 X pa : $6.95
1. Political science.
I. Title.

C49-8426

(50)   **Bibliographie du Québec: Liste mensuelle des publications québécoises ou relatives au Québec. 1968–**

This publication of Bibliothèque nationale du Québec offers monthly coverage of French Canadian publications. Scope includes works published in Québec, works deposited in Bibliothèque nationale du Québec, works published outside Québec which relate to that province. The first part covers books and pamphlets, arranged in a classified order; part two is devoted to government publications. Author, title, and subject indexing is supplied for both parts.
Sample entry:

-0-9999
FRANCESI, Wolfgang, 1999–
   Foules de pouvoir / Wolfgang Francesi.-Montréal: S.Del-
gieu, 2049. - xvi, 726p. ; 25 cm.
   Titre original: Crowds of power. - DL -0-999.
   ISBN 0-998989-01-X br.: $5.00
   1. Politique. I. Titre.
HM141   320   1-999999

(51)   **Canadian Books in Print. 1967–**

The University of Toronto Press publishes this annual guide to English-language Canadian books which are currently in print. The first volume is an author and title index. Since 1973, a second volume has provided subject indexing. Canadian publishers of all types—trade, small press, association, community group, etc.—are included. The 1977 edition listed more than 17,000 titles.

Earlier years of *CBIP* included French-language publications, but, beginning in 1973, scope was limited primarily to English-language books. This change was made to avoid duplication with *Répertoire de l'édition au québec,* which is an in-print index for French-language books published in Quebec.

AUSTRALIAN BIBLIOGRAPHY

The National Library of Australia has taken the lead in providing bibliographic coverage for that country. From 1937 to 1961, it published the *Annual Catalogue of Australian Publications,* which was superseded in 1961 by the Library's more comprehensive *Australian National Bibliography*. The National Library has also been active in retrospective bibliography. A retrospective national bibliography project, begun in 1974, has the objective of compiling a bibliography for 1901–1950, the only period for which a comprehensive Australian bibliographic record is lacking. (The master file for this project contains approximately 80,000 items, and 1985 is the projected completion date.) Between 1975 and 1978, the National Library issued a facsimile reproduction of the standard Australian bibliography for pre-1900 imprints—Sir John Ferguson's *Bibliography of Australia, 1784–1900*, in seven volumes.

(52)   Australian National Bibliography. 1961–

A weekly listing of "all books published in Australia or of Australian interest," the *Australian National Bibliography* also includes government publications and the first issue of new periodicals and newspapers. The first three issues of a month are classified listings, arranged by Dewey, with author-title-series indexing. The fourth issue each month includes the new classified listings for the week, together with a cumulation of the first three issues. Monthly cumulations have two indexes: (1) an author, title, and series index and (2) a detailed subject index, similar to the kind produced by the *British National Bibliography*. Monthly issues cumulate annually. The 1976 annual volume included 8,992 items.
Sample entry:

> 320 - Political science
>   Francesi, Wolfgang
>   Crowds of power [by] Wolfgang Francesi.-Melbourne:
>   Imaginary Books, 2049. - 400p. ill.; 25 cm.
>   Index.
>   ISBN 0 998989 01 X : $4.50 Aust.
>   1. Political science. II. Title

(53)   Australian Books in Print. 1956–

This commercial publication is now an annual list of "all available Australian titles," but title and frequency of publication have varied through the years. Announcements of the 1978 volume promise full ordering and bibliographic data on 42,000 entries.

FRENCH BIBLIOGRAPHY

This discussion of French bibliography has been limited to a small group of titles. Three general works (two catalogs of the Bibliothèque Nationale; Brunet's *Manuel*); two period bibliographies (Quérard's titles, covering 1700–1849, and Lorenz, 1840–1925), and two former current bibliographies, now merged (*Biblio* and *Bibliographie de la France*), have been included. For our purposes of a general introduction to French bibliography, however, many titles have been excluded. Those interested are directed to the latest issue of *Guide to Reference Books*.

(54) **Paris. Bibliothèque Nationale. Dépt. des imprimés. Catalogue général des livres imprimés de la Bibliothèque Nationale: Auteurs. 1897–**

As is the case in Great Britain and the United States, the catalog of the depository library of France is a major bibliography, not only of French works, but of books published abroad. It is not as comprehensive as either of the other two as regards type of materials covered, nor has the catalog ever been completed. Publication began in 1897 and by 1953, the letter "T" had been reached. In 1967, the volume covering "TURGAN-ULEY" was published, after 14 years in the "t's." In August 1973, the volume VINCA-VIRGINS was on the shelves of The University of Michigan's Graduate Library. Five years later, August 1978, the last volume that could be located was Volume 226 (WOR-WUK), published in 1977.

The early volumes are out of date, and there is no representation of the final letters of the alphabet. Furthermore, this catalog consists of entries for *personal authors only*. There are no entries for corporate bodies, for anonymous titles, documents, serials, or society publications. There are no added entries for secondary persons or bodies which might be thought to be the author.

This situation obtains because, in the 1894 report of the Commission des Bibliothèques Nationales et Municipales (which had been charged with the task of examining the state of the catalogs of printed books of the Bibliothèque Nationale), it was suggested that a series of catalogs be prepared: (1) a list of personal authors; (2) a second list of anonymous works and general titles issued by corporate bodies; (3) a third list, which would treat of certain special categories of publications—budgets, reports, etc.—which would be primarily official publications of corporate bodies.

This full set of catalogs is far from realization. For a work whose author is known, however, and which happens to have been published before the date of publication of the volume into which it fits alphabetically, the catalog is very satisfactory, being characterized by very careful and accurate work. The fact that it is not complete, and that the early parts are so far out of date, requires a greater reliance on complementary works than is the case in the United States.

Sample Entry:

FRANCESI (Wolfgang).—*Foules de pouvoir.* Discours prononcé dans l'église métropolitaine de Nôtre Dame de Paris, le 13 juillet 1794, jour de la réunion annuelle des citoyens qui furent électeurs en 1789, en commémoration de la prise de la Bastille et de la conquête de la liberté, par W. L. Francesi... —*Paris, Mame et fils,* 1794. In-18, 143 p., pl. et fig.   8y².51520

(55)   Paris. Bibliothèque Nationale. Dépt. des imprimés. Catalogue général des livres imprimés: auteurs, collectivités-auteurs, anonymes. 1960–64-   Paris, 1965–

Scope: For French works, includes all titles listed in *Bibliographie de la France* during the period, as well as any other titles cataloged by the Bibliothèque Nationale, whether or not the book was published during the 1960/64 period. (This would apply to books acquired by purchase or gift, rather than by legal deposit.) It includes not only those items listed in the *Bibliographie de la France's* general section, but also those listed in the parts devoted to theses, government publications, and auction catalogs. Foreign titles acquired by the Library would also be listed, regardless of date of publication. Periodicals are excluded, as there is a separate catalog of periodicals.

Arrangement: For the first time, corporate authors and anonymous works are included, which is a most happy enlargement of coverage. In addition to a wider array of main entries, the catalog includes secondary entries, where necessary, for joint authors, editors, writers of prefaces, translators, etc. Many title entries are also made for publications of corporate bodies.

Cross-references are supplied to aid in the identification of an author, especially where it is a corporate body which has a complicated name, or which has changed its name.

All these are presented in a single alphabetical list. Separate alphabets will be published for (1) Cyrillic; (2) Greek; and (3) Hebrew.

Note the many different formats for individual titles. What does this tell you about the method of publication employed?

Sample Entry:

FRANCESI (Wolfgang)
—Foules du pouvoir, par Wolfgang Francesi... — Rambouillet, l'auteur, 149 rue Madame de-Maintenon (Paris, impr. J. Grou), 1984. —In 4° (27 cm), non paginé, fig., couv. ill., multigraphié. 18,50 NF   4°R.9736 (1)

(56) **Brunet, Jacques, Manuel du libraire et de l'amateur de livres. Paris, Didot, 1860–80. 9 vols.**

Brunet's work is actually a universal bibliography of rare, important, or noteworthy books, but it is especially strong for French publications before the 19th century. His work has been highly esteemed as a prodigy of patience, exactness, erudition, and a monument of bibliography. The first five volumes are arranged alphabetically by author and anonymous title, while the sixth consists of a subject index, arranged according to Brunet's own bibliographical classification. The seventh and eighth volumes consist of supplementary lists and a subject index, while the ninth volume is actually not part of Brunet's list of titles, but Deschamps' dictionary of European cities and towns with their classical names, and, conversely, a list of classical place names with the modern European equivalent. The bibliography is selective. It serves, nevertheless, as an important supplement to the Bibliothèque Nationale's catalog. Brunet gives full bibliographical data, including author, title, place, publisher, date, size, and number of volumes. Notes which are often extensive give the record of editions and descriptions of important items (see the entry under the first Shakespeare folio).

Sample Entry:

FRANCESI (Wolfgang). *Foules de pouvoir,* en francoys, contenant quatre dialogues, fort antinques, joyeux et facetieux. *Lugduni, apud Anisonios,* 1677. 4 part. en 1 vol. pet. in-12. [3924]
Ces dialogues sont composés à la manière de Lucien. C'est un ouvrage allégorique assez piquant. Malheureusement l'autorité crut apercevoir, dans les allégories, des impiétés et des hérésies condamnables, et le livre fut déféré au parlement de Paris, qui en ordonna la suppression, et fit mettre en prison le libraire Anison. L'édition originale a été supprimée avec tant de soin, qu'on n'en connaît, avec certitude, qu'un seul exemplaire vend 350 fr. Gaignol, et 1200 fr. La Chappelle, et qui est maintenant dans la bibliothèque de la ville de Versailles. Pourtant, le catalogue de feu M**** (des Plances), *Avignon,* 1778, in-8., p. 15, en annonce un autre, rel. en. *v.f.t.d. bords et cordures,* avec la fameuse vignette de la Pauvreté; mais cette annonce parait s'appliquer à l'édition d'Amsterdam, 1732, dans laquelle on a réproduit le titre de 1677. Très-rares.

(57) **Quérard, Joseph Marie. La France littéraire, ou Dictionnaire bibliographique des savants, historiens, et gens de lettres de la France, aisi que des littérateurs étrangers qui ont écrit en français plus particulièrement pendant les XVIIIe et XIXe siècles. Ouvrage dans lequel on a inséré, afin d'en former une Bibliographie nationale complète, l'indication 1° des réimpressions des ouvrages français de tous les ages; 2° des diverses traductions en notre langue de tous les**

auteurs étrangers, anciens et modernes; 3° celle des réimpressions faites en France des ouvrages originaux de ces
mêmes auteurs étrangers, pendant cette époque. Paris, Didot, 1827–64. 12 vols.

This work consists of an author list, giving brief biographical
notes concerning the authors, with the usual bibliographical data for the
titles, plus bibliographical and historical notes. In addition, the last two
volumes (besides giving additions and corrections) are a list of the
pseudonymous and anonymous works of authors, under real name. The
period covered runs from 1700 to 1826. Emphasis is on works in the
field of literature, and so it is not actually a complete national bibliography.

Sample Entry:

> FRANCESI, (Wolfgang) jurisconsulte, né à Dunkerque en
> 1741, mort à Paris, le 7 avril 1817.
> —*Foules de pouvoir.* Paris, Laurens aîné, 18, 7, in-8.
>
> Édition la plus précieuse pour les gens de lettres, en ce que c'est la
> dernière revue par l'auteur, qui lui-même la nommait son édition favor-
> ite: on ne la trouve plus que par hassard. Il a éte tiré quelques
> exemplaires de cette édition sur papier fin de Holland, qui sont très-
> récherchés des amateurs (20,000 a 30,000 fr.), ainsi que quelques-uns
> sur papier fort.
>
> Après la publication de cette édition, l'éditeur s'étant aperçu que
> plusieurs fautes s'étaient glissées dans le commencement du texte,
> se décida à faire réimprimer les sept feuilles A-G, dans lesquelles il
> fit des corrections et des augmentations qui nécessitèrent un
> changement dans l'ordre de la pagination. La table des pièces et
> celles des matières ne correspondent plus avec les pages changées.
> Ces exemplaires son très précieux.

**(58) Quérard, Joseph Marie. La littérature française contempor-
aine, 1827–49. Le tout accompagné de notes biographiques
et littéraires. Paris, 1842–57. 6 vols.**

This work continues his earlier title and is arranged on the same
plan. Together the two titles cover 149 years, giving quite a range
chronologically.

Sample Entry:

> FRANCESI (Wolfgang), écrivain critique, conservateur de la
> Bibliothèque Mazarine, inspecteur de d'Académie de Paris,
> membre de l'Académie française.
> —*Foules de pouvoir,* discours prononcés dans la séance
> publique tenue par l'Académie française, pour le réception
> de M. de Francesi, le 17 avril 1827. *Paris, de l'impr. de F.
> Didot,* 1827, in-4 de 36 p.—Autre édit. *Paris, de l'impr. de
> Béthune,* 1827, br. in-8.

M. Francesi a fourni au Journal des débats un grand nombre d'articles de critique, signés A. Il avait quitté l'Académie par suite de tracasseries qu'on lui avait suscitées. Ses oeuvres sont pleines de frivoles argumentations, d'experience inexacts. Ses principales saillies sont puisées dans les lettres de Madame de Sévigné.

(59) Catalogue général de la librairie française. Paris, Lorenz, 1840–1925. 34 vols.

This work, usually cited as Lorenz, is the major bibliographical tool of the 19th century, continuing the work of Quérard. It is hoped that supplementary volumes will be issued to bring the coverage to 1933, the year in which *Biblio* began publication. Since Lorenz was intended to be a practical, commercial tool, literary notes were omitted. The list is primarily alphabetical by author, with catch-word subject indexes. An important feature of the work is its linking together of various works by an author through cross references from later to earlier volumes.

Sample Entry:

> FRANCESI (Wolfgang), professeur á l'Université du Michigan (États-Unis). (Voy. Tome xv, page 897).
> —*Foules de pouvoir.* in-8. 1807. H. Welter. 25fr. la 1re édition a paru en 1897.

From the Index:
> Politique; Brochures politiques.
> *Foules de pouvoir,* par Wolfgang Francesi. In-8. 1897.

(60) Bibliographie de la France. Paris, 1811 to 1970.

This current weekly bibliography (whose retrospective volumes, going back to 1811, form a substantial bibliography, the usefulness of which is diminished by the lack of cumulations) is based on the official copyright list of the Bibliothèque Nationale and reflects the careful cataloging of that institution. Unfortunately, its format presents some problems. The publication consists of three parts: (1) "Bibliographie officielle," which records the books, pamphlets, and documents received for copyright, and which is supplemented by separate parts, issued at irregular intervals. These extra parts include the following sections: A—Periodicals; B—Engravings, prints, and photographs; C—Music; D—Theses; E—Atlases, maps, and plans; F—Government publications. (2) "Chronique," consisting of notes and special features for the book trade. (3) "Annonces," publishers' announcements of new books, which are indexed cumulatively into *Livres de la semaine, Livres du mois, Livres du trimestre, Livres du semestre,* and *Livres de l'année.*

Since the titles are not listed until they have been cataloged, entries are often delayed for months after publication. Furthermore, the list does not include any works which have not been deposited for copyright.

Sample Entries:

(A)   AUTEURS
   Francesi (W.) 2084

(B)   3. SCIENCES SOCIALES
   2084. FRANCESI (Wolfgang).
     —Foules de pouvoir, par Wolfgang Francesi.—Paris,
     Les belles lettres (Besançon, Neo-typo), In-8° (24 cm),
     16p., carte. [D.L. 12934-62]
     [8° Z.34266 (37)
      (Annales litteraires de l'Université de Besançon. 37)

Sample Entries from Some of the Supplements

(A) From "Périodiques"
     N. SCIENCES JURIDIQUES, POLITIQUES,
         ÉCONOMIQUES ET SOCIALES
   N2. POLITIQUE
     100. *Foules de pouvoir.* Mensuel. Dir. Wolfgang
Francesi.
     N° 1, décembre 1960.—Guin, rue Lavoisier (impr. d'Au-
     ger). 45×32 cm. Le n° 0, 15 NF [D.L. 20-2-61]—N2b.
                     [Fol. Jo. 11708
(B) From the index to "Periodiques"
     Foules de pouvoir *100*
(C) From "Gravures, Estampes, et Photographies"

               I. AUTEURS

        A. GRAVURES ET LITHOGRAPHIES
   1. FRANCESI (Wolfgang).
   —Foules de pouvoir, lithogr. en coul., vers. 1961. [AA3]
          B. PHOTOGRAPHIES
   285. FRANCESI (Wolfgang)
     —100 phot.   [Oeuvre;—N.;—O.

(D) From the classified arrangement of "Gravures, Es-
    tampes," "etc."

       II. CLASSEMENT PAR SUJETS

      E. COSTUMES ET MOEURS
   510. *Foules de pouvoir,* album d'echantillons de
     tissus.—Paris, Société d'éditions de mode, 1962 et
     suiv. In-4°, f.g—
   N°1, mars 1962.—Printemps 1962—Été 1963.
                    [Th. 231, in-4°

(E) From the section "Musique"

MUSIQUE
1. MUSIQUE INSTRUMENTALE
1. Francesi, (Wolfgang).
—*Foules de pouvoir.* [pour piano]. Nouvelle édition
révue par H. Vaillant.—Nice, S. Delgieu (1961). In-4°, 12p.

[D.F.413]   B.N. [Vmg. 5965 (21)
                            Cons. [G. 9646 (21)

(F) From the section "Thèses"

Thèses 1961
VI.—LETTRES
Paris
4572. FRANCESI (Wolfgang).
—*Foules de pouvoir.* Recherches sur un région moins
developpée, vers 1854-vers 1871. Paris, Impr. nat.,
1961.—24 cm, 591p., fig., cartes.   [8° Lk. 1897
Thèse. Lettres. Paris. 1958

(61) Biblio; catalogue des ouvrages parus en langue française dans le monde entier. Paris, Hachette, 1933 to 1970.

The monthly *Biblio*, a world record of French language publications arranged in dictionary catalog style, lists titles sooner than the
Bibliographie de la France. *Biblio* uses the "Annonces" and "Bibliographie officielle" of the *Bibliographie de la France* as a base, but adds
works published abroad and those which are outside the copyright deposit. It is not as complete as *Bibliographie de la France* for non-book
materials, but its convenience of use leads many librarians to try it first
for a desired item. The annual volume cumulates the monthly list—with
additions—in the same dictionary arrangement,
Sample Entries:

Foules de pouvoir (Coll. Histoire de la vie politique,
185)
    FRANCESI, W. 58f. Gallimard

FRANCESI, Wolfgang
    Foules de pouvoir (Coll. Histoire de la vie politique, 185).
        17, 5 × 11. cxxxi, 195p. Rel.: 58fr. ['66] Gallimard.
    Réprod. de l'éd. orig., Bruxelles, Impr. Hayez, 1884.

POLITIQUE
    FRANCESI, W.
Gallimard

(62) Bibliographie de la France/Biblio. 1971–

The two titles just dispatched have now merged into a sort of
Siamese twin affair. The new publication shares the characteristics of
both. The new serial consists of the following parts:

1. A weekly publication, which continues the former weekly part of *Bibliographie de la France*. It is arranged by decimal classification. The titles are those received by the legal deposit section of the national library, and the cataloging represents BN cataloging. This first section continues the irregular addition of supplements for other materials. As of summer 1973, the following parts were being published (as occasion arose). A. Publications en série; B. Gravures, estampes et photographies; C. Oeuvres musicales; D. Thèses; E. Atlas, Cartes et plans; F. Publications officielles; G. Catalogues de ventes publiques.

This first weekly part (of the books) is indexed in two sections—an index of authors (including corporate authors), and an index of "anonymes." The weekly publication consists, in addition to this *Première partie (Bibliographie officielle),* of the *Chronique,* which continues as heretofore to consist of publishing news, historical articles ("Colette in the National Library"), copyright information, obituaries, lists of winners of literary prizes, etc.—a sort of "intersticed" *Publishers Weekly*); and, as a third part, the "Annonces" which are advertising pages by publishers.

2. The second part of this publication consists of the monthly cumulation, *Les livres du Mois. Bibliographie de la France/Biblio.* It is arranged as the weekly is, so one needs to add no more details to one's memories.

3. The third part is a new period bibliography, which used to be an index. It is now *Livres du Trimestre—Biblio.* It changes from the classified arrangement of *Bibliographie de la France* to the dictionary form of the old *Biblio*—by author, title, and subject.

4. The quarterly issues cumulate into *Les livres de l'année—Biblio,* which has the subtitle: "Bibliographie générale des ouvrages parus en langue française." To the works cataloged by the BN and registered for copyright, the editors of the annual add (during the course of the quarterly publications) material from "diverses sources," as, for example, titles from foreign bibliographies. They try to establish for each of these non-BN works entries which will follow international rules of cataloging.

(63)   In-Print Lists

Two works now report French books in print—*Répertoire des livres de langue française disponibles* and *La Catalogue de l'edition française (French Books in Print).* Both attempt to list books published worldwide in the French language.

GERMAN BIBLIOGRAPHY

German bibliography can be divided into three periods: 19th century and earlier; 20th century before World War II; and post World War II, with its division of Germany into two nations. The 19th century and earlier is well covered by three works (the earliest bibliographies are not being considered in this general discussion): (1) Heinsius' *Allgemeines Bücher-Lexikon* (1700–1892); (2) Kayser's *Vollständiges Bücher-Lexikon* (1750–1910), and (3) the Hinrichs firm's series, including weekly (1842–1915), quarterly (1846–1914), half-yearly (1798–1915), and polyennial issues (1851–1912).

The 20th Century period before World War II saw the assumption of the Hinrichs' series by the Börsenverein, the German book trade organization, and the supplanting of Heinsius and Kayser by the same publications. The weekly index, half-yearly, and five-year catalogs were continued, while the quarterly catalog was discontinued.

The second World War saw Germany divided into East and West Germany, each of which has attempted to publish bibliographies covering the total German output. In the German Democratic Republic, the Deutsche Bücherei at Leipzig and in the German Federal Republic, the Deutsche Bibliothek at Frankfurt-am-Main have continued the publication of the Börsenverein's bibliographies.

(64)   Heinsius, Wilhelm. Allgemeines Bücher-Lexicon, 1700–1892. Leipzig, 1912–04. 19 vols.

The first edition of Heinsius' work appeared at the end of the 18th century in four volumes (1793–98). It was based on publishers' and dealers' catalogs. The second edition (1812–13) revised and enlarged the first, in an attempt to make it more comprehensive and accurate. His fundamental principle of arrangement was to list alphabetically under author, when the author was known. His only exception was the listing of novels and plays in two separate sections under the chief word of the title even when author was known (although for the very famous authors, he made an exception to this exception and listed their works under their name in the author alphabet). When the author of a work—other than a play or novel—was not known, it was listed under the chief word of the title. He omitted engravings, maps, music, single sermons, dissertations, and ephemeral materials costing less than two groschen (unless they were by famous authors or important for other reasons). With the eighth volume (1823–34), the separate sections for plays and novels were discontinued. The period of coverage of the various volumes runs from four to seven years (excluding the basic four volumes, which covered the years 1700–1810). The long period of coverage—192 years—makes this a very extensive list, in spite of inaccuracies (of which Heinsius and his successors were aware. Heinsius complained bitterly of the inaccuracy of the publishers' catalogs themselves, on which he had to base his work, as well as of the cavalier attitude of some publishers toward the errors in their own catalogs).

Sample Entry:

> Francesi, W. L., *Mengen der Kraft;* sinnreicher Aussprüche
> aus d. Geschichte d. ält. u. neuern Zeit; ein Lesebuch f.
> Grosse und Kleine. 8°. Magdeburg, Lauban, 725   —10

(65)   Kayser, Christian Gottlob. Vollständiges Bücher-Lexikon, 1750–1910. Leipzig, 1834–1911. 36 vols.

Kayser runs roughly parallel to Heinsius for much of his period, with coverage beginning 50 years later and continuing 18 years longer. His work thus gives another long run of 160 years. Like Heinsius' work, this is primarily alphabetical by author, giving author, title, publisher, place, date, volumes, paging, series, and prices. Certain categories of works—handbooks, dictionaries, etc.—are gathered together under the category, rather than under the name of the compiler. Eleven volumes of subject indexes were also published. Kayser is generally conceded to furnish greater detail with more regularity than Heinsius or Hinrichs and is often found in order departments which have relegated those two sets to the stacks.

Sample Entries:

> (A) Francesi, Wolfgang, *Mengen der Kraft.* (iv, 395S.) gr. 18.
>   Wien, 905. F. Vahlen.
> (B) Francesi, Wolfgang. *Mengen der Kraft* (XV, 494S.), gr. 8.
>   Berlin 855. H. Berthold.

(66)   The Hinrichs'/Börsenverein series.

(1) *Hinrichs' Halbjahrs-Katalog* (1798–1915). The half-yearly catalogs consist of an alphabetical author list with subject indexes (catchword subjects). In the period before World War II (1915–1944) when the Börsenverein took over publication, the title was changed to *Halbjahrsverzeichnis der Neuerscheinungen des deutschen Buchhandels.* The half-yearly catalog has been continued in the post World War II period by the West German *Halbjahrsverzeichnis.*

(2) *Wöchentlichis Verzeichnis* (1842–1915). In 1842, Hinrichs added this weekly index as a more current record of German publications. The weekly list was continued by the Börsenverein and by both East and West German bibliographies after World War II.

(3) *Vierteljahr-Katalog* (1846–1914). The chronological coverage was filled out further with the appearance of this quarterly catalog in 1846. It was discontinued when the Börsenverein assumed publication of the Hinrichs' series and has not been resumed subsequently.

(4) *Fünfjahrs-Katalog* (1851–1912). The five-year cumulations of the Halbjahrs-Katalog were continued by the Börsenverein as *Deutsches Bücherverzeichnis* (1911–40), and are represented in the East German series as *Deutsches Bücherverzeichnis* and in the West German series as *Deutsches Bibliographie 1945–50*, etc.

Sample Entry:

(A) From the "Titelverzeichnis."
Francesi, Wolfgang: *Die Mengen der Kraft.* 5.Aufl. (111)
8° Lpzg, G. Messeburger, '11.   1.50d
(B) From the "Sachregister."
Kraft s.a. Kräfte.
Mengen der Kraft: Francesi

(67)   Gesamtverzeichnis des deutschsprachigen Schrifttums (GV): 1911–1965. 1976–   (In progress)

This retrospective bibliography of German-language publications is a cumulation and integration of main entries from sixteen previously-published bibliographies covering, collectively, the time period indicated in the title. Plans call for approximately two million German titles (including German, Swiss, and Austrian publications) to be abstracted and cited as they are found in the existing bibliographies. Author and title entries will be interfiled into a single alphabet, but entries will not be re-set. The publisher has projected a set of 150 volumes, with approximately 500 pages in each volume.

CURRENT GERMAN BIBLIOGRAPHY

West Germany (German Federal Republic)

The Deutsche Bibliothek in Frankfurt-am-Main prepares the *Deutsche Bibliographie* for publication. It attempts to list all books published in Germany and all books in the German language published abroad. It is issued in the following sequence:

(1) *Reihe A.* A weekly classified list with author and catchword subject indexes. Includes materials sold through the regular book trade. Indexes cumulate monthly and quarterly.

(2) *Reihe B.* A semimonthly list of materials outside the book trade. Index cumulates annually.

(3) *Reihe C.* A quarterly listing of maps. Index cumulates annually.

(4) *Halbjahres-Verzeichnis.* Semi-annual. Cumulates *Reihe A* and selected titles from *Reihe B.*

(5) *Deutsche Bibliographie; Fünfjahres-Verzeichnis. Bücher und Karten.* Polyennial. Cumulates *Reihe A,* selected titles of *Reihe B,* and *Reihe C.*

East Germany (German Democratic Republic)

The Deutsche Bücherei in Leipzig prepares the *Deutsche Nationalbibliographie,* which attempts to include all books published in Germany and all books in the German language published abroad. It is issued in the following sequence:

(a) Weekly. *Reihe A; Neuerscheinungen des Buchhandels,* which lists books published in the regular book trade. Classified, with author and catchword indexes.

(b) Bi-weekly. *Reihe B; Neuerscheinungen ausserhalb des Buchhandels.* Includes materials published outside the regular book trade, such as dissertations and society publications. Classified, with author and catchword indexes.

(c) Quarterly. Separate indexes (*Vierteljahrs-register*) to Reihen A and B.

(d) Annually. *Jahresverzeichnis des deutschen Schrifttums.* Cumulates Reihe A and B in two sections: (1) "Titelverzeichnis," listing works by author or title; (2) "Stich-und Schlagwortregister," listing works under catchword and subject.

(e) Polyennially. *Deutsches Bücherverzeichnis; Verzeichnis der in Deutschland, Österreich, der Schweiz, und im übrigen Ausland herausgegeben deutschsprachigen Verlagsschriften sowie der wichtigsten Veröffentlichungen ausserhalf des Buchhandels.* Cumulates the *Jahresverzeichnis,* listing works under author, anonymous title, and subject (in two sections).

(68)   In-Print Lists

A German in-print list, *Verzeichnis Lieferbarer Bücher* (1971/ 72–), covers West German, Austrian, and Swiss publications. It is also referred to as *German Books in Print.* It is sponsored and produced by the Börsenverein der Deutschen Buchhändler, the organization of booksellers and publishers.

BIBLIOGRAPHY

Besterman, Theodore. *A World Bibliography of Bibliographies....* 4th ed., rev. and enl. Lausanne, Societas Bibliographica, 1965–66. 5v.

British Library. *British Library News.* 1976– .

Canberra, Australia. National Library. *Annual Report.*

Downs, Robert B. and Frances B. Jenkins. *Bibliography; Current State and Future Trends.* Urbana, University of Illinois Press, 1967. 611p.

Gropp, Arthur Eric. *A Bibliography of Latin American Bibliographies.* Metuchen, N.J., Scarecrow Press, 1968. 515p. Supplement, 1971. 277p.

Lockhead, Douglas. *Bibliography of Canadian Bibliography.* 2d ed. Toronto, University of Toronto Press and Bibliographical Society of Canada, 1972. 312p.

McGeachy, John A., III. "The *Monthly Catalog*'s First Response to Its 1947 Congressional Charge." *Library Resources and Technical Services,* 20: 53–64, Winter 1976.

Malclès, Louise-Noëlle. *Manuel de bibliographie.* 2.éd. entièrement refondue et mise à jour. Paris, Presses Universitaires de France, 1969. 366p.

National Conference on the State of Canadian Bibliography, Vancouver, B.C., May 22–24, 1977. *Proceedings.* Edited by Anne B. Piternick. Ottawa, National Library of Canada, 1977. 514p.

Ottawa. National Library of Canada. *Annual Report of the National Librarian of Canada.* 1953– .

Ottawa. National Library of Canada. *National Library News.*

Sheehy, Eugene P. *Guide to Reference Books.* 9th ed. Chicago, American Library Association, 1976. 1015p.

Totok, Wilhelm and others. *Handbuch der bibliographischen Nachschlagewerke.* 4.,erw., völlig neubearb. Aufl. Frankfurt a.M., Klostermann, 1972. 367p.

U.S. Library of Congress. *Library of Congress Information Bulletin.*

Walford, A.J. *Guide to Reference Material.* 3d ed. London, Library Association, 1973–77. 3v.

Wees, Ian. "The National Library of Canada: The First Quarter-Century." *Canadian Library Journal,* 35:153–163, June 1978.

CHAPTER 11

Acquisitions

Introduction

Up to this point emphasis has been placed upon the selection of books and upon the problems involved in choosing the right materials for a given collection. A second area to be considered in the building of a library collection concerns the acquiring of the materials selected for purchase. This brings a whole new set of problems: finding out whether the materials are available, the best methods of purchasing, and the kinds of records necessary for controlling the order process.

Organization of Acquisitions

Although some libraries have acquisition functions scattered through two or more departments, the typical acquisition functions include bibliographic verification of all order requests (which may also include responsibility for collecting the tools—national and trade bibliographies, publishers' and dealers' catalogues, etc.—used in such verification); selecting the dealers to be used and preparing and forwarding orders to those dealers; maintaining complete, accurate and accessible files of materials on order or in process; updating and reviewing those files so as to claim or cancel orders which do not arrive on schedule; unpacking and sorting of orders as they are received, along with checking and approving of invoices; maintaining (or at least cooperating with the institution's business office in maintaining) records of payment and encumbrance of funds; and forwarding all newly-arrived materials, possibly with ownership marks already affixed, to the cataloging department.

No attempt will be made here to describe the acquisition system of any particular library. Instead, the various kinds of information needed to carry on acquisition work will be pointed out. Even the smallest library must exercise business-like procedures in keeping essential order records, and the larger the library, the more complicated those records will be. Nevertheless, certain records are common to both.

It is generally agreed that the work in any order department is largely clerical, although professional librarians are needed as well. Since a large part of the staff is non-professional, manuals of procedure will expedite the training of personnel in an area where there is considerable turnover. Certain characteristics should pertain to all staff members whether professional or clerical: accuracy, orderliness, resourcefulness, combined with speed, are among the essential requisites.

Since material is acquired both by purchase and by gift and exchange, these activities may be divided by method and handled separately. Gifts and exchanges are frequently combined. Another arrangement is by type of material, with separate sections for books, for serials, for documents, for microforms, for nonprint, etc. No matter how the division of work is arranged, it is well to remember that only simple and essential records should be kept.

Order Routines

Sources of materials to be ordered are various and differ from one type of library to another. Suggestions come in from the staff and readers, in addition to the titles approved during the process of selection. Replacements recommended by staff and departments compose another source. There is usually a want or consideration file (more elegantly referred to as the desiderata file) in the order department. In college, university and school libraries, the faculty recommendations for purchase are an important source of order requests. Once an order request has reached the order department, whatever its source, the problem is to verify the bibliographic information and to complete it if it is deficient in necessary information. This first necessary step comprises the searching of the title.

Searching is an activity in which both professionals and non-professionals participate and in which the qualifications of the detective play their part. A good knowledge of the details of bibliographic form, of the national and trade bibliographies, and—in the larger libraries, especially in college and university libraries—of foreign languages is essential. The searcher tries to verify the author's name (in good cataloging form), title, translator or editor (if any), publisher, edition, series (if any), number of volumes, date, list price. This information is entered on the order card.

Let us take an order request through a large university system, since it will have the widest variation in records and practices and fragmentation of collections, as well as sources of orders. Let us assume that a request for a group of titles has arrived from a professor in the history department. Before proceeding with the searching process, it may be enlightening to play the novelist and imagine how he/she

gathered these particular titles. Perhaps by reading professional journals, noting titles and putting them down on slips (some of these notices
may be announcements for books to be published at some future date;
ordering a book not yet in print can cause some confusion in the order
search). Perhaps by reading the *New York Times,* the London *Times,
Saturday Review, Harper's,* etc. and again busily noting titles and putting them down on order slips. (A dozen colleagues will be reading the
same sources at the same time and noting many of the same titles, none
aware, however, that others are doing the same thing.) Perhaps by
talking to various colleagues, sometimes at national meetings, who call
attention to unfamiliar titles. The professor puts down the names of the
authors and transcribes the titles, not always getting quite the correct
information and not always with the knowledge that the titles are part of
a series for which the library has a standing order. Finally the professor
decides to send this collection of titles over to the library to be ordered.
He/she submits them first for approval to the department head, who
initials them as a matter of course. The department head does not keep a
record of everything that each faculty member in the department orders,
so some of these titles may have been ordered in the past two weeks by
someone else in the department—or, for that matter, by several other
people.

The batch of requests arrives at the order department and is
handed over to a searcher. The first thing the searcher does is to determine whether these titles are already in the library, or whether they are
on order but have not yet arrived. It is at this point that the searcher may
fall into one of the pitfalls which await the unwary. The form of entry on
the order slip may not be the form of entry under which the book is
entered in the library's catalogs. The searcher may carefully search the
official catalog (in those libraries which maintain that file), may then
consult the outstanding order file to see if it is on order, and may finally
check in an orders-received file (which records those titles received but
not yet cataloged). Since he/she is searching under the wrong entry, no
record of the book will be found. (Through the years revisions have
occurred in the cataloging codes which determine how a work is entered
in a library catalog. This may make the search particularly challenging
in an old library with a large catalog.)

To obviate this chance of ordering a book which is already there,
it may be thought advisable to verify the title and author first in one of
the national or trade bibliographies, to determine that such a title actually exists and to discover what the correct main entry actually is. On
the other hand, the library may decide that the number of cases in which
such ambiguities arise is not great enough to justify verification of each
title first. All titles would be searched in the library's records first, and
then the residue, which had not been found, would be verified in the
bibliographies. Some examples of actual order requests may illustrate

the difficulties occasionally faced by a searcher in the effort to verify a title.

Some years ago, an order requested Churchill's *The Great Democracies.* This is actually volume four in his series on the history of the English-speaking peoples, which one university library had cataloged under the title of the set. No cards would be found for the individual titles. With Sir Winston there is perhaps no danger of failing to recognize the problem. But the monographic series, whose individual volumes are not analyzed by the library, offers a splendid opportunity for duplicating titles. The history professor, who has heard about a title at a national convention, might not realize that this was part of a large series, and would order by author and title. The searcher would find no entry under author, if the library had elected not to analyze the series. He/she would therefore send the order through. When it arrived, consternation might be created when it was discovered that this series was on standing order, and the library now had two copies of a title, where one would be sufficient. In large libraries, which order thousands of these series, the amount of duplication can become expensive.

A simpler example was the request for *Chinese Pottery and Porcelain,* Edinburgh, H.M. Stationers Office, 1955. This order request was not incorrect, merely incomplete. The searcher finally discovered that the entry was not under title, but rather under a corporate body: Edinburgh. Royal Scottish Museum.

Another not infrequent error is to cite a book under its sub-title, which is often more informative than the main title. A request for Carl Anton Dauten's *Fundamentals of Financial Management* may turn out to be a request for his *Business Finance, the Fundamentals of Financial Management.* If Mr. Dauten were a very prolific author, the searcher might miss the title filed under B and assert that the library did not have it.

The following grab bag of actual order requests will furnish further illustrations of the problems which confront the helpless searcher.

As Requested	*As Verified*
National Education Association Education and the Self-Contained Classroom	Snyder, Edith Roach, ed. The Self-Contained Classroom
Sitashov, Iurii Mikhailovich	Shashkov, Iurii Mikhailovich
Jervis, T. B. Travels in Kashmir	Huegel, Carl Alexander Anselm Travels in Kashmir, with Notes by T. B. Jervis
Huckaby, Calvin	Huckabay, Calvin
D'Olanda, Francisco Dialoghi Michaelangioleschi	Hollanda, Francisco de I Dialoghi Michelangioleschi

Hyderabad State.
  The Freedom Struggle in Hyderabad

Hyderabad, India (State).
  Committee Appointed for the
  Compilation of a History of the Freedom
  Movement in Hyderabad. The Freedom
  Struggle in Hyderabad

Sirotkovic, Jakov
  Economic Planning Yugoslavia

Sirotkovic, Jakov
  Privredno planiranje u Jugoslaviji

Silvert, Kalman H.
  The Conflict Society; Reaction and
  Revolution in Latin America

Silvert, Kalman H.
  Reaction and Revolution in Latin
  America; the Conflict Society

Fet, Aff A.
  Polnoe sobranie stixotvorenij, biblioteka
  poeta osnovana M. Gor'kim sol'saja
  serija 2-Oe izdanie

Shenshin, Afanasii Afanas'evich
  Polnoe sobranie [etc.]

Khadduri, Majid
  Islamic Jurisprudence

al-Shafi'i, Muhammad ibn Idris
  Islamic Jurisprudence

Gadoffre, Gilbert
  Ronsard par lui-même.

Ronsard, Pierre de
  Ronsard par lui-même

Rosen, Joseph
  Reagent chemicals and standards

Rosin, Joseph
  Reagent chemicals and standards

Rothschild, Lionel Walter
  A Classification of Living Animals

Rothschild, Nathaniel Meyer Victor
  A Classification of Living Animals

Rubin, I. R.
  Jordi

Rubin, Theodore Isaac
  Jordi

Rousset, Camille Felix Michel
  L'Algerie. Paris, 1900–04.

Rousset, Camille Felix Michel
  Commencement d'une conquête:
  l'Algerie de 1830 à 1840. 2.êd. 1900

Corporate bodies cause more than their share of misery to the unhappy searcher. A request for the American Institute of Accountants' *Accounting Terminology Bulletin* caused considerable trouble because the person requesting the serial did not realize—or did not indicate, at least—that it was published by the Committee on Terminology of the Institute. It was found under "American Institute of Accountants. Committee on Terminology." In the case of a large institution with many, many subdivisions, all of which publish heavily, it may become extremely difficult to locate an item if the subdivision does not appear on the order card.

Sometimes a perfectly standard-looking order causes problems. A request for Clara Mae Taylor's *Foundations of Nutrition,* 5th ed., caused some perturbation because Ms. Taylor turned out to be a later editor of a work which had been begun by someone else. The correct entry turned out to be Rose, Mary Davies Swartz. That author was dead by the time of the 5th edition, but the edition stayed under her name.

The ultimate—and, it is to be hoped, the unusual—difficulty that can be caused the harried searcher was described by the order librarian of one of the state universities. She described the arrival of a perfectly innocent-looking order: author, title, publisher, place, date— all complete and unsuspicious. A search was made, but the title could not be verified. Even the publisher could not be located. The order was returned with a request for the source of the title. Promptly, it returned with a citation to a legislative record. The journal was consulted: the data were all there as recorded. The title had been quoted by a legislator. Another search failed to reveal any information about the mysterious work. A letter was dispatched to the legislator, who finally wrote an embarrassed reply, explaining that he had needed a quotation to back up an argument, and that he had made up the title. This kind of request would probably be classified by the searcher among the "ghoulies, ghosties, and things that go bump in the night," from which one can only hope for deliverance.

Of course, these examples do not represent the bulk of order requests, which move through the order department without undue turmoil. But the large university library, which orders a substantial amount of foreign, peculiar, and unusual materials, far from the ordinary trade channels, affords the enthusiastic searcher much material against which he/she can match wits. One such dedicated soul remarked that it was the problems such as these that added zest to the task. Indeed, the detective work is sometimes of a high order.

To recapitulate: the searcher will check the order slip against the catalog to see if the library already has the title; will check against the outstanding order file to see if it is on order but has not yet arrived, and will check against the orders-received file or in-process file which keeps track of an item's status once it leaves the orders-received file, but before it is cataloged. If the searcher does not find it in these sources, he/she will check the trade bibliographies to get full bibliographic and ordering information. It may be well to note that these various files do not all exist as separate entities in every library—various permutations and combinations of them are found. The order will then be sent on to the functionary who will choose the dealer for the various items being ordered.

Choosing the Dealer

This is an important step, probably second to the selection of the books themselves. Libraries have three primary sources for purchase of current books: publishers, bookstores, and wholesalers (also called job-bers). Libraries do, in fact, buy from all three sources. The factors which are considered in deciding where it is most advantageous to buy are several: (1) Which gives the largest discount? (2) Which furnishes the speediest service? (3) Which will adapt billing to local accounting requirements? (4) Which is most accurate in filling orders and most prompt in rectifying mistakes? These factors do not always reside in any one of the three sources, and in some cases speed may be more impor-tant than discount, accounting procedures may take precedence over all other considerations, accuracy may be more important than speed or cost. As a result, a given library may, on occasion, order from all three sources.

The great difficulty in ordering from multiple sources comes from the fact that this procedure increases the paper work considerably. Separate orders to ten different dealers mean ten separate letters, ten separate shipments, ten separate invoices, ten separate payments. Sav-ing effected by shopping around and placing smaller orders at more favorable discounts may well be swallowed up by increased bookkeep-ing costs. Where speed in acquiring a title is the primary consideration (getting a reserve book for a college class which begins in five days, for example), nothing could be faster than walking across the street to the local bookstore and picking the book off the shelf. Here again, a more favorable discount may be sacrificed for the added service. The diffi-culty involved in placing all orders at a local bookstore (although this is done in some places because it is considered important to support local business) arises from the fact that bookstores with really large stocks of titles are few and far between. As the library moves out of the area of currently popular titles, its success in finding less popular items in the stock of the ordinary bookstore diminishes. In all questions of dis-counts, however, the librarian ought to face one issue squarely: should price be the only consideration, or should other factors—speed of ac-quisition, extra services furnished by the vendor, etc.—be taken into account? The cheapest purchase may not always be the best bargain.

Wholesalers receive a sizeable percentage of library orders. The advantage of dealing with the wholesaler is clear: the librarian places one order, receives one package, pays one bill, has only one person to deal with on service problems. The services offered to libraries by wholesalers have steadily expanded: special catalogs and lists have been compiled; prebound books will be supplied; notification as to the status of a book is made quickly; the special billing requirements of each library are observed; automated and, in some cases, on-line procedures for transmitting orders are available. Generally speaking, wholesalers have shown themselves willing to provide any service which could be organized on a mass-production basis.

The mass-production requirement emphasizes the basic nature of the wholesaler's business. Such a dealer buys multiple copies of large numbers of titles from many publishers and because of this is able to offer a better discount than the publisher can give the individual library ordering only one copy. The wholesaler can also offer a better discount on that one copy because of a special system for handling orders. This is essentially the wholesaler's specialty, as it is not the publisher's. This means that the wholesaler's savings in handling orders—which allow the offering of discounts—depend upon adherence to a routine, to something resembling an assembly-line treatment of orders. If the potential advantages of a wholesale system are to operate, it is imperative that those doing business with the wholesaler follow the wholesaler's recommended procedures.

Because improving the quality of the communication between librarians placing orders and wholesalers filling those orders is so important to the efficient operation of both groups, the Resources and Technical Services Division of the American Library Association encourages, through discussion groups and committees, meetings of librarians and bookdealers who are concerned with resolving mutual problems. One such joint committee has produced a set of "Guidelines for Handling Library Orders for In-Print Monographic Publications." These guidelines specify the form that library purchase-orders ought to take and the types of information that should be furnished about each item in order to identify it accurately. Suggestions for establishing claiming, cancellation, return, invoicing, and payment procedures are supplied. The guidelines also specify reasonable waiting periods for receipt of orders and include suggestions for improved reporting on the status of orders by the dealers.

Approval Plans and Blanket Order Plans

The place of blanket orders and approval plans in the broad picture of collection planning and development was discussed in Chapter 2, but it might be well to review some of the forms that such plans may take. When the library wishes to acquire the total output (or total output on certain subjects) of a publisher, a "publisher's standing order" may be arranged individually with each publisher involved. It is also possible to arrange through jobbers or wholesalers for the automatic shipment of new publications from specified publishers or in designated series. Wholesalers offer various kinds of standing order plans in which they will select and ship new publications of certain types. The type of plan sometimes referred to as a "jobber approval plan" usually involves selection and shipment (sometimes with advance notification) by the jobber of new publications which appear to fit some sort of collection description statement or subject selection profile supplied by the library. Although the terms "blanket order," "blanket approval," and "gathering plan" are not used consistently, they usually refer to agreements between libraries and dealers which incorporate one or both of these features—some degree of responsibility for selection given to the dealer and some degree of rejection and return privileges allowed to the library. "Standing orders," on the other hand, usually mean a firm commitment to buy on the part of the library. Any librarian planning to start an acquisition arrangement designated by any of the above terms ought to ascertain at the beginning of any discussion the dealer's understanding of the terms involved.

As an acquisition or procurement method, blanket plans of various kinds have been praised for being fast enough to supply books before they go out of print or before users requested them and for saving staff time and recordkeeping expense. On the opposite side of the argument are those who say that record-keeping becomes more difficult and that speed of acquisition is of no great consequence in a library with a sizeable cataloging backlog. The fact that most blanket plans are set up to supply one copy of a title causes concern in libraries where several branch libraries may want the same title. There is also an inherent danger, recognized by a number of libraries when one prominent jobber went out of business in the early 1970s, in placing large blocks of orders through one dealer. Even if there is only a slight deterioration in service, the effect on the library can be very unsettling. Whether or not a library is able to make efficient use of blanket plans as an acquisition method might depend on the relationship between the library and the business office of the parent institution, as well as on the quality of communication between library and dealer.

The most vulnerable aspect of the operation of a blanket plan appears to be the line of communication between the library and the jobber. In an ideal situation, the library defines its collection carefully; the jobber observes the definition of scope scrupulously; the library returns the few irrelevant books that slip by the jobber; and the jobber quickly makes any necessary adjustments in the profile. In the real world, problems arise at any of these points, beginning with the library's inability to specify subjects and levels of desired materials in terms that have the same meaning for the jobber. To both parties the question of whether the jobber makes a narrow or broad interpretation of the profile is an important one. If the interpretation is broad, then the library either receives and accepts much marginal material, thereby wasting part of the budget and probably creating weeding problems for the future, or the library receives and returns the unwanted materials, creating unnecessary work for both library staff and jobber and negating some of the arguments advocating the economy of blanket plans as ordering systems. On the other hand, if the jobber interprets the profile narrowly, the process appears to be very efficient, with the library receiving mostly materials that are wanted and making few returns. The hidden problem with this interpretation is that the jobber may be missing other items the library's selectors would have chosen if they had known that they existed. Missing such items at the time when they are easily available could mean an expensive out-of-print search later.

The loosening of fiscal control which the initiation of blanket order or approval plans brings has been a concern of many librarians, though some have seen the unallocated budget usually required by blanket plans as being a good opportunity to remove control of the book budget from the faculty. In general, the budget allocation and fund accounting systems of a library must be adjusted when the library enters into extensive blanket order arrangements.

Foreign Acquisitions

In most libraries of any size some order requests will be for materials published in foreign countries. When choosing a dealer for foreign publications, the acquisition librarian must decide whether to deal with an importer (a dealer based in the U.S. who specializes in foreign materials) or an exporter (a foreign dealer who may specialize in the materials of a particular country or group of countries). Although importers vary in their range of services—some handle monographs and serials, both in-print and out-of-print; some specialize in limited geographical areas or types of materials; some concentrate on what they list in their catalogs—in general they offer more service and charge more than exporters. An exporter may have lower overhead costs and may not charge as many extra service fees as an importer, but language problems may inhibit communication with dealers in some countries. Which way a library decides to go with its orders will depend on the average volume and type of foreign purchasing done and the library staff available to originate and monitor orders. A small library with few foreign purchases may find it easiest to do business with an importer, but a large library or one with a large volume of foreign acquisitions may prefer to establish a continuing relationship with exporters. Blanket plans for foreign materials have been popular since the 1960s and continue to be used in libraries where domestic blanket plans have been curtailed.

Bidding

Libraries supported by public funds may be restricted in their choices of dealers by local, state, or federal regulations. Such libraries may be required to obtain library materials through a competitive bidding system. Bidding may be either formal, requiring advertising, sealed bids, public opening of the bids, etc., or informal, requiring only that bids be obtained somehow from three or more dealers. Sometimes bidding may be required for lists of specific titles, but more often bids are based on an estimated volume of purchases (sometimes divided into categories such as adult trade, juvenile, scientific-professional, etc.) to be made in a specified period of time. The general advantages of bidding as a method for awarding public contracts are well-known, but the specific advantages or disadvantages of bidding as a method for acquiring library materials are hotly debated. It is doubtful that any librarian not required by law to obtain bids before choosing a dealer would voluntarily do so, but those librarians who do work in institutions with bidding regulations must learn the intricacies of the system in order to develop as efficient procedures as possible.

Preparing the Order

Systems of ordering will differ from library to library; some are strictly manual systems and others involve a high degree of automation. The manual procedure outlined here attempts to show the kinds of records and reports typically needed and is given as one example, not to be construed as the only possible method. It involves the use of multiple copy forms, sometimes called "fanfolds." They are 3 × 5 slips with inter-leaved carbons, or made of carbonless copying paper. With such forms, more than one copy can be made simultaneously. In a large system, the number of copies may be considerable. For the purpose of introducing certain order terms—and also to illustrate certain of the points which represent problems—we will take the reader through such a set of slips, with the warning that this particular form is not introduced as a model, but merely as an example.

The particular form we will follow involves the typing of ten slips in the fanfold. (Of course, only one typing is done on an electric typewriter, with the machine making nine additional copies simultaneously.) The slips consist of the following: (1) outstanding order file—on white; (2) fund slip—tan; (3) encumbrance release—green; (4) dealer purchase order—yellow; (5) dealer report slip—pink; (6) claim slip—orange; (7) official catalog—pink; (8) public catalog—pink; (9) labeling guide—white; (10) arrival notice—green. We hasten to remark that the various colors are means of quick identification and a help in sorting—we are by no means attempting to prescribe these particular colors for the individual type of slip! We suspect that a library might survive if its outstanding order file slip were yellow instead of white, its fund slip green instead of tan, etc., etc.

The following disposition is made of the slips when the order has been typed: (1) the dealer purchase order and dealer report slips are shipped off to the dealer as the order. (2) The fund slip is filed in the fund record, as an indication of the amounts charged against the fund but still outstanding. (3) The outstanding order slip—and all remaining slips—are filed in the outstanding order file to await arrival of the book.

The front of all slips would be identical (except for the legend at the bottom of the slip naming it and two additions to the encumbrance release slip). Bibliographic information is given (author, title, publisher, place, date, series, volumes), and in addition the following items are called for: order number; name of the fund on which the book is being purchased; name of the dealer; name of the library in the system to which the book is going; name of the person recommending purchase; date ordered; catalog number and item number, if the book was ordered from an o.p. catalog; estimated price.

Let us follow the dealer purchase order and dealer report slips along their path. The front, as was remarked in the preceding paragraph, would contain the same information as all other slips. But the back of the dealer purchase order would contain instructions to the dealer (these would vary widely from library to library, of course). The following legends appear on the sample we are using:

Invoice: Bill in DUPLICATE, referring to order number. Bill items on same FUND on one invoice (Fund is directly under order number on reverse side of this form.)

Shipping: Send accompanying report slip inside front cover of book; show full order number on all packages. Address shipments to:

Order Department
X Library
Z City, State; Zip Code

Report: Report slip is enclosed for your convenience in reporting on orders that can not be filled.

Series: If an item is part of a series and we have not so indicated, please report on pink slip before sending.

Billing instructions constitute an area in which dealers have to accustom themselves to great variation. Many libraries associated with state or city governments—or school boards—are bound by rigidly prescribed accounting rules which may demand notarized invoices, thirteen copies—the fourth of pink vellum, the sixth and eighth upside down, etc., etc. Sometimes dealers seem to prefer to ignore all instructions and proceed as they choose. No doubt excessively complicated systems may irk them considerably.

The report slip is most important to the library, but the dealer may not find it very impressive, and books may return without the slip. Of course, they can be identified by searching the outstanding order file, but on occasion the main entry under which the book is ordered may be in error, and if no report slip comes back, it may take some time to find where the outstanding order slip was filed. Note especially the last instruction concerning series. This is an effort to avoid the duplication caused by ordering under author and title a book which is in a series the library gets on standing order. If the library has failed to discover that the book is part of a series, it needs to know—and woe betide the careless searcher!

The front of the report slip—identical with all others. The legends on the verso of the slip:

```
┌─────────────────────────────────────────────────────────────────┐
│  If Book is Not Available Return This Slip to:                    │
│                             Order dept, X lib, etc.               │
│                                                                   │
│  _____Sold; order cancelled.                                    │
│                                                                   │
│  _____Not yet published              Order cancelled            │
│  _____Out of stock at publisher      —Will send                 │
│                                                                   │
│  _____Out of print, order cancelled                             │
│                                                                   │
│  _____Please confirm order:                                     │
│                                                                   │
│         1. Author's correct name is:                              │
│         2. Series:                                                │
│                                                                   │
│  _____Other                                                     │
└─────────────────────────────────────────────────────────────────┘
```

Perhaps the terms are reasonably self-explanatory, but it may be well to run straight down the list. "Sold; order cancelled" is clear enough, and the order cancelled will cause the library to withdraw the outstanding order slip. "Not yet published"—the problem of people sending in orders for books which have only been announced for publication. The dealer then has the option of cancelling the order or of holding it until the date of publication and sending. He also indicates the same options if the book is out of stock but the publisher will reprint at a given date: dealer either cancels, or holds order and fills it when publisher prints. Of course, if the dealer cancels in either of the two cases, the library will have to re-initiate the whole business after the appropriate date. "Out of print, order cancelled": clear enough. The "Please Confirm Order," however, is more interesting. Something is not in accord between the library's searchers and the dealer's searchers. If the library has ordered it under a different name (corporate body instead of personal author, personal instead of corporate, or some person other than the real author), it wants to know, in the event that it already has the book under the form the dealer has discovered. And, as was remarked a moment ago, any large system which orders many series on standing order wants to be informed if its searching has not identified a given book as one in a series.

To return, however, to the slips waiting in the library's files. The outstanding order file slip will not only furnish a record of the book's "outstanding" state, but will also serve to prevent undesired duplication of titles. The official and public catalog slips will be used to file into those catalogs when the book arrives, pending full cataloging. The labeling guide will go to the labelers' desk along with the book to instruct them as to the call number to be put on the spine. (This step has been modified in many libraries where prepared labels are now acquired from the same vendor—OCLC, for example—which supplies catalog cards.) The arrival notice will be sent to the person who recommended purchase of the book, to let him/her know it is now in the library. Many libraries might not prepare the catalog and labeling records at the point of writing up the order, but it does allow those forms to be prepared with the one, original order typing.

The encumbrance release slip and the fund slip are part of the accounting system. The encumbrance release slip has two items added to its front: the date received and the cost of the item (which replaces the estimated cost originally charged against the fund). The estimated cost had appeared on the fund slip, originally filed under the fund name to show encumbrances. When the item is paid, it is the amount on the encumbrance release slip which is used, and the fund slip is discarded.

The last slip in the batch is the claim slip, waiting in the outstanding order file against the day when it is discovered that a book which was ordered has not arrived. The verso of the claim slip contains the following legends:

We have not as yet received the title indicated on the reverse side of this slip. Please report by checking the appropriate box below. If the title has already been sent, please do not duplicate shipment.

☐ Shipped on
☐ Not yet published. Due   Will send.
☐ Out of print. Cancelling.
☐ Out of print. Searching
☐ Out of stock. Will send
    (Please give approximate date if possible.)
☐ Sold. Cancelling
☐ Other:

Multiple-copy order forms in various designs are available from commercial firms supplying libraries. The individual library, especially one with a large volume of acquisitions or peculiar record-keeping requirements, may find it necessary to devise its own forms to cover local procedures and files.

The acquisitions department, with its many business routines, is likely to be one of the first places in a library considered for automated operations. The whole system of ordering has been automated in some libraries; in others, only parts of the process have been so treated. Many libraries, of course, are finding it necessary to move away from extensive manually-maintained files of paper slips. If one thinks of the information that has been typed on order slips, one can quickly see that it could just as readily have been typed on a key-punch keyboard, producing a machine-readable record. It would also be relatively simple to assign a code number to each supplier of materials and then to store the address of each dealer in a machine-readable file. Punched cards for each order, coded by dealer, could then be fed into the computer, which would produce order requests by dealer and could simultaneously keep the accounts for each transaction by encumbering the separate funds coded into the cards and later debiting them for the actual amount spent. Periodically, the system would report exactly which items were on order and the status of each order; it could be programmed to write claim notices for items which had not arrived, report which items had been claimed and when, and keep all accounts current.

Automated acquisition systems, particularly locally developed ones, have been extensively reported in the literature, but because of improved equipment and programming techniques the details of the various systems change more quickly than the reports appear. Several of the larger wholesalers offer plans for automating library purchasing procedures, either through batch processing of orders in machine readable form or through direct on-line communication with computers at the wholesaler's headquarters. These systems vary in the extent to which they require special equipment, are regularly reviewed and improved, and are fully documented. A librarian who is considering automating an acquisition procedure ought, in addition to reading the literature and talking to dealers with systems to sell, to contact librarians in similar libraries where automated systems are operating.

Out-of-Print Titles

The ordering of library materials, particularly books, which are out-of-print presents a more complicated picture than the ordering of current trade publications. There are two general aspects to the problem of acquiring o.p. books. One involves the search by the library for a specific title which it wishes to acquire; the other involves searching the catalogs sent to the library by various o.p. dealers to see if anything is being offered which the library would like to buy.

To attempt to find a specific title in the o.p. market resembles the children's game of "Button, Button, Who's got the Button?" There are hundreds of o.p. dealers, and it is difficult to find which one has any given title at a particular moment. It is true that these dealers send copies of their catalogs to libraries, but the search through masses of the catalogs looking for a particular title can be tedious indeed. And it is also unfortunately true that the titles listed in a given catalog will soon be sold (at least the desirable titles will be), so that holding this year's catalog for next year's searching is not liable to produce satisfactory results. The library can take other steps to obtain the individual title. It can send the order to a dealer who specializes in that type of material, in the hope that it will be in stock or the dealer will be able to obtain it. There are also various searching services which will search for requested titles. Thirdly, there are publications in which libraries can advertise lists of titles wanted. Out-of-print dealers can then submit bids for those titles which they have in stock.

The second aspect of the o.p. business in libraries consists of checking dealers' catalogs for titles which the selector thinks might be desirable. The items checked are then searched in the library catalogs to see if they are already in the collection. If they are not, they are then ordered from the dealer. This procedure has its own special problems. The arrangement of dealers' catalogs and the amount of bibliographic information which they give varies greatly. Occasionally the catalogs are not arranged in any order, but are assembled helter-skelter—all subjects intermingled, no alphabetizing by author. Sometimes dealers are not very precise in differentiating one edition from another; some are very brief in identifying the author—occasionally giving only an initial for the forename—or the title—which is sometimes shortened until one cannot be sure that it is really the title wanted. In addition, the description of condition may be misunderstood, since a term like ''good condition'' is not very precise and may mean different things to the dealer and to the librarian. Speed in searching is essential, for the titles desired may be sold by the time the dealer receives the library's order. Some libraries send immediate requests to reserve a title until their order machinery can be set in motion.

There is another difficulty involved in dealing with the o.p. trade, but it is one which can only be mentioned, since there seems little that can be done about it. The same title may be advertised in several different catalogs over a period of a few months at considerably different prices. A librarian may be somewhat disconcerted to see a title which he/she has just purchased at $100 advertised by another dealer for $10. But the prices of o.p. materials, one can only conclude, are not regular and fixed: they represent the value which the item has in the eyes of the dealer. If a title seems overpriced, the library can always wait. But if it has long wanted the item, it may run the risk of seeing the next advertisement of it ask an even higher price.

If the item being considered for purchase by a library does not have to be in its original form, there are two other options available to the librarian—purchasing in reprint or in microform. Reprints may come from companies specializing in hardcover reprinting of materials no longer kept in stock by the original publishers or from companies such as University Microfilms International which offers "on-demand" xerographic or microfilm copies of out-of-print titles. Either of these approaches may at times cost more per title than buying through a secondhand dealer, but the frustration of determining who has a specific title will be less and the quality of paper in the reprint is likely to be better than in the original (though this depends on the place and period in which the original was published). A microform copy—either microfilm or microfiche—may be obtained from dealers specializing in this form of reproduction or, in some cases, may be obtained from another library. The cost may be less than for a hardcover reprint, but readers may not be as pleased with the choice.

Thanks to modern means of reproduction the librarian will often have a choice of format when acquiring out-of-print materials. The decision about format ought to be made on the basis of potential use (a microfilm copy of a reserve book would be inappropriate if a hardcover copy could be obtained), urgency of the request (searching the second-hand market may take years), and cost (in terms of staff time to locate the item and place the order as well as the list price of the item to be purchased).

One source of information about the secondhand book trade is the *AB Bookman's Yearbook,* issued annually by the *AB Bookman's Weekly* (itself an organ of the antiquarian trade). The section of the *Yearbook* called "The O.P. Market" contains a directory of specialist and antiquarian booksellers, with a subject index. Bowker's *American Book Trade Directory* contains a state by state, city by city listing of bookstores, including secondhand shops, with information on specialities.

Microforms

Microforms are usually ordered directly from the producers, who may be commercial or association publishers or other libraries which hold negative masters and are able to offer copying services. Compared to book and journal publishers, the number of micropublishers is relatively limited. Because of this and the different types of information which might be specified on the microform order (see Chapter 6 for a fuller discussion of this), some libraries merge into one position or department the responsibility for final selection decisions and ordering of microforms, and they separate this entirely from the library's regular order department. Other libraries may simply assign the primary responsibility for microforms to one individual in the order department. A basic tool for any librarian who has responsibility for microform selection and ordering is "Guidelines for Handling Library Orders for Microforms," published by the Resources Section of ALA's Resources and Technical Services Division in 1977.

When microform orders arrive, they must be inspected carefully to ensure that the material received is the material that was ordered. The checking of large sets is particularly important, because there is no other way to determine whether or not all the advertised units have been delivered. An ideal inspection would involve looking at each individual frame on every reel or fiche. This is tedious and time-consuming, but, based on the variation in quality which has existed in the past and the amount of money being invested in large sets, some librarians feel it is worth the effort.

Serials

Serial subscriptions will, of course, be handled through a routine separate from book ordering. Most serials come from sources other than trade publishers and the wholesaling function is handled by a separate group of vendors known as subscription agents. (Not all serials will be purchased. As with books, many may be available as gifts or through exchange.)

Librarians may choose to order serials directly from individual publishers, and for some publications—membership journals, very expensive indexing and abstracting services, investment and business services, certain directories, publications of societies and institutions, etc.—this is the recommended procedure. For other kinds of serials, the advantages of consolidating many titles in one order, thereby reducing correspondence and check-writing, may tempt the librarian to turn to a subscription agent.

Subscription agents offer a wide range of services, among which are the placing and renewing of subscriptions and claiming of missing issues. Some agents also automatically order all available title pages and indexes, attempt to retrieve funds from discontinued publications, handle address changes when a library or one of its branches moves, offer various kinds of reports to ease the difficulties of serials control, publish guides to serials, and maintain up-dating services for serials publication information. Most agents offer a "till forbidden" service, which means that the agent continues to renew subscriptions until a library sends specific instructions to the contrary. When a library is willing to start a "till forbidden" plan, some agents will work out a three-year cycle for the renewal of that library's subscriptions. This kind of plan allows the library to take advantage of the savings for three-year subscription rates offered by some popular magazines (scholarly journals are less likely to offer such savings.) There are also a few dealers who specialize in back issues, out-of-print or antiquarian stock.

Choosing a subscription agent is much like choosing a book jobber. Good service, fast and accurate, is usually the primary criterion. Although subscription agents may vary in the amount of their service charges, shopping around for the lowest price may be a money-losing proposition. Continuity of relations with a dealer is more important when purchasing serials than books. Changing from one agent to another usually means gaps in some subscriptions and duplications in others. This is one of the arguments against awarding serials contracts annually on the basis of bids.

Although bidding is less common than it once was, bidding regulations still exist for serial purchasing, as they do in some libraries for book purchasing. Bidding for serials purchasing involves submitting to various dealers a list of titles for which subscription renewals are desired, in order to get the lowest bid. This is an even more awkward procedure for serials than for books, since subscription lists are subject to frequent changes and so are subscription prices from publishers. Subscription agents—who may spend much time preparing a bid only to lose it or, worse yet, to win the contract and then be squeezed later by publishers' price increases—do not have anything good to say about bidding.

How the library maintains control of serial publications as they arrive, issue by issue, and are added to the collection is beyond the scope of this discussion. However, the way a library chooses to organize and up-date its records on serials holdings—records which show which titles are expected, which issues have arrived, the source (publisher or agent) and means (purchase, gift, exchange) by which the serial is obtained, which departmental or branch libraries hold the title, and various items of information about binding, cataloging, and payment, etc.—may determine where orders are placed and how much (if at all) they are distributed among several agents. Agents do differ in the extent to which they can accommodate and supplement a library's serials control procedures.

Gifts

Gifts are a valuable source of enriching the library's collection. They usually take the form of books or journals, although donations of money for purchase of materials are sometimes made. The gift of money poses few problems as the usual procedure of selection will be followed in its expenditure. In theory, at least, the same selection principles should be applied to gift materials as are applied in the library's own selection. This is sometimes difficult as the human factor, in the person of the donor, enters into the picture, and the librarian may have to adopt the role of the diplomat. Most librarians prefer to accept only gifts which have no strings attached. The no-strings-attached rule can avoid all sorts of difficulties which may arise because the donor wishes to insist on various kinds of restrictions. He/she may demand that no markings be put on the bindings, ask that the gift collection be kept intact as one unit (perhaps in its own special quarters), refuse to allow the library to dispose of any titles which are duplicates of titles already in the library, or oppose the discarding of any material which the library feels does not meet its standards of selection.

The librarian should be free to decide whether all or part of the gift should be integrated into the collection, discarded, exchanged, or sold. The donor should trust the librarian's judgment, for rare items will certainly be respected and treated as such. Gifts can be an important source for rare, unusual, or expensive items which the library budget cannot afford, but it is also true that the offerings of gifts may include much material which would only prove a burden to the library. Libraries have on occasion refused a gift collection because the cost of processing the materials exceeded the worth of the collection. Certainly there is need in every library for a policy regarding the acceptance of gifts. If such a policy does not exist, much duplication and added expense in handling materials may occur.

Patrons of the library, as well as members of Friends of the Library organizations, have proved effective sources for substantial gifts. When a gift is received, it should be acknowledged promptly. Various forms may be used, according to the importance of the material. Any gift warrants a personal letter from the librarian or the president of the library board. It sometimes happens that over a period of time a donor gives a series of books which are marked with special book plates. In that event, some member of the order department may have the responsibility for seeing that the plates are prepared and that they are properly inserted in each of the items of such a collection as it arrives (the collections are often memorial in nature).

The alert librarian should also be on the look-out for free materials from various sources. Publications such as *Public Affairs Information Service Bulletin, Vertical File Index,* and *Publishers Weekly* list free pamphlet material. It is possible to request that the library's name be put on the mailing lists of various government and private offices, organizations, and institutions which send free publications.

Duplicates and Exchanges

Duplicate materials tends to accumulate in every library. These are often sorted into different categories for disposal: (1) discards—

books which are worn out and are only fit to be sold as waste paper;
(2) duplicates which may be sold because their condition is satisfactory;
(3) exchanges, which comprise those which the library can exchange
with some other library to acquire materials not in the collection. Exchanges involve the development of some method of trading duplicate
materials with other libraries. The term "exchanges" also refers to the
process by which libraries connected with institutions which publish
their own materials exchange these publications for the works produced
by other institutions (as, for example, the exchange of one university's
publications for another, which is done on a wide scale, involving
international as well as intra-national exchanges). It is important that a
businesslike procedure for exchanges be set up, allocating the work to
one department, preferably to acquisitions. In actual practice, it has
sometimes been made the responsibility of the reference or circulation
departments.

The United Serials and Book Exchange, a well-known exchange
organization based in Washington, D.C., includes libraries of various
sizes and types and operates on an international basis. Formerly known
as the United States Book Exchange, it was established in 1948 as an
outgrowth of the American Book Center for War-Devastated Libraries,
which in turn had been created by the national library associations to
build up foreign library collections from duplicate books and periodicals
supplied by American libraries. The USBE acts as a pool for participating libraries which want to dispose of duplicate materials of value to
research in return for other materials which they do not hold. It is a
centralized warehouse where a participating library may send its duplicate materials with the least amount of labor and with the certainty that
they will be utilized in the best possible way. Many librarians have
found this service to be an excellent means of exchanging materials on
both a national and an international basis.

Exchanges may be facilitated through dealers and through certain associations of special libraries, such as the Medical Library Association, the American Association of Law Libraries, and the American Theological Library Association. Regional exchange programs,
sometimes directed by the state library agency, often provide for the
distribution of unneeded, but still worthwhile, duplicates.

BIBLIOGRAPHY

General

American Library Association, Bookdealer-Library Relations Committee. *Guidelines for
Handling Library Orders for In-Print Monographic Publications.* Chicago, 1973.
16p.

Ash, Joan and others. "Prediction Equation Providing Some Objective Criteria for the
Acquisition of Technical Reports by the College or University Library." *Library
Resources and Technical Services,* 17:35–41, Winter 1973.

Balke, Mary Noel. "Acquisition of Exhibition Catalogs." *Special Libraries*, 66:579–587, December 1975.

Bullard, Scott R. "The Language of the Marketplace." *American Libraries*, 9:365–366, June 1978. Short glossary.

Carter, John. *ABC for Book Collectors*. 5th ed. rev. London, R. Hart-Davis, 1972. 211p.

Cave, Roderick. *Rare Book Librarianship*. London, Clive Bingley, 1976. 168p. Includes chapter on acquisition.

Duckett, Kenneth W. *Modern Manuscripts; A Practical Manual for Their Management, Care, and Use*. Nashville, Tenn., American Association for State and Local History, 1975. 375p. Contains chapter on acquisitions.

Falk, Leslie K. *Procurement of Library Materials in the Federal Government; An Orientation Aid Prepared for the Federal Library Committee*. Washington, D.C., Federal Library Committee, 1968. 42p.

Ford, Stephen. *Acquisition of Library Materials*. Chicago, American Library Association, 1973. 237p. Covers all aspects of acquisitions.

Grieder, Ted. *Acquisitions: Where, What, and How*. Westport, Conn., Greenwood Press, 1978. 277p. Specific and practical suggestions based on experiences in a large university or research library. Emphasizes monographs and serials.

Haller, Margaret. *The Book Collector's Fact Book*. New York, Arco, 1976. 271p. List of terms relating to book trade.

Houghton, Bernard. *Technical Information Sources*. 2d ed. London, Clive Bingley, 1972. 119p. Covers patents, standards, and report literature.

Huleatt, Richard S. "Rx for Acquisitions Hangups." *Special Libraries*, 64:81–85, February 1973. Acquisitions in a special library.

Magrill, Rose Mary and Constance Rinehart. *Library Technical Services; A Selected Annotated Bibliography*. Westport, Conn., Greenwood Press, 1977. 238p. Contains sections on order procedures.

Melcher, Daniel. *Melcher on Acquisitions*. Chicago, American Library Association, 1971. 169p. Informal comments on jobbers, blanket plans, order procedures and a variety of other topics.

Peters, Jean. *Book Collecting; A Modern Guide*. New York, Bowker, 1977. 288p. Covers various aspects of the antiquarian book trade.

Peters, Jean. *Bookman's Glossary*. 5th ed. New York, Bowker, 1975. 169p. Terminology of book trade.

Raouf, Abdul and others. "A Performance Prediction Model for Bibliographic Search for Monographs Using Multiple Regression Technique." *Journal of Library Automation*, 9:210–221, September 1976. Study at University of Windsor.

Wulfekoetter, Gertrude. *Acquisition Work; Processes Involved in Building Library Collections*. Seattle, University of Washington Press, 1961. 268p. Practical approach to order, gift, and exchange procedures.

Relations with Dealers

Andresen, David C. "Book Discounts and Cost-Plus Pricing." *Library Resources and Technical Services*, 18:248–252, Summer 1974.

Boyer, Calvin J. "State-Wide Contracts for Library Materials: An Analysis of the Attendant Dysfunctional Consequences." *College and Research Libraries*, 35:86–94, March 1974.

Bromberg, Erik. "How the Birds (Pigeons) and Bees and Butterflies Do It; Avuncular Advice to a New Librarian About to Talk to His Purchasing Agent Who Has Already Signed a Book Buying Contract." *Special Libraries*, 61:168–170, April 1970.

Hensel, Evelyn and Peter D. Veillette. *Purchasing Library Materials in Public and School Libraries; A Study of Purchasing Procedures and the Relationships Between Libraries and Purchasing Agencies and Dealers*. Chicago, American Library Association, 1969. 150p.

Kim, Ung Chon. *Policies of Publishers; A Handbook for Order Librarians*. Metuchen, N.J., Scarecrow Press, 1978. 146p. Based on questionnaires returned from approximately 500 publishers.

Kim, Ung Chon. "Purchasing Books from Publishers and Wholesalers." *Library Resources and Technical Services*, 19:133–147, Spring 1975. Study based on 32 in-print titles.

Lincoln, Robert. "Vendors and Delivery: An Analysis of Selected Publishers, Publisher/Agents, Distributors, and Wholesalers." *Canadian Library Journal*, 35:51–57, February 1978. Study done at University of Manitoba.

Martin, Murray S. "The Series Standing Order and the Library." *Choice*, 10:1152–1155, October 1973. Points to consider before placing a standing order.

Roth, Harold L. "The Book Wholesaler: His Forms and Services." *Library Trends*, 24:673–682, April 1976. How jobbers operate.

Rouse, William B. "Optimal Selection of Acquisition Sources." *Journal of the American Society for Information Science*, 25:227–231, July–August 1974. Decision analysis approach.

Stokley, Sandra L. and Marion T. Reid. "A Study of Five Book Dealers Used By Louisiana State University Library." *Library Resources and Technical Services*, 22:117–125, Spring 1978.

Approval Plans and Blanket Orders

International Seminar on Approval and Gathering Plans in Large and Medium Size Academic Libraries, 1st, Western Michigan University, 1968. *Proceedings*. Edited by Peter Spyers-Duran. Kalamazoo, Mich., Western Michigan University Libraries, 1969. 142p. Includes papers on operating programs.

International Seminar on Approval and Gathering Plans in Large and Medium Size Academic Libraries, 2d, Western Michigan University, 1969. *Advances in Understanding Approval and Gathering Plans in Academic Libraries*. Edited by Peter Spyers-Duran and Daniel Gore. Kalamazoo, Mich., Western Michigan University, 1970. 220p. Collection of papers.

International Seminar on Approval and Gathering Plans in Large and Medium Size Academic Libraries, 3d, West Palm Beach, Fla., 1971. *Economics of Approval Plans*. Edited by Peter Spyers-Duran and Daniel Gore. Westport, Conn., Greenwood Press, 1972. 134p. Collection of papers.

McCullough, Kathleen. "Approval Plans: Vendor Responsibility and Library Research; A Literature Survey and Discussion." *College and Research Libraries*, 33:368–381, September 1972.

McCullough, Kathleen and others. *Approval Plans and Academic Libraries; An Interpretative Survey*. Phoenix, Ariz., Oryx Press, 1977. 154p. Report of a 1975 survey of 144 libraries.

Rebuldela, Harriet K. "Some Administrative Aspects of Blanket Ordering: A Response." *Library Resources and Technical Services*, 13:342–345, Summer 1969.

Thom, Ian W. "Some Administrative Aspects of Blanket Ordering." *Library Resources and Technical Services*, 13:338–342, Summer 1969.

For other citations on approval plans and blanket orders, see the bibliography which accompanies Chapter 2.

Foreign Acquisitions

Area Studies and the Library; The Thirtieth Annual Conference of the Graduate Library School, May 20–22, 1965. Edited by Tsuen-Hsuin and Howard Winger. Chicago, University of Chicago Press, 1966. 184p. Collection of papers on various areas.

Cylke, Frank K. *Selected Federal Library Programs for Acquisition of Foreign Materials*. Washington, D.C., Federal Library Committee, 1971. 22p. Summarizes programs of sixteen federal libraries.

Downs, Robert B. "The Significance of Foreign Materials for U.S. Collections: Problems of Acquisition." *Foreign Acquisitions Newsletter*, No. 34:1-7, Fall 1971.

Hotimsky, Constance M. *Acquisition of Russian Books*. London, Clive Bingley, 1974. 37p.

Institute on the Acquisition of Foreign Materials, University of Wisconsin-Milwaukee, 1971. *Acquisition of Foreign Materials for U.S. Libraries*. Compiled and edited by Theodore Samore. Metuchen, N.J., Scarecrow Press, 1973. 350p. Contains many short papers on sources of foreign materials and acquisition programs for specific areas.

Library Association. University, College, and Research Section. Conference, 1972, Morecambe, England. *Acquisition and Provision of Foreign Books by National and University Libraries in the United Kingdom*. Compiled by B. C. Bloomfield. London, Mansell, 1972. 217p. Collection of principal and supplementary papers.

Ligue des bibliothèques européennes de recherches. *Acquisitions from the Third World: Papers of the Ligue des bibliothèques européenes de recherche seminar 17-19 September, 1973*. Edited by D.A. Clarke. London, Mansell, 1975. 276p.

Orne, Jerrold. *The Language of the Foreign Book*. Chicago, American Library Association, 1976. 334p. Translates terms from fifteen European languages.

Publishers Association. *How to Obtain British Books: A Guide for Booksellers, Librarians and Other Professional Bookbuyers*. 8th ed. London, Whitaker, 1972. 130p. Lists of British publishers by type of books published, with representatives and agents abroad, and other details about British book distribution.

Stevens, Robert D. "Acquisitions for Area Programs." *Library Trends*, 18:385-397, January 1970.

Wertheimer, Leonard. *Books in Other Languages: How to Select and Where to Order Them*. Ottawa, Canadian Library Association, 1976. 129p. Handbook which includes bibliography of tools and directory of suppliers.

Out-of-Print Materials

American Book Trade Directory. 23d ed. New York, Bowker, 1978.

"Code of Fair Practices for Dealers and Librarians." In *AB Bookman's Yearbook*, 1972, Pt. 2, pp. 312-313. Newark, N.J., Antiquarian Bookman, 1972.

Cook, Sarah A. "The Selective Purchase of Out of Print Books: A Survey of Practices." *Library Resources and Technical Services*, 10:31-37, Winter 1966. Questionnaire survey of more than 300 libraries.

Hamann, Edmund G. "Out-of-Print Periodicals; The United States Book Exchange as a Source of Supply." *Library Resources and Technical Services*, 16: 19-25, Winter 1972.

Heppell, Shirley G. "A Survey of OP Buying Practices." *Library Resources and Technical Services*, 10:28-30, Winter 1966. Brief report from approximately 100 smaller academic libraries.

Kim, Ung Chon. "Comparison of Two Out-of-Print Book Buying Methods." *College and Research Libraries*, 34:258-264, September 1973.

Lynden, Fred C. and Arthur Meyerfeld. "Library Out-of-Print Book Procurement: The Stanford University Experience." *Library Resources and Technical Services*, 17:216-224, Spring 1973.

Mitchell, Betty J. "Methods Used in Out-of-Print Acquisition: A Survey of Out-of-Print Book Dealers." *Library Resources and Technical Services*, 17:211-215, Spring 1973.

Mitchell, Betty J. and Carol Bedoian. "A Systematic Approach to Performance Evaluation of Out-of-Print Book Dealers: The San Fernando Valley State College Experience." *Library Resources and Technical Services,* 15:215–222, Spring 1971.

Perez, Ernest R. "Acquisition of Out-of-Print Materials." *Library Resources and Technical Services,* 17:42–59, Winter 1973. Discusses various methods and surveys the literature.

Piekarski, Hala. "Acquisition of Out-of-Print Books for a University Library." *Canadian Library Journal,* 26:346–352, September–October 1969. Guidelines for establishing files and procedures.

Reichmann, Felix. "Bibliographical Control of Reprints." *Library Resources and Technical Services,* 11:415–435, Fall 1967. Alternative sources for o.p. books.

Reichmann, Felix. "Purchase of Out-of-Print Materials in American University Libraries." *Library Trends,* 18:328–353, January 1970. Pros and cons of various sources; classified bibliography.

Smith, Eldred. "Out-of-Print Book Searching." *College and Research Libraries,* 29:303–309, July 1968. Based on experiences at University of California at Berkeley.

Microforms

American Library Association. Resources and Technical Services Division. Resources Section. Bookdealer-Library Relations Committee. *Guidelines for Handling Library Orders for Microforms.* Chicago, American Library Association, 1977. 14p. (Acquisition Guidelines No.3)

Folcarelli, Ralph J. and Ralph C. Ferragamo. "Microform Publications: Hardware and Suppliers." *Library Trends,* 24:711–725, April 1976. Includes selected list of micro publishers.

Sullivan, Robert C. "The Acquisition of Library Microforms." *Microform Review,* 6:136–144, May 1977; 6:205–211, July 1977. Covers tools and procedures.

Veaner, Allen B. *The Evaluation of Micropublications: A Handbook for Librarians.* Chicago, American Library Association, 1971. 72p. (LTP Publication no. 17)

For other citations on microforms, see the bibliography which accompanies Chapter 6.

Serials

American Library Association. Resources and Technical Services Division. Resources Section. Bookdealer-Library Relations Committee. *Guidelines for Handling Library Orders for Serials and Periodicals.* Chicago, American Library Association, 1974. 16p. (Acquisition Guidelines No. 2)

Brown, Clara. *Serials Acquisition and Maintenance.* Birmingham, Ala., EBSCO, 1972. 201p. Practical approach; covers all activities of a non-automated serials department.

Brynteson, Susan. "Serial Acquisitions." In *Management Problems in Serials Work,* edited by Peter Spyers-Duran and Daniel Gore, pp. 50–65. Westport, Conn., Greenwood Press, 1974.

Brynteson, Susan. "Serial Acquisition: Old Problem—New Costs." *Library Scene,* 2:4–6; 39, Winter 1973. Emphasizes problems of communication between librarians and agents.

Buckeye, Nancy M. *International Subscription Agents.* 4th ed. Chicago, American Library Association, 1978. Information on agents handling subscriptions and standing orders.

Clasquin, Frank F. "The Claim Enigma for Serials and Journals." In *Management Problems in Serials Work,* edited by Peter Spyers-Duran and Daniel Gore, pp.

66–68. Westport, Conn., Greenwood Press, 1974. Same article appeared in *Library Scene,* 3:28–34, December 1974.

Clasquin, Frank F. "The Jobber's Side: Cost of Acquiring Periodicals." *RQ,* 10:328–330, Summer 1971. Explanation of service charges.

Clasquin, Frank F. "The Subscription Agency and Lower Serials Budgets." *Serial Librarian,* 1:39–43, Fall 1976. Argues that an agent can save the library money.

Doares, Juanita S. and others. *Report on a Survey of Subscription Agents Used by Libraries in New York State Conducted by the Technical Committee in 1970.* Albany, New York Library Association, Resources and Technical Services Section, 1971. 12p. (ED 061 950)

Huff, William H. "Serial Subscription Agencies." *Library Trends,* 24:683–709, April 1976. How agencies function.

Katz, William A. and Peter Gellatly. *Guide to Magazine and Serial Agents.* New York, Bowker, 1975. 239p. Directory of agents and discussion of serials acquisition fundamentals.

Kuntz, Harry. "Serials Agents: Selection and Evaluation." *Serial Librarian,* 2:139–150, Winter 1977.

Montag, Tom. "Stalking the Little Magazine." *Serial Librarian,* 1:281–303, Spring 1977. Acquisition problems and a list of aids.

Nientemp, Judith A. and Stanley R. Greenfield. "The Librarian . . . and the Subscription Agent." *Special Libraries,* 63:292–304, July 1972. Exchange of views on problems and ways to work together.

Osborn, Andrew D. *Serial Publications; Their Place and Treatment in Libraries.* 2d ed. rev. Chicago, American Library Association, 1973. 434p. Covers all aspects of serials in libraries.

Sineath, Timothy W. "Libraries and Library Subscription Agents." *Library Scene,* 1:28–30, Summer 1972. Concise review of pros and cons of using an agent.

Smith, Katherine R. "Serials Agents/Serials Librarians." *Library Resources and Technical Services,* 14:5–18, Winter 1970. Ways to choose and evaluate agents.

Government Publications

Gerard, James W. "Acquisition of United Nations Agencies Publications." *Illinois Libraries,* 55:147–150, March 1973. Describes activities of UNIPUB, Inc.

Hungerford, Anthos Farah. "U.S. Government Publications Acquisition Procedures for the Small Special Library." *Special Libraries,* 65:22–25, January 1974. Practical suggestions.

"Identifying and Acquiring Federal Government Documents." *Law Library Journal,* 65:415–442, November 1972. Panel presentations with discussion.

Kohler, Carolyn W. "Acquisition and Organization of International Documents in the University of Iowa Libraries." *Government Publications Review,* 2:245–251, 1975.

Locker, Bernard. "Expediting Acquisition of Government Documents." *Special Libraries,* 62:9;12–16, January 1971.

Morehead, Joe. *Introduction to United States Public Documents.* 2d ed. Littleton, Colo., Libraries Unlimited, 1978. 380p. Distribution system is among topics covered.

Mundkur, Mohini. "Some Selection and Acquisition Aids for Current State Documents." *Documents to the People,* 6:107–109, March 1978. Annotated.

Paulson, Peter J. "Government Documents and Other Non-Trade Publications." *Library Trends,* 18:363–372, January 1970. Acquisition problems.

Shaw, George A. "How to Locate Out-of-Prints, Hard-to-Get Documents." *Southeastern Librarian,* 24:28–29, Winter 1975.

Welsh, Harry E. "An Acquisitions Up-Date for Government Publications." *Microform Review,* 6:285–298, September 1977. Guide to sources for libraries which acquire government publications selectively.

Gifts and Exchanges

Ash, Joan. "The Exchange of Academic Dissertations." *College and Research Libraries*, 30:237–241, May 1969.

Association of Research Libraries. Office of University Library Management Studies. *SPEC Kit on Gifts and Exchange Function in ARL Libraries*. Washington, D.C., 1976. 129p. Examples of policies, procedures, etc.

Ball, Alice D. *The Role of the United States Book Exchange in the Nationwide Library and Information Services Network*. Washington, D.C., National Commission on Libraries and Information Science, 1975. 32p. (ED 114 104) Reviews history and operation of USBE (now United Serials and Book Exchange).

"Brief History of USBE." *Library Resources and Technical Services*, 14:607–609, Fall 1970.

Briggs, Donald R. "Gift Appraisal Policy in Large Research Libraries." *College and Research Libraries*, 29:505–507, November 1968. Results of a survey.

Collins, J.A. "The International Exchange Service." *Library Resources and Technical Services*, 10:337–341, Summer 1966.

Dobroski, Charles H. and Donald D. Hendricks. "Mobilization of Duplicates in a Regional Medical Library Program." *Medical Library Association Bulletin*, 63:309–318, July 1975.

Eggleton, Richard. "The ALA Duplicates Exchange Union—A Study and Evaluation." *Library Resources and Technical Services*, 19:148–163, Spring 1975.

Galejs, John E. "Economics of Serials Exchange." *Library Resources and Technical Services*, 16:511–520, Fall 1972.

International Exchange of Publications; Proceedings of the European Conference Held in Vienna from 24–29 April 1972. Edited by Maria J. Schiltman. Munich, Verlag Dokumentation, 1973. 135p.

Kanevskij, B.P. "The International Exchange of Publications and the Free Flow of Books." *Unesco Bulletin for Libraries*, 26:141–149, May 1972. Reviews past efforts and difficulties.

Kemp, Edward C. *Manuscript Solicitation for Libraries, Special Collections, Museums, and Archives*. Littleton, Colo., Libraries Unlimited, 1978. 208p. Techniques for soliciting gift materials.

Lane, Alfred H. "Gifts and Exchanges: Practicalities and Problems." *Library Resources and Technical Services*, 14:92–97, Winter 1970.

McCree, Mary Lynn. "Good Sense and Good Judgment: Defining Collections and Collecting." *Drexel Library Quarterly*, 11:21–33, January 1975. Examples of ways to handle gift offers.

Moran, Michael. "Foreign Currency Exchange Problems Relating to the Book Trade." *Library Resources and Technical Services*, 17:299–307, Summer 1973.

Pease, Mina. "A Reason for Being: A National Government Document Agency and the Exchange of Official Publications." *Government Publications Review*, 2:259–271, 1975. Reviews history of international document exchange.

Shinn, Isabella E. "Toward Uniformity in Exchange Communication." *Library Resources and Technical Services*, 16:502–510, Fall 1972.

"Statement on Appraisal of Gifts." *College and Research Libraries News*, 34:49, March 1973. Approved by ACRL Board of Directors.

"Statement on Legal Title." *College and Research Libraries News*, 34:49–50, March 1973. Approved by ACRL Board of Directors.

United Nations Educational Scientific and Cultural Organization. *Handbook on the International Exchange of Publications*. 3d ed. New York, 1964. 767p. Explains different types of exchange agreements.

PART III

MAINTENANCE

CHAPTER 12

Collection Evaluation

The librarian's responsibility for the collection does not end with the determination of users' needs, the setting of collection objectives, or even the selection of which books, journals, records, etc. to acquire. Collections must be continuously maintained by evaluating what has been obtained, weeding unneeded items, sending little-used materials to storage, and preserving the most valuable or most-used items in the collection.

Every librarian would like to be able to answer the question, "How good is my collection?" Materials are selected by different people over a long period of time. Librarians may vary in their conceptions of the purposes of the library and their interpretation and application of the general principles of selection. To decide how good any library collection is we must have information about three important factors: (1) what kinds of materials are in the collection and how valuable each item is in relation to other items which are not in the library; (2) the kind of community served, in order to decide whether the materials in the collection are actually appropriate to that clientele, regardless of how valuable they may be in terms of an abstract evaluation of their worth; (3) the purposes which that collection is supposed to accomplish, given that particular community of readers.

Collection evaluation must be a part of any large-scale library planning effort and is essential in any systematic approach to establishing collection development policy, rationalizing budget allocation, or undertaking weeding and storage projects. The collection may be evaluated in a one-shot, full-scale systematic project; it may be judged through a series of smaller projects; or the appraisal may involve a combination of projects. In some libraries collection evaluation is done daily, routinely, and almost subconsciously by individual librarians.

Various techniques can be used to get some idea of the worth of a collection. Some involve qualitative judgments. For example, users may be observed and questioned about how well the collection is meeting their particular needs. If there is a fairly regular stream of requests for titles which the library does not have, the librarian might conclude that there is a lack of correlation between the materials being purchased and the interests of the community. Of course, if readers are requesting cheap paperback editions or esoteric research materials, and the librarian does not think the library ought to be a source of such materials, he/she might conclude that no change in selection practice is warranted. But if the librarian discovers that substantial and worthwhile materials are being requested, materials which fit the library's collection objectives but have not been purchased by the library, he/she might well want to look into selection practices. Conversely, if the librarian observes on the shelves large numbers of titles which are never used, he/she might want to look into the selection practices. In such cases, it would appear—at first glance, anyway—that the collection is not adequate for serving the community.

The librarian may be moved by such observations to take more formal steps toward evaluating the collection, by conducting a questionnaire or interview survey among the users to determine exactly what kinds of information, or recreation, they hope to find in the library and how successful they have been in finding what they wanted. Users may be asked to report particularly on their failures, so that the reasons for these failures may be determined. Some of the comments made in the earlier chapter about the advantages and disadvantages of surveying the library's community apply here also.

Although some would agree that the opinions of most value in making a subjective, qualitative judgment of a collection are those of the students, faculty, researchers, general public, or staff members who use it regularly, some librarians prefer to call in subject specialists to conduct such an evaluation. Subject specialists, presumably, are familiar with the literature of their fields and can tell at a glance whether the important authors and landmark works are present in the collection. What such specialists may not always have as clearly in mind are the specific, special needs of the users of the particular collection.

Another qualitative approach to collection evaluation is to compare the collection against statements in published standards. Some library standards, such as those promulgated by national library associations, are concerned with setting minimum criteria for collections, services, staff, etc. in specific types of libraries. (See references at the end of this chapter for examples.) Although these statements of standards usually include quantitative guidelines, emphasis in recent years has been on the quality of the collection, especially as it might be judged in terms of the goals and objectives of the library in question. In addition to the type-of-library standards, there are sections on libraries and library collections in the statements of standards developed by regional and professional accrediting agencies. These standards also tend to emphasize quality of the collection, without offering many quantitative guidelines.

Use of Standard Lists in Evaluation

Perhaps the most widely used system of evaluating a collection is that which compares a library's holdings with one or more lists of selected titles. Such standard lists as the *Public Library Catalog* or *Books for College Libraries,* comprehensive subject bibliographies, selected lists of best books, and the catalogs of important libraries have been commonly used as guides to check the effectiveness of past selection policies. The assumption is made that such lists, which represent the composite judgment of many librarians, will pick up the most important titles in the several subject fields. Checking the library's holdings against a standard list produces a figure representing the percentage of the titles on that list which the library holds. (This figure, of course, does not indicate what percentage of the titles *ought* to be on the shelves.) Librarians may discover—to their comfort—that they have a large part of the titles on the list. Sometimes, however, this result could be predicted in advance. If the librarian uses *Books for College Libraries* as a buying guide, and then later evaluates the collection against it, a high correlation would seem inevitable.

The checklist method has been criticized because any checklist, it is asserted, represents an arbitrary selection of titles. All the titles on the list will not be of equal value, and some titles may be omitted which are better than the titles on the list. The smaller the list, the more arbitrary the selection is liable to be. One individual's list of the five best books in chemistry in the past fifty years might well fail to satisfy other selectors. A list of five hundred titles in chemistry, selected by three dozen experts in the field, with general agreement on the most valuable, would reduce the arbitrary character of selection considerably.

The checklist will, of course, say nothing about those titles which it does not list. The materials which a library has, but which are not on the standard list being used for checking, may be just as good as those which are on the list. But if the librarian finds groups of unlisted items, he/she may well want to make a further check on those titles to assure that they really are equivalent. The checklist will also fail to do a complete job in that it does not single out automatically those stocks of old and superseded items which the library may have gathered. The checklist method is useful only for estimating the strengths of a collection, to the degree that the collection approximates the selected lists.

Another criticism of the checklist is that although its titles may be authoritative, readable, and worthwhile, the list bears no necessary relationship to the particular community served by a given library. This is certainly a justifiable criticism, and it should emphasize the fact that this method must be used intelligently and not blindly. The degree of divergence will depend on the kind of list used. Checking the holdings of a branch library serving a factory labor community against the catalog of the Lamont Library, which is intended for the use of Harvard undergraduates, would make the disparity between the list and the community great indeed. But a general list, like the *Public Library Catalog,* would almost certainly reflect many of the reading interests of the ordinary community. No doubt it would not fit every community exactly, but this method makes no claim to absolute precision.

A variation of the practice of checking a library's holdings against a published subject bibliography or standard list is to construct such a checklist from the citations (footnotes, references, etc.) which appear in significant works in the field or fields of a library's interest. "Significant works" might include whatever is significant for the library in question—theses, state-of-the-art reviews, and faculty research publications for a large university library; textbooks and most-used journals for an undergraduate collection. In the case of citations in a thesis, research report, or literature review, the evaluation is based on whether or not the work could have been written in the library being surveyed. For an undergraduate collection, this type of evaluation assumes that a student should be able to locate the references which are cited in the books and journals used for class reading.

Comparing a library's holdings against a list is costly and time-consuming. It is probably most practical to think in terms of surveying only a part of the library collection, with the checking being limited to those areas about which doubt has arisen. Even here, the librarian must remember that the checking is only the beginning. It will furnish a rough guide, indicating that a certain percentage of a given group of titles (which have been judged to be reliable, important, or of interest to the general reader) is not available to the library's users. The librarian might then look more closely at the titles which the library has, to see if those not on the list are adequate substitutes. This could involve examining reviews. The librarian might also import—from the community or from some other library—experts in that subject field to evaluate those titles which are held and to make recommendations for purchase.

The list of titles in the guide which are not held by the library will furnish a group for consideration. Some may be ordered immediately; some may be put on a want-list for later purchase. The librarian will have to decide whether it is more important to fill in the gaps or to buy newer books which may be in greater demand. The gaps in the collection may also lead to closer consideration of selection practices and may raise fundamental questions concerning the purposes of the library. If the library has failed to buy a substantial number of titles which are judged by the compilers of the standard list to be important, the librarian might well wish to ask if the library has been placing too much stress on mere popularity of titles.

Quantitative Approaches to Evaluation

Quantitative methods may also be used in collection evaluation. The absolute size of a collection, the holdings of the library in certain subjects, the holdings of certain types of materials, the growth rate of the collection, the size of the collection in relation to the total number of users or potential users, the circulation rate of the collection (in whole or in part) and the money spent on the collection are examples of collection characteristics which may be expressed in quantitative terms for comparison with the performance of the library in previous years or with the holdings of other libraries of a similar size or type.

These quantitative measures have the advantage of being easy to collect and generally easy to explain to governing boards and users; but there are problems, too, in the lack of uniformity in the way such statistics are collected and reported and in the way they are interpreted. It is easy to compare the size of two collections; it is much more difficult to decide which of two collections is the better. It is usually assumed that a collection of four million items is better than one of four thousand. The chances seem better that a very large collection will have more material in any given subject field. Even in such a case, there is no assurance that a collection of five hundred carefully selected titles in a field like anthropology is poorer than a collection of five thousand randomly gathered titles. But if there are two collections of a million items each, how is one to tell which is the better collection?

In spite of the obvious difficulties in using quantitative approaches to collection evaluation, the last decade has seen an increased interest in such measures. One of the most prominent trends has been the development of formulas for determining collection adequacy. An example is the Clapp-Jordan formula, which was developed because the accepted standards for college libraries did not give enough guidance in estimating the minimum number of volumes that would be acceptable for libraries serving undergraduates. The Clapp-Jordan formula states the number of volumes required for a basic collection and also specifies the number of additional volumes which will be needed for each faculty member, student, and academic program. Others have worked with variables similar to those used by Clapp and Jordan—size and research activity of the faculty, curriculum profile of the institution, range and depth of programs, etc.—and have devised formulas for larger academic libraries. Some states have developed similar collection-size formulas for use in planning higher education budgets, and the latest (1975) revision of the ALA/ACRL standards for college libraries includes such a formula.

Public libraries also have been influenced by the trend toward describing collections in quantitative terms. One suggested technique involves drawing a sample of books published within a specified number of years and checking to see if the library owns each book and if the book is actually on the shelf. If a library owns a small percentage of the books checked, the assumption may be that either the budget or the current selection methods are inadequate. If, on the other hand, the library owns a fairly large percentage of the titles checked, but few of them are available on the shelf at the time of the test, the conclusion might be that more duplication of titles is needed. Similar tests may be conducted on the library's collections of periodicals and other materials.

Evaluating Total Resources

Another recent trend in collection evaluation is the tendency to look at total resource adequacy—the holdings of the collection being surveyed plus external resources which are also available to users of that library. One of the approaches here is to express in quantitative terms the library's ability to satisfy requests for a list of specific items. The Capability Index developed by Orr and his associates offers a way of rating a library's ability to deliver materials to its users by emphasizing the speed with which the library can supply an item, rather than by making counts or analyses of its holdings. If the list of items chosen for such a test is appropriate for the situation, the resulting Capability Index should give an indication of the library's capacity to respond to users' requests, not only through its own collection but also by effective use of cooperative arrangements and interlibrary loan. This method of collection evaluation emphasizes the interdependence of libraries, and the importance of such interdependence has been recognized in several recent statements of library standards.

When deciding how to approach collection evaluation, the librarian must consider the advantages and disadvantages of the various procedures. Any of the more objective approaches are likely to be expensive, because of the amount of staff time they require. On the other hand, subjective impressions of the collection may be easy to obtain but relatively worthless for some situations. The librarian must learn to balance the cost of the staff time needed to compile the data for an evaluation project against the potential value of the information collected.

The results of a survey of the collection furnish the librarian with facts upon which he/she can base decisions; they do not furnish an automatic mechanism for righting the wrongs of the collection. Survey results must be weighed in light of the purposes of the library, the clientele served, the funds available, and the nature of the gaps revealed. In the evaluation of collections, as in the original selection of materials, there is no substitute for intelligent and informed judgment.

BIBLIOGRAPHY

American Association of School Libraries. *Media Programs: District and School.* Chicago, American Library Association, Association for Educational Communication and Technology, 1975. 128p. Standards for school libraries; includes section on collections.

American Library Association. Resources and Technical Services Division. Resources Section. Collection Development Committee. "Guidelines for the Evaluation of Library Collections." 1977. 16p.

Association of College and Research Libraries. "Guidelines for Two-Year College Learning Resources Programs." *College and Research Libraries News,* 33:305–315, December 1972. Within the section on "Instructional System Components," there is a statement on materials.

Association of College and Research Libraries. "Standards for College Libraries." *College and Research Libraries News,* 36:277–279; 290–301, October 1975. Includes section on collections.

Association of Research Libraries. Office of University Library Management Studies. *SPEC Kit on Collection Assessment in ARL Libraries.* Washington, D.C., Association of Research Libraries, 1978. 103p. Examples of research libraries' approaches to collection evaluation.

Bonn, George S. "Evaluation of the Collection." *Library Trends,* 22:265–304, January 1974. Thorough review of methods.

Burnett, A. D. "Readers' Failure: A Pilot Survey." *Research in Librarianship,* 1:142–157, June 1967. Evaluation project at the University of Durham Library.

Cassata, Mary B. and Gene L. Dewey. "The Evaluation of a University Library Collection: Some Guidelines." *Library Resources and Technical Services,* 13:450–457, Fall 1969. Describes a project conducted at SUNY-Buffalo.

Clapp, Verner W. and Robert T. Jordan. "Quantitative Criteria for Adequacy of Academic Library Collections." *College and Research Libraries,* 26:371–380, September 1965. Proposes formulas for estimating minimum collections for college and junior college libraries.

Coale, Robert P. "Evaluation of a Research Library Collection: Latin-American Colonial History at the Newberry." *Library Quarterly,* 35:173–184, July 1965.

Dane, Chase. "Evaluating the Reference Collection." *Tennessee Librarian,* 17:3–11, Fall 1964.

DeProspo, Ernest R. and others. *Performance Measures for Public Libraries.* Chicago, American Library Association, Public Library Association, 1973. 71p. Includes quantitative approaches to materials availability.

Downs, Robert B. and John W. Heusman. "Standards for University Libraries." *College and Research Libraries,* 31:28–35, January 1970. Not a statement of standards, but an explanation of how statistics from groups of large libraries may be used.

Golden, Barbara. "A Method for Quantitatively Evaluating a University Library Collection." *Library Resources and Technical Services,* 18:268–274, Summer 1974. Describes project conducted at the University of Nebraska at Omaha.

Goldhor, Herbert. "Analysis of an Inductive Method of Evaluating the Book Collection of a Public Library." *Libri,* 23:6–17, 1973. Suggests a variation of list-checking method.

Hirsch, Felix E. "Standards for Libraries." *Library Trends,* 21:159–355, October 1972. Contains fourteen articles on standards for various types of libraries.

Lancaster, F.W. *The Measurement and Evaluation of Library Services.* Information Resources Press, 1977. 395p. See Chapter 5, "Evaluation of the Collection" (pp. 165–206), for a thorough review of methods and also Chapter 10, "The Relevance of Standards to the Evaluation of Library Service" (pp. 288–298).

Liesener, James W. *A Systematic Process for Planning Media Programs.* Chicago, American Library Association, 1976. 166p. Includes some aspects of collection evaluation in a school library media center.

Line, Maurice B. "The Ability of a University Library to Provide Books Wanted by Researchers." *Journal of Librarianship,* 5:37–51, January 1973. Example of a "reader failure" study.

McInnis, R. Marvin. "The Formula Approach to Library Size: An Empirical Study of Its Efficacy in Evaluating Research Libraries." *College and Research Libraries,* 33:190–198, May 1972.

McInnis, R. Marvin. "Research Collections: An Approach to the Assessment of Quality." *IPLO Quarterly,* 13:13–22, July 1971. Explains citation-checking method.

Mostyn, Gregory R. "The Use of Supply-Demand Equality in Evaluating Collection Adequacy." *California Librarian,* 35:16–23, April 1974. Suggests method for public libraries.

National Study of Secondary School Evaluation. *Evaluative Criteria for the Evaluation of Secondary Schools.* 4th ed. Washington, D.C., 1969. 356p. Section 6 contains questions and checklists for evaluation of collections.

Newhouse, Joseph P. and Arthur J. Alexander. *An Economic Analysis of Public Library Services.* Lexington, Mass., Lexington Books, 1972. 135p. Example of supply-demand evaluation of a public library collection.

Noble, Pamela and Patricia L. Ward. *Performance Measures and Criteria for Libraries; A Survey and Bibliography.* London, Public Libraries Research Group, 1976. 50p. (PLRG Occasional Paper No. 3) Annotated; includes section on "measuring library effectiveness."

Orr, Richard H. and others. "Developments of Methodologic Tools for Planning and Managing Library Services." *Medical Library Association Bulletin,* Pt. I & II, 56:235–267, July 1968; Pt. III, 56:380–403, October 1968; Pt. IV, 58:350–377, July 1970. Explains Document Delivery Tests which produce the Capability Index for a collection.

Orr, Richard H. and Arthur P. Schless. "Documents Delivery Capabilities of Major Biomedical Libraries in 1968: Results of a National Survey Employing Standardized Tests." *Medical Library Association Bulletin,* 60:382–422, July 1972. Application of the Document Delivery Test.

Ottersen, Signe. "A Bibliography on Standards for Evaluating Libraries." *College and Research Libraries,* 32:127–144, March 1971.

Penner, Rudolf J. "Measuring a Library's Capability. . . " *Journal of Education for Librarianship,* 13:17–30, Summer 1972. Application of the Documents Delivery Test in a library science collection.

Piternick, Anne B. "Measurement of Journal Availability in a Biomedical Library." *Medical Library Association Bulletin,* 60:534–542, October 1972. Example of a reader failure survey.

Pizer, Irwin H. and Alexander M. Cain. "Objective Tests of Library Performance." *Special Libraries,* 59:704–711, November 1968. Brief report on Capability Index for delivery of documents.

Raffel, Jeffry A. and Robert Shishko. *Systematic Analysis of University Libraries: An Application of Cost-Benefit Analysis to the MIT Libraries.* Cambridge, Mass., MIT Press, 1969. 107p.

Reichard, Edwin W. and Thomas J. Orsagh. "Holdings and Expenditures of U.S. Academic Libraries: An Evaluative Technique." *College and Research Libraries,* 27:478–487, November 1966. Develops a formula for collection adequacy.

Schofield, J.L. and others. "Evaluation of an Academic Library's Stack Effectiveness." *Journal of Librarianship,* 7:207–227, July 1975. Describes method to determine how and why readers fail to find what they want.

Stayer, Marcia S. "A Creative Approach to Collection Evaluation." *IPLO Quarterly,* 13:23–28, July 1971. Promotes citation-checking method.

Stecher, G. "Library Evaluation; A Brief Survey of Studies in Quantification." *Australian Academic Research Libraries,* 6:1–19, March 1975. Includes discussion of some collection evaluation techniques.

Tjarks, Larry. "Evaluating Literature Collections." *RQ,* 12:183–185, Winter 1972. Lists examples of bibliographies useful for checking.

Urquhart, John A. and J.L. Schofield. "Measuring Readers' Failure at the Shelf." *Journal of Documentation,* 27:273–286, December 1971. Explains survey technique and its compilation. See also next citation.

Urquhart, John A. and J.L. Schofield. "Measuring Readers' Failure at the Shelf in Three University Libraries." *Journal of Documentation,* 28:233–241, September 1972. Continues report in previous citation.

Voigt, Melvin J. "Acquisition Rates in University Libraries." *College and Research Libraries,* 36:263–271, July 1975. Includes a model for determining an adequate minimum acquisition rate.

Washington State Office of Interinstitutional Studies. *A Model Budget for Program 05 Libraries.* Olympia, Evergreen State College, 1970. 28p. (ED 051 866) Example of a state formula for determining collection size.

Webb, William. "Project CoED: A University Library Collection Evaluation and Development Program." *Library Resources and Technical Services,* 13:457–462, Fall 1969. Describes project conducted at the University of Colorado.

White, G. Travis. "Quantitative Measure of Library Effectiveness." *Journal of Academic Librarianship,* 3:128–136, July 1977. Several of the measures reviewed concern collection evaluation.

Williams, Edwin E. "Surveying Library Collections." In *Library Surveys,* edited by Maurice F. Tauber and Irlene R. Stephens, pp. 23–45. New York, Columbia University Press, 1967. Reviews types, purposes, and methods.

CHAPTER 13

Weeding and Storage

In libraries which do not pretend to become permanent depositories of all that has been published, weeding the collection becomes as important a part of the maintenance of the library as the initial selection. The importance of weeding has been underscored with great frequency in library literature, and impressive lip service has been paid to the process. Weeding is the removal of an item from the library's active collection for the purpose of either discarding it or sending it to storage. The reasons for weeding generally fall into two or three groups. Improved use of the library's resources (shelving space, staff required to maintain shelving, etc.) represents one justification for weeding. Little-used materials can be sent to a less expensive building for storage or can be put into compact storage in the main building. This may alleviate space problems and makes the servicing of the collection easier. Weeding is sometimes justified on the ground that service to users will be improved. Browsers can more easily find up-to-date and attractive materials, and the general appearance of the library will be improved. Occasionally, public or school librarians may feel the need to weed the collection so that it will not look overstocked to outsiders when budget request time comes.

As has been pointed out repeatedly, weeding is not practiced as often as it is preached. There seem to be a number of reasons for this state of affairs. First, librarians are likely to point out the cost involved in weeding. Deciding which books must go and arranging for their disposal takes time from some regular job; withdrawing the records costs money which could be used for other purposes. Some librarians have concluded that since weeding is so costly, it is best passed by in silence. There have been other reasons for avoiding the task of weeding. Librarians often take an exalted view of the book and hesitate to think of any book as "dead." Discarding a book is somehow immoral, approaching book-burning, vandalism, and wanton destruction. Furthermore, there is always the chance that the librarian may make a mistake and weed out a book which will be wanted the next day by some reader. How can one tell whether a book, which may not have been heavily used in the past, may not suddenly become very important? Certainly there is no sure way of learning about future demands.

Perhaps the most immediate, practical reason for failing to weed is simply lack of time. Beset by a dozen projects which are under way, plagued by lack of sufficient staff, busy and rushed and harried by the day-to-day demands of keeping the institution running, many librarians put off the task until some happier day, when they will have enough time. Eventually, of course, when they find there is just not enough space left in the library to cram in more books, they may be forced to do a rush job of weeding, and then they may fling themselves into the task, discarding furiously, perhaps without sufficient reflection. When they later discover their mistakes, weeding becomes even less attractive.

Organization of Weeding

How weeding is planned and conducted depends on the library in question—on the characteristics of its users, its objectives, its physical facilities and staff, and the age and type of collection it holds. Any cooperative agreements entered into by the library probably will affect weeding. The ideal library will have as comprehensive a plan for weeding the collection as for selecting new materials, and both aspects of collection development will be coordinated. Any thorough written policy for collection development will probably include a section on weeding (see Chapter 2).

Weeding should be a regular and continuing process. There are many arrangements which could accomplish this end. It might be desirable to allot one week of the year as the time for considering some part of the collection, with the librarian or librarians responsible for that part of the collection studying that group of books for those titles which have outlived their usefulness. It might be possible for the selectors to consider each new title in relation to the possibility of discarding one already on the shelves. If the new title really supersedes an older one, the older material might be withdrawn upon receipt of the newer. In some libraries, inventory time is used to identify titles for consideration for discard.

Library materials may be weeded because of their content (dated or no longer of interest), their physical condition (scratched, torn, generally ragged), their use patterns (declining or nonexistent), or a combination of these features. Research libraries will probably weed in order to discard only on the basis of physical condition, but will weed materials in order to send them to storage primarily because of low use. Popular or working collections may apply each of the three criteria.

Weeding Working Collections

In a general, non-research collection—school, public, small academic—there are certain categories of books which are the most obvious candidates for weeding. First, there are the duplicates of titles, purchased when the book was in heavier demand and now no longer needed. Ten or fifty or one hundred copies might be reduced to two or three. Superseded editions of books might well be eliminated, if the library is not attempting a historical collection of all the editions of a given title. Books that show signs of wear, books which have become dirty, shabby, or just plain worn out, might be replaced if their content is still significant. This might be the time to get rid of the mistakes in selection—books which were judged to be of interest and use but which turned out to be shelf-sitters. Books which have become obsolete in content, style, or theme should be eliminated by the library which aims at building a vital, useful collection. It is not always difficult to discover books which are now out-of-date. A medium-sized public library, discovering that the only work it has on the economic and political conditions of the Middle East is one published in 1950, might justifiably conclude that this book would not give its readers up-to-date information.

Let this distinction, however, be recalled again: there is a difference between a research collection and a working collection even in a public library. In the large public libraries, there may be extensive research collections; in the smaller, there may be special collections which are gathered for their historical importance, as, for example, collections on local history. One ought not to bring the principle of up-to-dateness to bear when looking hard and long at the local history collection. It is unhappily true that some basic collections have been hit hard by a librarian too intent on getting rid of everything which had not circulated in the past three years, or which had been published more than ten years ago. To seize one of these injunctions and apply it blindly is as futile as seizing and blindly applying a principle of book selection. Weeding of individual titles is not done in grand isolation, setting each book face to face with some weeding principle. There are a number of factors which must figure in the decision: relation of the book to other books on the same subject; money available for more satisfactory titles (if this is all one can afford, it may be better to act on the principle that something is better than nothing at all); consideration of the degree to which the library wants to represent older material; possible usefulness of the particular title to some special group or individual in the community—the list could be extended at length.

Weeding requires judgment, as did the original selection of a title; weeding in a particular library requires judgment based on factors which can be known only to the librarian of that particular library. The general injunctions for weeding, like the general injunctions for selecting, must be interpreted and adapted by type of library and type of material, and they will certainly be adapted by the type of librarian doing the job. In a small, working collection, the following suggestions for weeding might be useful. No one should seize upon these suggestions as an infallible formula: it is imperative that the librarian recognize them as suggestions and not laws.

General Reference Works: Bibliographies and encyclopedias are of little use after ten years, though exceptions may be made in specific instances; almanacs and yearbooks may be discarded when they are superseded.

Religion and Philosophy: Retain systems of philosophy, but discard historical and explanatory texts when superseded, older theology, old commentaries on the Bible, sectarian literature, sermons, and books on the conduct of life, popular self-help psychology, and other guides to living which are old or no longer popular. Be sure to take into account the use made of such materials, which will vary greatly from one library to another.

Social Sciences: Requires frequent revision, because much of the material will deal with problems of temporary interest, which can be replaced later by historical coverage of these topics. Economics, investments, taxation, etc. need careful watching. Historical works on economics, political science, education, transportation, etc. should be kept if there is demand. Generally, keep basic materials on customs and folklore; be guided by use.

Language: Discard old grammars, ordinary school dictionaries (rarely discard the larger dictionaries). Weed the rest of the collection on the basis of use.

Pure Science: Discard books with obsolete information or theories; all general works which have been superseded, unless they are classics in their field. All ordinary textbooks can usually be discarded after ten years, and some libraries discard after five. Botany and natural history should be inspected carefully before discarding. Astronomy dates rapidly.

Applied Science: Try to keep this section up-to-date by discarding older material. Five to ten years will date much of the material in such fields as medicine, inventions, radio, television, and business. For home economics, cookbooks, gardening, and some materials on crafts, etc., watch the use patterns.

Arts, Music, Hobbies, Etc.: Discard sparingly in the fine arts. Keep collections of music, engravings, fine illustrated books.

Literature: Keep literary history, unless it is superseded by a better title; keep collected works unless definitely superseded; discard poets and dramatists no longer regarded in literary histories and no longer read; discard the works of minor novelists whose works have not been re-issued and who are no longer of interests to readers.

History: Discard much contemporary writing which is now recorded in basic histories (as World War II materials), historical works which are only summaries and are not authoritative, and works of travel over ten years old, unless distinguished by the style or the importance of the author. Keep histories which have become literary classics. Keep anything related to local or regional history.

Biography: Keep collected biography, but individual lives of persons whose importance is no longer great may be discarded when demand declines. Keep anything that may be useful for local history.

Generally, the following classes should be inspected carefully as potential areas for drastic weeding: privately printed verse, memoirs, and essays; subjects not currently popular; unused or unneeded volumes of sets; publications of municipalities; multiple editions of books; incomplete runs of periodicals, or periodicals which are not indexed.

Weeding Research Collections

In a large library, such as the research collection of a university, weeding programs have often been resisted. Research collections have generally been built on the assumption that "bigger is better," although a practical look at the economic conditions of higher education has caused many librarians to question the validity of this assumption. Although some university librarians still believe that everything in a research collection will eventually be of use to some researcher, simple circulation counts have repeatedly shown that a small proportion of any collection, especially of a large research collection, accounts for a large percentage of the total circulation. This finding has been used to support the position that weeding, at least for the purpose of storage, is necessary even in research collections. Weeding decisions in these libraries are usually made on the basis of present demand and predicted future use.

The size of a research collection makes it impractical to consider individual items for weeding; consequently, much effort has been spent on trying to devise weeding and storage decision rules for groups of materials. Among the predictors of future use which have been tested in research libraries are the language in which the book or journal was published; the amount of time which has elapsed since it was published; the number of times it has been used (probably measured by the number of times it has circulated outside the library) since the library acquired it; and the amount of time it spends on the shelf between uses. No single criterion has been successful in predicting use for all kinds of materials and all subjects, but many librarians favor some measure of past use as the best way to predict future use for books and date of publication as an easy and relatively effective way to weed periodicals. The basic problem is to predict the point at which the cost (in shelf space, staff costs, and user frustration) of putting into and retrieving from storage a group of titles will fall below the cost of leaving them in the active collection.

Storage

Once little-used materials have been identified and withdrawn from the active collection, decisions must be made about how to store them. Some librarians put such materials into compact storage areas in the main library building; some send them to storage areas, possibly compact, in facilities separate from any of the library buildings used regularly by the public. The kind of storage used probably will depend on the money the library has available to invest in storage facilities, the probable costs of moving materials back and forth, the kinds of changes which may have to be made on library records to show the location of the material and estimates of how much users will be inconvenienced by the various kinds of storage.

In addition to storage planned by an individual library or library system, there is also the possibility of joining with other libraries in cooperative storage arrangements. In this case, the costs of maintaining the storage area may be shared and the little-used materials in each library can be available to users of any of the other libraries. Cooperative storage is often an integral part of cooperative acquisitions projects (see Chapter 9). Libraries accepting responsibility for collecting heavily on particular subjects may also agree to store what other cooperating libraries discard on those subjects. Even if storage is not a formal part of a cooperative plan, any cooperative acquisitions efforts of a library will probably have some effect on its weeding and storage program.

BIBLIOGRAPHY

Andrews, Theodora A. "The Role of Departmental Libraries in Operations Research Studies in a University Library—Part I: Selection for Storage Problems." *Special Libraries*, 59:519–524, September 1968. Considers fraction of collection to be stored and criteria for selecting the materials.

Ash, Lee. *Yale's Selective Book Retirement Program.* Hamden, Conn., Archon Books, 1963. 94p.

"Book Storage." Issue edited by Mary B. Cassata. *Library Trends*, 19:287–395, January 1971. Contains nine papers on various aspects of storage.

Bourne, Charles P. and Dorothy Gregor. "Planning Serials Cancellations and Cooperative Collection Development in the Health Sciences: Methodology and Background Information." *Medical Library Association Bulletin*, 63:366–377, October 1975. Offers five decision rules.

Brookes, B.C. "Growth, Utility and Obsolescence of Scientific Periodical Literature." *Journal of Documentation*, 26:283–294, December 1970. Specific groups of users must be considered when rating obsolesence of scientific literature.

Brookes, B.C. "Obsolescence of Special Library Periodicals." *Journal of the American Society for Information Science*, 21:320–329, September 1970. Suggests models to use in determining weeding policy.

Buckland, Michael K. "Are Obsolescence and Scattering Related?" *Journal of Documentation*, 28:242–246, September 1972.

Buckland, Michael K. *Book Availability and the Library User*. New York, Pergamon, 1975. 196p. Considers questions related to weeding, duplication, etc.

Buckland, Michael K. and others. *Systems Analysis of a University Library*. University of Lancaster Library, 1970. 110p. Operations research approach; implications for duplication policy.

Chen, Ching-Chih. *Applications of Operations Research Models to Libraries: A Case Study of the Use of Monographs in the Francis A. Countway Library of Medicine, Harvard University*. Cambridge, Mass., MIT Press, 1976. 212p. Includes implications for weeding and duplication.

Conger, Lucinda D. "Annex Library of Princeton University: The Development of a Compact Storage Library." *College and Research Libraries*, 31:160–168, May 1970.

Cooper, Marianne. "Criteria for Weeding of Collections." *Library Resources and Technical Services*, 12:339–351, Summer 1968. Developed at the Chemistry Library of Columbia University.

Crush, Marion. "Deselection Policy: How to Exclude Everything." *Wilson Library Bulletin*, 45:180–181, October 1970. Effect of typical selection criteria on popular books.

Durey, Peter. "Weeding Serials Subscriptions in a University Library." *Collection Management*, 1:91–94, Fall-Winter 1976–77. Experiences at the University of Auckland Library.

Ellsworth, Ralph E. *The Economics of Book Storage in College and University Libraries*. Metuchen, N.J., Association of Research Libraries and Scarecrow Press, 1969. 135p. Cost-analysis of twelve book storage systems.

Erlich, Martin. "Pruning the Groves of Libraro." *Wilson Library Bulletin*, 50:55–58, September 1975. Experiences of a public librarian; lists retention criteria.

Evans, G. Edward. "Limits to Growth, or the Need to Weed." *California Librarian*, 38:8–15, April 1977. Brief comments on reasons for weeding.

Farber, Evan Ira. "Limiting College Library Growth: Bane or Boom?" *Journal of Academic Librarianship*, 1:12–15, November 1975. Emphasizes differences between needs of college libraries and university libraries.

Fussler, Herman H. and Julian L. Simon. *Patterns in the Use of Books in Large Research Libraries*. Chicago, University of Chicago Press, 1969. 210p. Several possible predictors of use were tested against actual recorded use.

Gore, Daniel. *Farewell to Alexandria; Solutions to Space, Growth, and Performance Problems of Libraries*. Westport, Conn., Greenwood Press, 1976. Collection of ten papers presented at a 1975 conference; most discuss academic libraries.

Grundt, Leonard. "Nassau Community College Library Weeding Policy." *Unabashed Librarian*, no. 16:12, Summer 1975. Reprints policy adopted in May 1975.

Gupta, S.M. and A. Ravindran. "Optimal Storage of Books by Size: An Operations Research Approach." *Journal of the American Society for Information Science*, 25:354–357, November 1974.

Harrar, H. Joanne. "Cooperative Storage Warehouses." *College and Research Libraries*, 25:37–43, January 1964. Describes New England Deposit Library, Hampshire Inter-Library Center, and Midwest Inter-Library Center.

Harrar, H. Joanne. "Cooperative Storage." *Library Trends,* 19:318–328, January 1971.

Holland, Maurita P. "Serial Cuts vs. Public Service: A Formula." *College and Research Libraries,* 37:543–548, November 1976. Describes project at the University of Michigan Engineering-Transportation Library.

Lancaster, F.W. *The Measurement and Evaluation of Library Services.* Information Resources Press, 1977. 395p. Chapter 5 on "Evaluation of the Collection" also includes weeding and storage.

Lee, James D. "Book Storage as One Aspect of Cooperation." *Southeastern Librarian,* 21:161–168, Fall 1971.

Leimkuhler, Ferdinand F. and Michael D. Cooper. "Analytical Models for Library Planning." *Journal of the American Society for Information Science,* 22:390–398, November 1971. Operations vs. model; considers effects of collection growth on storage.

Line, Maurice B. "Half-Life of Periodical Literature: Apparent and Real Obsolescence." *Journal of Documentation,* 26:46–54, March 1970. Suggests ways to determine useful life of periodicals in various subjects.

Line, Maurice B. and A. Sandison. "Obsolescence and Changes in the Use of Literature with Time." *Journal of Documentation,* 30:283–350, September 1974. Literature review with 179 citations.

MacDonald, Mary Beth. "Weeding the Collection." *Unabashed Librarian,* no. 16:7–8, Summer 1975. Brief, practical suggestions for weeding.

McGaw, Howard F. "Policies and Practices in Discarding." *Library Trends,* 4:269–282, January 1956. Advantages, disadvantages, and traditional criteria.

McGrath, W. E. "Correlating the Subjects of Books Taken Out of and Books Used within an Open-Stack Library." *College and Research Libraries,* 32:280–285, July 1971. Results show a significant correlation.

McGrath, W.E. "Measuring Classified Circulation According to Curriculum." *College and Research Libraries,* 29:347–350, September 1968. Technique suggested for academic libraries.

McGrath, W.E. "Predicting Book Circulation By Subject in a University Library." *Collection Management,* 1:7–26, Fall-Winter 1976–77. Attempts to identify variables in a university environment which best predict use of books.

McGrath, W.E. "The Significance of Books Used According to a Classified Profile of Academic Departments." *College and Research Libraries,* 33:212–219, May 1972. Techniques for monitoring use.

Martin, Jess A. and Steven B. Manch. "Library Weeds." *Medical Library Association Bulletin,* 59:599–602, October 1971. Brief consideration of criteria and mechanics in a medical library.

Mattison, Lee. "Worn Book Checklist for Academic Libraries." *Library Resources and Technical Services,* 14:559–561, Fall 1970. Weeding of worn books at the University of Minnesota.

Maxim, Jacqueline A. "Weeding Journals with Informal Use Statistics." *De-Acquisition Librarian,* 1:9–11, Summer 1976.

Metcalf, Keyes D. "Compact Shelving." *College and Research Libraries,* 23:103–111, March 1962. Reviews ways to increase shelving capacity.

Metcalf, Keyes D. *Planning Academic and Research Libraries.* New York, McGraw-Hill, 1965. 431p. Chapter 8, "Housing the Collections" (pp. 133–174), contains a section on compact storage.

Morse, Philip M. "Demand for Library Materials: An Exercise in Probability Analysis." *Collection Management,* 1:47–78, Fall-Winter 1976–77. Includes consideration of effects of duplication.

Morse, Philip M. *Library Effectiveness.* Cambridge, Mass., MIT Press, 1968. 207p. Attempts to apply operations research methods to weeding and storage problems in libraries.

Muller, Robert H. "Economics of Compact Book Shelving." *Library Trends*, 13:433–447, April 1965.

Muller, Robert H. "Toward a National Plan for Cooperative Storage and Retention of Little-Used Library Materials." In *Resource Sharing in Libraries*, edited by Allen Kent, pp. 119–128. New York, Dekker, 1974.

Neufeld, John. "S-O-B: Save Our Books." *RQ*, 6:25–28, Fall 1966. Argues that preservation is more important than weeding.

Orne, Jerrold. "Storage and Deposit Libraries." *College and Research Libraries*, 21:446–452; 461, November 1960. Factors contributing to the need for storage facilities.

Perkins, David. "Periodicals Weeding, or Weed It and Reap." *California Librarian*, 38:32–37, April 1977. Describes cancellation project at California State University at Northridge.

Poller, Marian. "Weeding Monographs in the Harrison Public Library." *De-Acquisition Librarian*, 1:1,6–7, Spring 1976.

Reagan, Evelyn D. and others. "An Interim Solution to an Overcrowded Academic Library." *California Librarian*, 38:44–49, April 1977. Storage program at California Polytechnic State University at San Luis Obispo.

Rice, Barbara A. "Weeding in Academic and Research Libraries: An Annotated Bibliography." *Collection Management*, 2:65–71, Spring 1978.

Rosenberg, Betty. "Evaluation: Problems of Criteria and Methodology." *California Librarian*, 38:17–21, April 1977. Brief review of various methods.

Rouse, Roscoe. "Within-Library Solutions to Book Space Problems." *Library Trends*, 19:299–310, January 1971. Reports results of a survey of academic and public libraries.

Rush, Betsy. "Weeding vs. Censorship: Treading a Fine Line." *Library Journal*, 99:3032–3033, November 15, 1974. Weeding of children's collections.

Sandison, A. "Use of Older Literature and Its Obsolescence." *Journal of Documentation*, 27:184–199, September 1971. Argues that age is not the best criterion for weeding.

Seymour, Carol A. "Weeding the Collection: A Review of Research on Identifying Obsolete Stock." *Libri*, 22:137–148; 182–189, 1972. Reviews literature on weeding criteria for both monographs and serials.

Simon, Julian L. "How Many Books Should Be Stored Where? An Economic Analysis." *College and Research Libraries*, 28:92–103, March 1967. Discusses major variables in storage decision.

Slote, Stanley J. "An Approach to Weeding Criteria for Newspaper Libraries." *American Documentation*, 19:168–172, April 1968.

Slote, Stanley J. "Identifying Useful Core Collections: A Study of Weeding Fiction in Public Libraries." *Library Quarterly*, 41:25–34, January 1971. Tests weeding criteria on adult fiction in five libraries.

Slote, Stanley J. *Weeding Library Collections*. Littleton, Colo., Libraries Unlimited, 1975. 177p. Covers traditional approaches and also reviews research on objective weeding criteria.

Snowball, George J. and Joseph Sampedro. "Selection of Periodicals for Return to Prime Space from a Storage Facility." *Canadian Library Journal*, 30:490–492, November 1973. Describes project at Sir George Williams University, Montreal.

Spiller, David. "Stock Revision." In *Book Selection: An Introduction to Principles and Practice*, 2d ed. rev., pp. 88–111. London, Clive Bingley, 1974. Practical suggestions for evaluation and weeding.

Strain, Paula M. "A Study of the Usage and Retention of Technical Periodicals." *Library Resources and Technical Services*, 10:295–304, Summer 1966. Experiences of a special library.

Taylor, Colin R. "A Practical Solution to Weeding University Library Periodical Collections." *Collection Management*, 1:27–45, Fall-Winter 1976–77. Project conducted at Newcastle University Library.

Thompson, James. "Revision of Stock in Academic Libraries." *Library Association Record*, 75:41–44, March 1973. Advocates weeding for the purpose of storage.

Totten, Herman L. "Selection of Library Material for Storage: A State of the Art." *Library Trends*, 19:341–351, January 1971. Reviews research on objective criteria.

Trueswell, Richard W. "Determining the Optimum Number of Volumes for a Library's Core Collection." *Libri*, 16:49–60, 1969. Uses last recorded circulation date as indicator of use pattern.

Trueswell, Richard W. "A Quantitative Measure of User Circulation Requirements and Its Possible Effect on Stack Thinning and Multiple Copy Determination." *American Documentation*, 16:20–25, January 1965. Weeding using last circulation date.

Trueswell, Richard W. "User Circulation Satisfaction vs. Size of Holdings at Three Academic Libraries." *College and Research Libraries*, 30:204–213, May 1969. Uses last circulation date to indicate "core" collections.

Turner, Stephen J. "The Identifier Method of Measuring Use as Applied to Modeling the Circulation Use of Books from a University Library." *Journal of the American Society for Information Science*, 28:96–100, March 1977. Implications for weeding.

Voth, Sally and Mark E. Lipp. "Weeding of a Library Reserve Book Section: A Description of the Kansas State University Library System Using Floppy Diskettes." *Collection Management*, 1:78–89, Fall-Winter 1976–77.

Windsor, Donald A. "Core Versus Field Journals: A Method for Weeding During Changes in Research Needs." *De-Acquisition Librarian*, 1:1,5–6, Summer 1976.

Windsor, Donald A. "De-Acquisitioning Journals Using Productivity/Cost Rankings." *De-Acquisition Librarian*, 1:1,8–10, Spring 1976.

"Zero Growth; When Is NOT-Enough Enough? A Symposium." *Journal of Academic Librarianship*, 1:4–11, November 1975. Short comments by nine individuals.

CHAPTER 14

Preservation and Replacement

Discussion of preservation and replacement follows naturally after a discussion of weeding, because one of the reasons for weeding a collection is to identify the materials that are in poor physical condition. When an important, often-used item is found to be in such condition that it cannot be used either with pleasure to the borrower or without further damage to the item in question, preservation or replacement enter the picture. These appear to be the two alternatives. The item may simply be replaced—either with a new copy (if it is still available from the producer or publisher) or with a reproduction (done locally or commercially). The reproduction may not be in exactly the same format—a hardcover book may be put on microfilm, for example, or a phonodisc on audio cassette—but the content will be essentially the same. The other way to treat any library holding which is in poor physical condition is to preserve it in its original form. This is a costly alternative, but may be the only possibility in the case of rare and unique materials which are valued for physical, as well as intellectual, properties.

The extent to which a library must be concerned with preservation or replacement depends on the nature, age, and use of the collection. Some small, general collections, such as a branch of a public library system, might find that replacement, or even discarding without replacement, is the answer to all questions about worn books, torn journals, or scratched slides. However, most libraries have some materials—college archives or local history materials, for example—which are really intended to be kept indefinitely for research purposes. These are the materials that demand the most attention.

American librarians of the twentieth century have tended to emphasize the use of library materials rather than their preservation, but in recent years many have recognized that preservation and use are interrelated. All library materials will deteriorate in time, but the conditions of modern book manufacturing and our general environment are causing the rate of deterioration to be considerably faster than in the past. Materials must now be actively preserved in order to be available for use.

Those responsible for the collections of large research libraries have become quite vigorous in expressing concerns about the physical condition of their collections. No one really knows the full extent of the deterioration problem, but it is more serious than the average librarian may realize. Descriptions of the research collections of the New York Public Library as "the biggest junkpile on the North American continent" or of libraries in general as "well-staffed trash bins" sound too extreme to be believable, but less emotional research reports on the condition of selected samples of major research collections have tended to confirm the contention that a large number of books printed since about 1850 are quietly turning to dust.

Books and other materials suffer damage or deterioration because of several groups of factors, some inherent in the materials and others susceptible to control by the library. Library holdings may begin to deteriorate because of the organic materials from which they are made. Each type of material—paper, glue, plastic, etc.—that goes into the manufacture of a book, recording, or film has its own combination of physical and chemical properties and will present different preservation problems. The most obvious example of an internal preservation problem is the condition of the paper used in books. Because of the different contents and processes used to manufacture paper at different times and in different places, some books published twenty or thirty years ago may have yellow and brittle paper while those published two or three hundred years ago and stored in the same kind of environment may have relatively white and supple paper. These differences are due to the raw materials used in manufacture and are generally beyond the control of the librarian.

However, another group of factors influencing physical condition of library materials is external to the materials and is often within the library's control. These factors include all of the conditions surrounding the processing, storage, and use of the materials. For example, the levels of heat and humidity and the kind of lighting used in the area where materials are shelved and used can affect the rate of deterioration. Books stored in cool, dry, dark areas generally have a much longer life span than those housed in hot, humid, brightly-lighted areas. Constant levels of temperature and humidity are less harmful than fluctuating levels. The kinds of shelves or storage cabinets used, the ways materials are placed in those shelves or cabinets, the kinds of book return facilities provided, and even the procedures used by staff members responsible for processing and shelving materials are environmental factors which help determine the rate of deterioration of library materials.

Damage also comes from the users of library materials. Heavily-used items will eventually suffer damage even if users are careful, but any item may be ruined by one circulation to a careless user. No type of material which circulates is safe from possible destruction. Books which are tossed around, dropped in a puddle, or gnawed by the dog are as lost to the collection as are audiovisual materials which are handled carelessly and used on improper equipment. The effects of users on the physical condition of collections are generally beyond the control of librarians, but many libraries make attempts to educate their users in the problems and remedies.

Another group of preservation problems which face those responsible for collection maintenance includes the unpredictable and mostly uncontrollable emergencies and disasters which may strike a library. Fires, floods, storms, or even broken pipes within the building may lead to very extensive collection damage, especially from water. Again, these are generally beyond the control of the librarian, but it is possible to develop emergency plans for handling the collection and, in the case of fires, for preventing the disaster.

Organization for Preservation

While it is obvious that some aspects of collection deterioration can not be controlled by librarians, an organized approach to preservation can accomplish much more than random, spur-of-the-moment reactions to individual situations. There are certain basic decisions which should be made in advance of emergencies and priorities which should be set.

One of the first questions to be answered in a library which proposes to organize the attack on its preservation problems is the question of responsibility. Who is to have primary responsibility for preservation decisions? In recent years some large research libraries have appointed preservation officers to direct the whole effort. Smaller libraries can not afford such a full-time staff member, but it is still possible for an interested and knowledgeable librarian to be assigned the responsibility on a part-time basis. Some experts contend that the person charged with selection should also make the preservation decisions, since so many of the criteria are the same in both situations.

Related to the question of who should decide whether and how to preserve an item is the question of when the decision should be made. Again, some experts believe that preservation decisions should be made at the time the selection decision is made. Presumably, the selector has some idea about how his/her selection will be used and how permanent a part of the collection the new acquisition should be. If the material probably will not survive very long in its original format, should it be purchased in that format? If the answer is yes, then what can be done to protect it before it is ever used by the public?

Once a library begins to think seriously about preservation problems, it will probably find that a written record of policies and procedures is necessary. In considering its plan for preservation, a library needs to know a number of things which are related in one way or another to its overall collection development plan. What kinds of materials are in the collection? How are they used? Are any of the materials unique? Are they used by researchers from other cities or institutions? What is the present physical condition of the collection? Are some parts of it more worn and battered than others? If funds for preservation efforts are limited, as they doubtless will be, which part of the collection will receive attention first? How much will the library rely on replacement or reproduction as opposed to preservation of the original? Answers to many of these questions—which are only examples of the points to be considered in planning—depend on the original assessment of how the information (whatever its form) being added to the collection will be used. The type of information and its possible uses determine to a great extent the acceptable format in which it may be packaged.

Another aspect of organization for preservation of the collection involves the efforts which may be undertaken to inform the library's community of the problem and the possible solutions. Staff cooperation is essential and the cooperation of the public is highly desirable. In addition to informing everyone of ways in which staff and public can routinely assist the preservation effort, a comprehensive plan ought to include a disaster policy. If a major catastrophe strikes the library, which actions will be taken first and who will take them? Those librarians who have been through fires, floods, or other natural disasters recommend assigning responsibilities well before the event.

In small libraries a comprehensive, written preservation policy may seem unnecessary, but in any size or type of library there are certain basic things which may be done to prolong the useful life of the materials. Although it may be difficult to do, any library can at least try to keep temperature and relative humidity constant and the air in shelving and storage areas as clear as possible. Using ultraviolet filters on windows and lights will help. Shelvers may be taught to shelve materials properly, avoiding packing shelves too tightly or placing books with fore-edges down. When processing new materials, librarians should be careful about their use of tape or paper clips or other supplies which might react harmfully with the materials being added to the collection. Some potential physical problems can be identified and corrected before materials begin to circulate; others can be corrected quickly after they occur, so that they do not become major. The important thing is to be aware of the need to preserve the library's collection and to set up routine procedures which will at least not interfere with the achievement of that goal.

Cooperation in Preservation

Because the volume of library materials which are deteriorating is great, the diversity of materials and methods for preserving them is wide, and the resources to do the job are costly, some libraries are turning to cooperative arrangements for preservation. This is really a natural extension of cooperative acquisition and storage programs.

Some groups of libraries already cooperate in the microfilming of back files of journals and others are investigating the systematic microfilming or other reproduction of deteriorating monographs. In some cases, efforts are made by a group of libraries to identify the best original copy of certain important works so that the best copy may be placed on restricted circulation or otherwise preserved for future availability. In recent years a few regional restoration centers have been established—centers which have the expensive equipment and expert staff needed to carry out high quality repair and restoration.

The need for action on a wider front than the individual library was demonstrated in 1976, when the Library of Congress announced that it was developing plans for a national preservation program. The program as outlined at that time included three areas: the preservation of the intellectual content (probably by microfilming) of materials that do not need to be preserved in their original format; the preservation in original format of materials identified as rare and valuable in themselves; and the preservation (possibly by special storage or microfilming) of present and future publications which are printed on paper with a life-expectancy of fifty years or less.

The third aspect of the Library of Congress's preservation plan illustrates why preservation of library collections is an appropriate topic with which to conclude a book on building library collections. For reasons previously discussed, and highlighted again in the Library of Congress plan, many materials added to library collections have started to deteriorate by the time they are acquired. The librarian who wants to build an effective collection must be aware of the physical properties of the materials selected, as well as their potential use, and must be prepared to take the necessary steps to ensure that the intellectual content of the collection will be available when needed.

BIBLIOGRAPHY

Baker, John P. "Restoration of Library Materials." *Library Scene,* 3:4–6, December 1974. Managing a restoration program.

Banks, Paul N. "Cooperative Approaches to Conservation." *Library Journal,* 101:2348–2351, November 15, 1976. Possible advantages and disadvantages of regional conservation centers.

Banks, Paul N. "Environmental Standards for Storage of Books and Manuscripts." *Library Journal,* 99:339–343, February 1, 1974.

Banks, Paul N. "Some Problems in Book Conservation." *Library Resources and Technical Services,* 12:330–338, Summer 1968. Problems related to binding.

Capps, Marie T. "Preservation and Maintenance of Maps." *Special Libraries,* 63:457–462, October 1972. Discusses potential sources of damage.

Cunha, George M. and Dorothy Grant Cunha. *Conservation of Library Materials: A Manual and Bibliography on the Care, Repair and Restoration of Library Materials.* 2d ed. Metuchen, N.J., Scarecrow Press, 1971–72. 2v. First volume discusses materials, causes of damage, and prevention and repair. Second volume is a comprehensive bibliography.

Cutter, Charles. "The Restoration of Paper Documents and Manuscripts." *College and Research Libraries,* 28:387–397, November 1967. Review of methods.

Darling, Pamela W. "Developing a Preservation Microfilming Program." *Library Journal,* 99:2803–2809, November 1, 1974. Administrative and procedural considerations.

Darling, Pamela W. "A Local Preservation Program: Where to Start." *Library Journal,* 101:2343–2347, November 15, 1976. Thorough discussion of points to consider in developing a plan.

Darling, Pamela W. "Microforms in Libraries: Preservation and Storage." *Microform Review,* 5:93–100, April 1976. Considers use of microforms as a way of preserving content of deteriorating books and journals.

Davis, Douglas M. "Maintenance of Circulating Books in an Academic Library." *California Librarian,* 38:22–31, April 1977.

DeSomogyi, Aileen. "Access versus Preservation." *Canadian Library Journal,* 31:414–419, October 1974.

Deterioration and Preservation of Library Materials; The 34th Annual Conference of the Graduate Library School, August 4–6, 1969. Chicago, University of Chicago Press, 1970. 200p. Collection of papers on a variety of topics; also published in *Library Quarterly,* January 1970.

Dove, Jack. "Storage and Care." In *The Audio-Visual,* pp. 242–245. London, Deutsch, 1975. 300p.

Friedman, Hannah B. "Preservation Programs in New York State: Existent and Non-Existent." *Special Libraries,* 60:578–589, November 1969. Results of a questionnaire survey.

Grove, Lee E. "Paper Deterioration—An Old Story." *College and Research Libraries,* 25:365–374, September 1964. Historical review.

Horton, C. *Cleaning and Preserving Bindings and Related Materials.* 2d ed. rev. Chicago, Library Technology Program, American Library Association, 1969. 87p.

Kathpalia, Yash Pal. *Conservation and Restoration of Archive Materials.* Paris, Unesco, 1973. 231p.

King, Antoinette. "Conservation of Drawings and Prints." *Special Libraries,* 63:116–120, March 1972. Basic techniques.

Lane, Alfred H. "Reprints in the Preservation Picture and a Drift Aside." *Special Libraries,* 63:305–309, July 1972.

Library Binding Institute. *Library Binding Manual; A Handbook of Useful Procedures for the Maintenance of Library Volumes.* Edited by Maurice F. Tauber. Boston, 1972. 185p.

Lowell, Howard P. *Public Library Materials Conservation Project.* Boston, Bureau of Library Extension, Massachusetts State Department of Education, 1975. 40p. (ED 108 696)

Martin, John H. "Resuscitating a Water-Logged Library." *Wilson Library Bulletin,* 50:233–241, November 1975. Advice on what to do after a flood.

Middleton, Bernard C. *The Restoration of Leather Bindings.* Chicago, Library Technology Program, American Library Association, 1972. 201p.

Morris, John. *Managing the Library Fire Risk*. Berkeley, University of California, 1975. 101p.

National Fire Protection Association. *Protection of Library Collections*. Boston, 1970. 28p. Recommended ways to protect collections from fire.

Pakala, James C. "The Conservation of Library Materials." *Library Scene*, 7:2-5, March 1978. Brief review of problems and some attempted remedies.

Ready, William. "Deterioration Is Winning the Library Stakes." *Canadian Library Journal*, 35:201-207, June 1978. General review of the situation.

Ready, William. "Library Books Are Different." *Library Scene*, 2:23-27, December 1974. Argues for better bindings for important books.

Roberts, Matt. "Oversewing and the Problem of Book Preservation in the Research Library." *College and Research Libraries*, 28:17-24, January 1967.

Sellers, David Y. and Richard Strassberg. "Anatomy of a Library Emergency: How the Cornell University Library Dealt with Flood Damage and Developed Plans to Handle Future Emergencies." *Library Journal*, 98:2824-2827, October 1, 1973.

Seminar on the Application of Chemical and Physical Methods to the Conservation of Library and Archival Materials, May 17-21, 1971. Edited by George M. Cunha and Norman P. Tucker. Boston, Boston Athenaeum, 1972. 255p. Collection of papers.

Seminar on the Theoretical Aspects of the Conservation of Library and Archival Materials and the Establishment of Conservation Programs, October 1-5, 1973. Edited by Robert C. Morrison and others. New England Document Conservation Center and Boston Athenaeum, 1975. 351p. Collection of papers.

Shaffer, Norman J. "Library of Congress Pilot Preservation Project." *College and Research Libraries*, 30:5-11, January 1969.

Shelley, Karen Lee. "The Future of Conservation in Research Libraries." *Journal of Academic Librarianship*, 1:15-18, January 1976. Recommends possible administrative structure for a preservation program.

Smith, Richard D. "The Extension of Book Life." *Library Binder*, 18:36-40, December 1970. Discusses two methods.

Smith, Richard D. "Guidelines for Preservation." *Special Libraries*, 59:346-352, May-June 1968.

Smith, Richard D. "Maps, Their Deterioration and Preservation." *Special Libraries*, 63:59-68, February 1972.

Strassberg, Richard. "Fire and Water Damage; A Selective Bibliography on Preventative Measures and Restoration Techniques." *Cornell University Library Bulletin*, no. 181:31-33, January 1973.

Trelles, Oscar M. "Protection of Libraries." *Law Library Journal*, 66:241-258, August 1973.

U.S. Library of Congress. Office of the Assistant Director for Preservation. *Preservation Leaflets*. No. 1- , 1975- . First leaflet in series gives selected references; others cover various aspects of preservation.

U.S. Library of Congress. Preservation Office. "Deacidification, Lamination, and the Use of Polyester Film Encapsulation." *SLA Geography and Map Division Bulletin*, no. 99:46-48, March 1975.

Walker, Gay. "Preservation Efforts in Larger U.S. Academic Libraries." *College and Research Libraries*, 36:39-44, January 1975. Results of a survey.

Wardle, David B. *Document Repair*. London, Society of Archivists, 1971. 84p. Intended as a practical guide.

Waters, Peter. *Procedures for Salvage of Water-Damaged Library Materials*. Washington, D.C., Library of Congress, 1975. 30p.

PART IV

APPENDICES

APPENDIX A

Check List of Statements
On Selection Principles

In the first chapter, a selected group of traditional statements of principles was used to illustrate various attitudes toward the problems of selection which librarians have taken. This checklist is a summary in topical array of statements by various authors on this subject. It is recommended that this checklist be read through as if it were in narrative form. Such a reading will reveal a number of facts of interest: (1) the repetition of a given principle without change through the years; (2) the slight—but sometimes highly significant—alteration of some of the principles by succeeding authors; (3) the flat contradiction of one author by another—or of one author by himself or herself.

The author of each statement (and the date of the work from which it was taken) is given in parentheses following the statement. Complete bibliographical data will be found in the bibliography at the end of the checklist.

Purposes of the Library and Selection

1. Preceding a determination of book selection policy, every library should have a statement of library philosophy and over-all objectives of the individual library system. (PLD Reporter, 1955. Group 14)
2. The functions of the library determine the character of the book collection. (Bowerman, 1930)
3. Materials should be selected, retained, and discarded in the light of conscious objectives of each library. (Public Library Service, 1936)

Selection Policy Statements

4. Every library should have a written statement of policy, covering the selection and maintenance of its collection of books and nonbook materials. (Public Library Service, 1956)
5. Formulate a written book selection policy, prepared by the librarian and board jointly and adopted formally by the board. (PLD Reporter, 1955. Group 7)
6. Every library should have a concrete statement of book selection policy, as a basis for selecting material and for use in explaining the library's

policy as well as the exclusion or inclusion of specific items of material. (PLD Reporter, 1955. Group 13)

7. The first four sections of the Library Bill of Rights make an excellent statement of broad principles of book selection. (PLD Reporter, 1955. Group 12)

8. A broad statement of book selection policy should be followed by (1) a determination of the criteria in each field; (2) a statement of limiting factors governing book purchase; (3) a listing of techniques and screening tools. (PLD Reporter, 1955. Group 14)

9. Fix upon a policy of selection and stick to it until it has proved wrong, buying consistently along the line of this policy, until a better one is found. (Drury, 1930)

The Library's Users—Actual and Potential

10. The high purpose of book selection is to provide the right books for the right reader at the right time. (Drury, 1930)

11. The best reading for the largest number at the least cost. (Dewey, 1876)

12. Fewer books, responsibly selected, for all the library readers, at any cost. (Drury, 1930. Quoting ALA Board of Education for Librarianship, 3rd annual report, April 1927)

13. The first step in book selection should be to ascertain the reading interests of our readers. (Bonny, 1939)

14. As a responsibility of library service, books and other reading matter selected should be chosen for values of interest, information, and enlightenment of all the people of the community. (Library Bill of Rights, 1939)

15. Select books on subjects in which individuals and groups in the community have an interest. (Fairchild, 1903)

16. Select books on subjects in which individuals and groups in the community have a natural interest. (Bascom, 1922)

17. Book selection must be primarily in relation to the needs of the community which the library serves. (Bonny, 1939)

18. Study your community with care and try to provide something for all those who use or may be induced to use the library. (Bacon, 1907)

19. Study open-mindedly the community, endeavoring to analyze its desires, diagnose its ailments, provide for its wants, and satisfy its needs. (Drury, 1930)

20. Study your community and its needs. (PLD Reporter, 1955. Group 7)

21. The librarian should know the community to the extent of being aware of all potential demands. (PLD Reporter, 1955. Group 3)

22. Provide for the entire constituency, not simply those using the library. (Fairchild, 1903)

23. Provide for all the people in the community, not merely for those who are enrolled as borrowers (Bascom, 1922)

24. Provide for both actual and potential users. Satisfy the former's general and specific demands as far as possible; anticipate somewhat the demands which might or should come from the latter. (Drury, 1930)

Groups and Special Individuals

25. See to it that no race, nationality, profession, trade, religion, faith, or school of thought or local customs represented in the community is overlooked. (Fairchild, 1903)
26. So far as good books are obtainable and funds permit, represent in your selection every race, profession, trade, religious or political doctrine, interest, and local custom found in the community. Keep in mind, however, that the library is primarily an educational agent, and do not admit books containing harmful doctrines or teachings. (Bascom, 1922)
27. Purvey for recognized groups, reflecting every class, trade, employment, or recreation which develops a natural interest. (Drury, 1930)
28. Selection follows from conscious study of various groups. . . . Sensitivity to interests, early recognition of needs before they are clearly expressed, and catholicity of contact and viewpoint mark the librarian who keeps the collection in tune with its owners. (Public Library Service, 1956)
29. No one group should be served at the expense of another. (PLD Reporter, 1955. Group 10)
30. Selection must go beyond the requests of particular groups who have come to use the library regularly and reach out to segments in the population which do not as readily turn to this facility. (Public Library Service, 1956)
31. The book selector should further have in mind many *individuals* who are making active use of his collection of books and for whose special investigations he provides as occasion affords. (Drury, 1930)
32. Be willing to buy, as far as funds permit, the works asked for by specialists and community leaders. (Drury, 1930)
33. The public library is not to supply the specialist with his regular tools, but only with the general literature on his subject. (Bascom, 1922)
34. Select some books to meet the needs of only a few persons if by so doing society at large will be benefited. (Bascom, 1922)
35. Provide books which will be used by only a few people if they are likely, by the use of the books, to do original work of service to society. (Fairchild, 1903)
36. Sometimes buy a book wanted by a single reader. More often, borrow it for him from another library. (Bacon, 1907)
37. Do not sacrifice the interests of the student to those of the home reader. (Bascom, 1922)
38. If you have foreigners in your town, buy some books for them in their own language. (Bacon, 1907)

Standards of Selection

39. Erect suitable standards for judging all books, and strive to approximate them. (Drury, 1930)
40. Materials acquired should meet high standards of quality in content, expression, and format. (Public Library Service, 1956)
41. Books selected must be based on an established set of standards whether written or unwritten. (PLD Reporter, 1955. Group 11)

42. Select books which tend toward the development and enrichment of life. (Fairchild 1903; Bascom 1922; Haines 1950)
43. Select books that represent any endeavor aiming at human development— material, mental, or moral. (Drury, 1930)
44. Factual accuracy, effective expression, significance of subject, sincerity and responsibility of opinion—these and other factors must be considered and at times balanced one against the other. (Public Library Service, 1956)
45. Materials selected should be judged upon their authoritativeness and effectiveness of presentation. Each must be considered as a whole and not judged by any one of its parts. (PLD Reporter, 1955. Summary)
46. Secure any book which the library can use to advantage . . . for knowledge and information, for power and inspiration, for amusement and recreation, either now or in the future. (Drury, 1930)
47. The standard appropriate for one community might not apply in another. (PLD Reporter, 1955. Group 12)
48. Within standards of purpose and quality, collections should be built to meet the needs and interests of people. (Public Library Service, 1956)
49. The collection of the public library is inclusive and contains whatever materials contribute to the purposes of the library. (Public Library Service, 1956)
50. Selection of materials should be determined by usefulness and should not be limited by format. (Public Library Service, 1956)
51. Buy volumes that are suitable for the library purpose in format as well as in contents, being attractive and durable in binding, paper, and printing. (Drury, 1930)

Completeness; Proportion; Balance:
The "Well-Rounded Collection"

52. Do not strive for completeness. Select the best books on a subject, the best by an author. Do not get all of a series unless their merit or your need warrants it. (Bascom, 1922)
53. Do not buy an author's complete works if some of his books are worth your while to own and others are not. (Bacon, 1907)
54. Banish the idea of completeness except for an encyclopedic library or for a special collection. (Fairchild, 1903)
55. Do not strive for completeness in sets, series, or subjects unless convinced that it is necessary for real usefulness. (Drury, 1930)
56. Do not try to build up a "well-rounded" collection. Get what your readers need and want, or can be made to want. (Bacon, 1907)
57. Completeness is a practical impossibility. It is impossible to follow a scheme for balancing proportions of subject classes. (Drury, 1930)
58. Every library should be built up according to a definite plan on a broad general foundation. Its development must be flexible, but constant attention must be paid to the maintaining of just proportions as a whole, so that certain classes will not be overemphasized and others neglected. The needs of the library exist and should be met, as well as the needs of its readers. (Haines, 1950)

59. Keep a just proportion in the collection as a whole. (Bascom, 1922)
60. Have a good regard for proportion and balance, the most difficult task in book selection. (Fairchild, 1903)

Demand

61. Quality of materials must be related to the other two basic standards of selection, purpose and need. (Public Library Service, 1956)
62. Representation must be comprehensive of and in proportion to demand and not subject. (McColvin, 1925)
63. Demand is a large governing factor in selection. (Drury, 1930)
64. Provide for actual demand and anticipate any reasonable demands which may be made upon the library's resources. (Bonny, 1939)
65. The value of the demand is gauged by the extent to which the subject fosters the purposes of human endeavor, i.e., human development and happiness. (Drury, 1930)
66. Variety of demand arises from the complexity of human nature and ability represented in the community and from the several different aspects of any subject. (Drury, 1930)
67. The demand theory is not a good basis for book selection, but it affects selection. (PLD Reporter, 1955. Group 10)
68. In book selection, popular demand must be recognized to the extent of maintaining community interest and support of the library. (PLD Reporter, 1955. Summary)
69. Study your community and compare its needs with its demands. Welcome its recommendations, but use your judgment in following them. Be a leader, a guide, rather than a follower. (Bascom, 1922)
70. Restrain the unduly aggressive and recognize the inarticulate patron. Some demand that their every desire shall be satisfied and persist in recommending their hobbies; the unobtrusive also have rights. (Drury, 1930)
71. Buy no book without asking yourself whether in buying it you are not depriving your library of the chance to buy a better book that is in as great demand. (Bacon, 1907; Drury, 1930)
72. As a rule, prefer an inferior book that will be read to a superior book that will not be read. (Bascom, 1922; Haines, 1950)
73. Aim at getting the best on any subject, but do not hesitate to install a mediocre book that will be read in preference to a superior one that will not be read. (Drury, 1930)
74. Duplicate the best rather than acquire the many. (Drury, 1930)
75. This is the secret of the art of selecting: few titles, carefully chosen for the community's need and freely duplicated. (Dana, 1908)
76. It is better to buy ten extra copies of a wholesome book wanted by the public than one copy each of ten books which will not be read. But even the very small library can wisely spend a little of its money each year on scholarly books. (Dana, 1920)
77. Because of basic standards of the public library, it is impossible to satisfy all popular demands. Popular demand may include two types of material: that of more permanent value and that of temporary or superficial value.

We recommend that the emphasis in book selection policy be placed on securing a greater amount of worthwhile material, limiting the selection of other material as stringently as possible. (PLD Reporter, 1955. Group 8)

78. Popular demand must be considered, but should not serve as the primary criterion for purchase and duplication, for by so doing the library is selling short other interests in the community. (PLD Reporter, 1955. Group 3)

79. Do not think that because your library is tax-supported you must buy every book for which the taxpayers ask. Encourage people to make their wishes known. But you are not bound to buy every book called for, if you think it is a book the library should not own, any more than your local school board is bound to give a course in Chinese in the high school because the daughter of a certain taxpayer is going to China as a missionary. (Bacon, 1907)

80. Select some books of permanent value not immediately interesting to readers. (Fairchild, 1903)

81. Select some books of permanent value, regardless of whether or not they will be much used. (Bascom, 1922)

82. While demand is primarily the basis and reason for supply, remember that the great works of literature are foundation stones in the library's own structure and therefore select some books of permanent value regardless of whether or not they will be widely used. (Haines, 1950)

83. Buy good editions of standard works. Even a very small library may own a few attractive editions of great authors. (Bacon, 1907)

84. Stock the classics and the standards, ever and always, in attractive editions. (Drury, 1930)

Controversial Issues

85. Let the basis of selection be positive, not negative. Select books which will be of service to somebody; do not exclude books because somebody thinks they will do harm. (Fairchild, 1903; Bascom, 1922; Haines, 1950)

86. Select for positive use. A book should not be simply good, but good for something. It must do service. Question its usefulness if the best that can be said is "It can do no harm." (Drury, 1930)

87. There should be the fullest practicable provision of material presenting all points of view concerning the problems and issues of our times, international, national, and local. (Library Bill of Rights, 1939)

88. All sides of issues should be presented insofar as possible, within budget limitations, with as much authoritative background as is available. (PLD Reporter, 1955. Group 3)

89. The library collection should contain opposing views on controversial topics of interest to the people. (Public Library Service, 1956)

90. Controversial books relating to the local community should be selected. (PLD Reporter, 1955. Group 11)

91. The collection must contain the various opinions which apply to important, complicated, and controversial questions, including unpopular and unorthodox positions. (Public Library Service, 1956)

92. If a public library does not provide the means to study the several sides of issues, it is failing in one of its unique reasons for existence. This does not

necessarily imply numerical balance. Controversial materials kept in community libraries will naturally be limited to areas of controversy about which there is general concern. (Public Library Service, 1956)

93. The librarian should guard against taking the line of least resistance by avoiding issues, but meet them squarely. (PLD Reporter, 1955. Group 3)

94. The selection of all library materials should be as objective as possible. Selection which is affected by one's own beliefs is an act of censorship. (PLD Reporter, 1955. Summary)

95. Books or other reading matter of sound factual authority should not be proscribed or removed from library shelves because of partisan or doctrinal disapproval. (Library Bill of Rights, 1939)

96. In no case should any book be excluded because of the race, nationality, political or religious views of the writer. (Library Bill of Rights, 1939)

97. Care must be exercised that parts of the community do not unduly influence the collection, either positively or negatively. Selection must resist efforts of groups to deny access to materials on the part of other sections of the community, whether in the name of political, moral, or religious beliefs. (Public Library Service, 1956)

98. The library should not abdicate its responsibility for book selection to any individual or organization issuing restrictive lists. (PLD Reporter, 1955. Group 3)

99. Censorship of books, urged or practiced by volunteer arbiters of morals or political opinion, or by organizations that would establish a coercive concept of Americanism, must be challenged by libraries. (Library Bill of Rights, 1939)

100. If materials serve the purpose of the library, are of required quality, and relate to an existing need or interest, they should not be removed from the collection because of pressure by groups or individuals. (Public Library Service, 1956)

101. Do not refuse to buy a book because one or more people object to it. What no one objects to is probably valueless. A vital book, like a person of any vitality, is sure to antagonize someone. (Bacon, 1907)

102. No political or sectarian bias should influence the exclusion of good books. (Brown, 1937)

103. Do not pander to any sect, creed, or partisan taste. (Dana, 1920)

Sex and Morality

104. Questions of sexual morality are very difficult. If the librarian exercises the censorship of exclusion, he will be accused of prurience; if not exercised, he will be accused of exposing impressionable youth to immoral suggestion. (Brown, 1937)

105. What is immorality and what is immaturity every library authority will determine for itself. (Brown, 1937)

106. In selection, judgment should be based on the total effect of the piece of material and not on the presence of words, phrases, or situations which in themselves might be objectionable. (PLD Reporter, 1955. Group 13)

107. Do not reject a book on the opinion of a few narrow-minded people who think it harmful or even bad. (Bascom, 1922)

108. The hypersensitive objections of the narrow-minded (in matters of sex) must not be mistaken for genuine expressions of community views. (Brown, 1937)

109. The underlying principle of my own selection of books, for a library which is essentially for the people (as contrasted with a university library) is that books which speak truth concerning normal, wholesome conditions may be safely bought, however plain-spoken. While, on the other hand, books which treat of morbid, diseased conditions of the individual man, or society at large, are intended for the student of special subjects. Such are bought only after due consideration of the just relation of the comparative rights of the students and general readers. (West, 1895)

110. Avoid without censoring the ethically dubious. (Drury, 1930)

111. Buy few, if any, books that the majority of your clients would consider ethically dubious. If you buy any, restrict their circulation so that boys and girls will not draw them out. (Bacon, 1907)

112. One can always refuse to buy what is doubtful on the score of lack of funds. (Bacon, 1907)

113. There seems to be no reason why works which offend the current common views of morality should be purchased out of community funds. (Brown, 1937)

114. In the case of books with a sexual theme or treating of sex in an outspoken manner, if there are strong local opinions antagonistic to this type of book being on the public library shelves, the librarian should refrain from stocking such books. If, on the other hand, the books are of definite literary or other value, the librarian would be justified in taking a firm stand and insisting that they be kept in stock but supplied only upon special request to approved borrowers. (Bonny, 1939)

Religious and Political Problems

115. With political materials, librarians without being censors should still look for accuracy, integrity, and authority, always attempting to be aware of their own difficulty in being objective in such an emotionally charged field, particularly in regard to books covering recent happenings and current problems. (PLD Reporter 1955. Group 12)

116. About religious materials, it was agreed that the library should try to keep a balance, representing all religions and denominations as adequately as possible in its collection, that they should not buy and perhaps not even accept as gifts, books which were specifically denominational and not of general interest. (PLD Reporter, 1955. Group 12)

117. Of sectarian books get only those that are truly representative and likely to be used by the general reader, or at least by a considerable number of readers, and treat all sects alike. (Bascom, 1922)

Popular Materials and Fiction

118. We cannot justify swamping the library with ephemeral literature. When the supply of ephemeral books encroaches upon the satisfaction of the

needs of the student and the searcher after information, it should be stopped. (Bonny, 1939)

119. When legal, the rental collection may be used to provide ephemeral materials, reserving book funds for those of more enduring value. (PLD Reporter, 1955. Group 10)

120. Do not buy novels simply because they are popular. To follow that line is to end with the cheapest kind of stuff. Some librarians claim, erroneously, that they must buy to please the public's taste; that they can't use their own judgment in selecting books for a library which the public purse supports. Librarians are charged with getting the best ... not with suiting everybody. (Dana, 1920)

121. Do not aim too high—avoid trash, but do not buy literature which will not be read simply because it is "standard." Remember that the public library is popular in every sense of the word. (Dana, 1920)

122. No library could afford to set its standard of selection so high that it would reduce community interest in and support of the library, and there are important groups in the community to which light fiction means much. (PLD Reporter, 1955. Group 12)

123. Do not look down on fiction. Buy a good deal of it in a place where you are trying to induce people to use the library. It is good bait. Choose the best and duplicate. (Bacon, 1907)

124. In fiction, get the more popular of the wholesome novels found on the shelves of larger libraries. (Dana, 1920)

125. Do not be intolerant of fiction if it measures up to standard; it has educational as well as recreational value. (Drury, 1930)

126. It must be recognized that most public libraries find it necessary to buy some fiction and popular reading which is below the library's quality standards. (PLD Reporter, 1955. Group 1)

127. Perhaps it is a question of degree and gradualness of approach, and elimination gradually and consistently from the lower levels throughout the years. Some libraries, following this policy, have found themselves buying more copies of fewer and fewer novels. (PLD Reporter, 1955. Group 12)

128. Popular demand for fiction, not always of acceptable standards, creates a real problem. Librarians should try to meet demand but should not yield to popular pressure when books have been refused for definite reasons consonant with the library's objectives. (PLD Reporter, 1955. Group 12)

Children and Young People

129. Buy largely for children. Notice that I do not say: buy largely of juvenile books. There is too much pre-digested mental food for babes on the market today. Shun all but the best of it, and give the children some of the great books of all times. (Bacon, 1907)

130. Buy largely for children. They are the library's best pupils. They are more easily trained to enjoy good books than their elders. (Dana, 1920)

131. Since guidance is implicit in selection of materials for children and young people, book selection policy may differ among these and the adult groups. (PLD Reporter, 1955. Summary)

132. Teen-agers should participate in selecting their own materials and in deciding on the purchase of controversial materials for their own department. (PLD Reporter, 1955. Group 10)

Gifts

133. Gifts to the library should be judged upon the same basis as purchased materials. (PLD Reporter, 1955. Summary)
134. In controversial and sectarian subjects, gifts may be accepted when purchase is undesirable. (Haines, 1950)

Local History

135. Buy, or better, beg all books or pamphlets relating to your town or written by townspeople. Secure church and town reports, club programs, etc. Build up a little local history collection no matter how small your library. (Bacon, 1907)
136. Local interest should be fostered by buying freely books on local history and books by local authors. (Dana, 1920)
137. Develop the local history collection; the items will be sought for in the library if anywhere in the world. (Drury, 1930)
138. Make your collection of local history as extensive and useful as possible. (Haines, 1950)

Nonbook Materials

139. Nonbook materials should be an integral part of the collection, and, within limits of availability and usefulness, should be provided to the same degree of range and inclusiveness as books. (Public Library Service, 1956)
140. For nonbook materials, considerations of physical and technical excellence, as shown in quality of photography and sound, must be considered. (Public Library Service, 1956)

Relationship to Other Libraries

141. The character and emphasis of the public library collection should be influenced by the existence of other library collections in the community and area. (Public Library Service, 1956)
142. The ability of any library to meet all demands from its own holdings is limited. Needs beyond the resources of a given library can be met from those of other libraries. (PLD Reporter, 1955. Group 6)
143. Do not duplicate valuable books in other libraries in your town, if these are easily accessible to the public. (Bacon, 1907)
144. Extensive use of interlibrary loan is recommended for books of limited use. (PLD Reporter, 1955. Group 4)

145. Husband resources through cooperation, local, regional, and national. (Drury, 1930)

Weeding

146. Systematic removal from the collection of material no longer useful is essential to maintaining the purposes and quality of resources. (Public Library Service, 1956)
147. The discarding of materials requires the same degree of attention as initial selection and deserves careful study. (PLD Reporter, 1955. Group 13)
148. Discard or refrain from adding books (other than the classics and standards) for which there is no actual or anticipated demand. (Drury, 1930)
149. Annual withdrawals from the collection should average at least 5 per cent of the total collection. (Public Library Service, 1956)

Administration of Selection

150. Selection must be an orderly, co-ordinated process. (Public Library Service, 1956)
151. Maintain, so far as possible, promptness and regularity in supplying new books. (Haines, 1950)
152. So apportion the library funds as to obtain books of the highest quality for the greatest number of people. (Drury, 1930)
153. Keep within the budget, knowing the total amount available and maintaining a just but not rigid proportion among the allotments. (Drury, 1930)
154. It is very important for the selector to have at hand at all times a record of the amount of money available for purchases. (Drury, 1930)

Sources of the Selection Statements
Used in this Appendix

A.L.A. *Library Bill of Rights*. [See Appendix B]

Bacon, Corinne. "Principles of Book Selection." *New York Libraries*, v. 1, Oct. 1907, p. 3–6.

Bascom, Elva Lucille. *Book Selection*. Chicago, ALA, 1922.

Bonny, Harold Victor. *Manual of Practical Book Selection for Public Libraries*. London, Grafton, 1939.

Bowerman, George Franklin. *Censorship and the Public Library*. New York, Wilson, 1931.

Brown, James Duff. *Manual of Library Economy*. 5th ed. London, Grafton, 1937.

Dana, John Cotton. *A Library Primer*. New York, Library Bureau, 1920.

Dana, John Cotton. "Selection and Rejection of Books." *Public Libraries*, v. 13, 1908, p. 177–8.

Dewey, Melvil. "The American Library Association." *Library Journal*, v. 1, 1877, p. 247.

Drury, Francis K. W. *Book Selection*. Chicago, ALA, 1930.

Fairchild, Mary Salome (Cutter). "Book Selection." *Public Libraries*, v. 8, 1903, p. 281.

Haines, Helen. *Living with Books*. 2d ed. New York, Columbia Univ. Press, 1950.

McColvin Lionel Roy. *The Theory of Book Selection for Public Libraries*. London, Grafton, 1925.

PLD Reporter No. 4, 1955. "Book Selection; Proceedings of a Work Conference, 1955." Ed. by S. Janice Kee and Dorothy K. Smith. Chicago, ALA, 1955.

Public Library Service; a Guide to Evaluation with Minimum Standards. Chicago, ALA, 1956.

West, Theresa H. "Improper Books; Methods Employed to Discover and Exclude Them." *Library Journal*, v. 20, 1895, p. C32.

APPENDIX B

Statements of A.L.A. Council Related to Intellectual Freedom

THE FREEDOM TO READ

The freedom to read is essential to our democracy. It is continuously under attack. Private groups and public authorities in various parts of the country are working to remove books from sale, to censor textbooks, to label "controversial" books, to distribute lists of "objectionable" books or authors, and to purge libraries. These actions apparently rise from a view that our national tradition of free expression is no longer valid; that censorship and suppression are needed to avoid the subversion of politics and the corruption of morals. We, as citizens devoted to the use of books and as librarians and publishers responsible for disseminating them, wish to assert the public interest in the preservation of the freedom to read.

We are deeply concerned about these attempts at suppression. Most such attempts rest on a denial of the fundamental premise of democracy: that the ordinary citizen, by exercising his critical judgment, will accept the good and reject the bad. The censors, public and private, assume that they should determine what is good and what is bad for their fellow-citizens.

We trust Americans to recognize propaganda, and to reject it. We do not believe they need the help of censors to assist them in this task. We do not believe they are prepared to sacrifice their heritage of a free press in order to be "protected" against what others think may be bad for them. We believe they still favor free enterprise in ideas and expression.

We are aware, of course, that books are not alone in being subjected to efforts at suppression. We are aware that these efforts are related to a larger pattern of pressures being brought against education, the press, films, radio and television. The problem is not only one of actual censorship. The shadow of fear cast by these pressures leads, we suspect, to an even larger voluntary curtailment of expression by those who seek to avoid controversy.

Such pressure toward conformity is perhaps natural to a time of uneasy change and pervading fear. Especially when so many of our apprehensions are directed against an ideology, the expression of a dissident idea becomes a thing feared in itself, and we tend to move against it as against a hostile deed, with suppression.

This statement and those that follow are reprinted by permission of the American Library Association.

345

And yet suppression is never more dangerous than in such a time of social tension. Freedom has given the United States the elasticity to endure strain. Freedom keeps open the path of novel and creative solutions, and enables change to come by choice. Every silencing of a heresy, every enforcement of an orthodoxy, diminishes the toughness and resilience of our society and leaves it the less able to deal with stress.

Now as always in our history, books are among our greatest instruments of freedom. They are almost the only means for making generally available ideas or manners of expression that can initially command only a small audience. They are the natural medium for the new idea and the untried voice from which come the original contributions to social growth. They are essential to the extended discussion which serious thought requires, and to the accumulation of knowledge and ideas into organized collections.

We believe that free communication is essential to the preservation of a free society and a creative culture. We believe that these pressures towards conformity present the danger of limiting the range and variety of inquiry and expression on which our democracy and our culture depend. We believe that every American community must jealously guard the freedom to publish and to circulate, in order to preserve its own freedom to read. We believe that publishers and librarians have a profound responsibility to give validity to that freedom to read by making it possible for the readers to choose freely from a variety of offerings.

The freedom to read is guaranteed by the Constitution. Those with faith in free men will stand firm on these constitutional guarantees of essential rights and will exercise the responsibilities that accompany these rights.

We therefore affirm these propositions:

1. *It is in the public interest for publishers and librarians to make available the widest diversity of views and expressions, including those which are unorthodox or unpopular with the majority.*

Creative thought is by definition new, and what is new is different. The bearer of every new thought is a rebel until his idea is refined and tested. Totalitarian systems attempt to maintain themselves in power by the ruthless suppression of any concept which challenges the established orthodoxy. The power of a democratic system to adapt to change is vastly strengthened by the freedom of its citizens to choose widely from among conflicting opinions offered freely to them. To stifle every nonconformist idea at birth would mark the end of the democratic process. Furthermore, only through the constant activity of weighing and selecting can the democratic mind attain the strength demanded by times like these. We need to know not only what we believe but why we believe it.

2. *Publishers, librarians and booksellers do not need to endorse every idea or presentation contained in the books they make available. It would conflict with the public interest for them to establish their own political, moral or aesthetic views as a standard for determining what books should be published or circulated.*

Publishers and librarians serve the educational process by helping to make available knowledge and ideas required for the growth of the mind and the increase of learning. They do not foster education by imposing as mentors the patterns of their own thought. The people should have the freedom to read and consider a broader range of ideas than those that may be held by any single librarian or publisher or government or church. It is wrong that what one man can read should be confined to what another thinks proper.

3. *It is contrary to the public interest for publishers or librarians to determine the acceptability of a book on the basis of the personal history or political affiliations of the author.*

A book should be judged as a book. No art or literature can flourish if it is to be measured by the political views or private lives of its creators. No society of free men can flourish which draws up lists of writers to whom it will not listen, whatever they may have to say.

4. *There is no place in our society for efforts to coerce the taste of others, to confine adults to the reading matter deemed suitable for adolescents, or to inhibit the efforts of writers to achieve artistic expression.*

To some, much of modern literature is shocking. But is not much of life itself shocking? We cut off literature at the source if we prevent writers from dealing with the stuff of life. Parents and teachers have a responsibility to prepare the young to meet the diversity of experiences in life to which they will be exposed, as they have a responsibility to help them learn to think critically for themselves. These are affirmative responsibilities, not to be discharged simply by preventing them from reading works for which they are not yet prepared. In these matters taste differs, and taste cannot be legislated; nor can machinery be devised which will suit the demands of one group without limiting the freedom of others.

5. *It is not in the public interest to force a reader to accept with any book the prejudgment of a label characterizing the book or author as subversive or dangerous.*

The ideal of labeling presupposes the existence of individuals or groups with wisdom to determine by authority what is good or bad for the citizen. It presupposes that each individual must be directed in making up his mind about the ideas he examines. But Americans do not need others to do their thinking for them.

6. *It is the responsibility of publishers and librarians, as guardians of the people's freedom to read, to contest encroachments upon that freedom by individuals or groups seeking to impose their own standards or tastes upon the community at large.*

It is inevitable in the give and take of the democratic process that the political, the moral, or the aesthetic concepts of an individual or group will occasionally collide with those of another individual or group. In a free society each individual is free to determine for himself what he wishes to read, and each group is free to determine what it will recommend to its freely associated members. But no group has the right to take the law into its own hands, and to impose its own concept of politics or morality upon other members of a democratic society. Freedom is no freedom if it is accorded only to the accepted and the inoffensive.

7. *It is the responsibility of publishers and librarians to give full meaning to the freedom to read by providing books that enrich the quality and diversity of thought and expression. By the exercise of this affirmative responsi-*

bility, bookmen can demonstrate that the answer to a bad book is a good one, the answer to a bad idea is a good one.

The freedom to read is of little consequence when expended on the trivial; it is frustrated when the reader cannot obtain matter fit for his purpose. What is needed is not only the absence of restraint, but the positive provision of opportunity for the people to read the best that has been thought and said. Books are the major channel by which the intellectual inheritance is handed down, and the principal means of its testing and growth. The defense of their freedom and integrity, and the enlargement of their service to society, requires of all bookmen the utmost of their faculties, and deserves of all citizens the fullest of their support.

We state these propositions neither lightly nor as easy generalizations. We here stake out a lofty claim for the value of books. We do so because we believe that they are good, possessed of enormous variety and usefulness, worthy of cherishing and keeping free. We realize that the application of these propositions may mean the dissemination of ideas and manners of expression that are repugnant to many persons. We do not state these propositions in the comfortable belief that what people read is unimportant. We believe rather that what people read is deeply important; that ideas can be dangerous; but that the suppression of ideas is fatal to a democratic society. Freedom itself is a dangerous way of life, but it is ours.

This statement was originally issued in May of 1953 by the Westchester Conference of the American Library Association and the American Book Publishers Council, which in 1970 consolidated with the American Educational Publishers Institute to become the Association of American Publishers.

LIBRARY BILL OF RIGHTS*

The Council of the American Library Association reaffirms its belief in the following basic policies which should govern the services of all libraries.

1. As a responsibility of library service, books and other library materials should be chosen for values of interest, information and enlightenment of all the people of the community. In no case should library materials be excluded because of the race or nationality or the social, political, or religious views of the authors.

2. Libraries should provide books and other materials presenting all points of view concerning the problems and issues of our times; no library materials should be proscribed or removed from libraries because of partisan or doctrinal disapproval.

3. Censorship should be challenged by libraries in the maintenance of their responsibility to provide public information and enlightenment.

---

*The *Library Bill of Rights* is now under revision, which is expected to be completed in 1979. All of the following statements that are based on the *Library Bill of Rights* will subsequently be reviewed in the light of that revision.

4. Libraries should cooperate with all persons and groups concerned with resisting abridgment of free expression and free access to ideas.

5. The rights of an individual to the use of a library should not be denied or abridged because of his age, race, religion, national origins or social or political views.

6. As an institution of education for democratic living, the library should welcome the use of its meeting rooms for socially useful and cultural activities and discussion of current public questions. Such meeting places should be available on equal terms to all groups in the community regardless of the beliefs and affiliations of their members, provided that the meetings be open to the public.

Adopted June 18, 1948.
Amended February 2, 1961, and June 27, 1967, by the ALA Council.

INTELLECTUAL FREEDOM STATEMENT

An Interpretation of the *Library Bill of Rights*

The heritage of free men is ours.
In the Bill of Rights to the United States Constitution, the founders of our nation proclaimed certain fundamental freedoms to be essential to our form of government. Primary among these is the freedom of expression, specifically the right to publish diverse opinions and the right to unrestricted access to those opinions. As citizens committed to the full and free use of all communications media and as professional persons responsible for making the content of those media accessible to all without prejudice, we, the undersigned, wish to assert the public interest in the preservation of freedom of expression.

Through continuing judicial interpretations of the First Amendment to the United States Constitution, freedom of expression has been guaranteed. Every American who aspires to the success of our experiment in democracy—who has faith in the political and social integrity of free men—must stand firm on those Constitutional guarantees of essential rights. Such Americans can be expected to fulfill the responsibilities implicit in those rights.

We, therefore, affirm these propositions:
1. We will make available to everyone who needs or desires them the widest possible diversity of views and modes of expression, including those which are strange, unorthodox or unpopular.

   Creative thought is, by its nature, new. New ideas are always different and, to some people, distressing and even threatening. The creator of every new idea is likely to be regarded as unconventional—occasionally heretical—until his idea is first examined, then refined, then tested in its political, social or moral applications. The characteristic ability of our governmental system to adapt to necessary change is vastly strengthened by the option of the people to choose freely from among conflicting opinions. To stifle nonconformist ideas at their inception would be to end the democratic process. Only through continuous weighing and selection from among opposing views can free individuals obtain the strength needed for intelligent, constructive decisions and actions. In short, we need to understand not only what we believe, but why we believe as we do.

2. We need not endorse every idea contained in the materials we produce and make available.

We serve the educational process by disseminating the knowledge and wisdom required for the growth of the mind and the expansion of learning. For us to employ our own political, moral, or esthetic views as standards for determining what materials are published or circulated conflicts with the public interest. We cannot foster true education by imposing on others the structure and content of our own opinions. We must preserve and enhance the people's right to a broader range of ideas than those held by any librarian or publisher or church or government. We hold that it is wrong to limit any person to those ideas and that information another believes to be true, good, and proper.

3. We regard as irrelevant to the acceptance and distribution of any creative work the personal history or political affiliations of the author or others responsible for it or its publication.

A work of art must be judged solely on its own merits. Creativity cannot flourish if its appraisal and acceptance by the community is influenced by the political views or private lives of the artists of the creators. A society that allows blacklists to be compiled and used to silence writers and artists cannot exist as a free society.

4. With every available legal means, we will challenge laws or governmental action restricting or prohibiting the publication of certain materials or limiting free access to such materials.

Our society has no place for legislative efforts to coerce the taste of its members, to restrict adults to reading matter deemed suitable only for children, or to inhibit the efforts of creative persons in their attempts to achieve artistic perfection. When we prevent serious artists from dealing with truth as they see it, we stifle creative endeavor at its source. Those who direct and control the intellectual development of our children— parents, teachers, religious leaders, scientists, philosophers, statesmen— must assume the responsibility for preparing young people to cope with life as it is and to face the diversity of experience to which they will be exposed as they mature. This is an affirmative rsponsibility that cannot be discharged easily, certainly not with the added burden of curtailing one's access to art, literature, and opinion. Tastes differ. Taste, like morality, cannot be controlled by government, for governmental action, devised to suit the demands of one group, thereby limits the freedom of all others.

5. We oppose labeling any work of literature or art, or any persons responsible for its creation, as subversive, dangerous, or otherwise undesirable.

Labeling attempts to predispose users of the various media of communication, and to ultimately close off a path to knowledge. Labeling rests on the assumption that persons exist who have a special wisdom, and who, therefore, can be permitted to determine what will have good and bad effects on other people. But freedom of expression rests on the premise of ideas vying in the open marketplace for acceptance, change, or rejection by individuals. Free men choose this path.

6. We, as guardians of intellectual freedom, oppose and will resist every encroachment upon that freedom by individuals or groups, private or official.

It is inevitable in the give-and-take of the democratic process that the political, moral and esthetic preferences of a person or group will conflict occasionally with those of others. A fundamental premise of our free society is that each citizen is privileged to decide those opinions to which he will adhere or which he will recommend to the members of a privately organized group or association. But no private group may usurp the law and impose its own political or moral concepts upon the general public. Freedom cannot be accorded only to selected groups for it is then transmuted into privilege and unwarranted license.

7. Both as citizens and professionals, we will strive by all legitimate means open to us to be relieved of the threat of personal, economic, and legal reprisals resulting from our support and defense of the principles of intellectual freedom.

Those who refuse to compromise their ideals in support of intellectual freedom have often suffered dismissals from employment, forced resignations, boycotts of products and establishments, and other invidious forms of punishment. We perceive the admirable, often lonely, refusal to succumb to threats of punitive action as the highest form of true professionalism: dedication to the cause of intellectual freedom and the preservation of vital human and civil liberties.

In our various capacities, we will actively resist incursions against the full exercise of our professional responsibility for creating and maintaining an intellectual environment which fosters unrestrained creative endeavor and true freedom of choice and access for all members of the community.

We state these propositions with conviction, not as easy generalizations. We advance a noble claim for the value of ideas, freely expressed, as embodied in books and other kinds of communications. We do this in our belief that a free intellectual climate fosters creative endeavors capable of enormous variety, beauty, and usefulness, and thus worthy of support and preservation. We recognize that application of these propositions may encourage the dissemination of ideas and forms of expression that will be frightening or abhorrent to some. We believe that what people read, view, and hear is a critically important issue. We recognize, too, that ideas can be dangerous. It may be, however, that they are effectually dangerous only when opposing ideas are suppressed. Freedom, in its many facets, is a precarious course. We espouse it heartily.

Adopted by the ALA Council, June 25, 1971.

HOW LIBRARIES CAN RESIST CENSORSHIP

An Interpretation of the *Library Bill of Rights*

Libraries of all sizes and types continue to be targets of pressure from groups and individuals who wish to use the library as an instrument of their own tastes and views. The problem differs somewhat between the public library, with a responsibility to present as wide a spectrum of materials as its budget can afford, and the school or academic library, whose collection is designed to support the educational objectives of the institution. Both, however, involve the freedom of the library to meet its professional responsibilities to the whole community.

To combat censorship efforts from groups and individuals, every library should take certain measures to clarify policies and establish community relations. While these steps should be taken regardless of any attack or prospect of attack, they will provide a firm and clearly defined position if selection policies *are* challenged. As normal operating procedure, each library should:

1. *Maintain a definite materials selection policy.* It should be in written form and approved by the appropriate regents or other governing authority. It should apply to all library materials equally.

2. *Maintain a clearly defined method for handling complaints.* Basic requirements should be that the complaint be filed in writing and the complainant be properly identified before his request is considered. Action should be deferred until full consideration by appropriate administrative authority. [Upon request, the Office for Intellectual Freedom will provide a sample complaint form adapted from one recommended by the National Council of Teachers of English.]

3. *Maintain lines of communication with civic, religious, educational and political bodies of the community.* Participation in local civic organizations and in community affairs is desirable. Because the library and the school are key centers of the community, the librarian should be known publicly as a community leader.

4. *Maintain a vigorous public relations program on behalf of intellectual freedom.* Newspapers, radio and television should be informed of policies governing materials selection and use, and of any special activities pertaining to intellectual freedom.

Adherence to the practices listed above will not preclude confrontations with pressure groups or individuals but may provide a base from which to counter efforts to place restraints on the library. If a confrontation does occur, librarians should remember the following:

1. Remain calm. Don't confuse noise with substance. Require the deliberate handling of the complaint under previously established rules. Treat the group or individual who complains with dignity, courtesy and good humor. Given the facts, most citizens will support the responsible exercise of professional freedom by teachers and librarians, and will insist on protecting their own freedom to read.

2. Take immediate steps to assure that the full facts surrounding a complaint are known to the administration and the governing authority. The

school librarian should go through the principal to the superintendent and the school board; the public librarian, to the board of trustees or to the appropriate governing authority of the community; the college or university librarian, to the president and through him to the board of trustees. Present full, written information giving the nature of the complaint and identifying the source.

3. Seek the support of the local press when appropriate. The freedom to read and freedom of the press go hand in hand.

4. Inform local civic organizations of the facts and enlist their support when appropriate. Meet negative pressure with positive pressure.

5. In most cases, defend the *principle* of the freedom to read and the professional responsibility of teachers and librarians. Only rarely is it necessary to defend the individual item. Laws governing obscenity, subversive material and other questionable matter are subject to interpretation by courts. Responsibility for removal of any library materials from public access rests with this established process.

6. Inform the ALA Office for Intellectual Freedom and other appropriate national and state organizations concerned with intellectual freedom of the nature of the problem. Even though censorship must be fought at the local level, there is value in the support and assistance of agencies outside the area which have no personal involvement. They can often cite parallel cases and suggest methods of meeting an attack.

The principles and procedures discussed above apply to all kinds of censorship attacks and are supported by groups such as the National Education Association, the American Civil Liberties Union and the National Council of Teachers of English, as well as the American Library Association. While the practices provide positive means for preparing for and meeting pressure group complaints, they serve the more general purpose of supporting the *Library Bill of Rights,* particularly Article III which states that: "Censorship should be challenged by libraries in the maintenance of their responsibility to provide public information and enlightenment." Adherence to this principle is especially necessary when under pressure.

Adopted February 1, 1962; revised January 28, 1972, by the ALA Council.

EXPURGATION OF LIBRARY MATERIALS

An Interpretation of the *Library Bill of Rights*

Library materials are chosen for their value and interest to the community the library serves. If library materials were acquired for these reasons and in accordance with a written statement on materials selection, then to expurgate must be interpreted as a violation of the LIBRARY BILL OF RIGHTS. For purposes of this statement, expurgation includes deletion, excision, alteration or obliteration. By such expurgation, the library is in effect denying access to the complete work and the full ideas that the work was intended to express; such action stands

in violation of Article II of the LIBRARY BILL OF RIGHTS which states that
"no library materials should be proscribed or removed from libraries because of
partisan or doctrinal disapproval."

The act of expurgation has serious implications. It involves a determination by an individual that it is necessary to restrict the availability of that
material. It is, in fact, censorship.

When a work is expurgated, under the assumption that certain sections
of that work would be harmful to minors, the situation is no less serious.
Expurgation of any library materials imposes a restriction, without regard to the
rights and desires of *all* library users.

Adopted February 2, 1973 by the ALA Council

REEVALUATING LIBRARY COLLECTIONS*

An Interpretation of the *Library Bill of Rights*

The continuous review of library collections to remove physically deteriorated
or obsolete materials is one means to maintain active library collections of
current interest to users. Continued reevaluation is closely related to the goals
and responsibilities of libraries and is a valuable tool of collection building. This
procedure, however, is sometimes used as a convenient means to remove materials thought to be too controversial or disapproved of by segments of the
community. Such abuse of the reevaluation function violates the principles of
intellectual freedom and is in opposition to Articles I and II of the LIBRARY
BILL OF RIGHTS, which state that:

> As a responsibility of library service, books and other library materials selected
> should be chosen for values of interest, information and enlightenment of all
> the people of the community. In no case should library materials be excluded
> because of the race or nationality or the social, political, or religious views of
> the authors.

> Libraries should provide books and other materials presenting all points of
> view concerning the problems and issues of our times; no library materials
> should be proscribed or removed from libraries because of partisan or doctrinal
> disapproval.

The American Library Association opposes such "silent censorship," and recommends that libraries adopt guidelines setting forth the positive purposes and
principles for reevaluation of materials in library collections.

Adopted February 2, 1973 by the ALA Council

---

*The traditional term "weeding," implying "the removal of a noxious growth," is
purposely avoided because of the imprecise nature of the term.

RESOLUTION ON CHALLENGED MATERIALS

An Interpretation of the *Library Bill of Rights*

WHEREAS, The LIBRARY BILL OF RIGHTS states that no library materials should be proscribed or removed because of partisan or doctrinal disapproval, and

WHEREAS, Constitutionally protected expression is often separated from unprotected expression only by a dim and uncertain line, and

WHEREAS, Any attempt, be it legal or extra-legal, to regulate or suppress material must be closely scrutinized to the end that protected expression is not abridged in the process, and

WHEREAS, The Constitution requires a procedure designed to focus searchingly on the question before speech can be suppressed, and

WHEREAS, The dissemination of a particular work which is alleged to be unprotected should be completely undisturbed until an independent determination has been made by a judicial officer, including an adversary hearing,

THEREFORE, THE PREMISES CONSIDERED, BE IT RESOLVED, That the American Library Association declares as a matter of firm principle that no challenged library material should be removed from any library under any legal or extra-legal pressure, save after an independent determination by a judicial officer in a court of competent jurisdiction and only after an adversary hearing, in accordance with well-established principles of law.

Adopted June 25, 1971 by the ALA Council

RESTRICTED ACCESS TO LIBRARY MATERIALS

An Interpretation of the *Library Bill of Rights*

Restricting access of certain titles and certain classes of library materials is a practice common to many libraries in the United States. Collections of these materials are referred to by a variety of names such as "closed shelf," "locked case," "adults only," or "restricted shelf" collections.

Three reasons generally advanced to justify restricted access are:

(1) It provides a refuge for materials that belong in the collection but which may be considered "objectionable" by some library patrons;
(2) It provides a means for controlling distribution of materials which allegedly should not be read by those who are not "prepared" for such materials by experience, education, or age;

(3) It provides a means to protect certain materials from theft and mutilation.

Though widely used—and often practical—restricted access to library materials is frequently in opposition to the principles of intellectual freedom. While the limitation differs from direct censorship activities, such as removal of library materials or refusal to purchase certain publications, it nonetheless constitutes censorship, albeit a subtle form. As a form of censorship, restricted access violates the spirit of the LIBRARY BILL OF RIGHTS in the following ways:

(1) It violates that portion of Article II which states that "... no library materials should be proscribed ... because of partisan or doctrinal disapproval."

The word "proscribed," as used in Article II, means "suppressed." Restricted access achieves *de facto* suppression of certain materials.

Even when a title is listed in the card catalog with a reference to its restricted shelf status, a barrier is placed between the patron and the publication. Because a majority of materials placed in restricted collections deal with controversial, unusual, or "sensitive" subjects, asking a librarian or circulation clerk for them is an embarrassment for patrons desiring the materials. Because restricted collections are often composed of materials which some library patrons consider "objectionable," the potential user is predisposed to thinking of the materials as "objectionable," and is accordingly inhibited from asking for them. Although the barrier between the materials and the patron is psychological, it is nonetheless a tangible limitation on his access to information.

(2) It violates Article V which states that, "The rights of an individual to the use of a library should not be denied or abridged because of his age. . . . "

Limiting access of certain materials to adults only abridges the use of the library for minors. "Use of the library" includes use of, and access to, library materials. Such restrictions are generally instituted under the assumption that certain materials are "harmful" to minors, or in an effort to avoid controversy with parents who might think so.

The librarian who would restrict the availability of materials to minors because of actual or suspected parental objection should bear in mind that he is not *in loco parentis* in his position as librarian. The American Library Association holds that it is the parent—and only the parent—who may restrict his children—and only *his* children—in reading matter. The parent who would rather his child did not read certain materials or certain kinds of materials should so advise the child.*

When restricted access is implemented to protect materials from theft or mutilation, the use of the practice may be legitimate. However, segregation of materials to protect them must be administered with extreme attention to the rationale

---

*See also FREE ACCESS TO LIBRARIES FOR MINORS, adopted by the ALA Council, June 30, 1972.

for restricting access. Too often only "controversial" materials are the subject of such segregation, leading to the conclusion that factors other than theft and mutilation were the true considerations. The distinction is extremely difficult to make, both for the librarian and the patron.

Selection policies, carefully developed on the basis of principles of intellectual freedom and the LIBRARY BILL OF RIGHTS, should not be vitiated by administrative practices such as restricted access.

Adopted February 2, 1973 by the ALA Council

FREE ACCESS TO LIBRARIES FOR MINORS

An Interpretation of the *Library Bill of Rights*

Some library procedures and practices effectively deny minors access to certain services and materials available to adults. Such procedures and practices are not in accord with the LIBRARY BILL OF RIGHTS and are opposed by the American Library Association.

Restrictions take a variety of forms, including, among others, restricted reading rooms for adult use only, library cards limiting circulation of some materials to adults only, closed collections for adult use only, and inter-library loan service for adult use only.

All limitations in minors' access to library materials and services violate Article V of the LIBRARY BILL OF RIGHTS, which states that, "The rights of an individual to the use of a library should not be denied or abridged because of his age...." Limiting access to some services and materials to only adults abridges the use of libraries for minors. "Use of the library" includes use of, and access to, all library materials and services.

Restrictions are often initiated under the assumption that certain materials are "harmful" to minors, or in an effort to avoid controversy with parents who might think so. The librarian who would restrict the access of minors to materials and services because of actual or suspected parental objection should bear in mind that he is not *in loco parentis* in his position as librarian. Individual intellectual levels and family backgrounds are significant factors not accommodated by a uniform policy based upon age.

In today's world, children are exposed to adult life much earlier than in the past. They read materials and view a variety of media on the adult level at home and elsewhere. Current emphasis upon early childhood education has also increased opportunities for young people to learn and to have access to materials, and has decreased the validity of using chronological age as an index to the use of libraries. The period of time during which children are interested in reading materials specifically designed for them grows steadily shorter, and librarians must recognize and adjust to this change if they wish to maintain the patronage of young people.

The American Library Association holds that it is the parent—and only

the parent—who may restrict his children—and only *his* children—from access
to library materials and services. The parent who would rather his child did not
have access to certain materials should so advise the child.

The word "age" was incorporated into Article V of the LIBRARY
BILL OF RIGHTS as a direct result of a preconference entitled "Intellectual
Freedom and the Teenager," held in San Francisco in June, 1967. One recommendation of the preconference participants was, "That free access to all books
in a library collection be granted to young people." The preconference generally concluded that young people are entitled to the same access to libraries and
to the materials in libraries as are adults and that materials selection should not
be diluted on that account.

This does not mean, for instance, that issuing different types of borrowers' cards to minors and adults is, *per se,* contrary to the LIBRARY BILL OF
RIGHTS. If such practices are used for purposes of gathering statistics, the
various kinds of cards carry no implicit or explicit limitations on access to
materials and services. Neither does it mean that maintaining separate children's
collections is a violation of the LIBRARY BILL OF RIGHTS, provided that no
patron is restricted to the use of only certain collections.

The Association's position does not preclude isolating certain materials
for legitimate protection of irreplaceable or very costly works from careless use.
Such "restricted-use" areas as rare book rooms are appropriate if the materials
so classified are genuinely rare, and not merely controversial.

Unrestrictive selection policies, developed with care for principles of
intellectual freedom and the LIBRARY BILL OF RIGHTS, should not be
vitiated by administrative practices which restrict minors to the use of only part
of a library's collections and services.

Adopted by the ALA Council, June 30, 1972.

SEXISM, RACISM AND OTHER -ISMS IN LIBRARY MATERIALS

An Interpretation of the *Library Bill of Rights*

Traditional aims of censorship efforts have been to suppress political, sexual or
religious expressions. The same three subjects have also been the source of most
complaints about materials in library collections. Another basis for complaints,
however, has become more and more frequent. Due, perhaps, to increased
awareness of the rights of minorities and increased efforts to secure those rights,
libraries are being asked to remove, restrict or reconsider some materials which
are allegedly derogatory to specific minorities or which supposedly perpetuate
stereotypes and false images of minorities. Among the several recurring "isms"
used to describe the contents of the materials objected to are "racism" and
"sexism."

Complaints that library materials convey a derogatory or false image of a minority strike the personal social consciousness and sense of responsibility of some

librarians who—accordingly—comply with the requests to remove such materials. While such efforts to counteract injustices are understandable, and perhaps even commendable as reflections of deep personal commitments to the ideal of equality for all people, they are—nonetheless—in conflict with the professional responsibility of librarians to guard against encroachments upon intellectual freedom.

This responsibility has been espoused and reaffirmed by the American Library Association in many of its basic documents on intellectual freedom over the past thirty years. The most concise statement of the Association's position appears in Article II of the LIBRARY BILL OF RIGHTS which states that "Libraries should provide books and materials presenting all points of view concerning the problems and issues of our times; no library materials should be proscribed or removed because of partisan or doctrinal disapproval."

While the application of this philosophy may seem simple when dealing with political, religious or even sexual expressions, its full implications become somewhat difficult when dealing with ideas, such as racism or sexism, which many find abhorrent, repugnant and inhumane. But, as stated in the FREEDOM TO READ STATEMENT,

> It is inevitable in the give and take of the democratic process that the political, the moral, or the aesthetic concepts of an individual or group will occasionally collide with those of another individual or group. In a free society each individual is free to determine for himself what he wishes to read, and each group is free to determine what it will recommend to its freely associated members. But no group has the right to take the law into its own hands, and to impose its own concept of politics or morality upon other members of a democratic society. Freedom is no freedom if it is accorded only to the accepted and the inoffensive. . . . We realize that application of these propositions may mean the dissemination of ideas and manners of expression that are repugnant to many persons. We do not state these propositions in the comfortable belief that what people read is unimportant. We believe rather that what people read is deeply important; that ideas can be dangerous; but that the suppression of ideas is fatal to a democratic society. Freedom itself is a dangerous way of life, but it is ours.

Some find this creed acceptable when dealing with materials for adults but cannot extend its application to materials for children. Such reluctance is generally based on the belief that children are more susceptible to being permanently influenced—even damaged—by objectionable materials than are adults. The LIBRARY BILL OF RIGHTS, however, makes no distinction between materials and services for children and adults. Its principles of free access to all materials available apply to every person, as stated in Article V, "The Rights of an individual to the use of a library should not be denied or abridged because of his age, race, religion, national origins or social or political views."

Some librarians deal with the problem of objectionable materials by labeling them or listing them as "racist" or "sexist." This kind of action, too, has long been opposed by the American Library Association in its STATEMENT ON LABELING, which says,

If materials are labeled to pacify one group, there is no excuse for refusing to label any item in the library's collection. Because authoritarians tend to suppress ideas and attempt to coerce individuals to conform to a specific ideology, the American Library Association opposes such efforts which aim at closing any path to knowledge.

Others deal with the problem of objectionable materials by instituting restrictive circulation or relegating materials to closed or restricted collections. This practice, too, is in violation of the LIBRARY BILL OF RIGHTS as explained in RESTRICTED ACCESS TO LIBRARY MATERIALS which says,

> Too often only "controversial" materials are the subject of such segregation, leading to the conclusion that factors other than theft and mutilation were the true considerations. The distinction is extremely difficult to make, both for the librarian and the patron. Unrestrictive selection policies, developed with care for the principles of intellectual freedom and the LIBRARY BILL OF RIGHTS, should not be vitiated by administrative practices such as restricted circulation.

The American Library Association has made clear its position concerning the removal of library materials because of partisan or doctrinal disapproval, or because of pressures from interest groups, in yet another policy statement, the RESOLUTION ON CHALLENGED MATERIALS:

> The American Library Association declares as a matter of firm principle that no challenged material should be removed from any library under any legal or extra-legal pressure, save after an independent determination by a judicial officer in a court of competent jurisdiction and only after an adversary hearing, in accordance with well-established principles of law.

Intellectual freedom, in its purest sense, promotes no causes, furthers no movements, and favors no viewpoints. It only provides for free access to all ideas through which any and all sides of causes and movements may be expressed, discussed and argued. The librarian cannot let his own preferences limit his degree of tolerance, for freedom is indivisible. Toleration is meaningless without toleration for the detestable.

Adopted February 2, 1973 by the ALA Council

STATEMENT ON LABELING

An Interpretation of the *Library Bill of Rights*

Because labeling violates the spirit of the LIBRARY BILL OF RIGHTS, the American Library Association opposes the technique of labeling as a means of predisposing readers against library materials for the following reasons:

1. Labeling[1] is an attempt to prejudice the reader, and as such it is a censor's tool.

2. Although some find it easy and even proper, according to their ethics, to establish criteria for judging publications as objectionable, injustice and ignorance rather than justice and enlightenment result from such practices, and the American Library Association must oppose the establishment of such criteria.

3. Libraries do not advocate the ideas found in their collections. The presence of a magazine or book in a library does not indicate an endorsement of its contents by the library.

4. No one person should take the responsibility of labeling publications. No sizable group of persons would be likely to agree either on the types of material which should be labeled or the sources of information which should be regarded with suspicion. As a practical consideration, a librarian who labels a book or magazine might be sued for libel.

5. If materials are labeled to pacify one group, there is no excuse for refusing to label any item in the library's collection. Because authoritarians tend to suppress ideas and attempt to coerce individuals to conform to a specific ideology, the American Library Association opposes such efforts which aim at closing any path to knowledge.

Adopted July 13, 1951
Amended June 25, 1971, by the ALA Council

RESOLUTION ON GOVERNMENTAL INTIMIDATION

WHEREAS, The Principle of intellectual freedom protects the rights of free expression of ideas, even those which are in opposition to the policies and actions of Government itself; and

WHEREAS, The support of that principle is guaranteed by the First Amendment, thus insuring Constitutional protection of individual or collective dissent; and

WHEREAS, Government, at whatever level, national, state, or local, must remain ever vigilant to the protection of that principle; and

---

[1] "Labeling," as it is referred to in the STATEMENT ON LABELING, is the practice of describing or designating certain library materials, by affixing a prejudicial label to them or segregating them by a prejudicial system, so as to pre-dispose readers against the materials.

WHEREAS, Government, although properly empowered to promulgate, administer, or adjudicate law, has no right to use illicitly its legally constituted powers to coerce, intimidate, or harass the individual or the citizenry from enunciating dissent; and

WHEREAS, The illegitimate uses of legitimate governmental powers have become increasingly a matter of public record, among them being the misuse of the Grand Jury and other investigative procedures, the threat to deny licenses to telecommunications media, the indictment of citizens on charges not relevant to their presumed offenses, and the repressive classification, and hence denial, of documentary material to the very public taxed for its accumulation; and

WHEREAS, These illicit uses not only constitute an abrogation of the right to exercise the principle of freedom of expression but also, and perhaps more dangerously, prefigure a society no longer hospitable to dissent;

NOW THEREFORE BE IT RESOLVED, That the American Library Association, cognizant that in the scales of justice the strength of individual liberty may outweigh the force of power, expresses its unswerving opposition to any use of governmental prerogative which leads to the intimidation of the individual or the citizenry from the exercise of the constitutionally protected right of free expression, and

BE IT FURTHER RESOLVED, That the American Library Association encourage its members to resist such improper uses of governmental power, and

FURTHER, That the American Library Association supports those against whom such governmental power has been employed.

Adopted February 2, 1973 by the ALA Council

APPENDIX C

Guidelines for the Formulation of
Collection Development Policies

The Collection Development Committee of the Resources Section, Resources and Technical Services Division, American Library Association, was organized to provide a focus in ALA for activities relating to collection development, and, in particular, to: study the present resources of American libraries and the coordination of collection development programs; develop guidelines for the definition of selection policies; evaluate and recommend selection tools for collection development; and recommend qualifications and requisite training for selection personnel. In partial response to these charges, the committee at its New York meeting of 9 July 1974 appointed task forces comprised of committee members and consultants to prepare guidelines for the following collection development activities: formula budgeting and allocation; the formulation of collection development policies; the development of review programs designed to assist in the solution of space problems; and the description and evaluation of library collections. The *Guidelines for the Formulation of Collection Development Policies* which follow were prepared by task-force members Thomas Shaughnessy, Hans Weber, and Sheila Dowd (chairman), and were submitted to the committee for revision at its meetings of January and July 1975. They were further revised at the committee's meeting of 19 January 1976 and were then approved for submission to the executive committee of the Resources Section. They were approved as a "preliminary edition" dated March 1976 by the executive committee on 19 July 1976 and were approved by the Board of Directors of RTSD by a mail ballot in August 1976 (seven for publication, one opposed, two not voting).

1. INTRODUCTION

1.1 Purpose.

The committee offers these *Guidelines for the Formulation of Collection Development Policies* in the belief that collection development policy statements must be comprehensible, and that they must be comparable,

Prepared by the Collection Development Committee, Resources Section, Resources and Technical Services Division, American Library Association. Reprinted by permission of the Resources and Technical Services Division, American Library Association.

particularly if they are to prove useful in the implementation of long-range goals for sharing of resources.

1.2 Objectives.

The immediate aims of the designers of these *Guidelines* are, to identify the essential elements of a written statement of collection development policy, and to establish standard terms and forms for use in the preparation of such policies.

1.3 Need.

Widespread budgetary constraints and the growth of interlibrary cooperation in resources-sharing call for analysis of collection activity in universally comprehensible terms.

1.4 Scope.

The committee has attempted to provide an instrument that will be of use to libraries of all kinds and sizes in formulating statements of their collection development policies. Some elements of the *Guidelines,* however, will of necessity be more applicable to larger libraries.

1.5 Audience.

The *Guidelines* are intended to help library administrators and collection development librarians to produce a document that can serve as both a planning tool and a communications device. The resulting policy statements should clarify collection development objectives to staff, users, and cooperating institutions, enabling them to identify areas of strength in library collections; and by this means should facilitate the coordination of collection development and cooperative services within an area or region.

1.6 Methodology.

The *Guidelines* have been submitted to the committee in open meeting at several Midwinter and Annual Conferences. The group discussions, in which numerous visitors have participated, have resulted in extensive revisions of the initial drafts.

1.7 Assumptions.

1.7.1 A written collection development policy statement is for any library a desirable tool, which: (a) enables selectors to work with greater consistency toward defined goals, thus shaping stronger collections and using limited funds more wisely; (b) informs users, administrators, trustees and others as to the scope and nature of existing collections, and the plans for continuing development of resources; (c) provides information which will assist in the budgetary allocation process.

1.7.2 It is desirable that form and terminology of collection development policy statements be sufficiently standardized to permit comparison between institutions.

1.7.3 Libraries have acknowledged the impossibility of building totally comprehensive collections, and will increasingly need to rely on cooperative activities. Collection development policy statements will assist cooperative collection building, and will also, in the absence of precise bibliographic tools such as union catalogs, be of value to users and user-service units in locating materials.

1.8 Definitions.
    1.8.1 Levels of collection density and collecting intensity codes. The codes defined below are designed for use in identifying both the extent of existing collections in given subject fields (collection density) and the extent of current collecting activity in the field (collecting intensity).

        A. Comprehensive level. A collection in which a library endeavors, so far as is reasonably possible, to include all significant works of recorded knowledge (publications, manuscripts, other forms), in all applicable languages, for a necessarily defined and limited field. This level of collecting intensity is that which maintains a "special collection"; the aim, if not the achievement, is exhaustiveness.

        B. Research level. A collection which includes the major source materials required for dissertations and independent research, including materials containing research reporting, new findings, scientific experimental results, and other information useful to researchers. It also includes all important reference works and a wide selection of specialized monographs, as well as a very extensive collection of journals and major indexing and abstracting services in the field.

        C. Study level. A collection which is adequate to support undergraduate or graduate course work, or sustained independent study; that is, which is adequate to maintain knowledge of a subject required for limited or generalized purposes, of less than research intensity. It includes a wide range of basic monographs, complete collections of the works of more important writers, selections from the works of secondary writers, a selection of representative journals, and the reference tools and fundamental bibliographical apparatus pertaining to the subject.

        D. Basic level. A highly selective collection which serves to introduce and define the subject and to indicate the varieties of information available elsewhere. It includes major dictionaries and encyclopedias, selected editions of important works, historical surveys, important bibliographies, and a few major periodicals in the field.

        E. Minimal level. A subject area which is out of scope for the library's collections, and in which few selections are made beyond very basic reference tools.

           Note: Definitions of collecting levels are not to be applied in a relative or ad hoc manner (that is, relative to a given library or group of libraries) but in a very objective manner. Consequently it is quite likely that a large number of libraries will not hold comprehensive collections in any area. Similarly, academic libraries which do not support doctoral programs, or other types of libraries which are not oriented toward specialized research, may not have any collections that would fall within the research level as defined herein.

The definitions are proposed to describe a range and diversity of titles and forms of material; they do not address the question of availability of multiple copies of the same title.

1.8.2 Language codes.

The following codes should be used to indicate languages in which material is collected. Libraries wishing a greater refinement of this data may sub-code with the MARC language codes.

F. All applicable languages (i.e., no exclusions)
G. English
H. Romance languages
J. Germanic languages
K. Slavic languages
L. Middle Eastern languages
M. Asian languges
N. African languages
P. Other languages

2. GUIDELINES

2.1 Principles governing formulation and application of collection development policies.

    2.1.1 Libraries should identify the long- and short-range needs of their clientele, and establish priorities for the allocation of funds to meet those needs. A collection development policy statement is an orderly expression of those priorities as they relate to the development of library resources.

        Note: The collection development policy statement addresses the question of breadth and depth of subject coverage. Libraries will need to formulate separate statements of policy relating to duplication of materials; and such additional policy statements must be given consideration in fund allocation.

    2.1.2 Collection development policy statements should be reviewed at regular intervals to insure that changes in user needs are recognized, and that changing budgetary situations are confronted.

    2.1.3 A library's collection development policy should be coordinated with those of appropriate other libraries, whether in a hierarchy of dependence, or in a division of responsibility among equals. A collection development policy statement should assist librarians to select and de-select in conformity with regional needs and resources.

2.2 Elements of a collection development policy statement.

    2.2.1 Analysis of general institutional objectives, including:

        (1) Clientele to be served
        (2) General subject boundaries of the collection

      (3) Kinds of programs or user needs supported (research, instructional, recreational, general information, reference, etc.)

      (4) General priorities and limitations governing selection, including:

         (a) degree of continuing support for strong collections

         (b) forms of material collected or excluded

         (c) languages, geographical areas collected or excluded

         (d) chronological periods collected or excluded

         (e) other exclusions

         (f) duplication of materials (generally treated; but see also 2.1.1, Note)

      (5) Regional, national, or local cooperative collection agreements which complement or otherwise affect the institution's policy.

2.2.2 Detailed analysis of collection development policy for subject fields. The basic arrangement of this analysis is by classification; a parenthetical subject term follows the class number for ease of interpretation. A suggested minimum of refinement of the Library of Congress classification on which to structure the analysis is the breakdown into approximately 500 subdivisions used in: *Titles Classified by the Library of Congress Classification: Seventeen University Libraries*. Preliminary ed. Berkeley, General Library, University of California, 1973. (A list of the classes used in that survey is appended to these guidelines.) For Dewey or other classifications, a comparably refined breakdown should be attempted.

    Note: This recommendation indicates a minimal refinement of classification analysis needed to permit interinstitutional comparisons. Many libraries will prefer to analyze their collections in greater detail.

For each subject category (ie., classification number or group of numbers), indicate the following:

(1) Level of collecting intensity codes to indicate:

    (a) existing strength of collection

    (b) actual current level of collection activity

    (c) desirable level of collecting to meet program needs

(2) Language code or codes

(3) Chronological periods collected

(4) Geographical areas located

(5) Forms of material collected (or excluded)

(6) Library unit or selector with primary selection responsibility for the field

2.2.3 Detailed analysis of collection development policy for form collections.

    In some libraries special collection development policy statements are required for certain forms of materials, where policy governing the collection of those materials differs from the library's general policy for subject collections. Some examples of forms for which special policy statements may be needed include:

(1) Newspapers

(2) Microform collections
(3) Manuscripts
(4) Government publications
(5) Maps
(6) Audio-visual materials
(7) Data tapes

Where possible, it is desirable that the basic structure of the policy statement for a form collection follow subject classification; but with some form collections it will be necessary to use another primary arrangement (kind of material, area, etc.). For example, the policy statement for a map collection might be divided first into ''general maps,'' ''topographic maps,'' ''thematic maps,'' ''raised relief maps,'' etc., with subdivision by area classification; that for a newspaper collection might be primarily by political division.

Whatever the basic structure chosen, the detailed analysis of collection development for a form collection should include the elements identified in 2.2.2 (1)-(6) above.

2.2.4 Indexes.

The information in the policy statement should be made accessible for a wide variety of purposes. To this end an index should be appended which correlates subject terms to class numbers. Individual libraries may also wish to index by academic programs, library units, or other key words or concepts.

INDEX

Index